INTERNATIONAL SOCIAL MOVEMENT RESEARCH

Volume 4 • 1992

SOCIAL MOVEMENTS AND VIOLENCE: PARTICIPATION IN UNDERGROUND ORGANIZATIONS

INTERNATIONAL SOCIAL MOVEMENT RESEARCH

SOCIAL MOVEMENTS AND VIOLENCE: PARTICIPATION IN UNDERGROUND ORGANIZATIONS

Series Editor: BERT KLANDERMANS
Department of Social Psychology
Free University of Amsterdam

Volume Editor: DONATELLA DELLA PORTA
Wissenschaftszentrum Berlin
für Sozialforschung

VOLUME 4 • 1992

JAI PRESS INC.

Greenwich, Connecticut *London, England*

55 Old Post Road, No. 2
Greenwich, Connecticut 06830

JAI PRESS LTD.
The Courtyard
28 High Street
Hampton Hill, Middlesex TW12 1PD
England

ISBN: 1-55938-445-X

Manufactured in the United States of America

CONTENTS

PART III. WOMEN'S STUDIES

PART IV. COMPARATIVE STUDIES

LIST OF CONTRIBUTORS

Margaret M. Braungart	State University of New York Health Science Center at Syracuse
Richard G. Braungart	Department of Sociology Syracuse University
Martha Crenshaw	Department of Government Wesleyan University
Donatella della Porta	Wissenschaftszentrum Berlin für Sozialforschung
Maria Jose Moyano	Department of Political Science The University of Vermont
Friedhelm Neidhardt	Wissenschaftszentrum Berlin für Sozialforschung
Luisa Passerini	Department of History University of Turin
Peter Waldmann	Department of Sociology University of Augsburg
Robert W. White	Department of Sociology Indiana University
Gilda Zwerman	Department of Sociology State University of New York at Old Westbury

PART I

THEORIES AND METHODOLOGIES

INTRODUCTION: ON INDIVIDUAL MOTIVATIONS IN UNDERGROUND POLITICAL ORGANIZATIONS

Donatella della Porta

THE RESEARCH ON INDIVIDUAL MOTIVATIONS IN UNDERGROUND POLITICAL ORGANIZATIONS

The opening volume of this series on "International Social Movement Research"—*From Structure to Action* (Klandermans, Kriesi and Tarrow 1988)—emphasized the need for research on political mobilization which links processes occurring at different analytical levels, and identifies connections between social conflits and individual involvement. The contributors to this volume have attempted to fill this need, following several suggestions from the earlier volume to look at a very special kind of political organization: underground groups. I hope that this collection of papers can broaden the understanding of a phenomenon—normally referred to as "terrorism"—that sociological investigation has, so far, done little to illuminate, despite the enormous number of essays devoted to the topic. The need for deeper insight into individual motivations in the underground—or on "terrorism" tout court—is easy to substantiate. According to one recent commentator, this field

International Social Movement Research, Vol. 4, pages 3-28.

ISBN: 1-55938-445-X

of study is characterized by "a disturbing lack of good empirically-grounded research" (Gurr 1988, p. 115) and by "naive descriptions, speculative commentary and prescriptions for 'dealing with terrorism' which would not meet minimum research standards in the more established branches of conflict and policy analysis" (Gurr 1988, p. 143). Weakness and bias are even more visible in the studies on "terrorists," which have produced the impression that, to quote Zwerman's essay in this volume, several authors are "more concerned with generating antipathy toward the subject than with theory or scholarship." Especially in the seventies, when terrorist activities peaked in several countries, the majority of scientific as well as journalistic works presented "terrorists" as crazy people or cold-blooded murderers. In most of these works: "well-known personalities of the terrorist scene [were] utilized as show-pieces for propagating the authors' own ideas . . . to denounce the offenders simply as paranoids, neurotics, or psychopaths" (Rasch 1979, p. 79). Analysts therefore showed little interest in explanations of individual motivations, which were considered irrelevant or simply untruthful. To interview militants was then deemed a sign of dangerous symphathy for, or even connivance with, political criminals.

In the 1980s, attitudes changed. The perception of what was sometimes called "the end of the terrorist emergency" provided a more congenial atmosphere for research projects focusing precisely on the nature of the individual motivations in the underground. The papers collected in this volume report the results of several of these research projects. All the contributions attempt to link individual motivations with structural conditions and group dynamics, focusing in particular on the "social construction of reality" (Berger and Luckmann 1966) taking place in the underground. Underlying this research is the assumption that a phenomenon such as terrorism cannot be understood unless we take into account the interactions between structural conditions and symbolic meaning, "objective" and "subjective" reality, public activities, and private life.

Research in the sociology of knowledge has identified multiple realities. Our perceptions are influenced by the frames we use to understand events; events themselves are not "objective": they can be "fabricated" or simply misinterpreted. Thus, for a number of reasons experiences are vulnerable to manipulation (see, e.g., Goffman 1974). Further, the formation of perceptions and images is an interactive process. Because what is perceived as real produces real consequences, individual motivations evolve through, as it were, the concatenation of different subjective realities. From different perspectives, the studies in this book examine individual choices and rationale for such choices, as they emerge from the transformation of "historical" facts in the individual or subcultural mind, from the effects of some dramatic public event on the activist's private life, and from the activist's perceptions of the external world. A primary object of the book is therefore to explain the distinctive—socially constructed—"reality" shared by members of the underground.

This purpose is reflected in the methodological approach shared by all the researchers whose work is represented in this volume: that is, the use of biographical materials that enable us to see "inside" the underground organizations. Several of these studies—in particular those of White, Moyano, Passerini, Zwerman, and della Porta—are based on in-depth interviews with former or current members of underground organizations. The remaining studies rely on written sources, such as newspapers, autobiographies, police archives, and trial records. These different research techniques produced slightly different results. Printed sources provided more information on the external environment in which the underground organizations developed; life-histories offered a more "inward," subjective perspective; and semistructured interviews focused on opinions. But because they share the biographical method, all these essays produced highly comparable information about the macro-, meso-, and micro-processes that shape individual motivations in the underground.

The primary aim of this volume is therefore to approach the phenomenon of "terrorism" through the understanding of individual motivations and perceptions, and to present some results of a methodology rarely applied to the study of political radicalism (della Porta 1987, 1990b). In addition, the authors attempt to provide material for a comparative analysis in a field in which it is particularly needed. Labels such as "terrorism" or "underground political organizations" in fact describe a range of very disparate phenomena: right-wing and left-wing groups, political violence in democratic and authoritarian regimes, class-oriented and ethnically based conflicts. Not only do the underground organizations differ according to their goals, they also have varying organizational models and favor different forms of action. Any attempt to develop interpretative hypotheses about "terrorism" is therefore destined to fail without a typology that can identify their range of application.

Although this collection of papers does not attempt to describe all the main terrorist organizations, it provides a large sample of studies on the different forms of political violence which developed in the last two decades. The various contributions examine underground organizations in European countries—Northern Ireland, Spain, West Germany, Italy, and France—and in America—the United States, Canada, and Argentina. In assembling information on different national cases, we hope to "relativize" and specify hypotheses and explanations.

This intention is expressed in the structure of the volume. In Part I, this introduction and Crenshaw's paper offer observations toward a theory on individual motivations in underground organizations. In the remainder of this introduction, I discuss some results of the research presented in this volume, analyzing in particular the ways in which individual motivations are affected by the activists' social networks, the political environment's predispositions to violence, and the totalizing commitment required by terrorist organizations.

Crenshaw presents some hypotheses on decision making in underground groups, and then deduces several conclusions about the counterproductive effects of over-repressive antiterrorist policies.

Part II consists of three case studies of different forms of underground organizations. Braungart and Braungart describe the environmental conditions and group dynamics that can explain individual motivations in the left-wing Weather Underground in the United States, an organization that emerged from the radicalization of the protest of the 1960s. White examines one of the oldest terrorist organizations in Europe, the Irish Republican Army, studying the development of "injustice" frames based on ethnic discrimination in a special group of militants: those living in the Irish Republic. And Moyano's interviews with Argentinian militants on the context and dynamics of political violence reveal the workings of yet another type of underground organization—the South American "guerrilla."

Part III contains two papers on women's studies in the field. Zwerman, a sociologist and psychotherapist, analyzes images of militant women in the academic field, in antiterrorist agencies, and in the feminist press, and compares them with the self-images of militants in the various American underground organizations she is studying in a project on American female prisoners. The oral historian Passerini reflects on the imagery and mentality of the Italian female militants whose life histories she collected during a seminar in the Turin prison.

Part IV makes an explicit attempt to develop typologies of underground organizations. Comparing left-wing and right-wing militants in West Germany, Neidhardt emphasizes the wide range of differences in the mobilization capacity of the various underground groups. Waldmann's study of left-wing and ethnic organizations reveals, in addition, significant differencies in the nature of membership in the two kinds of groups. In my own comparison of life histories of Italian and West German militants, I stress the relevance of historical circumstances and national contexts—such as the legitimation of political violence—in predisposing the individuals to engage in terrorism.

INDIVIDUAL MOTIVATIONS AND SOCIAL NETWORKS IN UNDERGROUND ORGANIZATIONS

On Psychological Characteristics: A Critique of Some Prejudices and Stereotypes

In the past, commentators have often explained participation in underground groups as the manifestation of some psychological pathology, such as personality dependence, low intelligence, egocentrism (Livingstone 1982; Wasmund 1986), and as a frustrated attempt to build a positive identity

(Billig 1984; Ivianski 1983; Russel and Miller 1983; Knutson 1981; Schmidtchen 1981). These claims have never been substantiated by empirical research. Even in the few cases in which militants have been given personality tests, the subjects were individuals who had passed through two "total institutions"—the clandestine organization and the prison system—which had influenced their personalities (della Porta 1988, p. 156). In accord with a more recent trend in research all the papers in this volume share the assumption that no specific personality traits are "typical" of terrorists. As Braungart and Braungart state, militants are impelled to engage in destructive action not because of a "single orientation toward aggression" but for a "variety of reasons."

In addition, past research has found no sign of any typical pattern in the primary socialization of militants, no sign of particular family problems or of an authoritarian upbringing. On the contrary, Passerini's subjects, for example, remembered their childhood as serene and happy. My research among Italian militants confirms Passerini's findings: 85% of a total of 29 former militants described their family atmosphere as "good" or "very good." Moreover, the interviews indicate that, far from conflicting with the values of their parents the radical commitment of the young activists often reflected a continuity with the political traditions of their families (significantly, this relation appear to hold true among protest activists as well [see, e.g., Keniston 1968]). In fact, more than half of the militants of left-wing underground organizations grew up in left-wing families (della Porta 1990a).

Thus personality traits and family pathologies turn out to be very poor predictors of the propensity to engage in radical political activism. And comparative analysis shows that the extent to which a given society resorts to psychopathological explanations reflects the degree of political violence that society will tolerate. Waldmann observed, for instance, that in societies in which ethnic groups operate, the militants are generally perceived as demonstrating positive personality traits—determination, initiative, leadership ability—and are seen as integrated into their society. In societies in which underground organizations are more isolated from their environment, however, analysts favor interpretations of militance that stress pathological characteristics. Thus, in West Germany, for example, "the efforts at interpretation by psychological, psychiatric or psychoanalytical theories outnumber those afforded by sociology and political science" (Rasch 1979, p. 79).

Social Networks and Political Motivations

Pathological personality types or deficient primary socialization, therefore, do not seem to account for motivations to join underground organizations. But, all the contributors to this volume agree, one further stage in the socialization process *is* highly relevant: the construction of peer groups during adolescence. That social networks play a vital role in political socialization as well as in personality building is not a new finding. Many empirical studies on social movements have shown that social movements recruit in dense social networks and, more particularly, among individuals who are already members of preexisting formal and informal groups. Further, friendship ties within social movement organizations have proven to be a prime inducement to participation (see, e.g., Zald and Ash 1966; Wilson 1973; Snow, Zurcher and Ekland-Olson 1980; Reynaud 1982; Snow and Machalek 1983; Klandermans 1984). Past research has already revealed the function of these ties in the evolution of political involvement: they provide a sense of cohesiveness in the face of opposition from the surrounding community, they encourage a desire for acceptance and cognitive coherence which produces conformity; and they filter political messages and information (Keniston 1968; see also Verba 1961).

Indeed, earlier research has demonstrated that participation in interpersonal networks is very important in all stages of involvement in the underground. In the case of the German and Italian militants, it was clear that the more time an individual spent on political activities, the more contact he or she had with political comrade-friends. And as his or her friendship ties became stronger, the value of the political activities increased (see my paper in this volume and also della Porta 1990a). Among the Irish militants, too, friendship and political ties were intertwined: as one militant interviewed by White declared, for instance, "most of my friends developed from . . . my political involvement." Thus an individual's participation in militant activities increased at an "incredible speed," as the Italian and German militants said, and in a natural and almost unconscious way.

It was precisely these affective ties that prompted activists to make the transition from nonmilitant groups to the underground. For one thing, underground organizations were founded by cliques of friends (see, e.g., Franceschini, Buffa and Giustolisi [1988], on the Red Brigades) or, in some cases, by what Moyano has called "family dynasties," composed of couples and several siblings. Moreover, recruitment to the underground took place via the same channels that provided recruits for nonmilitant groups: "entering in the area of the armed struggle presupposed previous relational networks" (Novaro 1988, p. 287). Many German and Italian militants, for example, explained that joining an underground organization was an act either of solidarity with a friend "in danger" (in prison or in clandestinity) or of revenge for the death of a fellow comrade during a "militant" action (see my paper in this volume and also della Porta 1990a). In some cases, these affective ties developed during activities in the so-called organizations of solidarity with political prisoners, which in West Germany represented almost the only channel of recruitment for the second generation of left-wing terrorists.

Loyalty to the peer group was therefore an important motive as activists moved toward an ever-deepening political commitment (for a similar analysis on commitment in religious sects, see Lofland and Stark [1965]). They forged this commitment by dismissing all ties with outsiders, thus restricting themselves to relations within the group. Integration in the friendship networks within the social movement—in what Useem (1972) called "movement solidarity"—enabled activists to shift from their moderate initial stance to a radical political position. As McAdam (1986) observed about the passage from low-risk to high-risk activities in general, increased interactions within activist networks, ideological socialization and construction of an activist identity all served to enforce an individual's commitment. Commitment was thus "self-generating" (Becker 1960).

Although affective networks always play a role in politics, they operate in a special way in underground organizations, for in this context strong ties are more important than weak ties, which represent the primary channel of expansion for nonmilitant social movement organizations (Granovetter 1973). In underground organizations illegality produces a risk and so a need for secrecy; and, as in other secret societies, this need becomes the single most important determinant of the organization's structure and strategy (Erikson 1981). Recruitment in the underground therefore depends on strong confidence ties between recruitors and recruitees. Consequently, the possibilities for recruitment for the underground groups are always limited.

Furthemore, social networks have a peculiar function in maintaining loyalty to terrorist organizations. One characteristic of affective ties among comrade-friends in the underground is their intensity. Relations within the small community are given particular prominence, Passerini notes; and individual identities are so embedded in the group that the militants believe it is not possible to live outside the group or, indeed, it is not worth living outside it. In this volume, Moyano suggests that, in the isolation of clandestinity, the guerrillas' comrades served as a functional surrogate for their families, with whom they could not keep in contact. In the underground, as in high-risk secret societies (Erikson 1981), the excitement of shared risks strengthened friendships among the members. As a former Argentinian militant recalled, "you had people around you whom you knew would be ready to die in order to save you." Danger and isolation thus hightened emotional intensity.

Scholars have offered various explanations for the "strength" of these bonds. One of these explanations focuses on the degree of affective identification required by the total changes in an individual's life that adherence to an underground organization creates. As Berger and Luckmann observe, processes of re-socialization, or "alternations,"

> resemble primary socialization, because they have radically to reassign reality accents and, consequently, must replicate to a considerable degree the strongly affective identification with the socializing personnel that was characteristic of childhood. They are different from primary socialization because they do not start *ex nihilo*, and as a result they must cope

> with a problem of dismantling, disintegrating the preceding nomic structure of subjective reality (Berger and Luckmann 1966, p. 157).

Thus, the new values must be mediated to the individual through "significant others" with whom he or she has established strong affective identifications: "No radical transformation of subjective reality (including of course identity) is possible without such identification, which inevitably replicates childhood experiences of emotional dependency on significant others" (Berger and Luckmann 1966, p. 157). Activists entering the underground, like individuals in other "novitiate" phases, "nihilated" those who inhabited their world before their conversion; in Berger and Luckmann's words, "People and ideas that are discrepant with the new definitions of reality are systematically avoided" (1966, p. 159).

A second explanation for the intensity of friendships in the underground is related to the militants' youth. Peer groups, we know, exert a different kind of influence in the different stages of an individual's life. Because the activists' participation in underground organizations often coincided with their search for emotional independence from the family, their loyalty to the peer group—an important element in the evolution of an adult personality—was especially strong. We can understand why underground organizations attract the young—youth is perhaps the only characteristic "terrorists" share—when we remember that young people are relatively unconstrained by obligations, responsibilities, and conventions, and that the underground mentality depends on certain psychological characteristics of adolescence. As the Braungarts' research on the Weathermen makes clear, such typically youthful characteristics as energy, utopianism, the need for autonomy, openness to experimentation, a search for identity and fidelity are conducive to total adherence to a "negative identity" and enhance the attraction of the "adventure" in the underground. Several other militant groups described in this volume also emphasized "adventure" and "action." The imagery of Italian militants, Passerini observed, revealed a great sensitivity to spectacular effects and a preoccupation with the illusion of an intense, free, and thoughtless life. Several former members of the underground quoted in this volume said they felt they were living "in a movie" or "in science fiction." Moreover, the biographies disclose the militants' fascination with action as opposed to "mere talking," and their positive emphasis on what Passerini has called "rebellion."

Having emphasized the importance of friendship ties throughout the process of political socialization—from the individual's first experiences of protest activism, to the radicalization of this experience, to his or her participation in the underground—and having observed the vital role that affective ties play in clandestine organizations, we must consider another question: how are the networks of "rebels" created? Focusing on affective ties provides only a partial explanation of individual motivations, since they cannot account for the specific form that social networks take. In the following section, then, I focus on the environmental conditions that make an individual receptive to the use of political violence.

INDIVIDUAL MOTIVATIONS AND THE ESCALATION OF POLITICAL CONFLICTS

Social Origins of the Underground Organizations' Activists

In looking for explanations of individual motivations at a macroanalytical level, we must consider the hypotheses that posit a correlation between political violence and social strata. One such hypothesis holds that political deviance—as well as other kinds of deviance—is accepted more readily in the marginal strata of the population, than in any others. And its general "subculture of violence" (Wolfgang and Ferracuti 1967) makes it hospitable to specifically political forms of violence as well. Lacking legal means to challenge the system, individuals in the marginal strata would also have a higher propensity for violence. But at least in the historical cases discussed in this book, this hypothesis did not hold true.

Proponents of a second, quite opposite, hypothesis focus on the middle class, maintaining that the radicalization of a working-class ideology in a middle-class environment is a psychological device to "compensate" for bourgeois origins. Apropos of the Weathermen, for instance, the Braungarts refer to one source that explains the behavior of these militants as a reaction to the cognitive dissonance created by the contrast between their own comfortable backgrounds and their awareness of poverty and racism. This hypothesis too proved misleading. First, several ethnic underground organizations—Waldmann cites the IRA and ETA—were composed mainly of militants from the lower or lower-middle classes. Further, Neidhardt's comparative study shows that right-wing terrorists came from poorer backgrounds than did their left-wing counterparts and were less educated than the left-wing terrorists. The hypothesis also misrepresents left-wing ideological terrorism. My research on more than 1,000 Italian militants, for instance, shows that only a few had an autonomous "bourgeois" profession (about 9%, including 2.2% who were lawyers); a larger group came from the new middle class (30%, about 5% of whom were teachers); but the highest number (41.8%) had working class positions (della Porta 1990a).

Generalizing from the Italian case, we can state that "terrorists belong to different social groups; no single social class is responsible for their production and reproduction, for their ideology or for their behavior" (Pasquino and della Porta 1986, p. 180). The social origins of terrorists varies with the organization and with the context. In our cases, political violence does not seem to depend on a subculture of violence among "poor people" or on a frustrated reaction of bourgeois revolutionaries. Rather, the social origins of the militants of terrorist organizations reflect those of the protest movements in which they were recruited. Accordingly, we should examine the dynamics of those social movements.

Social Protest and Political Violence

In traditional studies, terrorism has been defined according to its more singular aspects: terrorism, it is said, uses an "intolerable" level of violence, aims at "scaring" people, and breaks the "rules of the game" (della Porta 1983). Without denying these singularities, the research collected in this volume demostrates that underground organizations can be seen as part of a larger "social movement sector" (as defined in Garner and Zald [1983]). The definition of a social movement organization as "a self-conscious group which acts in concert to express what it sees as the claims of challengers by confronting elites, authorities, or other groups with these claims" (Tarrow 1989; see also Zald and McCarthy 1987) aptly characterizes the underground political organizations studied in this volume, for they clearly were "self-conscious groups" that expressed what they saw as "the claims of challengers." They were founded by social movement activists—often as a result of splits in social movement organizations—as a by-product of those interactions between challengers and opponents which constitute the essence of a social movement (Tilly 1984, p. 299). And not only did the militants perceive themselves as part of the social movement sector, the social movement activists (from whom the underground drew its new recruits) often recognized the militants as "comrades"—albeit as "comrades who were wrong."

The contributors to this volume agree that future terrorists can be described as small minorities within larger political subcultures or countercultures. The militants of the underground themselves defined their role as that of actors in a political conflict. Of course, as Waldmann rightly states, ethnic and leftwing terrorists operated within quite different political contexts. Ethnical militants reacted to what they perceived as an external threat coming from a power foreign to their own ethnic, regional, or religious group, with which they identified deeply. The left-wing militants, in contrast, rejected their own society and, in their search for an alternative, came to identify with external groups. Despite this difference, however, ethnic and left-wing militants did have something in common: the existence of—smaller or larger—networks of political activists for which political violence gradually became an everyday experience.

In all the cases analyzed in this book, protest repertoires gradually escalated toward violence. In the United States, protest actions became more and more radical after the Democratic convention in Chicago and the uprisings at

Columbia University in 1968. In 1970, when the Weathermen went underground, as many as 5,000 bombing attempts for political reasons occurred. In Italy, the number of protest events characterized by organized and small-group violence increased dramatically during the first half of the 1970s (della Porta and Tarrow 1987). When the student movement declined in West Germany, the hope that the newly elected SPD government would adopt a reformist policy impelled several activists to return to conventional politics. But after a few years the activists became disillusioned and violence escalated during "squatting" incidents in houses and youth centers in the big cities (Klein 1980). In Ulster, the nonviolent civil rights movement faded away in the face of a violent opposition. And in Argentina, although reformers had some hope at the beginning of the sixties, political interactions soon degenerated into physical fights, and a bloody repression decimated the democratic opposition.

These environmental conditions fostered the rise not only of some underground organizations but also, to paraphrase Garner and Zald (1983), of national "terrorist sectors" composed of several clandestine groups, sometimes competing, sometimes collaborating with each other. In most of the historical cases dealt with in this volume, terrorist organizations claimed to represent the same social groups. Furthermore, adversaries—or countermovements—also organized in the underground. In Italy throughout the 1970s brutal conflicts escalated among young members of right-wing and left-wing nonunderground groups who fired at each other, sometimes killing each other, right in front of the high schools. Neo-Nazis and "anti-fascists" clashed in West Germany at the end of the 1970s. Civil rights advocates opposed the Ku Klux Klan in the United States. In Ulster and in the Basque country, armed groups of "loyalists" attacked IRA and ETA members respectively, setting off a spiral of violent reciprocal revenge. And in Argentina, Moyano shows, on the day of the Peron's definitive return street fights between rightists and Montoneros triggered an escalation of violence (during which 16 people died and 433 were wounded). A few months later, the terrorist anticommunist alliance (Triple A) was founded and began persecuting democratic Argentinians, driving the Montoneros further and further underground.

In these volatile climates, individual motivations for joining the underground proliferated. The atmosphere of violence had a particular influence on those who were just beginning to take an interests in political activities. Braungart and Braungart observe, for example, that the Weathermen and the older SDS leaders grew up under qualitatively different historical conditions: the nonviolent SDS in a period that valued peaceful protest; the militant Weathermen in a period accostumed to radical forms of action. Similarly, in West Germany and Italy, activists, socialized to politics in the violent first half of the 1970s and enrolled in the underground in the second half of that decade, formed a "second generation" of terrorism more populous and more violent than the first.

We can explain this self-sustaining proliferation of motivations for engaging in political violence in various ways. First, through experience, activists gradually acquired "skills," and structures for the use of violence were gradually created. The case of the New Left groups in Italy provides an illustration: as a result of their street fights with police and right-wing radicals, more or less autonomous "marshal bodies" sprang up within their main organizations. Through shisms and secessions, these small groups themselves sometimes became the foundation of underground groups (Novelli and Tranfaglia 1988; della Porta 1990a). These radicalized small groups also formed the reservoir for recruitment for the underground organizations. Similarly, the biographies of German militants testify to a (in Neidhardt's words) "militarizing" effect of involvement in radical legal groups, an effect that helped to "presocialize activists to militancy."

In addition to refining martial skills and creating structures for violence, the experience of daily fights with adversaries transformed the activists' attitudes toward politics. Physical conflicts with opponents produced a kind of battle spirit toward politics, much like that which emerged in the street violence between young communists and Nazi storm troopers in the early 1930s in Berlin. As Merkl reports: "According to accounts on both sides, the street fighters were motivated far more by the escalating physical confrontations than by ideological beliefs . . . the reality of the clashes had a great deal more to do with aroused emotions, brawny fists, and weapons than with these ideological concepts" (1986, p. 43). Street fights, then, produced ex post facto justifications and rationalizations for violence. As the biographies describe in detail, the militants engaged in long debates on the different "right" forms of violence; nevertheless, the empirical boundaries between "right" violence and "wrong" violence, "defensive" violence and "offensive" violence, "mass" violence and "elite" violence remained quite vague.

As attitudes and behaviors became radicalized, the "armed struggle" became easier for activists to accept—so much so that, as Passerini notes in her essay, several activists came to consider violence as "natural" and were able to move into the underground so smoothly that they did not perceive they had made an important choice. In most of the biographies I analyzed, the militants were unable to isolate a particular moment in which they decided to join the underground. Because the perceptions and attitudes of the young militants were similar to those that dominated their political environments, joining the underground was not a traumatic step for them. And because they saw only marginal difference between the normal and the deviant (on this point, see Matza [1969]), they could not clearly perceive any "deviation" from the norms. For the activists, the reality of everyday life—that is, the "reality par excellence," in which "the tension of consciousness is highest" (Berger and Luckmann 1966, p. 21)—created the conditions for a gradual acceptance of violence as a political means. Justifying violence was thus an integral part of constructing alternative systems of values and norms. As Passerini clearly illustrates, shared representations of the reality then "short-circuited" with the "primacy of action" mythicized by the young militants.

The Effects of Antiterrorist Policies

Political conflicts are often further radicalized by the effects of antiterrorist policies. Several of the papers in this volume examine what in terms of the sociology of deviance could be defined as the role of deviance-control institutions in selecting those who will become deviant and in helping to create a "deviant" personality. In the late 1960s and early 1970s, state institutions often reacted to protest in over-repressive ways. To cite just one by no means extreme example: in the United States, Braungart and Braungart recall, the Nixon administration countered social protest by escalating surveillance, resorting to intimidation, establishing special congressional committees to investigate leftists, using informants and infiltrators, approving FBI controls over all SDS members, and creating the CIA's "operation chaos." In this way, it not only prosecuted illegal political behavior, but "criminalized" protest. Zwerman notes that the Reagan administration implemented a similar policy in the 1980s, when "terrorists" were defined as those who "support" or are "associated" with terrorist groups or "activities," engage in "previolent" forms of protest, and commit actions that have the "potential" to "evolve" into terrorism. This vague definition makes even noncriminal political behavior a possible target of repression. All the countries surveyed in this volume present similar examples of "criminalizing" the opposition. Moreover, in such countries as Argentina and Italy, many people believed that state apparatuses were involved in protecting the radical Right and thus in a "dirty war" against the political opposition on the Left.

Although they were intended to isolate the radical Left, the repressive measures of these governments often produced the opposite effect. First, they delegitimized the state not only by creating "injustice frames" (Gamson, Fireman and Rytina et al. 1982) but also by arousing the sense of an "absolute injustice" (Manconi 1988)—that is, the belief that the state had committed the most serious violation of the rules of the game. Following the delegitimation of the state, which was then perceived as an "unfair" enemy that used brutal repression, activists entered the underground. The interviews with the militants provided several examples of a sense of deep "injustice." For the Irish republicans, the British policy of "internment"—the imprisonment of suspected IRA members without trial—reinforced the image of the central authorities as illegitimate (White 1989). The Italian militants saw the neo-fascist massacre of Piazza Fontana as a turning point, proof that the state, which was alleged to have taken part in the terrorist plot, had violated its own democratic rules. Perceptions of an "absolute injustice" varied with the degree to which violent behavior was tolerated in the different countries and periods. In West Germany, a country with a very low tolerance for political violence, the death of the protestor Benno Ohnesorg and the attempt on the life of the student movement leader Rudi Dutschke were sufficient to produce the feeling that, as Baumann (1976) said, "they were firing at you." In an authoritarian regime such as that of Ongania's Argentina in the sixties, the shocking sense of a deep injustice grew out of the much more dramatic acts of military brutality, vividly described by Moyano: the "Cordobazo" (with 14 protestors killed), the "Viborazo" (with other 2 protestors killed), and the cold-blooded murder of 16 guerrillas in an Argentinian prison.

The fear of being the direct target of repression also impelled activists to join underground groups. In their biographies, several Italian militants recounted that they decided to join an underground organization only after the police began to pursue them (they joined in order to find support for escaping arrest) or after they had been arrested and had shared a prison cell with members of terrorist groups. A few members of the West German radical groups that supported the "political prisoners" said that they had felt harrassed or endangered by close police scrutiny and had reacted by joining the underground. Another impetus that often pushed rank-and-file militants deeper into the underground was the very severe penalties that the courts imposed for acts of political violence, such as the condemnation of some Weathermen, as early as in 1970, for a crime as serious as "conspiracy." Thus for many activists joining a terrorist formation was what Crenshaw calls an "unforeseen consequence" of nonterrorist actions.

Accordingly, the material effect of the "ban"—in Matza's (1969) words—was to "force" activists into contact with more experienced militants who were already engaged in clandestine activities. The ban had relevant psychological effects as well. Zwerman, for instance, observes that, among the American underground groups, getting arrested often "initiated" activists of radical groups "into their status as terrorists" and into an "array of exceptional, erratic, experimental procedures." The common reaction of these militants was to hide their feelings and fears behind what Zwerman calls a "grandiose self-definition" of their own heroic role and of the imminent revolution. In addition, many of the biographies of German and Italian militants indicate that harsh prison conditions and long sentences made them determined to stick to their "freedom-fighter" identity, which allowed them to see themselves as soldiers of a revolution that would soon free them. Imprisonment in high-security sections produced what Passerini calls a rigidity in memory and an "inability to go forwards or backwards." And, Crenshaw notes, coercive counterterrorist reactions often made terrorism self-sustaining insofar as these measures proved the militants' expectations of hostility to be correct, reinforced injustice frames, and set off a spiral of revenge. Over-reactions to political violence fostered what the neo-Chicago school has called "secondary deviance"—the identification of a "specifically deviant" individual with his or her "primary" deviation—and therefore the identification with the underground organization. The militants thus adopted alternative systems of norms and values, roles and rules, in order to transform stigma into prestige symbols (Goffman 1963).

INDIVIDUAL MOTIVATIONS AND POLITICAL SOCIALIZATION IN THE UNDERGROUND

We have already noted that the resources and meaning that foster underground organizations are produced by a variety of processes. The primary determinants of the militants' perceptions and behavior, however, can be traced to the very same characteristics of the terrorist groups. For underground groups as for religious sects, "the 'whys' or 'reasons' for joining arise out of the recruitment itself" (Snow, Zurcher and Eckland-Olson 1980, p. 799). The experience inside the terrorist organizations was then what shaped their dispositions. All the papers in this volume underline the relevance of the particular group situation the individual encounters on joining the underground. As the Braungarts emphasize, the real transformation in individual motivations begins within the terrorist organizations. "Terrorist" motivations are largely a product of what Crenshaw calls the "psychology of small, radical, illegal groups."

State control agencies usually operate on the assumption that underground organizations are criminal groups. Without denying the validity of this assumption, I feel it is necessary to point out another characteristic of these organizations which helps explain their behavior: they are ideological groups. In a study based on autobiographical materials concerning members of Russian underground groups in the second half of the nineteenth century, Nahirni tried to define the particular characteristics of ideological groups: they are, he said, groups "which require their members to orient themselves to one another primarily in terms of some central symbols and ideas" (Nahirni 1962, pp. 397-398). The distinctive feature of these groups is the members' total commitment to a cause, to which they must subordinate all personal ties. This description aptly characterizes underground political organizations as well.

Structures in the Underground: "Greedy Institutions"

The obvious peculiarity of terrorist organizations is that they are underground. This characteristic has a profound effect on individual motivations: underground groups demand the total involvement of their members. Like the "greedy institutions" analyzed by Coser, they "seek exclusive and undivided loyalty and they attempt to reduce the claims of competing roles and status positions on those they wish to encompass within their boundaries" (Coser 1974, p. 4). To enforce loyalties, terrorist groups developed negative incentives, such as the threat of punishment for traitors. More effectively, they developed a value system in which, as in an army (so Crenshaw notes), betrayal was considered the most serious violation of group norms.

Terrorist organizations devoted much energy to developing systems of rules that their members had to respect at all times. The "handbooks for urban guerrillas" produced by most of the groups went well beyond the "logistic" needs of clandestinity. Their main effect was to ensure the organization's control of its members through domination on the more private aspects of their lives. The underground groups required their members to provide such extreme "testimony" of commitment as the total renunciation of privacy regarding both material and affective ties (and, in the case of the Weathermen, even in sexual relations). Lacking a private life, the militants experienced what Passerini calls the loss of individual identity, which in turn compelled them to rely more and more on the group. A reduced sense of the self obscured their perception of personal responsibility.

Once having joined an underground group, he or she would be required to participate at increasingly demanding levels of activity, whether in terms of the risk or the time involved. Militants usually began their careers in the underground by distributing leaflets or renting an apartment. The longer they remained underground, the more likely they were to end up in participating in robberies and assassinations. In their biographies, several militants testify to the accelerating effect that a warrant of arrest had on their promotion in the internal hierarchy of the underground: from rank-and-file members they rapidly advanced to national leaders. Moreover, many recall the time they spent in the underground as a period of frenetic activism: they organized attacks, wrote documents, looked for refuge, and planned to free their comrades. The result of this "24-hours-a-day" commitment to the organization was, as one Italian militant put it, the lack of any time for "thinking," for critically reflecting on the sense of the crimes the terrorists had carried out. The biographies of the Italian and German militants demostrate that this process of material and emotional involvement culminated in the militants' almost complete identification with a "community of the armed struggle."

Another factor that strengthened total commitment in the underground was the militants' isolation from external channels of information. It is well known that the kind of clique to which people belong determines to a large extent the political message they receive and the ideological appeals they translate into concrete action. Earlier research has established that the media alone are not an effective conduit for political information; such information acquires meaning and relevance only when it is channeled through social networks (Smith, Lasswell and Casey 1946; McPhail 1971; McPhail and Miller 1973). The more "total" the activists' involvement in a political network, the more insulated they were from information that could threaten their political beliefs. As my comparative analysis of Italian and German militants illustrates, the militants' source of values and information rapidly shrank to the small circles of those who were underground. As a result, they lost a sense of reality, constructing images that were increasingly remote not only from the "dominant" culture but also from the counterculture. And because they were so isolated from external reality, the militants of the underground groups had great difficulty in perceiving the defeat of their project.

The degree to which these processes of commitment governed an underground organization seemed to vary according to the organization's degree of isolation. Waldmann notes, for example, that left-wing groups were far more isolated from their environment than were ethnic groups. In ethnic organizations, peer groups in the underground enforced the same norms and values that prevailed in their environment, whereas in left-wing groups, members had to enforce an alternative value system. As several studies indicate, however, under the pressure of internal conflicts and the specialization of state repression, all the underground groups tended to become more and more isolated and ended up concentrating their efforts simply on their survival.

Commitment to a Cause: Ideologies in the Underground

Individual motivations were also shaped by the characteristics of the ideologies of the underground groups. Using a typology proposed by Sartori (1969), we can identify the major formal peculiarities of these ideological systems: they refuse factual arguments, they are abstract, they base their appeal on emotions, and they are accessibile to only a very small public. In order to ensure total commitment, underground ideologies exalt "powerful," strong, and abstract ideas. Because proponents of these ideologies never refer to the preconditions and the progression of a revolutionary process, the ideological beliefs seem "impermeable" to external defeats. In the underground, as in secret societies, symbolism and rituals which are needed to legitimize alternative authority, render the ideologies particularly rigid (Simmel 1950). Terrorist groups develop special languages, cryptic to anyone outside the group but possessing a highly symbolic value for their members.

Some of these characteristics can exist, to a different degree, in social movement organizations as well. Students of social movement ideologies have, for instance, defined social movement ideologies as "dogmatic" and have observed that motivating radical behavior requires a high degree of "certainty" about the external world (Gerlach and Hine 1970). Moreover, they noted that it is to a movement's advantage to maintain a certain level of ambiguity, which enables leaders to escalate their requests in order to keep protest alive after initial victories or to conceal moments of weakness (Gerlach and Hine [1970]; on a similar phenomenon in religious sects, see Lofland and Stark [1965]). Researchers have also stressed the positive role that rhetoric and rituals play in social movement organizations that must substitute symbolic for material incentives.

Nevertheless, social movement ideologies differ from underground ideologies in many ways. Social movement organizations, which hope to reach a large public, must try to balance the need for internal coherence with the often conflicting need for communication with external elements (Boucher 1977); underground groups, which are essentially insular organizations, focus mainly on internal functions. Their ideologies are what Moyano calls "an instrument for internal consumption." Consequently, the more isolated the groups are, the more abstract, ritualistic and inaccessible to factual argument their ideologies become. The experience of the German and the Italian militants indicate that the less time and energy they gave to recruitment, the more ingrown they became, abandoning the imagery and the language they shared with the counterculture and constructing an "alternative" reality. The Montoneros' "hedge theory"—according to which Peron supported the guerrilla but could not express his support because of his wife and the Right—exemplifies the extremes this "loss of the sense of reality" can reach.

The ideologies of underground organizations exhibit certain peculiarities in their political content as well as in their form. Members of the underground organizations, like members of other political groups, develop ideologies in order to define the organization's field of action and its role in it—that is, "the reasons for its existence, the embodiment of its values, its analysis of society and its prescriptions for change" (Boucher 1977, p. 25). Terrorist organizations, including right-wing groups, do not act randomly or because they are "bloodthirsty." On the contrary, they devote a great deal of energy to the elaboration of what Crenshaw called a "cognitive restructuring," through which reprehensible conduct is presented as honorable. Historical, linguistic, and religious "macronarratives" that justify violence are encompassed in eclectic ideological frames (Toloyan 1987). Processes of "frame amplification" (Snow et al. 1986) allow militants to accept the "armed struggle" on the basis of social movement discourses.

Frame amplification is evident in underground ideologies, first of all, in their elitist self-definition of the actors. It has been noted, in fact, that small radical organizations in general favor the image of a close community of the elect, emphasizing purity rather than proselytization, exclusivity rather than expansion (O'Toole 1975). The militants of the underground organizations described in this book "amplified" this claim of belonging to an "elite," although an "alternative" one. When they were linked to a larger social movement, they presented themselves as the "vanguard of the revolutionary masses." When they were isolated, they claimed to be the only "beacon" of resistance opposing the total dominion of capitalism. And we find that the German and Italian militants, for example, justified the use of violence through highly abstract and simplified images of the world in which small elites of "freedom fighters" were in charge of administering the real "justice." According to Crenshaw, the self-images of an "elite with high consciousness" and of the "hero" were widespread among the militants.

Elitism accomplished an important function: it made isolation appear to be a positive, self-imposed quality. An organization's lack of support became a sign of superiority, rather than an indication of its mistakes and defeat. Members cultivated their differences from others as proof of their being among the few "elect." Similarly aristocratic conceptions of self-identity are characteristic of other small totalistic groups, such as secret societies (Simmel 1950; Hazelrigg 1969) and sects (Niebuhr 1937; Wilson 1959).

Frame amplification is evident as well in the way terrorist groups define their adversary. Social movement ideologies, it has been said, tend to adopt a dicotomous image of the world, based on an inward-outward definition (Gerlach and Hine 1970). They represent the movement's counterculture as enacting "collective dramas" or rhetorical "phantasy themes" in which the actors in the conflict are "heroes" and "villains" and the setting consist of "profane" and "sacred" ground (Rogers 1985a, 1985b). The peculiarity of underground organizations is that they amplify the dichotomous confrontation. First, they define an "absolute" enemy. Among the Italian militants, Passerini observes, the widely accepted idea of "militant" antifascism provided the rationale for a process of frame amplification that would justify violence. The enemies were "fascist" and therefore responsible for all the enormities of the Mussolini dictatorship. In an even more abstract way, the terrorists described the victims of their attacks as "wheels of the capitalist machine" and therefore as responsible for all capitalist evil. The militants denied the possibility that there could be any mediate positions between the two adversaries. In the words of Ulrike Meinhof, the world is divided into "human beings and pigs." Their conflict is not reconcilable. The dichotomous image of conflict was "amplified" into an image of military war. Both the German and the Italian militants described how they perceived reality in military terms: they adopted a military jargon to define the external world; they divided the world into dangerous and free zones; and they judged successes and defeats in a military way.

Like the term "partisan" applied to forces in a war (Schmitt 1975) the terrorists' image of an "absolute enemy" imply an alternative "legal" system, while denying the legitimacy of a foreign ruler or a political regime because of its "crimes." Moreover, in order not to appear inhuman, anyone who assumes the the self-appointed right to kill requires an absolutely evil enemy as justification. Contrasting one's own behavior with the more "inhuman" acts of the enemy is a technique for displacing responsibility. Dehumanizing the enemy is a way to deny any responsibility for one's victims (Crenshaw 1988). In other words, the war analogy allows for a suspension of normal values and behavior. As a result, the social and political dimensions of the activists' motivations gradually dissipate, and the "military" metaphor becomes real and self-sustained in the militants continuous clashes with the state apparatuses. As Crenshaw has observed, terrorist and counterterrorist groups tend to become mirror images of each other, each consciously imitating the other. Thus, both underground groups and antiterrorist policies become more and more "militarized," each side fueling the violence of the other and so reducing the possibility of political solutions to the conflict.

To conclude, we should note that some organizational processes and dynamics typical of underground groups appear as well in the legal activism of social movements. In social movements as in the underground, activists construct "new" cultures, and commitment transforms the individual's private life. Social movements also produce collective identities to which the members willingly subordinate their own identities or roles. Further, social movements, Roots (1983) has observed, are particularly sensitive to the participants' structure of perceptions and the distribution of knowledge. Collective identities and the activists' motivations to participate are enforced by the integration of the individual into a movement counterculture built on alternative value systems and social structures. Activism in the social movement organizations strongly influences the "lenses" through which reality is perceived, information is selected, and motivations are produced.

Terrorist organizations, of course, differ from other social movements organizations in significant ways—most of which arise from the terrorists' isolation from the external world and from their almost daily use of criminal forms of action. Nevertheless, because it is important for empirical research on social movements to analyze the effects of organizational structure and violent interactions on activists' motivations, the study of underground organizations is entirely relevant, for like a kind of magnifying glass, it can clarify processes and dynamics that may also be present—though to a different degree—in nonunderground political organizations.

CONCLUSION

In this introduction, I have surveyed some of the major results of research on individual motivations in underground organizations. In the first part, I stressed that to understand differential recruitment and escalation of commitment in terrorist groups as well as in social movement organizations, we must look not at the psychological characteristics of the activists but at their relational positions. Accordingly, we examined the role personal networks played in the different stages of an activist's involvement in radical politics, including the decision to join the underground. The militants' youth and the high risks involved in militance in the underground appeared as factors that strengthened affective ties with comrade-friends.

Friendship ties, however, could not account for the environmental conditions that allowed for the radicalization of action strategies. As we saw, several processes contributed to the escalation, both symbolic and actual, of political conflict. To identify these processes, we examined some of the ways in which physically violent interactions and state repression affected the prominent images in political countercultures. The networks in which the underground organizations found their recruits were part of a larger political counterculture. As protest strategies confronted counterstrategies, the repertoires of collective actions expanded and became increasingly violent. In this process, activists developed new skills and new structures for carrying out violent action. The second generation of activists, which was socialized to politics after violence had become accepted in larger or smaller wings of the social movement sector, thus accepted radical action as routine. Moreover, the militants' attitudes toward politics changed, and they began to find justifications for the more radical forms of action which developed in their everyday experiences. As a result of its over-repressive counterstrategies, the state was perceived throughout the counterculture as nondemocratic and unfair. A "military attitude" toward political conflicts became pervasive.

These processes underwent a qualitative change in the underground organizations. Once an activist was recruited into an underground group—having been compelled to join by a combination of individual motives and environmental preconditions—the very specific conditions of participation in such a group determined the characteristics of further commitment. As "greedy institutions," these groups required a total commitment from their members, thus isolating them from the outside world and making them completely dependent on the organizations. Accordingly, the individual's value systems and perceptions of the external world became those of the group, and his or her motivational structure was transformed. By internalizing the groups rigid ideological systems, characterized by extreme elitism and "absolute" enmity, the militants accepted the definition of the situation as a war. This militaristic outlook in turn shaped their perceptions and motivations.

These findings, among others presented in the essays that compose this book, can greatly improve our understanding of individual militance in underground groups. By integrating macro-, meso- and micro-processes, we can in fact explain the complex mechanisms through which reality is constructed in the underground. The biographical method allows us to follow the gradual evolution of political commitment and of images of social conflict. Given this framework, we have been able to offer much more comprehensive explanations for individual motivations in underground than we could devise with models of "strategic" but "evil" behavior or of "craziness." Thus we have arrived at some important answers to the main question that students of underground organizations often ask: How do "normal" activists evolve into "terrorists"?

This collection presents some of the first research to adopt the biographical method. But the sociological literature on individual motivations in the underground contains several gaps, and much remains to be done. The first gap lies in the amount of material we have on militants in different forms of underground organizations. The comparative papers in this volume indicate that the degree to which a terrorist organization is isolated from its external environment differs significantly with the type of organization. But we have still to make a comparative assessment of the effects of the various forms of underground organizations on the motivational dynamics of their members. To make a systematic comparison, however, we will need to collect and analyze much more biographical material.

A second major gap in the literature is an "exogenous" one. We will be able to state what is "typical" of underground groups only when we have gathered enough biographical material on those activists in the broader countercultures—indeed, the majority—who did not join underground groups. With few exceptions (see della Porta [1990b] for a review), research on the life histories of social movement activists is almost nonexistent. Another serious deficiency in social movement research is the lack of studies on the effects of movement participation on the individual, or on "the ongoing dynamics of individual activism" (McAdam, McCarthy and Zald 1988, p. 729). Following this line of thought, Neidhardt and Rucht (1990) have stressed the need for studying the characteristics of the subcultural milieus of social movements—of their network structures and alternative life styles. Only by working within this broad research frame, can we hope to understand fully the evolution of individual motivation from nonviolent to radical forms of action.

We can identify a third major gap as the underdevelopment of methodologies appropriate for the study of the interactive dynamics that explain individual motivations. While researchers have elaborated sophisticated techniques to measure causal correlations, they have done much less for an empirical study of complex sets of interactions. Rational strategic action has received far more attention than self-sustaining escalation produced by miscalculations, which, according to several studies, were often the source of political violence. Commentators have singled out a similar deficiency in the sociology of social movements, namely the underdeveloped state of knowledge on the dynamics of collective action once the movement has emerged (McAdam, McCarthy and Zald 1988). In particular, social movement research has paid surprisingly little attention to the interactions between social movement organizations and their opponents and has neglected the black-and-white perceptions of reality these interactions tend to produce (Klandermans 1989, p. 302). Indeed, one of the main areas for future research is the analysis of the ways in which specific conflicts escalate into "metaconflicts" as movement and countermovement strategies interact (Neidhardt and Rucht 1990). The more information on these dynamics that becomes available, the more urgent the need for methodological techniques to analyze the empirical data and for appropriate concepts to transform the new findings into theoretical knowledge. The authors of this book hope to stimulate both empirical research and reflection on methodological and theoretical tools suitable for analyzing apparently "absurd" phenomena.

ACKNOWLEDGMENTS

This volume was compiled while I was a research associate first at the European University Institute in Florence and, later, at the Wissenschaftszentrum Berlin für Sozialforschung. I am grateful to both institutions for their support. A Career Development Award of the Harry Frank Guggenheim Foundation enables me to continue my research in the field of political violence. My thanks to Bert Klandermans and Dieter Rucht for helpful suggestions on a previous draft of this introduction. Allan Silver kindly provided me with bibliographical references and comments on "ideological groups." I am also grateful to Martha Linke who has edited with care and competence the English text of several contributions.

REFERENCES

Baumann, M. 1976. *Tupamaros Berlin-Ouest* [Tupamaros West Berlin]. Paris: Les Presses d'aujourd'hui.

Becker, H. S. 1960. "Notes on the Concept of Commitment." *American Journal of Sociology* 66:32-40.

Berger, P. and T. Luckmann. 1966. *The Social Construction of Reality: A Treatise in the Sociology of Knowledge.* Garden City, NY: Anchor Books.

Billing, O. 1984. "The Case History of a German Terrorist." *Terrorism* 7:1-10.

Boucher, D. 1977. "Radical Ideologies and the Sociology of Knowledge: A Model for Comparative Analysis." *Sociology* 11: 25-46.

Coser, L. A. 1974. *Greedy Institutions: Patterns of Undivided Commitment.* New York: Free Press.

Crenshaw, M. 1988. "The Subjective Reality of Terrorists: Ideological and Psychological Factors in Terrorism," Pp. 12-46 in *Current Perspectives on International Terrorism,* edited by R. O. Slater and M. Stohl. London: Macmillan.

della Porta, D. 1983. "Le cause del terrorismo nelle società contemporanee" ["The Causes for Terrorism in Contemporary Societies]." Pp. 9-47 in *Terrorismo e violenza politica. Tre casi a confronto: Stati Uniti, Germania e Giappone* [Terrorism and Political Violence. A Comparison of Three Cases: United States, Germany and Japan], edited by D. della Porta and G. Pasquino. Bologna: Il Mulino.

———. 1987. "Storie di vita e movimenti collettivi. Una tecnica per lo studio delle motivazioni alla militanza politica" ["Life Histories and Collective Movements. A Technique for the Study of Motivation in Political Activism"]. *Rassegna italiana di sociologia* 28:105-131.

———. 1988. "Recruitment Processes in Clandestine Political Organizations: Italian Left-Wing Terrorism." Pp. 155-169 in *New Social Movements in Western Europe and the United States.* edited by B. Klandermans, H. Kriesi and S. Tarrow. Greenwich, CT: JAI Press.

———. 1990a. *Il terrorismo di sinistra* [Left-wing Terrorism]. Bologna: Il Mulino.

———. 1990b. *Biographies of Social Movement Activists: State of the Art and Methodological Problems.* Paper presented at the ECPR Joint Sessions, Bochum, April.

della Porta, D., and S. Tarrow. 1987. "Unwanted Children. Political Violence and the Cycle of Protest in Italy, 1966-1973." *European Journal of Political Research* 14:607-632.

Erikson, B. H. 1981. "Secret Societies and Social Structures." *Social Forces* 60: 188-210.

Franceschini, A., P. Buffa, and F. Giustolisi. 1988. *Mara, Renato ed io. Storia dei fondatori delle Brigate Rosse* [Mara, Renato and I. The Story of the Red Brigades' Founders]. Milan: Mondadori.

Gamson, W. A., B. Fireman and S. Rytina. 1982. *Encounters with Unjust Authorities.* Homewood, IL: Dorsey Press.

Garner, R. and M. N. Zald. 1983. *Social Movement Sector and Systemic Constraints: Toward a Structural Analysis of Social Movements.* CRSO Working Paper no. 238. University of Michigan.

Gerlach, L. P. and V. Hine. 1970. *People, Power, Change: Movements of Social Transformation.* New York: Bobbs-Merrill.

Goffman, E. 1963. *Stigma: Notes on the Management of Spoiled Identity.* Englewood Cliffs, NJ: Prentice-Hall.

________. 1974. *Frame Analysis. An Essay on the Organization of Experience.* Cambridge: Harvard University Press.

Granovetter, M. 1973. "The strength of weak ties." *American Journal of Sociology* 78:1360-1380.

Gurr, T. R. 1988. "Empirical Research on Political Terrorism: The State of the Art and How it Might Be Improved." Pp. 115-154 in *Current Perspectives on International Terrorism,* edited by R. O. Slater and M. Stohl. London: MacMillan.

Hazelrigg, L. E. 1969. "A Reexamination of Simmel's 'The Secret and the Secret Society': Nine Propositions." *Social Forces* 47: 323-330.

Ivianski, Z. 1983. "A Chapter in the Story of Individual Terror: Andrey Zhelyabol." Pp. 85-96 in *Perspectives on Terrorism,* edited by L.Z. Freedman and Y. Alexander. Wilmington, DE: Scholarly Resource Inc.

Keniston, K. 1968. *Young Radicals: Notes on Committed Youth.* New York: Harcourt, Brace and World.

Klandermans, B. G. 1984. "Mobilization and Participation in Social Movements: A Socio-Psychological Expansion of the Resource Mobilization Theory." *American Sociological Review* 49:583-600.

________. 1989. "Introductions." Pp. 1-17; 21-32; 117-128; 215-224; 301-314 in *Organizing for Change,* edited by B. Klandermans. Greenwich CT: JAI Press.

Klandermans, B.G., H. Kriesi, and S. Tarrow (eds.). 1988. *From Structure to Action: Comparing Social Movement Research Across Cultures.* Greenwich CT: JAI Press.

Klein, H.-J. 1980. *La mort mercenaire. Temoignage d'un ancient terroriste ouest-allemand* [The Mercenary Death: Testimony of a West-German Former Terrorist]. Paris: Seuil.

Knutson, J. N. 1981. "Social and Psychological Pressures Toward a Negative Identity: The Case of an American Revolutionary Terrorist," Pp. 105-150 in *Behavioral and Quantitative Perspectives on Terrorism,* edited by Y. Alexander and J. M. Gleamson. New York: Pergamon Press.

Livingstone, N. C. 1982. *The War Against Terrorism.* Lexington, KY: Lexington Books.

Lofland, J. and R. Stark. 1965. "Becoming a World-Saver: A Theory of Conversion to a Deviant Perspective." *American Sociological Review* 30:362-374.

Manconi, L. 1988. "Il nemico assoluto. Antifascismo e contropotere nella fase aurorale del terrorismo di sinistra" [The Absolute Enemy: Anti-fascism and Counter-Power at the Dawn of Left-Wing Terrorism]. *Polis* 2:259-286.

Matza, D. 1969. *Becoming Deviant.* Englewood Cliffs, NJ: Prentice-Hall.

McAdam, D. 1986. "Recruitment to High-Risk Activism: The Case of Freedom Summer." *American Journal of Sociology* 92:64-90.

McAdam, D., J.D. McCarthy and M. Zald. 1988. "Social Movements." Pp. 695-737 in *Handbook of Sociology*, edited by N. J. Smelser. Beverly Hills, CA: Sage.

McPhail, C. 1971. "Civil disorder participation: A critical examination of recent research." *American Sociological Review* 36:1058-1073.

McPhail, C., and D. Miller. 1973. "The Assembling Process: A Theoretical and Empirical Examination." *American Sociological Review* 38:721-735.

Merkl, P. H. 1986. "Approaches to the Study of Political Violence." Pp. 19-59 in *Political Violence and Terror. Motifs and Motivations*, edited by P. H. Merkl. Berkeley: University of California Press.

Nahirni, V. C. 1962. "Some Observations on Ideological Groups." *American Journal of Sociology* 67:397-405.

Neidhardt, F. and D. Rucht. 1990. "The Analysis of Social Movements: The State of the Art and Some Perspective for Further Research." In *Research on Social Movements: The State of the Art in Western Europe and the USA*, edited by D. Rucht. Frankfurt/M. and Boulder: Campus and Westview Press.

Niebuhr, R. H. 1937. "Sects." Pp. 624-631 in *Encyclopaedia of the Social Sciences*, Vol. 13. New York: Macmillan.

Novaro, C. 1988. "Reti amicali e lotta armata" [Friendship Networks and Armed Struggle]. *Polis* 2:287-320.

Novelli, D. and N. Tranfaglia. 1988. *Vite sospese. Le generazioni del terrorismo.* [Suspended Lives: The Generations of Terrorism]. Milan: Garzanti.

O'Toole, R. 1975. "Sectarianism in Politics. Case Studies of Maoists and Leninists." Pp. 162-190 in *Sectarianism: Analysis of Religious and Non-religious Sects* edited by R. Wallis. New York: Wiley.

Pasquino, G. and D. della Porta. 1986. "Interpretations of Italian Left-Wing Terrorism." Pp. 169-189 in *Political Violence and Terror. Motifs and Motivations*, edited by P. H. Merkl. Berkeley: University of California Press.

Rasch, W. 1979. "Psychological Dimensions of Political Terrorism in the Federal Republic of Germany." *International Journal of Law and Psychiatry* 2:79-85.

Reynaud, E. 1982. "Identites collective et changement social: les cultures collectives comme dynamique d'action." *Sociologie du travail* 2: 159-177.

Rogers, K. L. 1985a. *Decoding a City of Words: Fantasy Theme Analysis and the Interpretation of Oral Interviews*. Paper.

———. 1985b. "Words Testify in Spite of Us": The Experience of CORE As a Subculture. Unpublished paper.

Roots, C. A. 1983. "On the Social Structural Sources of Political Conflict: An Approach from the Theory of Knowledge." *Research in Social Movements, Conflict, and Change*. 5:33-54.

Russel C. A. and B. H. Miller. 1983. "Profile of a terrorist." Pp. 45-59 in *Perspectives on Terrorism*, edited by L. Z. Freedman and Y. Alexander. Wilmington, DE: Scholarly Resource Inc.

Sartori, G. 1969. "Politics, Ideology, and Belief System." *American Political Science Review* 63:398-411.

Schmidtchen, G. 1981. "Terroristische Karrieren" [Terrorist Careers]. Pp. 14-77 in H. Jaeger, G. Schmidtchen, and L. Suellwold, *Lebenslaufanalysen* [Analysis of Life Careers]. Opladen: Westdeutscher.

Schmitt, C. 1975. *Teoria del partigiano. Note complementari al concetto di politica* [Theory of the Partisan. Complementary Notes to the Concept of Politics]. Milan: Il saggiatore.

Simmel, G. 1950. "The Secret and the Secret Societies." Pp. 345-376 in *The Sociology of George Simmel*, edited by K. H. Wolff. New York: Free Press.

Smith, B. L., H. D. Lasswell, and R. D. Casey. 1946. *Propaganda, Communication, and Public Opinion. A Comprehensive Reference Guide*. Chicago: University of Chicago Press.

Snow, D. A. and R. Machalek. 1983. "The Convert As A Social Type." Pp. 259-289 in *Sociological Theory*, edited by R. Collins. San Francisco: Jossey-Bass.

Snow, D.A., E. B. Rochford, S. K. Worden, and R. D. Benford. 1986. "Frame alignment processes, micromobilization, and movement participation." *American Sociological Review* 51: 464-481.

Snow, D.A., L. A. Zurcher, and S. Ekland-Olson. 1980. "Social networks and social movements: A microstructural approach to differential recruitment." *American Sociological Review* 45:787-801.

Tarrow, S. 1989. *Struggle, Politics, and Reform: Collective Action, Social Movements, and Cycle of Protest.* Western Societies Program Occasional Paper no. 21, Ithaca NY.

Tilly, C. 1984. "Social Movements and National Politics." Pp. 297-317 in *Statemaking and Social Movements: Essays in History and Theory*, edited by C. Bright and S. Harding. Ann Arbor: University of Michigan Press.

Toloyan, K. 1987. "Culture Narrative and the Motivation of the Terrorist." *Journal of Strategic Studies* 10:217-233.

Useem, M. 1972. "Ideological and Interpersonal Change in the Radical Protest Movement." *Social Problems* 19:451-469.

Verba, S. 1961. *Small Groups and Political Behavior. A Study of Leadership.* Princeton: Princeton University Press.

Wasmund, K. 1986. "The Political Socialization of West German Terrorists." Pp. 191-228 in *Political Violence and Terror: Motifs and Motivations*, edited by P. H. Merkl. Berkeley: University of California Press.

White, R. W. 1989. "From Peaceful Protest to Guerrilla War: Micromobilization of the Provisional Irish Republican Army." *American Journal of Sociology* 94:1277-1302.

Wilson, B. R. 1959. "An Analysis of Sect Development." *American Sociological Review* 24:3-15.

Wilson, J. 1973. *Introduction to Social Movements.* New York: Basic Books.

Wolfgang, M. and F. Ferracuti. 1967. *The Subculture of Violence.* London: Tavistock.

Zald, M. and R. Ash. 1966. "Social Movement Organizations: Growth, Decay, and Change." *Social Forces* 44:327-341.

Zald, M., J. D. McCarthy, et al. 1987. *Social Movements in an Organizational Society.* New Brunswick, NJ: Transaction.

DECISIONS TO USE TERRORISM: PSYCHOLOGICAL CONSTRAINTS ON INSTRUMENTAL REASONING

Martha Crenshaw

Terrorism is often considered the result of a strategic choice based on instrumental reasoning (Crenshaw 1990; DeNardo 1985). In this perspective, terrorism is analyzed as a form of political violence designed to affect the attitudes of specific audiences whose reactions determine political outcomes. Terrorism is interpreted as a calculated course of action, chosen from a range of alternatives according to a ranked set of values. The efficacy of terrorism as a means of political influence is assumed to be the primary criterion of choice. Decision makers in the organizations that use terrorism are supposed to rely on explicit strategic conceptions to guide group behavior. These conceptions then become the focus of analysis. To explain a particular terrorist action, one asks what strategic purpose it was meant to accomplish.

Like all rational choice explanations of political action, this one is incomplete. My intention is not to contest the premise that terrorism is often strategic behavior, but to describe possible psychological barriers to purely strategic calculation in underground organizations. Psychological factors influence both the initiation and the conduct of terrorism and may be the source

International Social Movement Research, Vol. 4, pages 29-42.

ISBN: 1-55938-445-X

of actions that are incomprehensible if interpreted strictly as external goal-oriented behavior. We may be misled if we assume that such outcomes are the result of deliberate choice. Psychological interactions within underground organizations can provoke groups to action that is counterproductive in terms of long-term goals. Although psychological factors may occasionally reinforce the grounds for decisions that are instrumentally based, they may also interfere with strategic calculation of ends and means. I ask how group dynamics and collective belief systems influence the use of terrorism by making it possible, motivating it, determining its forms, and instigating its escalation or decline.

Any such analysis must be sensitive to variations in context. Terrorism is the resort of numerous groups acting in terms of different social and political situations, ideological backgrounds, and prospects of ultimate success. Yet there is a psychology of small, radical, illegal conspiracies that distinguishes them from other political and social actors. The hypotheses I suggest may be applicable primarily to underground organizations without substantial ethnic or other ascriptive constituencies and which are consequently isolated from society. Groups that are closed rather than open to contacts outside the group may be less likely to be strategic in their reasoning.

GROUP DYNAMICS

The appropriate focus for a psychological explanation is the interaction of individuals within the group, not individual personality. The idea of terrorism as the product of mental disorder or psychopathology has been discredited. In a recent review of the literature, Maxwell Taylor concludes that it is inappropriate to think of the terrorist as mentally ill in conventional terms and that the individual psychology of the terrorist cannot be characterized in general (Taylor 1988). Such groups recruit selectively and exclude aspirants who are undisciplined or untrustworthy. Furthermore, the group takes on an independent collective identity that transcends individual characteristics. Radical organizations typically unite people of different backgrounds and temperaments. Participation in the extremist group and commitment to a collective belief system, rather than any shared propensity for violence or inclination toward aggression, bind members together. As Albert Bandura (1979, p. 338) notes, "it requires conducive social conditions rather than monstrous people to produce heinous deeds." Jerrold Post (1987, pp. 25-26) also emphasizes that " once individuals join a terrorist group individual differences disappear in the face of the powerful unifying forces of group and organizational psychology" and that "group psychology provides a powerful explanation for this uniformity of behavior within the diverse population of terrorist groups." Thus the topics of most interest to the researcher are group recruitment and socialization processes, not individual personality characteristics prior to joining the group.

For political oppositions, the initial decision to use terrorism against the state usually requires a transition to clandestine life in the underground, a decision that in many contexts is irreversible. "The roads of retreat are all closed; one blows up all the bridges behind one in the truest sense of the word," explains Michael "Bommi" Baumann, a member of a West German terrorist group (Baumann 1977, p. 109). The move to the underground may even be precipitated by acts of nonterrorist violence. For example, the West German Red Army Fraction's attempt to rescue Andreas Baader from prison resulted in the accidental killing of a guard and thus criminality and illegality: "From this point on there was no going back but only the 'forward escape'" (Wasmund 1986, p. 199).

The transition to clandestinity requires total commitment from an inner core of militants. Some undergrounds form a kind of counterculture, resembling that of religious cults or youth gangs. Illegality isolates the members of the group from society and encourages the development of distinctive values, norms, and standards of behavior. The collectivity usually demands the complete obedience of members. For reasons of security as well as discipline, the organization usually prohibits personal relationships outside the group. Contacts with the outside world are mediated through the institutions of the group. Insiders are trusted; outsiders are distrusted.

Relationships of leaders to followers in the group may contribute to the isolation of the group from society and to the growth of interdependence among members. A leader of the Uruguayan Tupamaros, in a prison interview with a journalist, explained that rather than trying to select recruits who possessed specific traits, the "Movement" tried to "proletarize" the new member: "the most important thing is to create in him a feeling of dependence on the group. He has to be aware of the fact that he cannot be self-sufficient—that the others are essential to him" (Gilio 1972, p. 137). In addition to explicit indoctrination procedures, the structure of an underground organization creates dependence on a central leadership, because, for security reasons, it is essential to restrict knowledge of the overall organizational structure. Leaders usually control contacts with the outside world as well as the dissemination of information within the group. The authority of leaders within extremist undergrounds may be based on command of ideology (intellectual authority), operational expertise (military authority), or charisma (personal authority). Leaders also base their authority on the ability to manipulate incentives for followers. These incentives are both political—the ability to move the group toward accomplishment of collective goals—and psychological. For example, threatening expulsion from the group or from the inner circle is a powerful way of inhibiting dissent. In addition, leaders are under pressure to conform to group norms and to preserve ideological purity. Their freedom of action is thus limited.

In general, the members of such organizations are not suddenly converted to terrorism but acquire their commitment gradually, often through belonging to a group, set of friends, or family unit that collectively turns to terrorism. That is, people are recruited into terrorism through personal associations that precede or accompany political commitment. With regard to the West German left-wing groups, Klaus Wasmund (1986, p. 204) notes that "Most terrorists, in fact, have ultimately become members of terrorist organizations through personal connections with people or relatives associated with appropriate political initiatives, communes, self-supporting organizations, or committees—the number of couples, and brothers and sisters is astonishingly high." Leonard Weinberg and William Lee Eubank found in Italy that "it seems reasonable to suspect that the decision to become a terrorist was often not that of individual choice. Likely it involved a decision, and a gradual one at that, by a primary group whose members reached consensus over the desirability of violent political engagement" (1987, p. 83). Ties to other members of the group are independent of commitment to collective goals. As a consequence, the importance of the group to the individual is heightened. Loyalty is primarily to the group or entity, not to abstract objectives or ideology. At the least, the individual is unable to separate these two emotional and cognitive commitments—the one to friends, the other to ideals.

Therefore the pressures toward cohesion and uniformity that exist in all primary groups are likely to be intensified under the circumstances of underground life. Solidarity is all the more critical because the group usually lives under conditions of acute threat and high stress. Exposure to danger increases cohesion. The tension created by the underground situation may lead to high levels of anxiety, aggravated by fatigue. Such conditions decrease a group's ability to identify alternatives, estimate costs and benefits, assess outcomes, evaluate audience perspectives, and adjust to changes in the environment (Holsti 1972, pp. 7-25).

Furthermore, underground organizations usually suffer high rates of attrition. The death or imprisonment of group members may lead to the activation of the defense mechanism of identifying with the lost comrade. Through a process of introjection, the remaining members of the group take on the values of the dead or captured members (Janis 1968, pp. 84-85). As a result, adherence to group standards is strengthened because abandonment would be viewed as an act of disloyalty. In some ways, the behavior of members of such groups resembles that of soldiers under combat conditions. Disloyalty to one's comrades constitutes betrayal, the most serious violation of group norms.

Thus deviation from group standards is probably rare because of mutual interdependence, peer pressure, sensitivity to betrayal, and security risks. Ordinarily, members of these groups seek above all to avoid the disapproval of their peers. Dissent is emotionally painful. Both external danger and internal dissent may stimulate a need for reassurance, leading the faithful and loyal members to become more dependent on the group, its leaders, and collective beliefs. Thus where factionalism occurs—and it is common to many groups such as the Palestinian and Basque movements—solidarity within "survivor" groups may be intensified. Furthermore, the dissenters who form new factions are also likely to feel acutely dependent on the new group because they have sacrificed so much to join. The high entrance fee is likely to discourage exit (Hirschman 1970).

Whereas some groups such as the IRA permit their members to leave the group so long as they do not inform on it, others punish defection as "betrayal." There are then physical as well as psychological penalties associated with exit. One would expect dissent to be even more distressful under circumstances of high personal risk, which includes the prospect of punishment from the government as well as retribution from one's comrades.

BELIEF SYSTEMS

A key role of the leadership is to develop or maintain a collective belief system that links overall ideological orientation to the environment in which the group operates. Ascertaining what terrorists believe is not a simple task (Crenshaw 1988). Appropriate sources are difficult to acquire. It is difficult to distinguish motive from rationalization. The beliefs of violent extremists are often quite complex as well as hard to know. Nevertheless, understanding how underground groups view the world and themselves is essential to explaining terrorism. In particular, one must ask if their perceptions of the effects of their actions on audiences become distorted because of simplifying beliefs that guide action. For example, Alessandro Silj (1979) observed that the Italian Red Brigades "lost perspective on the situation" upon entering the underground; their misinterpretation of the likely reactions of relevant audiences resulted from isolation. "In part, the very logic of clandestinity, the dynamic of a process which, once set in motion, was irreversible, contributed to such a misperception" (Silj 1979, p. 115). Mistakes—particularly the false expectation that the Italian government was on the verge of collapse in 1971—were encouraged by the movement into the underground.

The sharpest and clearest aspect of the beliefs that may be conducive to terrorism is identification and characterization of the enemy. In a pattern that is typical of much social conflict, the enemy is portrayed as an undifferentiated and monolithic entity, usually an abstraction such as a system or a class. Wasmund (1986, pp. 215, 218) observes that "a friend-enemy mentality exists which is typical of all totalitarian groupings" and that the enemy is a figure that symbolizes everything "bad." The stereotypical enemy is both unrelentingly hostile and morally corrupt. Society as well as the state may be perceived as the enemy—the bourgeoisie, for example, or capitalism. The enemy may even be international; multinational imperialism is often a common enemy of the radical right and the radical left.

The self-image of the terrorist is ambivalent, even contradictory. Terrorists need to see themselves as doing good, to justify their actions, and to maintain morale. Consequently "auto-propaganda" may be more critical to group survival than are attempts to persuade external audiences, whether governments, constituencies, or likeminded groups (Cordes 1988). The users of terrorism often see themselves as victims, but also as an avant-garde acting on behalf of victims of injustice. They act for "the people" who are unable to act for themselves. They are simultaneously victims and righteous avengers, targets of oppression and soldiers. This conviction may be strengthened by the belief that they do not stand to gain personally from their efforts. Altruism and self-sacrifice are dominant themes, yet the key metaphor in terrorist literature is struggle and combat. A strong trace of millenarianism, with its faith in personal redemption through violence, is evident (Rapoport 1987).

Beliefs about enemy and self overshadow references to the actual victims of terrorism, whose deaths or injuries are usually blamed on others (governments who refuse to heed warnings, for example). They do pay attention, however, to the audiences for terrorism and interpret the world in causal terms (Hopple and Steiner 1984). The image of the "people" in Western democracies, for example, is based on imperfect assumptions of benevolence and ignorance. The physical victims of terrorism, whatever their personal identity, are never seen as members of the social classes whom the terrorists claim to represent.

The sources of these beliefs, which justify terrorism, lie in political culture and in psychological needs. Beliefs are selectively derived from the group's political, social, and cultural environment and thus reflect prevailing ideologies as well as socialization patterns. The intellectuals who lead or participate in groups that use terrorism are rarely philosophical or ideological innovators. Beliefs also serve important psychological needs, such as compensation for an inability to deal with aggressive feelings. They may aid in the external attribution of blame and the projection of hostility onto the enemy. Ideological rationalizations may mask a form of generational rebellion against authority displaced onto political figures. The low self-esteem exhibited by some individuals in these groups and their view of the enemy as omnipotent may be signs of developmental immaturity. The fact that most terrorists are young provides some support for this hypothesis. People who commit acts of violence may also need to neutralize guilt—guilt over their victims, survivor guilt when comrades are lost, or guilt over aggressive impulses toward parents or surrogate authority figures.

Psychological research in different theoretical traditions suggests that individual beliefs are likely to be stable rather than volatile. Even greater stability should characterize collective attitudes that are constantly reinforced by group interaction. Theories of cognitive consistency indicate that individuals absorb only information that supports their beliefs, ignore disconfirming evidence, fail to recognize value conflicts, and neglect to reconsider decisions once they are reached. Other approaches emphasize the emotional conflict that lies behind decision making. The more costly the consequences of a decision, the more painful the reassessment. Members of the groups who use terrorism may engage in what Irving Janis and Leon Mann call "defensive avoidance" (Janis and Mann 1977). Ego involvement in prior commitments is bound to be strong, and the cost of abandoning them unacceptably high. Furthermore, the nature of a belief system itself may preclude change. The least systematic beliefs are the most resilient, and the least empirically relevant are the most incontrovertible because they cannot be tested or falsified. Vague and distant long-term goals can be an advantage. "True believers" are not by nature skeptical (Snow and Machalek 1982).

It is also possible that the resort to terrorism precedes and consequently determines beliefs. That is, rather than acting as a result of preconceptions, people may act impulsively or unthinkingly and then rationalize their actions. "Self-perception theory" is based on the assumption that individuals use their own actions as a guide to the formation of attitudes and beliefs, through a process of self-inference (Larson 1985, pp. 42-50). Engaging in terrorism, perhaps because of coincidence or group pressures, leads the individual to adopt beliefs and images that explain the moral necessity and practical efficacy of terrorism. Once convinced that terrorism is intellectually justified, an individual is persuaded in retrospect that the initial use of terrorism was based on prior ideological beliefs. Because terrorism is extreme behavior, usually condemned by society, it is important for the individual to generate an explanation for it. When terrorists are students, the need to intellectualize terrorist activity may be particularly strong. Groups formed of people with diverse social backgrounds (such as the Provisional IRA) may feel less need for intellectual rationalizations or self-inference. The Provisional IRA appears to feel that the reasons for terrorism are self-evident.

Jeanne Knutson (1980) effectively described the relationship between group pressures and rigid but subjective belief systems: "Doubts are muted and are continuously attacked by the group, which employs great psychological pressure toward conformity. Basic concepts are challenged with great difficulty . . . . There is no real debate over primary assumptions (p. 213)." The group seeks a "homogeneous level of . . . thought which stifles self-doubt and a consideration of alternatives (p. 213)." She quoted one of her interviewees as admitting that "we were increasingly losing our grip on reality" and that cutting off contacts with the outside world led to a "group personality" with its own deadly internal momentum (pp. 213-214). She concluded, "In such an atmosphere, group actions take on a predetermined, fatalistic quality in which *responsibility* for the occurrence of specific actions is progressively shifted onto the opposition players in the government, general social forces, or an inactive populace, and terrorist players come to experience themselves as guided by an externally perceived necessity" (p. 214; also Wasmund 1986, pp. 218-220). The cohesiveness of the group strengthens adherence to beliefs, and in turn beliefs reinforce solidarity.

IMPLICATIONS FOR THE PRACTICE OF TERRORISM

These psychological factors have important implications for terrorist behavior. On a general level, members of groups may act simply to maintain a collective identity and thus seek to keep the group alive whatever its political accomplishments. Baumann (1977, p. 76) explains, "I saw that it was going to go a hundred percent wrong . . . . I only participated out of solidarity." Dependence on the group is likely to lead members to value the approval of other members of the group more than the achievement of long-term political goals. Thus an objective definition of success, predicated on the achievement of political ends, may not be appropriate. When extremist organizations such as ETA and the Provisional IRA persist despite objective failure, one must ask whether or not simply keeping the group together has become more important than a Basque homeland or a united Ireland.

One consequence of the centrality of the group is that motives that unite its members, such as vengeance, take precedence over instrumental calculations, which can be deeply divisive. Newman and Lynch (1987) argue that terrorism may be a "cycle of violence" fueled by vengeance, leading to its self-perpetuation. They argue that the only possible common ideology associated with terrorism is one of vengeance, a code of conduct that shapes behavior. The code of vengeance embodies its own justification, giving the terrorist not only a moral claim but an obligation. Terrorism thus becomes a sophisticated modern form of feuding. Vengeance, which is motivated by a sense of injustice and of powerlessness, is based on the principle of reciprocity. Escalation occurs because the act of retribution is never an exact match for the original offense. Those who administer it cannot resist adding an element of coercion, trying to make the response to perceived injustice sufficiently strong to deter counterretribution. The avenger develops identity through violence, thus generating a process without limits. Only vengeance can defend one's honor, which is an essential component of identity.

The intense loyalty that members of the underground group feel for each other, a loyalty strengthened by bonds of kinship or personal affection, makes revenge imperative when government security forces kill or imprison comrades. Such an outcome is highly likely once a group resorts to terrorism, which is bound to provoke a repressive government reaction. Because revenge motivates both sides, terrorism and the response to terrorism create an independent and self-contained logic. Eventually repression from the authorities provokes actions intended only to avenge comrades, not to change the positions of government or society (Silj 1979, p. 219). Revenge is part of a process of using violence in order to strengthen group cohesiveness, confirm beliefs about self and world, and maintain group morale and individual self-esteem. These needs are frequently characterized in terms of upholding "honor."

Jerrold Post (1987, p. 33) notes, moreover, that government "retaliation may actually strengthen the group and promote increased terrorist activity" because the terrorists' worldviews are confirmed and their cohesiveness is enhanced by threat and shared danger. Coercive government responses thus make terrorism self-sustaining because the terrorists' expectations of hostility are proved right. Terrorism can then be justified as defensive. But, as noted earlier, governments may not be able to control their own response or prevent the development of a cycle of vengeance and retribution. Once terrorism begins, both sides are likely to lose control.

Terrorist and counter-terrorist forces are often mirror images of each other. Each consciously imitates the other—terrorists act as "armies," while national armies develop specialized elite intervention forces that operate covertly. Each side's reputation is caught up in the struggle. The purpose of terrorism and of repression becomes to outdo the other. Each small, self-contained, and specialized unit tends to become autonomous from central authority. Examples include the Combat Organization of the Socialist Revolutionary Party in Russia, combatting the czarist secret police or Okhrana, and the Algiers terrorist units of the FLN against the French paratroopers. In these situations, the phenomenon of the double agent or agent-provocateur takes on special importance as the communication link between the two sides. The role of the informant or double agent remains a "neglected category" for analysis, as Gary T. Marx claimed (1974).

Because internal conflict threatens group cohesion and identity, leaders may try to deflect aggression onto external targets. For example, one reason for the creation of the Black September organization was apparently to absorb the intense frustration of younger militants over the Palestinian expulsion from Jordan in 1970. Arafat apparently decided to permit, if not direct, terrorism outside the Middle East in order to prevent internal dissent within Fatah.

Furthermore, adherence to the group and to its standards helps to overcome guilt. Even if group values are internalized, some individuals will experience anxiety and self-doubt. Peer pressure encourages members of the group to commit actions they would normally find morally reprehensible, such as killing children. Distress engendered by guilt leads to greater dependence on the group, increased group influence over the individual, and consequently more terrorism. The unpleasant prospect of accepting responsibility and suffering remorse may then prevent the individual from leaving the group.

The collective belief system can aid in assuaging guilt. Albert Bandura explains that "People do not ordinarily engage in reprehensible conduct until they have justified to themselves the morality of their actions. What is culpable can be made honorable through cognitive restructuring. In this process, reprehensible conduct is made personally and socially acceptable by portraying it in the service of moral ends" (1979, p. 351). He refers to mechanisms such as contrasting one's behavior with the more inhumane practices of one's enemy (palliative comparison), using euphemistic language to disguise violence and make it respectable, obscuring the consequences of one's actions, dehumanizing the enemy, blaming the victim, or displacing responsibility onto others or in fact onto a collective instrumentality. All collective arrangements, he notes, obscure individual responsibility. He further explains that "people frequently engage in violent activities not because of reduced self-control but because their cognitive skills and self-control are enlisted all too well through moral justifications and self-exonerative devices in the service of destructive causes" (p. 356). In effect, the beliefs of terrorist actors serve as a mechanism of "moral disengagement" (Bandura 1987). Upon entering an underground organization, the individual does not undergo a psychological conversion but comes to see violence as morally sanctioned.

Legal and military terms of discourse reinforce the image of the terrorist as the impersonal agent of larger forces. In the euphemistic language of terrorism, victims are "executed" after "trials." Terrorism becomes "urban guerilla warfare." Seeing oneself as a victim makes it hard to conceive of others as victims or oneself as an aggressor. The idea of acting on behalf of an oppressed but faceless constituency (the proletariat, the Third World, or prisoners) justifies practices that would be abhorrent if performed out of pure self-interest. William Ascher (1986), in interviewing Armenian and Irish supporters of terrorism (admittedly not the terrorists themselves) identifies moral indignation as a critical attitude and links it to "disinterestedness" or "distance": the less one has to gain personally from the outcome of violence, the more sincere and righteous one feels.

Psychological considerations may also explain the particular form terrorism takes. Hostage taking, for example, can be interpreted rationally as a form of coercive bargaining, a means of compensating for the greater power of governments, since weakness is not a disadvantage in situations of blackmail (Crenshaw 1990). Yet, it is also possible that a desperate need to free imprisoned comrades genuinely motivates hostage taking. "Second generation" successor groups in West Germany and Italy devoted themselves to freeing imprisoned "historic" or "founding" leaders. The demand for the release of prisoners may thus be sincere rather than a disguise for publicity-seeking behavior. Dependence on the group and its leaders, fear of a hostile government, or survivor guilt, may combine to make hostage takers feel desperate. Hostage taking may also be a search for recognition by the government, a result of the terrorists' collective self-image as powerless victims (Knutson 1980).

The desire to avoid responsibility for violent outcomes may also affect the form of terrorism. Terrorists wish to blame casualties on the government. The attribution of blame begins with an assignment of responsibility and a judgement about causality (Shaver 1985; Bandura 1987, p. 23). Terrorists may not see themselves as morally accountable because they believe that they did not originally intend or foresee a negative outcome. Their initial expectations upon seizing hostages, for example, are optimistic because they believe that the government will comply. Terrorists may be likely to think that governments have a certain knowledge of the outcome if concessions are refused. Furthermore, one way of reducing cognitive dissonance, induced by having to choose between the two negative options of killing hostages or giving up, is to believe that the only escape from the dilemma rests with the opponent (Holsti 1972). The terrorists are also likely to see themselves as having been coerced, rather than seeing the government as having been blackmailed. They do not perceive the killing of hostages as a voluntary action but as something the government compelled them to do. Terrorists can thus not only exonerate themselves but feel self-righteous and see their image of the evil state confirmed.

Similarly, in leaving bombs a group may accept responsibility but not blame, which perhaps reveals an interesting ability to separate these two processes. Maria McGuire, an early member of the Provisional IRA, describes a car-bomb in Belfast in 1972 that killed six and injured 146 people. In this case, the Provisionals falsely accused the security forces of deliberately muddling the telephoned warning in order to discredit the IRA. McGuire continues, "despite blaming the security forces, the movement 'accepted responsibility" for the explosion, and it was a curious thing that the Provisionals felt that by doing so they somehow atoned for the casualties . . . . I admit that at times I did not connect with the people who were killed or injured in such explosions. I always judged such deaths in terms of the effect they would have on our support, and I felt that this in turn depended on how many people accepted our explanation" (1973, p. 113).

In barricade and hostage situations, where stress and tension are high, hostage takers may be prone to panic. Their behavior, Janis and Mann (1977) would suggest, is likely to be erratic. They are tempted to precipitous action. If all choices appear unpleasant and time pressures are severe, their judgement will be poor. The responsibility for averting disaster will be seen to rest with the government. For example, during incidents such as the takeover of the Achille Lauro or the attempted hijacking of a Pan Am jet in Karachi, the aggressive behavior of the hijackers may have been the result of loss of emotional control, not deliberate calculation. What an instrumental approach would interpret as sequential killing of hostages in order to reinforce the credibility of a threat, a psychological approach would interpret as a panic reaction. The so-called Stockholm Syndrome, a shorthand term for the hypothesis that with time hostages and their captors will become attached to each other because of the phenomenon of identification with the aggressor, is thus unlikely to operate. Hostage takers or kidnappers are acting as agents of a group on which they are emotionally dependent in the extreme; letting the group down is probably a worse alternative than killing hostages of whom one has grown reasonably fond or even confronting death. The relationship with the group also enables the hostage takers to think of themselves as impersonal agents of the collective entity and thus avoid assuming individual responsibility.

The escalation of terrorism to greater levels of destructiveness may also result from psychological processes. For example, it is possible that the "risky shift" that research in experimental social psychology finds characteristic of small groups applies to political undergrounds (Crenshaw 1986, p. 397). Participation in group discussions leads to a heightened propensity to take risks. The individual's reluctance to let the group "down" or lose face in the eyes of peers may encourage this process. Yet, we also know that most groups are risk-averse in the sense of selecting soft, unprotected targets. The expansion of targets toward increasingly innocent victims is a form of escalation. A group setting facilitates brutalization. Participation in terrorism conditions and desensitizes the individual. Discomfort with violence is overcome by performing it. Routine sets in. Thus the absence of conditioning may impede the adaptation of "second generation" recruits who enter the group after its values have been formed. They may be the most likely defectors. On the other hand, candidates for membership in established organizations may be attracted to violence, while the founding members were attracted to the group.

To note the phenomenon of brutalization, however, is not to claim that all members of such groups actually participate in or are capable of participating in physical violence. Only a few elite members of the underground organizations are sharpshooters or bombers; most are support personnel. Role differentiation enables many members of the group to dissociate themselves from violence. Responsibility is diffused through the division of labor (Bandura 1987). Few group members confront their victims face-to-face. Reluctance to deal personally with victims may partially explain the popularity of bombings as opposed to other forms of terrorism.

Moreover, a common method of dealing with stress is to focus narrowly on the task at hand, rather than to reflect on the implication of one's actions (Roth 1982, pp. 52-53, referring to Finz 1975). This psychological defense or coping mechanism becomes less necessary as the task becomes habitual. Both compartmentalization and routinization reduce the discomfort an individual might initially feel upon committing an act of terrorism. When terrorists claim that they are only "soldiers," they are trying to achieve detachment and impersonality as well as to legitimize their actions.

CONCLUSIONS

This analysis suggests that a radical group's decision to enter the underground and isolate itself from society may be a decisive event in the development of terrorism. In circumstances where this decision entails extreme isolation from social support networks, clandestinity strengthens solidarity and dependence on group beliefs that justify violence. The more terrorism is used, the more it needs to be justified by moralistic attitudes. It may develop into a cycle of vengeance and retribution that is self-defeating.

Furthermore, this analysis suggests that justifications for terrorism and emotional support, both provided by the group, are critical. From this point of view, terrorism is likely to end when the bonds that link members of the group to each other are dissolved or when beliefs that justify violence break down or are discredited. But, as Franco Ferracuti has observed, "What happens in the mind of the terrorist who decides to abandon terrorism is not known" (1987, p. 13). Future research should focus on the psychology of dissent and of exit, as well as on the personal interactions and collective beliefs of groups.

ACKNOWLEDGMENTS

An earlier version of this paper was presented to the Twelfth Annual Scientific Meeting of the International Society of Political Psychology, Tel Aviv, June, 1989.

REFERENCES

Ascher, W. 1986. "The Moralism of Attitudes Supporting Intergroup Violence." *Political Psychology* 7, 3:403-425.

Bandura, A. 1979. "Psychological mechanisms of aggression." In *Human Ethology: Claims and Limits of a New Discipline,* edited by M. von Cranach, K. Froppa, W. Lepenies, and D. Ploog. Cambridge: Cambridge University Press.

________. 1990. "Mechanisms of Moral Disengagement." In *Origins of Terrorism: Psychologies, Ideologies, Theologies, States of Mind,* edited by W. Reich. Cambridge: Cambridge University Press and Woodrow Wilson International Center for Scholars.

Baumann, B. 1977. *Wie Alles Anfing–How it all Began: The Personal Account of a West German Urban Guerilla.* Vancouver: Pulp Press.

Cordes, B. 1988. "When Terrorists Do the Talking: Reflections on the Terrorist Literature." In *Inside Terrorist Organizations* edited by D. Rapoport. New York: Columbia University Press.

Crenshaw, M. 1986. "The Psychology of Political Terrorism." In *Political Psychology,* edited by M. G. Hermann. San Francisco: Jossey-Bass.

________. 1988. "The Subjective Reality of the Terrorist: Ideological and Psychological Factors in Terrorism." In *Current Perspectives on International Terrorism,* edited by R. O. Slater and M. Stohl. New York: St. Martin's.

________. 1990. "The Logic of Terrorism: Terrorism As a Product of Strategic Choice." In *Origins of Terrorism: Psychologies, Ideologies, Theologies, States of Mind,* edited by W. Reich.

Cambridge: Woodrow Wilson International Center for Scholars and Cambridge University Press.

DeNardo, J. 1985. *Power in Numbers: The Political Strategy of Protest and Rebellion.* Princeton: Princeton University Press.

Ferracuti, F. 1990. "Ideology and Repentance: Terrorism in Italy." In *Origins of Terrorism: Psychologies, Ideologies, Theologies, States of Mind,* edited by W. Reich. Cambridge: Cambridge University Press and Woodrow Wilson International Center for Scholars.

Finz, W. D. 1975. "Strategies for Coping with Stress." In *Stress and Anxiety.* Vol.2, edited by I. G. Sarason and C. D. Spielberger. New York: Wiley.

Gilio, M. E. 1972. *The Tupamaros.* London: Secker and Warburg.

Hirschman, A. O. 1970. *Exit, Voice, and Loyalty: Responses to Decline in Firms, Organizations, and States.* Cambridge: Harvard University Press.

Holsti, O. R. 1972. "Crisis, Stress and Decision Making." In *Crisis Escalation War.* Montreal: McGill-Queen's University Press.

Hopple, G. W. and M. Steiner. 1984. *The Causal Beliefs of Terrorists: Empirical Results.* McLean, VA: Defense Systems, Inc.

Janis, I. 1968. "Group Identification Under Conditions of External Danger." In *Group Dynamics: Research and Theory,* edited by D. Cartwright and A. Zander, 3rd ed. New York: Harper and Row.

Janis, I. L. and L. Mann. 1977. *Decision-Making: A Psychological Analysis of Conflict, Choice, and Commitment.* New York: Free Press.

Knutson, J. 1980. "The Terrorists' Dilemmas: Some Implicit Rules of the Game." *Terrorism: An International Journal* 4(1-4):195-222.

Larson, D. 1985. *Origins of Containment: A Psychological Explanation.* Princeton: Princeton University Press.

Marx, G. T. 1974. "Thoughts on a Neglected Category of Social Movement Participant: The Agent Provocateur and the Informant." *American Journal of Sociology* 80(2):402-440.

McGuire, M. 1973. *To Take Arms: My Year with the IRA Provisionals.* New York: Viking Press.

Newman, G. R. and M.J. Lynch. 1987. "From Feuding to Terrorism: The Ideology of Vengeance." *Contemporary Crises* 11:223-242.

Post, J. M. 1987. "Rewarding Fire with Fire: Effects of Retaliation on Terrorist Group Dynamics." *Terrorism: An International Journal* 10: 23-36.

Rapoport, D. C. 1990. "Messianic Sanctions for Terror." In *Origins of Terrorism: Psychologies, Ideologies, Theologies, States of Mind,* edited by W. Reich. Cambridge: Cambridge University Press and Woodrow Wilson International Center for Scholars.

Roth, W. T. 1982. "The Meaning of Stress." In *Victims of Terrorism,* edited by F. M. Ochberg and D. A. Soskis. Boulder, CO: Westview.

Shaver, K. G. 1985. *The Attribution of Blame: Causality, Responsibility, and Blameworthiness.* New York: Springer-Verlag.

Silj, A. 1979. *Never Again Without a Rifle: The Origins of Italian Terrorism.* New York: Karz.

Snow, D. A. and R. Machalek. 1982. "On the Presumed Fragility of Unconventional Beliefs." *Journal for the Scientific Study of Religion* 21:15-26.

Taylor, M. 1988. *The Terrorist.* London: Brassey's.

Wasmund, K. 1986. "The Political Socialization of West German Terrorists." In *Political Violence and Terror: Motifs and Motivations,* edited by P. H. Merkl. Berkeley: University of California Press.

Weinberg, L. and W.L. Eubank. 1987. *The Rise and Fall of Italian Terrorism.* Boulder, CO: Westview Press.

PART II

CASE STUDIES

FROM PROTEST TO TERRORISM:
THE CASE OF SDS AND THE WEATHERMEN

Richard G. Braungart and Margaret M. Braungart

> June, 1969. Enter the Weathermen. . . . It swooped from giddy Third Worldism to a call for "antipig self-defense" movements and "cadre organization" on the way to a "Marxist-Leninist party" and "armed struggle." . . . Compared to the general run of SDS members . . . , they came from wealth; they were used to getting what they demanded, stamping their feet if they had to, wriggling away without punishment (Gitlin 1987, pp. 384-385).

> October, 1969. [T]he Weathermen blew up the statue commemorating the police victims of the Haymarket bombings a century before. On October 8 . . . the Weathermen were running through the Gold Coast [in Chicago], smashing expensive cars and shop windows. It was the beginning of three days of steady rampages (Hayden 1988, pp. 360-361).

> Early 1970s. [T]he Weather Underground at the height of its activities . . . claimed responsibility for a number of bombings—including an explosion at the U.S. Capitol (McGrath 1981, p. 32).

> October, 1981. [A] group of armed robbers tried to pull off "the big dance"—the code name they gave to a planned armed robbery of over a million dollars from a Brink's truck in Nyack, New York . . . two police officers and a Brink's guard were killed, and several men and women were captured. The best known was Kathy Boudin . . . who . . . was the most prominent political fugitive still at large (Frankfurt 1983).

International Social Movement Research, Vol. 4, pages 45-78.

ISBN: 1-55938-445-X

These were the Weathermen—a fringe group of the youthful 1960s political generation that mobilized to challenge the status quo and tried to change the course of politics in the United States. The result of a takeover of the Students for a Democratic Society (SDS) in 1969, the Weathermen was spearheaded by bright, energetic youth, mostly from affluent backgrounds, who attended some of the most prestigious colleges and universities in the United States. This was a group that delighted in acrimonious rhetoric, applauded terrorist tactics, and eventually went underground to carry out a revolution against "Amerika," taking credit for over 25 bombings in the United States in a five-year period (Schlagheck 1988). Though small in number, the Weathermen became the focus of considerable government and media attention in the late 1960s and early 1970s.

The young people that joined the Weathermen were not the disadvantaged and downtrodden in America who had plenty of cause for anger, but were youth that appeared to "have it all." Despite their privileged backgrounds, the Weathermen relished in statements such as, "We are the incubation of your mother's nightmare." They talked of "turning New York into Saigon" and "smashing the pig inside ourselves," and they devoted several years to trying to engineer a revolution in America that clearly had little sympathy, support, or following (Jacobs 1970; Sale 1973; Gitlin 1987). The question is why?

Although there have been a number of descriptive accounts of the Weathermen and their activities, not much systematic effort has been devoted to explaining the Weathermen—why the group emerged from SDS in 1969 as part of the 1960s Generation, why it became a clandestine organization involved in acts of terrorism, and why young people from affluent and educated backgrounds decided to participate in the group? In order to address these questions, this study examines the formation of the Weathermen and the motivations of its members.

The term motivation often is taken to mean psychological motivation, but it is argued here that attempts to understand the Weathermen need to go beyond the individual level of analysis. Especially when trying to understand a group of young people actively involved in politics during a certain era, consideration must be given to the larger sociohistorical context and to the dynamics of the political group to which the young activists belong. What is needed is a social psychological approach that incorporates analysis at the individual, societal, and group levels in order to provide a broad perspective on political activist groups such as the Weathermen.

To accomplish this task, the origins, organization, and activities of the Weathermen are described as background information on the group. Second, psychological, sociohistorical, and group dynamic explanations are examined as each of these approaches provides a perspective on the Weathermen and the motivations for their behavior. Comparisons are made with SDS, the forerunner of the Weathermen, to try to identify why the 1960s generation became increasingly hostile and violent, and why the Weathermen became one of the few clandestine political youth groups to have operated in the United States. The intent is to develop a broad framework for evaluating youthful political groups in order to better understand the dynamics of political generations and the motivations of their participants.

FROM PROTEST TO TERRORIST POLITICS

The Origins of the Weathermen

The Weathermen evolved out of one of the largest and most visible New Left organizations of the 1960s—the Students for a Democratic Society (SDS). Full of idealism, SDS formed in 1962 at a conference in Michigan and codified its values and purposes in *The Port Huron Statement* (Students for a Democratic Society 1964). Authored largely by Tom Hayden, the document began, "We are people of this generation, bred in at least modest comfort, housed now in universities, looking uncomfortably to the world we inherit" (Students for a Democratic Society 1964, p. 3). Under the banner of "participatory democracy," SDS advocated a "more human capitalism," antidiscrimination, support for third world peoples, and university reform. Referring to themselves as the "beloved community," this group of radical intellectuals, many of whom found socialist ideas appealing, spent their time organizing educational and economic development projects in various cities throughout the United States, headed South to be part of the civil rights struggle, and by mid-decade were staging marches, sit-ins, teach-ins, student strikes, and demonstrations to demand university reform and an end to the war in Vietnam (Sale 1973; Gitlin 1987; Miller 1987; Hayden 1988).

As the Vietnam War continued to escalate in the mid1960s and racism in the North seemed as intractable as that in the South, "protest" politics appeared to be having little tangible effect, with the result that SDS moved toward a new phase of "resistance" politics. The goal at this stage, according to Todd Gitlin (1987, p. 252), former activist leader of SDS, was to "conduct yourself in a disorderly way, close off the streets, retreat when attacked, make interesting trouble, and protect yourself." The year 1968 was a pivotal one for SDS—described in a 1989 special issue of *Time* magazine as "a knife blade that separated past from future." Political violence spiraled in America: the Tet offensive by the Viet Cong in what was perceived to be the unending Vietnam war; assassinations of Martin Luther King, Jr. and Robert Kennedy; flash-fires of rioting in urban areas across the country and heightened black militancy; the burning of hundreds of 1-A draft classification records at a Catonsville, Maryland Selective Service office by the Berrigan brothers and seven other priests; and the notorious student uprising at Columbia University, led by the confrontational Mark Rudd of SDS. Events came to a head in August 1968 at the Democratic Party Convention, as young people from a plethora of New Left groups and Mayor Richard Daley's police declared war on each other in the streets of Chicago. "Shoot to kill," Daley was quoted as saying (Gordon and Gordon 1987, p. 455).

Soon after the Democratic Convention, talk in SDS turned to revolution and "smashing the state," with a new kind of "all-or-nothing politics" taking hold (Braungart 1988). At the same time, problems were increasing within SDS, with a growing decline in tolerance for alternative views, a "frustrating intellectualization" of political problems, a coercive parliamentary manipulation of meetings, and a disaffection among SDS women for the rampant male chauvinism in the group (Gitlin 1987; Young 1977). Factional struggles abounded over ideology and tactics, played out on a grand scale at the June 1969 SDS convention in Chicago. One prominent faction was Progressive Labor (PL) that argued for a working-class perspective necessary to bring about the revolution in America, whereas other factions demanded that SDS be more concerned with racism and the need for armed struggle.

At the 1969 SDS Convention, an 11-member committee was charged by the national SDS office to write a position paper challenging PL. The resulting 16,000-word statement was titled "You Don't Need a Weatherman to Know Which Way the Wind Blows," a line from one of singer Bob Dylan's 1965 songs—a song, commented Sale (1973, p. 559), appealing to the "SDSian soul," with its overtones of "antiauthoritarianism and youthful independence." In contrast to the 1962 *Port Huron Statement*, the 1969 Weatherman manifesto began, " . . . the main struggle going on in the world today is between US imperialism and the national liberation struggles against it . . . . The goal is the destruction of US imperialism and the achievement of a classless world" (Jacobs 1970, pp. 51-52). All-out support was advocated for black liberation and for opening a new front against American foreign policy by establishing urban-based collectives. The diatribe included a quote from Lin Piao, "Long Live the Victory of People's War!"

Calling themselves the "Weathermen," the group quickly gained control at the SDS convention. At center stage was the charismatic Bernardine Dohrn, described as "chorus-line figured, articulate law-school graduate . . . " and "the object of many an SDS male's erotic fantasy . . . who fused the two premimum images of the movement: sex queen and streetfighter" (Gitlin 1987, pp. 385-386). After tiresome rounds of factional bickering, Dohrn seized the microphone, demanded that PL be expelled, and stalked off stage, leading a walk-out of about 700 participants chanting, "Power to the people, power to the people; Ho! Ho! Ho Chi Minh!" The major SDS factions caucused at various locations in Chicago. A slate of candidates from the different factions was announced, with the top three leadership positions in SDS won by Weathermen Mark Rudd, Bill Ayers, and Jeffrey Jones. These were the second generation SDS, who came to the organization in 1966 or thereafter, eschewing the tedious radical intellectualizing of the SDS founders in favor of all-or-nothing, action politics. The election results signaled the demise of SDS and a several-year foray into a more vituperative style of youth politics, infused with elements of terrorism and secrecy (Jacobs 1970; Sale 1973; Gitlin 1987).

Organization and Activities

Once formed, the leaders of the Weathermen, known as the Weather Bureau, took over the SDS National Office in Chicago and changed the name of SDS's journal *New Left Notes* to *Prairie Fire*. Gitlin (1987, p. 386) commented that initially the Weathermen made revolution look like fun, with their LSD, sexual orgies, celebration of the presumed guerrilla exploits of five-year-old Marion Delgado who derailed a train in Calfornia, and songs like "I'm dreaming of a white riot" (to the tune of "White Christmas") and "When You're a red, you're a red all the way" (to the tune of "All the Way"). In this first phase of its organization, the Weathermen attempted to implement a two-pronged program: (1) urban action projects designed to awaken and recruit working-class youth to revolution; and (2) anti-Vietnam War actions (Sale 1973; Unger 1974). Estimates of the numbers of young people involved in the Weathermen vary, ranging from a high of about 3,000 to a low of 200. Organized into collectives, members of the Weathermen were assigned to various cities such as Chicago, New York, Seattle, Newark, Denver, and Cleveland, among others, to carry out "urban action projects." The collectives were able to function on relatively little money, with funding acquired through personal saving accounts, part-time jobs, stealing credit cards, and some money donated from the central office (Sale 1973; Franks 1981). Women were at the forefront of many of the Weather actions, taking sizable risks in their struggle for feminist recognition (Stern 1975; Alpert 1981; Gitlin 1987).

The Weathermen championed "politics by action," drawing inspiration from the black power movement, especially the Black Panthers. Uncomfortable about their "white-skin privilege," the Weathermen attempted to win the respect of the black movement and to prove themselves as legitimate white revolutionaries by outraging middle-class America. Noted Hornblower and Valentine (1980, p. A2): "They believed that if they proved, through violent acts, that they were not wimpy middle-class intellectuals, but 'guerrillas fighting behind enemy lines,' working-class youths would rise and join them." To that end, the Weathermen planned a series of provocative actions for the late summer and fall of 1969—raiding two Detroit junior colleges to "rap" with students about imperialism, racism, and the excesses of capitalism; staging a "jailbreak" and rally outside a Pittsburgh high school; and spray-painting public buildings and statues with political slogans. As Gitlin (1987, p. 391) described, "They . . . talked about 'kicking ass' and 'getting us a few pigs,' and dared the local kids to fight."

The Weathermen's most ambitious project at this stage was the Days of Rage in Chicago. Under the slogan "Bring the war home," the Weathermen spent four days trashing property, bombing a statue honoring police in Haymarket Square, and skirmishing with Chicago police, doing thousands of dollars worth of property damage in the wealthy Gold Coast section. Weatherwomen were highly instrumental in these "actions," and police responded with force. Injuries, arrests, and indictments followed, with total bail for the Weathermen amounting to 2.3 million dollars (Sale 1973). Though the Weathermen declared victory, Black Panther Fred Hampton called their actions "adventuristic, opportunistic and custeristic" (Unger 1974, p. 174). Membership declined in the Weathermen, as SDS campus chapters closed down or changed their name.

These early actions, which also included passing out leaflets and marching the National Liberation Front (NLF) flag around in various cities, did not have the intended effect of inspiring thousands of young working-class youth, especially blacks, to join the ranks of the revolutionary force—quite the reverse. Although some youth joined in the Weathermen escapades, such events more likely met with open hostility, not only from the public and community but from bands of youth who declared the Weathermen crazy and chased collectives out of their neighborhoods. Weathermen were not easily daunted, however. As an example, at one high school when students started fighting against the Weathermen, a Weatherman remembered yelling in fear to Cathy Wilkerson, "This is terrible," to which she yelled back in surprise, "Oh no, this is terrific. People are communicating" (Hornblower and Valentine 1980).

With the two-pronged Weathermen program largely a failure and SDS in a shambles, the Weatherman organization intensified its strategy and began converting the group into a clandestine organization devoted to guerrilla warfare and bombing (Unger 1974). Bernardine Dohrn announced, "revolutionary violence is the only way. Now we are adopting the classic guerrilla strategy of the [Uruguayan] Tupamaros . . . in the technically most advanced country in the world" (Young 1977, p. 276). In order to forge "instant" revolutionaries, the Weathermen turned inward, focusing the group's energies on reconstructing the personal lives of its members.

Individualism and personal privacy were declared "out" in the collectives; shared drugs and sex were "in," and Weather members were expected to give themselves over totally to the group. Endless self-criticism sessions, labeled "Weatherfries," were initiated in each collective, personal possessions went to the group, and mongamous relations, including marriages, were to be "smashed," since, it was argued, such relationships put women in a dependent position relative to men. Experimentation with sex and drugs was promoted "to establish new connections both personal and political." As a Weatherman pamphlet extolled, "We're . . . knowing our bodies as part of our lives, becoming animals again after centuries of repression and uptightness" (Sale 1973, p. 624). Such behaviors among some members, especially homosexuality, estranged many Weathermen who left the group. This was a time when the organization was under threat both externally and internally: externally from police and FBI surveillance, indictments for offenses, and fear of infiltration; internally by a growing feminist movement and enormous ego battles among the leadership (Jacobs 1970; Sale 1973; Unger 1974; Hayden 1988).

The last public event of the Weathermen before going underground was the National War Council, held in Flint, Michigan, in December 1969. About 400 people attended, some of whom were infiltrators, curiosity or thrill-seekers, or "hangers-on" (Sale 1973; Gitlin 1987). Rhetoric and style escalated to a new level of nastiness at Flint, as politics was transformed into theatrics, partially to help build an illusion of strength (Jacobs 1970). Mass meetings were billed as "wargasms," and much of the time was spent on alcohol, pot, and sex; practicing karate exercises; and singing songs about trashing, bomb throwing, and killing "pigs" (Unger 1974). A kind of Alice-in-Wonderland, Queen of Hearts logic prevailed. One debate at the meeting concerned whether killing white babies was correct, and John Jacobs declared to the audience, "We're against everything that's 'good and decent,' in honky America. We will burn and loot and destroy." It was here that Bernardine Dohrn made her infamous remark about the Charles Manson gang killings, "Dig it. First they killed those pigs, then they ate dinner in the same room with them, then they even shoved a fork into the victim's stomach, Wild" (Unger 1974, p. 181).

Another phase was launched in "Weatherpolitics." War was declared on the state by building a self-styled Red Army, and collectives were broken down further into cells or "focos" to go underground. Observed Gitlin (1987, p. 395), "The world having failed their analysis, they rejected it." In February 1970, the SDS Chicago office was closed and its files sold to the Wisconsin Historical Society. Contacts with family and friends were severed, identities were changed, and the organization was renamed the "Weather Underground" (a name much more palatable to Weatherwomen). Going underground was an honored tradition among some of the Weathermen's most revered political organizations, such as the Tupamaros, who the Weathermen saw as heroes for their Robin Hood style politics. In small groups, members moved to city apartments or to isolated rural areas, often rotated by orders from the Weather Bureau (Sale 1973; Stern 1975; Alpert 1981). Isolation was not complete, however, with informal contacts made with families and friends through post-office boxes and pay phones. A network of support was provided by above-ground activists who would transfer messages and supply quick cash, while an organization in Canada for U.S. military deserters helped with border crossings and false identification papers (Franks 1981).

The need for heightened violence and bombing in America was justified by the Weathermen. As Mike James harangued a crowd in Chicago:

> Non-violent marches have their place, but they won't bring about the changes necessary for freedom. Capitalism won't crumble because of moral protest .... They've got the guns, we've got the people .... The time will come when we'll have to use guns. Don't let that hang you up. Some of you say violence isn't human. Well, taking oppression isn't human; it's stupid. You only live one time, so you'd better make it good and make it liberating .... Violence, when directed at the oppressor, is human as well as necessary (Sale 1973, p. 631).

The most active of the Weather Underground bombing groups was the New York City cell that included Cathy Wilkerson, Kathy Boudin, Diana Oughton, Terry Robbins and Ted Gold—all from wealthy backgrounds (Unger 1974). On February 21, 1970, this group was said to be responsible for setting off three firebombs at Judge John Murtagh's home (Murtagh was the presiding judge for a trial of a group of New York Black Panthers). However, on March 6, a bomb, which was to be planted at Columbia University, was being assembled in the basement of a fashionable Greenwich Village townhouse belonging to Wilkerson's vacationing father. But something went wrong, and the bomb and house exploded, killing Gold, Oughton, and Robbins, while Wilkerson and Boudin escaped to a neighbor's house (Unger 1974; Franks 1981). Several days later, three commercial buildings in New York City were bombed, and at the end of the month police raided a Kenmore Avenue apartment where Dohrn and Jacobs had stayed, which was described as a "bomb factory" (Sale 1973).

In the first part of May 1970, following Nixon's decision to invade Cambodia, waves of student protest erupted throughout the United States, which climaxed with the killing of six students by National Guard and police at Kent State University and Jackson State University. From the underground, Dohrn issued the first Weather communique in late May—a nihilistic statement fusing the youth culture and politics:

> All over the world, people fighting Amerikan imperialism look to Amerika's youth to use our strategic position behind enemy lines to join forces in the destruction of the empire .... We fight in many ways. Dope is one of our weapons .... Guns and grass are united in the youth underground .... If you want to find us, this is where we are. In every tribe, commune, dormitory, farmhouse, barracks and townhouse where kids are making love, smoking dope and loading guns—fugitives from Amerikan justice are free to go ... (Jacobs 1970, pp. 508-510).

She went on to warn that the Weather Underground soon would attack "a symbol or institution of Amerikan injustice," and some 19 days later, a bomb exploded at New York City police headquarters. A second communique followed that blamed the police for murdering blacks and brutalizing "Latin and white youth on the Lower East Side."

> The pigs in this country are our enemies . . . . Every time the pigs think they've stopped us, we come back a little stronger and a lot smarter . . . . They build the Bank of America, kids burn it down. They outlaw grass, we build a culture of life and music. The time is now. Political power grows out of a gun, a Molotov, a riot, a commune . . . and from the soul of the people (Jacobs 1970, p. 512).

The Weathermen were not the only ones bombing. During the 1969-1970 school year, there were 174 major bombing attempts on campus and more than 70 off campus attributed to the white left—an eight-fold increase from 1968-1969; nationally, estimates of bombings and attempts reached nearly 5,000 from January 1969 to April 1970 (Sale 1973, p. 632).

Concomitant with the bombing episodes were intensive investigations carried out by police, the FBI, and U.S. Attorney's Office. According to Schlagheck (1988), every member of SDS and the Weather Underground was investigated by the FBI, while the CIA's "Operation Chaos" for movement surveillance, that had been established under the Johnson Administration, was expanded under the Nixon Administration. Gitlin (1987, p. 378) recounted:

> The Nixon administration used militants (including agents provocateurs) to taint moderates, on the principle that the more destructive the protest, the easier it was to discredit. It authorized wiretaps, grand jury investigations, felony prosecutions. It tried to intimidate news media . . . . State and local police contributed their own burglaries, stole mailing lists, instigated harassment by landlords and disconnection by phone companies. Eventually, even mild liberals were placed on a White House "enemies list."

During early April a federal grand jury in Chicago indicted 12 key Weathermen leaders for crossing state lines with the intention of inciting riots, and for assorted charges stemming from inflammatory remarks in speeches, in addition to hitting a policeman (Sale 1973, p. 648). In July 1970, a Detroit federal grand jury indicted 13 Weathermen (some of whom were already indicted in previous cases) on conspiracy charges, and Dohrn made the FBI's most-wanted persons list. Then on July 26 in celebration of a Cuban national holiday, a bomb went off in the entrance of a Bank of America branch on Wall Street, with the Weather Underground taking credit. Two Viet Cong flags were left at the scene, and a third communique was issued, ending with the message to Attorney General John Mitchell, "Don't look for us, Dog; We'll find you first" (Jacobs 1970, p. 515).

In September 1970, the Weathermen arranged the escape of Dr. Timothy Leary, guru of the drug culture, who had been sentenced to ten years for marijuana possession in California's San Luis Obispo prison. A fourth communique followed that hailed Leary for "creating a new culture on the barren wasteland that had been imposed on this country by Democrats, Republicans, Capitalists, and creeps." The statement ended with "Our organization commits itself to the task of freeing these prisoners of war. We are outlaws, we are free" (Jacobs 1970, p. 517). Leary issued his thanks in the *San Francisco Good Times*:

> There is a time for peace and the time for war . . . . I declare that World War III is being waged by short-haired robots whose deliberate aim is to destroy the complex web of free willed life by the imposition of mechanical order . . . . Total war is upon us. Fight to live or you'll die (Jacobs 1970, pp. 517-519).

Bombings continued in the United States, with the Weather Underground taking credit for some of these, which included the Army Mathematical Research Center at the University of Wisconsin where a graduate student was killed, courthouses in California and Long Island, the Senate men's restroom in the U.S. Capitol, the Pentagon, ITT corporate offices, and the U.S. State Department (Unger 1974; Schlagheck 1988). Nonetheless, clandestine life became increasingly wearing, with no real revolution in sight. As Alpert recounted in a letter to "Sisters in the Weather Underground" published in *Ms.* magazine in 1973 (Alpert 1973, p. 88), "My first year underground was very hard. Expecting to die for the Revolution in a matter of months, I was unprepared to find myself not only alive but living a rather unadventurous and secluded existence less than a year after 'disappearing.'" Infighting persisted underground over issues such as feminism versus chauvism, staying underground versus surfacing, and whether to direct violence at select targets with no killing or to engage in kidnap and assassination like the Red Brigades in Italy (Hornblower and Valentine 1980).

By 1974, however, the momentum was gone, despite occasional issues of *Prairie Fire*. Some observers date the end of the Weathermen in 1976, although isolated urban guerrilla groups continued activities. By the late 1970s, there were two remaining groups: the Prairie Fire collective, which favored surfacing from underground life; and the May 19th Coalition (May 19 is the birthday of Ho Chi Minh and Malcolm X), which wanted to become part of a black terrorist army (Franks 1981; McGrath 1981). In 1979, a police raid on a Hoboken, New Jersey apartment uncovered another "bomb factory," attributed to Jeff Jones and Eleanor Raskin of the Weather Underground. In 1981, a reminent underground group that included David Gilbert, Judith Clark, and Kathy Boudin, robbed a Brinks truck in Nyack, New York, and killed a guard and two police officers (one of whom was the first black policeman in Rockland County). The gang was caught. Gilbert and Clark were convicted of murder and sentenced to 75 years in prison. Boudin, who plead guilty to robbery and murder, was given 25 years to life in prison (Frankfurt 1983; Gitlin 1987).

Throughout the late 1970s, Weathermen members left the underground, and in the early 1980s, some of its more prominent leaders abandoned fugitive life: Rudd surfaced in 1977, was fined $2,000 and given two-years probation;

Wilkerson surrendered in 1980 and was given a three-year term in a New York state prison; in 1980 Dohrn surfaced and was fined and put on probation, while Ayers's charges were dropped. Dohrn and Ayers married in 1982 and have two sons (McGrath 1981, pp. 30-34; *Newsweek*, 1985, p.15). As Franks (1981, p. 36) summarized:

> [These] white radicals . . . traveled down a long spiral: from idealistic students to peaceful protestors to rioters trashing the streets to revolutionary cadres bent on shedding their "white-skin privilege" to fugitives planting bombs in empty buildings to women and men accused of assassinating the very "people" they said they were fighting for.

The question why young people decided to join the Weathermen and carry out such actions is explored in the next section of this study on motivation, organized around psychological, sociohistorical, and group dynamic explanations.

MOTIVATIONS OF THE WEATHERMEN

Psychological Explanations

There are several possible psychological explanations for the Weathermen and their behavior. First, the Weathermen were part of the 1960s generation, and since generational movements are carried out by youth, then it must be asked whether there is something about the stage of youth that makes young people receptive to political movements and extremist behavior? Second, because some of the Weathermen were involved in terrorist acts, then, in keeping with the terrorist literature, consideration must be given to personality characteristics—including the possibility that their personalities were pathological. And third, since many of the Weathermen were from affluent professional homes, it seems reasonable to ask if their family background and parents' politics could be at the root of some of the Weathermen's attitudes and behavior. Each of these psychological explanations is considered as it pertains to the Weathermen.

It has been argued that youthful political movements are partially rooted in the life-cycle developmental characteristics of youth: high energy levels, improved cognitive skills, heightened political awareness, the need for self independence or "genital primacy," and a socioemotional search for identity, fidelity, and a place in society (Erikson 1968; Keniston 1968; Feuer 1969; Braungart and Braungart 1986). While these are characteristics that help explain why young people in general are prone to create generational movements—whether in politics, literature, science, or other fields—in order to understand the motivations of any specific youthful political group such as the Weathermen, it is necessary to explore the way in which these developmental tasks were approached and carried out.

Typical of the stage of adolescence and youth are important new cognitive developments: the ability to think abstractly, a wider awareness of possibilities and alternatives, and a greater recognition of the world of politics (Erikson 1968; Gallatin 1980; Vander Zanden 1989). And although research has indicated that adolescent political conceptions are often untested and somewhat simplistic, Adelson reported that among some of the highly politicized young, their ideals are not diffuse but are "highly organized, intellectualized, systematic, and a bit blood-thirsty. It's a cold-blooded sort of utopianism: *we* know what to do, and *we* are going to do it" (Adelson 1987, p. 93).

Adelson's remarks describe well the cognitive political thinking of the Weathermen. In comparison to SDS's statements and writings, those of the Weathermen were often more categorical, rigid, over-simplified, and "bloodthirsty." For example, when asked in a *Life* magazine interview, "What do you hope to obtain by bombing?" the anonymous Weatherman responded:

> We are revolutionaries, not reformists. We are not trying to frighten the Establishment, we are trying to destroy it, so that a just society can be built based on human values, not financial or commercial values. . . . Ours is an attempt to attack capitalism, racism, exploitation—directly and militarily. These are not attacks on individuals who work in these offices or happen to be there. It is the use that the buildings are put to that we are attacking (*Life* 1970, p. 30).

The Weathermen, said SDS leader Tom Hayden (1988, p. 358), "had no patience for the complicated moral and political philosophizing of the Port Huron Generation." Another SDS member commented about Weatherwoman Cathy Wilkerson, "She was driven by guilt about being born white and privileged . . . . Any doubts about radical theory were thought to be signs of weakness, so she would draw herself further and further into a fantasy world about the way the world works. You could never have an intellectual discussion with her" (Hornblower and Valentine 1980, p. A2).

The youthful search for identity, fidelity, and a place in society was carried out in a distinct fashion by the Weathermen, which differed from youth in general and from their predecessors in SDS. According to Erikson (1968), an important aspect of adolescent identity development involves experimentation, and this was one of the Weathermen's appeals. As Hayden (1988, p. 359) observed: "there was an attraction about them, a sinister one, for many radicals. The mystery of what was out there, beyond normal experience, was magnetic to some from bourgeois backgrounds." Thus, youth who wanted to indulge in personal exploration and experience high risk were drawn to the Weathermen, who provided, encouraged, and justified going beyond the bounds of convention into a never-never land of forbidden pleasures and acts. Youthful experimentation with drugs, sex, life styles, and violence was endorsed in the Weather collectives and at their meetings. Personal experimentation was then tied to political experimentation. As one radical told a reporter, "No one knows whether terrorism will work . . . . No one has really tried it yet." Another described the Weathermen as "an experiment to see if an underground can be set up in this country" (*Newsweek* 1970, pp. 27, 36).

Besides experimentation, part of youthful identity formation may involve an identity crisis, which occurs when young people lose their way and suffer what Erikson (1968) termed "identity diffusion." In the process, the young person may embrace a negative identity, which Erikson said is evident in a "scornful and snobbish hostility toward the roles offered as proper and desirable in one's family or immediate community," and which may be due to "the excessive ideals either demanded by morbidly ambitious parents or indeed actualized by superior ones" (Erikson 1968, p. 175). As Franks (1981) described them, the Weathermen were youth who, though nurtured by advantaged backgrounds, thought that if you were not poor, black, and hungry, your conscience should suffer.

> White-skin privilege. Rich bitches. Spoiled kids. Bourgeois liberals. The young radicals of the Vietnam era set out to prove that such phrases did not apply to them (Franks 1981, p. 44).

They had to reject their bourgeois past, and one way to accomplish that task was to take on a negative identity.

The Weathermen offered what many of these youth thought they needed. In fact, much of the basis for the Weathermen's recruitment rested on the group's style rather than on a coherent persuasive argument (Gitlin 1987). Role models for the group were often outlaws, and the experimental nature of their cultivated negative identity has been described by SDS leader and historian Carl Oglesby.

> They knew they were crazy . . . . Terry [Robbins] and Billy [Ayers] had this Butch Cassidy and Sundance attitude—they were blessed, they were hexed, they would die young, they would live forever . . . . I believe they thought they looked cute, and that everybody would know it was basically a joke. The next minute, they were lost in it and couldn't get out (Gitlin 1987, pp. 386-387).

Problems with identity and identity diffusion may also explain the Weathermen's enthusiasm for going underground. As Weatherwoman Susan Stern (1975, p. 244) recounted in her autobiography:

> I was about to jump off, make a clean break, split. Soon there would be no more Susan Stern. She would be dead, and the person she had been would have another face, another color hair, another name, another past. She would invent it, build it, engineer it to be exactly what she wanted it to be, what she had never been . . . . Susan Stern Sham would end finally, finally she would end.

Another part of the search for identity involves a quest for meaning in life, which some youth, Erikson (1968) noted, try to find by linking their personal lives to politics. As one Weatherman expressed it, "You give meaning to your life by fighting the system" (*Newsweek* 1970, pp. 26-30). Susan Stern (1975, p. 275) echoed the theme:

> I want to join with the black liberation movement, and struggle with the Vietcong. They are all building a new kind of life in the midst of war and they sing while they work, because their life has meaning. They're not cogs in the wheel any more; they are the wheel and they are rolling onto their own heritage, and those are the people I want to identify with.

For a number of youth, the Weathermen may have provided a way station in their struggle for personal identity. The Weatherman organization was a totalistic group where the self and personal responsibility could be abandoned, and to fill the void, the group offered a kind of patched-together, utopian political thought and prescriptions for behavior. As Kanfer (1981, p. 32) commented, "Dylan furnished the phrases, Che [Guevara] and [Regis] Debray the shibboleths, Timothy Leary the smoke, Marcuse the philosophy." Moreover, according to Crenshaw (1986, p. 394), for those involved in groups that engage in terrorist acts:

> To individuals already suffering from identity confusion, the attention paid them by the government not only confirms a negative identity but makes them feel like "somebody." They are gratified to be sufficiently important to be the object of excessive attention, even if that attention is negative. Harassment or surveillance is preferable to being ignored by society.

At the same time, the decision to leave the Weather Underground may have rested partially on a desire to have one's old identity again. As Jane Alpert (1981, p. 314) recounted, "At the Albuquerque HEW office I had applied for a new Social Security card in the name of Carla Weinstein—Weinstein because, after two years 'passing,' I wanted my Jewish identity back . . . ." Thus, there is strong evidence that much of the Weathermen's psychological motivation had to do with their youthful cognitive style and their quest for identity through experimentation, negative identity, and trying to finding meaning in life. The evidence for the role of personality factors in distinguishing Weathermen's behavior is less clear.

One dimension of personality that needs to be considered is aggression, since much of the style, rhetoric, and actions of the Weathermen were highly aggressive. To a greater extent than in SDS, the Weathermen had a penchant for what Fromm (1973) termed "malignant aggression": a preoccupation with destruction (self, relationships, society, America)—often evident in their writings, language, humor, style, and actions. However, it has been cautioned in the terrorist literature that while aggression may be part of the psychological make-up of terrorists, it is not clear to what extent such aggression is derived from the inner personality of individual members or has been "assumed" (willed or cultivated) because of group norms and pressure (Crenshaw 1986). In addition, while the Weathermen displayed a fascination for aggression and violence, it is another matter whether this characteristic was a dominant feature of all personalities in the group. For example, Knutson (1981) interviewed West German terrorists and reported there was an ambivalent attitude toward violence; for many, creating fear was less important than demonstrating commitment to a cause through self-sacrifice.

In addition, Crenshaw (1986, p. 387) pointed out that "rather than being attracted to the inherent violence of terrorism, some individuals are seduced by the lures of omnipotence and grandeur to compensate for feelings of inferiority or impotence;" thus, terrorism may be one response to a lack of self-confidence. Feelings of inferiority predominate both the Stern (1975) and Alpert (1981) accounts of life with the Weathermen. Stern's longing for recognition and elitism is evident in one passage where she describes being in jail with Bernardine Dohrn but feels too intimidated to approach Dohrn.

> But she was still the high priestess. Whatever quality she possessed, I wanted it. I wanted to be cherished and respected as Bernardine was. More than that I wanted to know Bernadine. I wanted to be an aristocrat too (Stern 1975, p. 144).

Rather than a single orientation toward aggression, it is likely there was a variety of attitudes represented within the Weathermen, with members engaging in destructive actions (rhetoric, behavior, self, others, political) for a combination of reasons.

Besides aggression, there have been a number of additional personality characteristics attributed to individuals who commit acts of terrorism, some of which include low self-esteem, high aspirations, goal-directed behavior, high stress-seeking and risk-taking, impatience, uncompromising attitudes, a tendency to blame others, and fear of anonymity (Jenkins 1980; Crenshaw 1986). However, Bell (1980, pp. 201-202) noted that there seems to be a lot of faith in but very little evidence for a terrorist personality profile, and Laqueur (1987) commented that while some terrorists may be stress-seeking, hostile, and unstable, others have none of these personality traits.

A related issue is whether those who engage in terrorism have personalities that are pathological, but the consensus in most of the terrorist literature is that only a minority are certifiably "disturbed," partially because groups are not likely to tolerate highly irratic, unpredictable behavior, and they require a certain amount of stability among their members in order to plan and carry out terrorist acts (Storr 1978; Lebow 1980). Accounts of the Weathermen written by Stern (1975) and Alpert (1981) document how the Weather Bureau readily weeded out those who threatened the group in any way. Stern herself was under suspicion by Mark Rudd and other leaders for being emotionally unstable and was dismissed from the Weathermen at one point. Although few terrorists who operate in groups may be truly pathological, Crenshaw (1986) pointed out there may be elements of neuroticism, both for individuals within the group and the group as a whole.

In a general sense, however, personality is not a useful predictor of participation in groups such as the Weathermen, since a variety of different personalities were represented in the group. Second, a number of individuals who possessed these same traits did not join the Weathermen or any terrorist group and could be found in diverse careers (Laqueur 1987). And third, it does not appear that only certain types of personalities were drawn to the Weathermen, since it has been observed that personalities changed as a result of affiliation with the group. For example, Hayden (1988, p. 422) commented:

> I had seen personality changes in the Weathermen and Panthers as they struggled to become "tools of necessity." They became drained of human feelings, in readiness to die or perhaps kill, to accept personal oblivion for an ideology.

Hayden (1988, p. 359) further described his friend Terry Robbins, whose personality changed after becoming a Weatherman from "a shy introvert to a devilish charmer exuding a charisma of violence."

Along with developmental and personality considerations, an examination of individual political motivations requires a discussion of family background characteristics—the kinds of families that produced offspring who joined the Weathermen. One salient feature of the Weathermen was that they came from affluent homes, which differed somewhat from the backgrounds of the early SDS group. As Gitlin (1987, p. 385) contrasted: Whereas the initial SDS organizers—the first generation SDS—were "the children of public-school teachers, professors, accountants, and the like," the Weathermen "came from wealth."

For example, Bill Ayers's father was the chairman of the Board of the Commonwealth of Illinois electrical combine; Kathy Boudin's father was a well-known attorney who defended political leftists; Diana Oughton's father was a banker in a small Midwest town who was also a Republican state legislator; Cathy Wilkerson's father owned ratio stations; Mark Rudd's father had been a Lieutenant Colonel in the Army Reserves and sold real-estate; and Bernardine Dohrn's father was a Hungarian immigrant, who moved the family from Chicago to the Milwaukee suburbs (Sale 1973; Gitlin 1987). One of Cathy Wilkerson's associates commented, "It used to be a joke in the movement that you can't get into the Weathermen unless your parents are millionaires" (Hornblower and Valentine 1980, p. A2).

Part of the dynamic for these Weathermen from privileged homes may have been rooted in the youthful developmental need to become independent and in the generational desire to go beyond one's parents (Bettelheim 1963; Erikson 1968). As Franks (1981, p. 44) observed about two Weatherwomen:

> Diana [Oughton] could not become richer than her father, but she could become poorer—and purer. Kathy [Boudin] who grew cynical about the law, had to go one step farther than her radical father; she had to find a more powerful—and forbidden—way to fight injustice.

Sheltered, protected, supported, and accustomed to getting their own way at home, these Weathermen felt invincible, knowing little of life's fears or harshness (Franks 1981; Gitlin 1987).

Not all Weathermen came from affluence, of course; some were from middle- and lower-middle-class homes. Yet, it may not have been family income per se that was important. What bound both the affluent and not-so-affluent youth together in the Weathermen was their feeling of guilt: regardless of class background, "all had the illusion of great—and shameful—advantage" (Franks 1981, p. 44). A kind of cognitive dissonance was created between their awareness of poverty, racism, and the exploitation of humanity in society, relative to their own comfortable, secure personal backgrounds. Their attempt to reduce this tension was by linking their individual lives to revolutionary politics.

Besides economic background, the political socialization literature indicates that parents' politics have an important bearing on offspring political views. And in keeping with this literature, parents' politics was found to be a key predictor of the political behavior of SDS leaders—who tended to come from left-wing, liberal, or Democratic homes (Flacks 1967; Braungart 1979; Braungart and Braungart 1988). The leaders of the Weathermen, on the other hand, came from more mixed political backgrounds—Republican, Democrat, liberal, leftist, and pacifist (Sale 1973; Franks 1981).

Like personality, however, family background leaves much to be desired as a predictor of why some young people join extreme political groups. First, the overwhelming majority of youth from privileged homes did not join the Weathermen or any other political or terrorist group. Second, the Black Panthers and Symbionese Liberation Army, which operated around the same time as the Weathermen and employed similar tactics and rhetoric, had very different family backgrounds from the Weathermen (Laqueur 1987). The limitations of many of these psychological explanations indicate the need to go beyond the individual level of analysis and examine additional factors. As social psychologists have pointed out, individual behavior often has less to do with dispositional characteristics than with situational factors and the larger social context (Forsyth 1983).

Sociohistorical Explanations

In attempting to explain the groups that arise within a political generation, besides psychological factors and youthful developmental characteristics, consideration must be given to sociohistorical forces, such as (1) cohort effects—the shared socialization experiences of an age group as its members grow up together in a society during a certain time in history; and (2) period effects—the historical events and trends occurring as a generationtakes form and mobilizes around a certain set of sociopolitical issues (Knoke 1984; Braungart and Braungart 1986, 1989b; Delli Carpini 1986). Both of these factors are important to understanding the attitudes and behavior of the Weathermen, particularly why the Weathermen became increasingly extreme and violent.

There are several dimensions of the cohort effect to consider in relation to the Weathermen. One distinguishing characteristic of most political generations in history was that they were part of a large-size birth cohort (Moller 1972; Wallimann and Zito 1984). The 1960s generation was an extraordinarily large birth group—sometimes referred to as the Baby Boom—born during the post-World War II years. As Ryder (1965, p. 845) noted, "Any extraordinary size deviation is likely to leave an imprint on the cohort as well as on the society." And, as teenagers in the 1950s, the first wave of baby-boom youth made a difference, vexing their elders by creating a lively, rebellious youth culture of music, dress, and language, and applauding antiheroes such as Marlon Brando, James Dean, and Elvis Presley. As the cohort reached college age from 1960-1970, the size of the youth population (ages 17-24) increased by 52 percent, and more youth than ever before went off to college, escalating college and university enrollments by 121 percent in a decade (Ryder 1974).

A cohort also shares a particular set of socialization experiences as its members grow up together in a society at a similar stage in life-cycle development. The baby-boom cohort came of age during the postwar years when America was changing rapidly, with increasing suburbanization, new technology, bureaucratization, and corporate consolidation, coupled with a growing GNP, white-collar labor force, and middle class (Current, Williams, Freidel, and Brinkley 1983). Yet, in contrast to the growing affluence and changing technology, the baby-boom cohort also shared fearful images of World War II, Nazi atrocities, the atomic bomb, and the Cold War.

According to generational theorists, it is these cohort experiences that provide the basis for the formation of a generational consciousness (Mannheim 1952; Ortega y Gasset 1961; Esler 1984). Mannheim (1952) made the distinction between a cohort, as an age group "in itself," and a generation, as an age group "for itself." The importance of shared growing-up experiences, generational awareness, and the generation gap is reflected in the writings of the early SDS organizers. The *Port Huron Statement* began with a section called "Agenda for a Generation;" part of Todd Gitlin's (1987) explanation for why he and other members of SDS became active in politics rests heavily on the collective memories of their growing-up years during the 1950s; and Tom Hayden as editor of the campus newspaper in his college days wrote:

> The present student generation was born on the brink of war and has never seen their country at more than wobbling peace.... Theirs is a generation ... stultified and frustrated by intense cold war pressures, particularly as those pressures have been illustrated in the unique concept of The Bomb (Miller 1987, p. 51).

Hayden (1988, pp. 178-179) was well aware too of the consequences of differential sociohistorical experiences for his father's versus his own generation:

> What became known as the generation gap stemmed from the very different world views of those of my father's era and my own. My father's generation believed—correctly—that they had defended democracy against *foreign* despotism; we believed we were defending democracy from its enemies at home.... In my generation's world view, the most apparent and unwanted invaders were our own armed forces—"white boots marchin' in a yellow land," as Phil Ochs sang—the very opposite of the dynamics of World War II.

However, the Weathermen—or second generation SDS—were born a few years later than the youth who formed SDS, and although also part of the baby-boom cohort, had a slightly different set of cohort experiences. The teenage years of many Weathermen were not the 1950s but the 1960s (Gitlin 1987; Hayden 1988). As Weatherwomen Cathy Wilkerson commented, "Our revolutionary consciousness was the result of growing up in the age of the atom bomb, of growing up in the '60s. We are who we are because Malcolm X was around teaching, and Rap Brown . . . " (Hornblower and Valentine 1980).

Yet, such shared cohort experiences are not sufficient to explain the formation of an active political generation. Another important factor is the sociohistorical context or period effect—the events and trends at any given time in history that affect all age groups in society—which has been found to have considerable influence on the formation, activities, and demise of various political generations in history (Braungart and Braungart 1989b). It is significant that SDS formed in the early 1960s and the Weathermen in the late 1960s. The historical influences were qualitatively different for these two groups, which may partially explain why the Weathermen turned to violence.

The significant events that influenced the formation of SDS occurred in the early 1960s, which represented an opening-up era in American history, as the youthful President John F. Kennedy led the country away from the "old," the conservative, and the domination of privatist interests of the 1950s to the "young," the progressive, and public spiritedness of the 1960s (Klapp 1975;

Schlesinger 1986). It was a decade that began with the civil rights struggle in the South, full of hope that social inequities could be corrected and a firm conviction that the world could become a better place through human effort. These were the social and political forces that influenced the organization of SDS in 1962, and in keeping with the spirit of the times, much of SDS's early efforts were devoted to implementing its shibboleth of "participatory democracy" through civil rights, community action programs, and university reform efforts.

However, events and trends began to shift with the Kennedy assassination and Johnson presidency. Increasing numbers of U.S. troops were committed to fight in Vietnam, and events worsened on the domestic front. The civil rights movement headed North to become an acerbic black power movement, and as the Vietnam war escalated, so did youthful protests against the war and against the draft. By the mid 1960s, the baby-boom cohort crowded many college campuses and worked to change the *in loco parentis* policies of university administrations. All the while, the ubiquitous youth culture was dividing over a number of issues: activists versus nonactivists; the druggies, hippies, and flower children versus the collegiates; the feminists versus the traditionalists and chauvinists; the gays versus the straights; the black power movement versus the "honkies." America was heating up, as the mix of events and trends spiraled and escalated; actions were met with counteractions.

The events of 1968 set the stage for the entrance of the Weathermen in the United States. The 1968 Democratic Convention in Chicago and ensuing Chicago conspiracy trial along with the Columbia University uprising oriented the New Left in America toward direct action, confrontation, disruption, and violence and provided the meeting ground for many of the Weathermen's leaders (Gitlin 1987; Hayden 1988). Frustrated over the intransigent American elitist system (government, corporate, university), protesting groups often spearheaded by SDS, intensified their tactics, while authorities countered with heightened rigidity, force, and surveillance, which political youth characterized as "repressive" and "fascistic." For example, according to Sale (1973, p. 406), the extent and scope of the 1968 Pentagon protest demonstration caught the Johnson Administration by surprise, despite the government's "elaborate plans and surveillance." After the demonstration, the Adminstration responded in a number of ways, including escalating surveillance, reclassifying students involved in draft resistance as 1-A and getting them sent to Vietnam, handing down indictments against protestors, and setting up special Congressional committees to investigate left-wing organizations such as SDS. Local FBI and police units deployed student informers and infiltrators as well as undercover agents at the campus level. Exaggeration and overreaction on both sides kept the momentum going—a dynamic that helped assure Nixon's election to the presidency under the banner of "law-and-order" (Hayden 1988; Schlagheck 1988).

The youth culture and political activism in America were part of a larger global trend of heightened youthful activity that was becoming increasingly utopian, violent, and revolutionary. Terrorism was on the increase in the world, and extremist youth groups applauded and copied the style and actions of some of these terrorist groups—most notably Germany's Baader-Meinhof gang, Italy's Red Brigade, and the Japanese Red Army that terrorized and murdered in the 1960s and 1970s (Carroll 1978). Worthy of note was the high female participation in these terrorist-styled youth groups, which one West German criminologist attributed to "deficiencies in their socialization process," characterizing these women as "more out of touch with reality than male terrorists, and as a result some become even more fanatical extremists" (Getler 1977, p. A15). More likely, the aggressive participation of women in these groups, including the Weathermen, was rooted in the larger struggle for feminist identity and recognition that was a dominant issue in the late 1960s and 1970s (Stern 1975; Hayden 1988).

These were some of the historical events and trends that influenced the evolution of the Weatherman organization as distinct from SDS in 1969. Once formed, other specific events were associated with the Weathermen's decision to become a clandestine organization and to engage in acts of bombing. The idea of going underground did not originate with the Weathermen. In the late 1960s and early 1970s, the Black Panthers were going underground, the Berrigan brothers were contemplating going underground, and many American draft evaders were hiding out as fugitives in Canada and Sweden (Hayden 1988). In addition, there was a further hardening of the lines between youth and the government following Nixon's invasion of Cambodia in 1970 when massive student disruptions occurred across the country and protesting students were killed at two universities. Foreshadowing the Watergate affair, the Nixon Administration intensified the pressure on student political groups initiated by President Johnson; not only did the government engage in surveillance and infiltration but in harassement and entrapment. These practices later were cited by a Senate investigating committee as "excessive," involving serious breaches of law that jeopardized democratic values (Schlagheck 1988, pp. 102-103). In addition, Weathermen were incensed over two events related to the Black Panthers—Bobby Seale was bound and gagged at the Conspiracy 8 trial and later hustled off to jail, and two other Black Panther leaders were killed by police in an early morning raid.

Despite these polarizing and increasingly violent events, it was becoming clear in late 1969 that there was not much support for the Weathermen's "white revolution." The Weather Bureau then decided to shift away from the idea of a mass youth revolution in favor of an elitist one and formed a clandestine organization. Stern (1975, pp. 202-203) recounted how the Weather Bureau explained their decision to the group:

> . . . there was no longer any hope for white youth. American defeatism had conquered; they were not willing to struggle for themselves, let alone the peoples of the world. Weatherman, with a clear vision of what had to be done, could wait no longer. To hold back now would be to fail the Vietnamese, the blacks, and the revolution.

Going underground meant that the tactics employed by the Weathermen were to be more destructive. Since American society could not be saved, it would have to be destroyed. The dark side of politics held seductive appeal to the Weathermen. "We have to force the disintegration of society, creating strategic armed chaos where there is now pig order," Weathermen wrote before going underground in "Revolution in the 70s" (Jacobs 1970, p. 366). Hayden (1988, p. 360) summarized the difference in perspectives between SDS and the Weathermen:

> Revolutionaries like the Weathermen, having given up on changing American society, thought of themselves as a "fifth column" or, in Malraux's phrase "doomed executioners." There would be no social revolution in America, just wreckage . . . . While I was still very much a child of Port Huron, they were war orphans. As I said in a bitter argument with Terry [Robbins of the Weathermen], they were not the conscience of a generation, but its id, finally surfacing.

Underground they went in the early 1970s, with several of their cells highly active in bombing. But the event that shook the Weathermen's confidence was the townhouse explosion in March 1970 that killed three members. Stern's (1975, p. 238) response was:

> Those were people who were real . . . . I was horrified that they had blown themselves up, that they had not known enough, that they had made a mistake when a mistake was deadly. But their deaths were instructive to me . . . . No mistakes. No more children's crusade. To go up against serpents . . . you must be a serpent yourself.
>
> "The times were driving people toward madness," said Hayden (1988, p. 420).

But several years later, American politics had become less divisive, and life underground had become tedious for many Weatherpeople. As Alpert (1981, pp. 327-328) remembered, "By 1974, the Weathermen were of little interest to prosecutors . . . I no longer believed, as I had in 1970, that the country was in any way ready for a revolution, leftist or otherwise." In the latter 1970s and early 1980s, most members of the Weather Underground quit clandestine life to live above ground. Rank-and-file members Stern and Alpert tired of an underground existence, became saddened and lonely as some of their friends abandoned the revolution, and longed for their old contacts. In 1977, it was reported that a split occurred among Weather Underground leaders about whether, how, and when to surface. One faction hatched a plan by Jeff Jones in 1975, which was called "inversion," or the process of emerging from fugitive life in order to enlist above-ground radicals into the cause. According to statements made by the dissenting leadership, which included Bernardine Dohrn, the plan involved having lawyers prepare a defense, and showing the film "Underground" to "sanitize the image of the organization and to raise money for legal defense" (*New York Times* 1977, p. 22).

From the late 1970s through the 1980s well-known Weather leaders, such as Mark Rudd, Bernardine Dohrn, Bill Ayers, and Cathy Wilkerson surfaced from the underground. The Weather Underground did not cease to exist, however. The "last gasp" of the Weather Underground was the 1981 Brinks robbery. The robbery was bungled, a guard and two policemen were shot, and Kathy Boudin, Judith Clark, David Gilbert of the May 19th Coalition faction of the Weathermen, along with several others possibly from the Black Liberation Army, were caught, charged, and sentenced for their crimes (Franks 1981; McGrath 1981; Gitlin 1987).

While it is apparent that historical-period effects influenced both the formation of the Weathermen and their activities, in order to more fully understand the Weatherman organization and decisions, an important consideration is the group itself. Committing acts of terrorism, Crenshaw (1986, p. 385) noted, "is a result of group interaction as much as individual choice." As the terrorist literature has indicated, the group is a major source of radicalization for individual members, providing the rationale, norms, and reinforcement for extreme behavior (Braungart and Braungart 1983; Wasmund 1983). In the next section, attention is given to the group dynamics within the Weathermen that indicate why some youth joined the group and document the pronounced group effect of the Weathermen on individual members.

Group Dynamic Explanations

One question of interest is how young people became involved in the Weathermen organization. Many of the leaders came directly from SDS, but recruitment of rank-and-file members into the Weathermen appears to have been less based on radicalized individuals seeking out extremist groups to join than on friendship and personal-network factors. Studies of terrorist groups, entry into SDS, and accounts of those who joined the Weathermen indicated that individuals, some of whom were not initially radical or political, became involved in the group because of friends and lovers, or they drifted into the group under fortuitous circumstances (Wasmund 1983; Laqueur 1987; Braungart and Braungart 1988). The stage of youth is a time in life where peer associations and the group are especially important, with many of the Weathermen exhibiting a high need for group affiliation. Once a member, these youth found a sense of identification and belonging. As one newcomer to the Weatherman expressed it:

> It struck me, at a meeting I went to, that they were a family. A big, very tight family. I wanted to be part of that. People were touching each other. Women together, men together. They were beautifully free. I felt that they were experiencing a whole new life-style that I really hadn't begun to understand. They were so full of life and energy and determination and love (Sale 1973, p. 625).

The Weathermen was more than just a membership group; it was a highly committed reference group that demanded the total involvement of the individual. New members perceived themselves to be under close scrutiny or "test"—another dynamic that is characteristic of terrorist groups (Wasmund 1983). This kind of reference group quickly gains control over individual members' perceptions, attitudes, and behavior, especially for the highly ego-involved members. Experiments in group psychology have demonstrated the effects of groups on their members. For example, individual group members tend to relinquish their personal norms for those of the group (Sherif 1936), they conform to group pressure (Asch 1955) and roles (Zimbardo 1975), they commit distasteful, abhorent acts because they are told to do so (Milgram 1974) and are conforming to group norms and practices (Sherif and Sherif 1969; Turner and Killian 1987). Group effects such as these are predicted to be even more pronounced in self-selected or intact radical political groups (Stephan 1985; Tajfel and Turner 1986).

The Weathermen organization was an important source of political socialization for many of its members. And, it was often *after* joining the group that many individuals became more radicalized and extreme in their behavior. For example, Alpert (1981, p. 122) described:

> As Sam and I became closer to each other, I became drawn into the world of radical politics which I had admired from the outside for so many years and to which I'd never quite managed to gain entry on my own . . . . As I adopted the radicals' viewpoint for myself, I came to see all antiestablishment uprisings as aspects of a world revolution . . . . Instead of feeling anxiety that the world order I'd grown up with was breaking down, I came to welcome the prospect, identifying my own discontent with that of rebels around the globe and cheering for our eventual victory.

Totalistic groups such as the Weathermen provide clear, simplistic structure for the members' lives. To some individuals, part of the initial appeal of the Weathermen was the feeling of belonging and giving one's self over to the group. For the drifters, the timing of group affiliation came when they felt their lives to be "in transition," with the Weathermen attracting some individuals who were Vietnam veterans, recently divorced or from a broken relationship, and college drop-outs (Stern 1975; Alpert 1981). Part of the attraction to the Weathermen may also have been the excitement of being in a group environment where conventional values are eschewed, with the group "giving permission" to young people—along with positive reinforcement—for engaging in a variety of taboo behaviors, both personal and political. The Weathermen was a high risk-taking, extremist group, and as social psychological studies have demonstrated, individuals are more apt to support extreme types of behavior sanctioned by the group than they would if acting alone (Myers and Lamm 1976; Forsyth 1983). This kind of strong group support may partially explain why these youth from middleand upper-middle-class families and prestigous schools could discard conventional norms to engage in the highly experimental and destructive acts promoted by the Weathermen.

It is worthy of comment that some of the most extreme and violent actions in the Weathermen were conducted by women—as was also the case in the Baader-Meinhof gang and Red Brigades. No doubt the charismatic Bernardine Dohrn was a compelling role model for women in the group, but much of the explanation for women's behavior may rest in the feminist movement of that particular time in history, with Weatherwomen feeling that they had to prove their toughness to group members in their fight for recognition and respect. While the male-female struggle within the group was an ongoing battle, Hayden (1988) pointed out that relative to other political activist groups operating during that time, the Weathermen was a group where women had relative freedom and could act out their conflicts and hostilities. Yet, as several Weather Underground members—one a female and the other a male—admitted years later: "We've made many mistakes . . . . Male supremacy undermined us;" and "The Weather Underground has always emphasized that men and women had to struggle together . . . . But macho attitudes were largely responsible for our downfall" (Boeth 1977; Hornblower and Valentine 1980).

What helped to sustain the Weatherman organization was group conflict. The Weathermen were constantly "at war" with some "enemy": at its formative stage it was SDS and the other factions within SDS; during its rampage stage in the summer and fall of 1969, it was bourgeois white America; and in the clandestine stage it was the state (government, FBI-CIA, police) and the corporate sectors. The enemy was given focus by the Weathermen's vitriolic language, evident in its communiques and statements, such as when Mark Rudd told the audience at the National War Council, "It's a wonderful feeling to hit a pig" (Sale 1973, p. 628). As Gitlin (1987, p. 390) observed, "Language became a cudgel in this shadow play." Having an enemy to hate and vilify facilitated group solidarity and provided a target for group energy and efforts to maintain organizational momentum. Escalating the level of intergroup conflict, as the Weather Bureau did, also helped divert attention from the ongoing intragroup conflict to some outside enemy.

Because the Weathermen was a totalistic group and in continual conflict with the authorities, the group was able to exert a powerful influence over individual members' perception, thinking, and behavior—a dynamic that facilitates distorted social judgments and destructive behavior at both the individual and group levels (Sherif and Sherif 1969; Forsyth 1983). Group-based evaluations were exaggerated—termed the assimilation-contrast effect—providing the basis for stereotyping, unrealistic expectations, negative intergroup attitudes, dehumanization of outgroups, and the promotion of conflict that once established becomes difficult to end (Stephan 1985; Tajfel and Turner 1986; Braungart and Braungart 1989a). Similar group dynamics occurred within the Nixon Administration and local police forces. Distortion effects were further heightened within the Weathermen when it became a clandestine organization. As Gitlin (1987, p. 395) observed, "The more insulated . . . from counterarguments and complicated reality, the easier it was to hold onto abstract revolutionary schemes. The Weathermen developed this hermetic tendency to a coarse art."

As with groups engaging in terrorist actions (whether substate, nihilist, issue-oriented, or the government), the individual is socialized into committing destructive acts by the reference group (Braungart and Braungart 1983; Wasmund 1983; Crenshaw 1986). In the Weathermen, individual identities were broken down ("Weatherfries"), along with morality and personal concerns about harming others through violence. Encouraging Weather members to abandon personal misgivings was partially facilitated through extensive sexual and drug experimentation, with the group totally controlling the individual's life, even in the sexual area. The Weathermen readily supplied the rhetoric and rationale as well as the positive reinfocement for unconventional or destructive behavior. As Alpert (1981, p. 194) recounted:

> In the same way I had convinced myself that sexual possessiveness was reactionary, I was now trying to overcome my scruples against bombings, which I was convinced were a residue of the same bourgeois upbringing. I was afraid to seem cowardly: I didn't want Sam or anyone else to accuse me of timidity or conservatism, and I didn't want to be excluded from Sam's plans for the future.

Weathermen absolved the individual of guilt by justifying harmful actions. As one said, "It's not a question of whether to use violence or not. There's no other way" (*Newsweek* 1970, p. 27). Proving oneself and gaining status in the group was achieved through destructive acts, and engaging in behavior against one's better judgment to impress the group is a theme echoed in several personal accounts (see Stern 1975; Alpert 1981). Yet, as with terrorist or criminal organizations, after participating in such instrumental and illegal activity, even if the individual no longer wants to be part of the group, alternatives to the group are increasingly restricted and the path back to conventional society and a positive identity becomes blocked. Susan Stern (1975, pp. 208-209) described the burden of underground life as well as the Weathermen's inability to read reality:

> There was no escape . . . . We were alone and isolated. We constituted a fraction of a fraction of the population at large. Everyone was disgusted with the Weathermen. The dream had turned into a nightmare . . . . We were finished, but we didn't know it yet. The end was coming swiftly, but no one warned us. Ignoring the reality, we filled our minds with visions of the new underground . . . . I was living science fiction. It was the loneliest, most morbid time of my life.

In reviewing Stern's book, *With the Weathermen*, Brownmiller (1975, p. 6) observed, "But the real story here is one of group tyranny over individual lives." In the end, what weakened the Weathermen had far less to do with government harassment than with the faceless existence of underground life, the convoluted "Weatherlogic," and infighting within the group.

WHY THE WEATHERMEN?

In this study it has been suggested that in order to more fully understand the formation and motivations of a youthful political group such as the Weathermen, a social psychological approach is needed. Toward that end, a framework was developed, organized around psychological, sociohistorical, and group dynamic explanations. Combining macro and micro levels of analysis, each approach suggested certain key concepts and relationships that were applicable to explaining the Weathermen and their behavior. Some of the major results are summarized in Table 1.

A Social Psychological Assessment

From a psychological perspective, focusing on the develpmental processes of youth provided more information about the Weathermen's motivations and behavior than did a search for similar personality traits or a terrorist personality profile. The journey into "Weatherpolitics" by individual members appeared to be strongly rooted in resolving the developmental issues of the stage of youth. Young people drawn to the Weathermen tended to engage in a categorical all-or-nothing style of political thinking, struggled with identity formation, and found the personal and political experimentation as well as the negative identity offered by the Weatherman appealing and exciting. Often coming from well-to-do families, a number of youth who became members of the Weathermen were deeply concerned with resolving the dissonance between their own relative comfort and the poverty, exploitation, and misery of those less fortunate in America and the third world. Many of the young people who joined the Weathermen were looking for meaning in their lives and linked their personal lives to politics by affiliating with this highly controlling and contentious political youth group. Consideration of psychological features, while necessary, does not appear sufficient to explain the Weathermen's attitudes and actions.

Table 1. Social Psychological Framework for Assessing Motivations of the Weathermen

Level of Analysis	*Weatherman Organization*
Psychological	
Development	Cognitive style categorical, "blood-thirsty," ideological-utopian
	Identity diffuse, experimental, and negative, with a search for meaning in life
Personality	Mixture of personality types and traits in the group
	Some individuals innately aggressive, while others less aggressive but conformed to group pressure
	Some individuals' personalities changed as result of group membership
Family Background	Many from affluent or middle-class backgrounds, who felt guilty about their comfort relative to the poor
	Parents politics mixed: Democrat, liberal, Republic, radical-chic, pacifist
Sociohistorical	
Cohort Effects	Grew up as part of the large baby-boom cohort
	Came of age as teenagers during turbulent 1960s when black power movement and Vietnam War were important issues
Period Effects	Violent late 1960s: international terrorism and extremist youth groups active in Europe and Japan; assassinations of Martin Luther King, Jr. and Robert Kennedy; 1968 Democratic Convention; Columbia University uprising
	Increasingly unpopular Vietnam war continued
	Youth culture highly experimental and cynical
	Competing activist movements (feminist, black power, gay rights) view for attention
	Domestic politics polarized, fragmented, and conflict oriented under Nixon Administration
	Intensive government surveillance of youthful political activists in an era of widespread student protests
Group Dynamics	
Affiliation	Joined through friends, lovers, or by chance
Strucutre	Totalistic reference group: authoritarian and isolated, enhancing group effect on individual
Dynamics	Intensive intergroup and intragroup conflict
	Distorted perception, judgment, and behavior
	Negative role models and destructive behavior reinforced

Much of the behavior of the Weathermen and its members had to do with the the larger sociohistorical context, including both cohort and period effects.

One important sociohistorical influence involved growing up as members of the large baby-boom cohort, who were teenagers during the tumultuous 1960s when racial conflict and the Vietnam war were divisive issues in American society. These middle- and upper-middle-class youth appeared especially attuned to the violent, unjust, and shrill America in which they came of age, and their political attitudes and style were a partial reflection of their interpretations and responses to the cohort influences of their youth in the 1960s. As college students and young adults in the late 1960s and early 1970s, the Weathermen's rhetoric and style was a partial outcome of their political socialization experiences and psychological needs.

Another type of sociohistorical influence on the Weathermen included the particular mix of events and trends in the late 1960s and early 1970s as the group organized and took political action. The formation of the Weathermen stemmed largely from the escalating political polarization, fragmentation, and violence, coupled with the failure of SDS and other leftist political groups to effectively bring about the changes that had concerned many youth since the early 1960s in the areas of civil rights/racism, the Vietnam War-U.S. imperialism, and university reform. Global trends such as the heightened youthful revolutionary and terrorist political activity helped sustain the momentum of the Weathermen, while on the domestic front the Weathermen were strongly influenced by the black power movement, the feminist struggle, and the Nixon Administration's Vietnam policy, surveillance, and distain for youthful protest.

These were among the unique period effects that contributed to the the escalation of the Weathermen's tactics and strategy as well as the Weather Bureau's decision to become a clandestine organization engaging in acts of violence and terrorism. However, as the political issues shifted in the mid-1970s, the activities of the Weatherman organization subsided, and most Weather leaders and rank-and-file members began to emerge from their underground life. Only a few Weathermen remained fugitives, such as those who attempted the Brinks robbery—an act that Franks (1981, p. 46) described as "a chilling perversion of every purpose they had ever had: the children of the rich killing the less privileged in the name of revolution."

Mediating between the individual members and society was the Weathermen group, which was both strongly affected by social and political events and in turn exerted a dominant influence over the personalities, attitudes, and behavior of its participants. Often joining because of friends or lovers, part of the appeal of the Weathermen was the group's ability to meet the affiliative needs of youth. As a highly controlling reference group, the Weathermen provided a vehicle for many young individuals to abandon their weak identities, give themselves over to the group, and find meaning in life. The self-selected isolation of the group, its intensive inter and intragroup conflict further enhanced the power of the group over its members. Distorted social judgments and extremist political behavior were the result, as the group interpreted (distorted) reality, romanticized revolution, encouraged the violation of conventional society's taboos, and offered support for engaging in destructive personal and political behavior.

From SDS to the Weathermen

To help put these findings in clearer perspective, comparisons can be made between the Weathermen and SDS, which are of interest in this study, since SDS helped launch the 1960s Generation in the United States, whereas the Weathermen are often credited with bringing the 1960s political generation to an end. Though both groups were part of the New Left movement in the stormy 1960s, the style and tactics of the two groups differed, partially due to the unique interplay among sociohistorical, group, and psychological forces. Especially important to understanding the behavior of SDS and the Weathermen were their somewhat different locations in history. SDS, whose members were slightly older than the Weathermen and had grown up as teens in the late 1950s, organized during the the optimistic early 1960s in the United States. Members of the second generation SDS, the Weathermen came of age during the more dramatic and divisive later 1960s, with the organization evolving out of the frustrations of the student left in 1969 in an era of heightened political conflict and rage.

Both SDS and Weathermen participated in and contributed to the momentum of the 1960s generation, but, of critical importance, each had emerged from a different starting point and had acted and reacted to a different set of escalating societal and political conditions. The Weathermen became active during a time when the larger student movement had intensified its activity and expanded to more college and university campuses. The tactics that had been "radical" in the early phases of SDS, by the late 1960s had become "conventional;" therefore, in order to keep the New Left Movement going, more extreme tactics were required, especially since a variety of new groups and causes (feminism, gay rights, Yippies, black power) were vying for public attention.

While the momentum and mix of historical events and trends strongly affected the origins of SDS and Weathermen, a significant factor accounting for differences in their organizations and actions was the group effect. Although those joining either SDS or the Weathermen often entered for similar reasons—friends, lovers, fortuitous circumstances—once involved in their respective groups, individual members were exposed to a specific set of sociohistorical conditions and group dynamics that influenced the identities, attitudes, and behavior of their members. An important difference between SDS and the Weathermen was the totalistic structure of Weathermen, which became more pronounced when the group became a clandestine organization.

Both SDS and the Weathermen attempted to transform politics, but the Weathermen attempted to transform individual members as well. The Weathermen had special appeal to youth struggling with an identity crisis who were drawn to a revolutionary group that espoused an over-simplified, utopian, and violent form of politics. These were some of the same reasons given by SDS leaders Tom Hayden (1988) and Todd Gitlin (1987) for *not* joining the Weathermen, although they, like many of their Weathermen friends, were highly frustrated over the events and issues in the late 1960s.

The impact of a political generation is not curtailed when a particularly active era such as the 1960s has ended. There are "spillover effects," especially on the lives of a political generation's participants. Although both SDS and the Weathermen activists have aged and society has changed markedly since the 1960s and early 1970s, the political loyalty and outlook of these former activists remains partially "frozen" in generational time, continuing to reflect the orientation and style of their respective groups. Now middle-aged, Tom Hayden, founder and former leader of SDS, closed his book *Reunion* (1988, p. 507) with the statement:

> Times filled with tragedy are also times of greatness and wonder, times that really matter, and times truly worth living through. Whatever the future holds, and as satisfying as my life is today, I miss the sixties and always will.

A more caustic analysis came from several Weathermen entering mid-life. Noted Cathy Wilkerson after leaving the underground: "I have the same commitment to struggle . . . . It is 1980, but the conditions still exist which caused colonized peoples to fight for liberation . . . "(Hornblower and Valentine 1980, p. A2). Said Bill Ayers upon surfacing from the underground in 1980: "It's a system built on genocide and slavery and oppression, a system that poisons the earth and cripples future generations for profit . . . " (*Syracuse Herald Journal* 1980, p. A11). SDS and the Weathermen were part of the same 1960s Generation and shared a fervent commitment to radical left-wing politics. But as the 1960s decade wore on and SDS's aspirations to reform and radicalize society were thwarted, the way was paved for the Weathermen's journey into clandestine politics and terrorist tactics. The Weathermen, like the Queen of Hearts in *Alice in Wonderland*, had only one solution for settling difficulties both great or small. "Off with their heads!" the Queen would say, "without even looking round."

REFERENCES

Adelson, J. 1987. "Children and Other Political Naifs." Pp. 88-102 in *Growing and Changing*, edited by E. Hall. New York: Random House.

Alpert, J. 1973. "Mother Right: A New Feminist Theory." *Ms.*, August, pp. 52-55, 88-94.

________. 1981. *Growing Up Underground.* New York: Morrow.

Asch, S. E. 1955. "Opinions and Social Pressure." *Scientific American* 193:31-35.

Bell, J. B. 1980. "The International Scientific Conference on Terrorism, Berlin." *Terrorism: An International Journal* 3:201-202.

Bettelheim, B. 1963. "The Problem of Generations." Pp. 64-92 in *Youth: Change and Challenge*, edited by E. H. Erikson. New York: Basic.

Boeth, R. 1977. "The Return of Mark Rudd." *Newsweek* (September 26), p. 34.

Braungart, R. G. 1979. *Family Status, Socialization and Student Politics.* Ann Arbor, MI: University Microfilms International.

________. 1988. "Journey into All-or-Nothing Politics." *Contemporary Sociology* 17(November):733-737.

Braungart, R. G. and M. M. Braungart. 1983. "Terrorism." Pp. 299-337 in *Prevention and Control of Aggression*, edited by Center for Research on Aggression, Syracuse University. New York: Pergamon.

________. 1986. "Life Course and Generational Politics." *Annual Review of Sociology* 12:205-231.

________. 1988. "The Life-Course Development of Left- and Right-Wing Youth Activist Leaders from the 1960s." Paper presented at the Annual Scientific Meeting of the International Society of Political Psychology, Secaucus, New Jersey, July 1-5.

________. 1989a. "Generational Conflict and Intergroup Relations as the Foundation for Political Generations." Pp. 107-30 in *Advances in Group Processes* (Vol. 6), edited by E. J. Lawler and B. Markovsky. Greenwich, CT: JAI Press.

________. 1989b. "Political Generations." Pp. 281-319 in *Research in Political Sociology* (Vol. 5), edited by R.G. Braungart and M.M. Braungart. Greenwich, CT: JAI Press.

Brownmiller, S. 1975. "With the Weathermen." *New York Times Book Review* (June 15), p. 6.

Carroll, R. 1978. "Inside the Red Brigades." *Newsweek* (May 15), pp. 43-44, 49.

Crenshaw, M. 1986. "The Psychology of Political Terrorism." Pp. 379-413 in *Political Psychology*, edited by M. G. Hermann. San Francisco: Jossey-Bass.

Current, R. N., T. H. Williams, F. Freidel, and A. Brinkley. 1983. *American History: A Survey.* 6th ed. New York: Knopf.

Delli Carpini, M. X. 1986. *Stability and Change in American Politics: The Coming of Age of the Generations of the 1960s.* New York: New York University Press.

Erikson, E. 1968. *Identity: Youth and Crisis.* New York: Norton.

Esler, A.. 1984. "'The Truest Community': Social Generations as Collective Mentalities." *Journal of Political and Military Sociology* 12:99-112.

Feuer, L. 1969. *The Conflict of Generations.* New York: Basic.

Flacks, R. 1967. "The Liberated Generation: An Exploration of the Roots of Student Protest." *Journal of Social Issues* 23:52-75.

Forsyth, D.R. 1983. *An Introduction to Group Dynamics.* Monterey, CA:Brooks/Cole.

Frankfurt, E. 1983. *Kathy Boudin and the Dance of Death.* New York: Stein and Day.

Franks, L. 1981. "The Seeds of Terror." *New York Times Magazine* (November 22, pp. 34-38, 44, 46).

Fromm, E. 1973. *The Anatomy of Human Destructiveness.* New York: Holt, Rinehart and Winston.

Gallatin, J. 1980. "Political Thinking in Adolescence." Pp. 344-382 in *Handbook of Adolescent Psychology*, edited by J. Adelson. New York: Wiley.

Getler, M. 1977. "Women Play Growing Role in Slayings By West Germany's Terrorist Groups." *Washington Post* (August 6), p. A15.

Gitlin, T. 1987. *The Sixties: Years of Hope, Days of Rage.* New York: Bantam.

Gordon, L. and A. Gordon. 1987. *American Chronicle: Six Decades in American Life.* New York: Atheneum.

Hayden. T. 1988. *Reunion: A Memoir*. New York: Random House.

Hornblower, M. and P. Valentine. 1980. "Cathy Wilkerson: The Evolution of a Revolutionary." *Washington Post* (July 15), p. 2.

Jacobs, H,, ed. 1970. *Weatherman*. New York: Ramparts.

Jenkins, B. M. 1980. "The International Scientific Conference on Terrorism, Berlin." *Terrorism: An International Journal* 3:246-250.

Kanfer, S. 1981. "The Politics of the Playpen." *New Republic* (December 23), 30-32.

Keniston, K. 1968. *Young Radicals*. New York: Harcourt, Brace and World.

Klapp, O. E. 1975. "Opening and Closing in Open Systems." *Behavioral Science* 20:251-257.

Knoke, David. 1984. "Conceptual and Measurement Aspects in the Study of Political Generations." *Journal of Political and Military Sociology* 12:191-201.

Knutson, J. N. 1981. "Social and Psychodynamic Pressures Toward a Negative Identity: The Case of an American Revolutionary Terrorist." Pp. 105-50 in *Behavioral and Quantitative Perspectives on Terrorism*, edited by Y. Alexander and J. M. Gleason. New York: Pergamon.

Laqueur, W. 1987. *The Age of Terrorism*. Boston: Little Brown.

Lebow, R. N. 1980. "The Origins of Sectarian Assassination: The Case of Belfast." Pp. 41-53 in *International Terrorism: Current Research and Future Directions*, edited by A. D. Buckley and D. D. Olson. Wayne, NJ: Avery.

Life. 1970. March 27, p. 30.

Mannheim, K. 1952. "The Problem of Generations." Pp. 276-320 in *Essays on the Sociology of Knowledge*, edited by Paul Kecskemeti. London: Routledge and Kegan Paul.

McGrath, P. 1981. "Return of the Weathermen." *Newsweek* (November 2), pp. 30-34.

Milgram, S. 1974. *Obedience to Authority*. New York: Harper and Row.

Miller, J. 1987. *Democracy in the Streets*. New York: Simon and Schuster.

Moller, H. 1972. "Youth as a Force in the Modern World." Pp. 215-223 in *Youth and Sociology*, edited by Peter K. Manning and M. Truzzi. Englewood Cliffs, NJ: Prentice-Hall.

Myers, D. G. and H. Lamm. 1976. "The Group Polarization Phenomenon." *Psychological Bulletin* 83:602-627.

Newsweek. 1970. March 23, pp. 27-36.

———. 1985. November 2, p. 15.

New York Times. 1977. January 16, p. 22.

Ortega y Gasset, Jose. 1961. *The Modern Theme*. New York: Harper and Row.

Ryder, N. B. 1965. "The Cohort as a Concept in the Study of Social Change." *American Sociological Review* 30:843-861.

———. 1974. "The Demography of Youth." Pp. 45-61 in *Youth: Transition to Adulthood*, edited by the Panel on Youth of the President's Science Advisory Committee. Chicago: University Chicago Press.

Sale, K. 1973. *SDS*. New York: Random House.

Schlagheck, D. M. 1988. *International Terrorism*. Lexington, MA: D.C. Heath.

Schlesinger, A. M., Jr. 1986. *The Cycles of American History*. Boston: Houghton Mifflin.

Sherif, M. 1936. *The Psychology of Social Norms*. New York: Harper Torchbooks.

Sherif, M. and C. Sherif. 1969. *Social Psychology*. New York: Harper and Row.

Stephan, W. G. 1985. "Intergroup Relations." Pp. 599-658 in *Handbook of Social Psychology* (vol. 2), edited by G. Lindzey and E. Aronson. New York: Random House.

Stern, S. 1975. *With the Weathermen*. New York: Doubleday.

Storr, A. 1978. "Sadism and Paranoia." Pp. 231-239 in *International Terrorism in the Contemporary World*, edited by Marius Livingston. Westport, CT: Greenwood.

Students for a Democratic Society. 1964. *The Port Huron Statement*. New York: Students for a Democratic Society.

Syracuse Herald Journal. 1980. December 4, p. A11.

Tajfel, H. and J. C. Turner. 1986. "The Social Identity Theory of Intergroup Behavior." Pp. 7-24 in *Psychology of Intergroup Relations*, edited by S. Worchel and W. G. Austin. Chicago: Nelson-Hall.

Turner, R. H. and L. M. Killian. 1987. *Collective Behavior*. 3rd. ed. Englewood Cliffs, NJ: Prentice-Hall.

Unger, I. 1974. *The Movement: A History of the American New Left, 1959-1972*. New York: Dodd Mead.

Vander Zanden, J. W. 1989. *Human Development*. 4th ed. New York: Knopf.

Wallimann, I. and G. V. Zito. 1984. "Cohort Size and Youthful Protest." *Youth and Society* 16:67-81.

Wasmund, K. 1983. "The Political Socialization of Terrorist Groups in West Germany." *Journal of Political and Military Sociology* 11:223-240.

Young, N. 1977. *An Infantile Disorder? The Crisis and Decline of the New Left*. Boulder, CO: Westview.

Zimbardo, P. 1975. "Transforming Experimental Research into Advocacy for Social Change." Pp. 33-66 in *Applying Social Psychology*, edited by M. Deutsch and H. A. Hornstein. Hillsdale, NJ: Erlbaum.

POLITICAL VIOLENCE BY THE NONAGGRIEVED:

EXPLAINING THE POLITICAL PARTICIPATION OF THOSE WITH NO APPARENT GRIEVANCES

Robert W. White

Research on social protest and political violence almost exclusively concentrates on the activities of people with obvious grievances, for example, African-Americans in the United States. Most social protest movements, however, include supporters who do not have obvious grievances. For example, Von Eschen and colleagues (1971, pp. 540-541) document the involvement of white Catholic and Protestant clergy in the U.S. civil rights movement; these people were not directly discriminated against because of their race. Similarly, U.S. students currently involved in antiapartheid activities have not been directly harmed by the South African government.

Why people with no apparent grievances participate in political violence is the focus of this paper. The analyses examine why residents of the Irish Republic do and do not support the political violence of the Provisional Irish Republican Army (IRA). The IRA and its political wing, Sinn Féin, limit most of their activities to Northern Ireland, and draw most of their recruits and

International Social Movement Research, Vol. 4, pages 79-103.

ISBN: 1-55938-445-X

supporters from this geographic location. Both organizations, however, have a significant level of support in the Irish Republic, even though residents of this geographic area are not subject to the grievances that are usually invoked as causes of support for the IRA.[1] For example, Birrell (1972) examines whether or not the socioeconomic deprivation of Northern Irish Catholics prompts IRA support. Similarly, Hewitt (1981, 1983, 1985, 1987) and O'Hearn (1983, 1985, 1987; see also Kovalcheck 1987), debate whether Nationalism or economic grievances produce support for the IRA in the North of Ireland. These factors do not directly affect IRA supporters in the Irish Republic. By default, then, these explanations of support for the IRA must be incomplete. This paper seeks to fill this void.

THEORETICAL BACKGROUND: THE POLITICS OF THE NONAGGRIEVED

Argument One: Relative Deprivation and Equity Arguments

"Relative deprivation" explanations of political violence posit that "something" takes place (e.g., a sharp drop in the standard of living) which causes a perceived difference between expected and achieved outcomes (e.g., income) for a given individual. This difference purportedly causes frustration in the individual which leads to aggression. One outlet for this aggression is political violence (e.g., Davies 1962; Gurr 1970). "Equity" authors focus on reactions to inequity. The basic proposition of equity theory is found in the following equation presented in Adams (1965, p. 273)[2]:

$$\frac{\text{A's rewards less A's costs}}{\text{A's investments}} = \frac{\text{B's rewards less B's costs}}{\text{B's investments}}$$

Distributive justice, or equity, exists when for two persons in an exchange relationship the profit (rewards from the relationship minus the costs of the relationship) of each person is proportional to the investment (e.g., education or effort) of each person. If the two ratios are unequal, then each person experiences a "feeling of injustice," and one person experiences deprivation (Adams 1965, p. 273). When individuals perceive that they are participating in inequitable relationships, "they become distressed" and try to restore equity (e.g., Walster, Walster, and Berscheid 1978, p. 6; also see, Utne and Kidd [1980]). Involvement in political violence by those experiencing deprivation is one method of alleviating distress, and attempting to restore equity (see Walster et al. 1978, pp. 50-56).

A straightforward interpretation of either the relative deprivation or the equity perspective cannot account for the behavior examined below. To begin, virtually all theory and research on relative deprivation concern grievances that produce frustrations which directly and immediately affect individuals, not "third parties" (see, for example, the discussion in Gurney and Tierney [1982]). Equity theory addresses the reaction to injustice of "observers" with the argument that third party observers of inequity also experience distress. This reaction, however, is expected to be "less intense" than the reaction of those immediately affected by inequity (Walster et al. 1978, pp. 60-65). The data examined below involve active supporters of political violence, a behavior that is extreme, and "intense." This suggests that the equity explanation of third party observer support for political violence is inadequate (see also Martin and Murray [1983]).

Aspects of both the relative deprivation and equity perspectives may be used to develop an extended argument which may explain why people not directly affected by grievances still engage in protest. This argument is consistent with these two perspectives in that distress caused by a violation of justice expectations remains a key motivator of protest. The argument differs from the perspectives described earlier in that the justice violation is viewed as one involving social issues so that even "third parties" are directly affected by social injustice.

In the relative deprivation and equity conceptualizations a person compares an outcome for him or herself against either an expected outcome for him or herself (relative deprivation), or the outcome for some other, similar, person (equity). For present purposes this must be broadened so that the comparison is one of the life situation of other individuals against some general standard of social justice. From this view, individuals assess the allocation of rewards from the social structure of a given society when they determine what is fair (e.g., Rawls 1971). With such an assessment an individual may not be the victim of injustice, but his or her standard of justice may still be violated if some other person is seen to experience an injustice (i.e., an unfair allocation of rewards). If such a standard of justice is violated normative standards of fairness or moral obligation may then motivate participation in activities like social protest (Moore 1978; Marwell and Ames 1979; Zurcher and Snow 1981, pp. 458-460). From this view the violation of an abstract level of justice may prompt the participation in social protest of individuals who, apparently, have not experienced injustice.

Argument Two: Resource Mobilization and Political Process Arguments

The resource mobilization (McCarthy and Zald 1973, 1977; Tilly 1978) and political process (McAdam 1982) perspectives were developed in response to deprivation arguments. Because these two perspectives place less emphasis on grievances per se, this literature is more easily extended to account for the political participation of the nonaggrieved. From these perspectives grievances are viewed as relatively constant within a given population and they are, therefore, only a necessary cause of involvement in social protest (McCarthy and Zald 1973, 1977; Jenkins and Perrow 1977; Tilly 1978; Jenkins 1983). In and of themselves grievances do not motivate participation in political protest, their impact is mediated by more important factors that determine involvement in social protest.

Mobilization and political process research suggests that two key factors, social connections among potential and active social movement members and expectations of social movement success, influence the political participation of the nonaggrieved. Research on networks and social solidarity suggests that even if an individual recognizes that others are victims of injustice this recognition has an impact only if the injustice affects other persons with whom the individual experiences solidarity relations (Fireman and Gamson 1979; Snow, Zurcher, and Ekland-Olson 1980; McAdam 1986; della Porta 1988; see also Deutsch 1975). The importance of solidarity relations is demonstrated in Markovsky's (1985) finding that the victims of injustice protest collective injustices more than personal injustices under conditions of high group identification.

Other research suggests that unless individuals perceive that an injustice can be effectively countered then there is no response to the injustice (Lawler 1975; McAdam 1982; Klandermans 1984). Utne and Kidd, in reviewing literature pertaining to third party reactions to inequity, agree with this view. In describing the influence of expectations of success on the reactions of the nonaggrieved they state: "It seems . . . that a third party observer is most likely to intervene when he can do something for an individual that the individual cannot do for himself" (Utne and Kidd 1980, p. 86).

Thus, mobilization and political process arguments suggest that the political participation of the nonaggrieved results in part from social ties that link the nonaggrieved to the aggrieved. Further, political participation of the nonaggrieved should also depend on the belief that the political activities of the aggrieved, in combination with the nonaggrieved, are efficacious.

Using these two extended arguments as guidelines I examine why the nonaggrieved support political violence. The analysis is divided into two general sections, one concerning the political motivations of Irish Republican Army supporters who live in the Irish Republic, the other concerning the political motivations of those involved in mainstream, constitutional, politics in the Irish Republic. The investigation of the motives of IRA supporters focuses on their knowledge of living conditions in the North of Ireland, and their social ties to active IRA supporters prior to their own decision to support the IRA. The investigation of those involved in mainstream politics addresses why they do not support the IRA, and their belief, in contrast to the beliefs of the IRA supporters, that IRA violence will not lead to the reunification of Ireland.

DATA AND PROCEDURES

The Irish Republican Army has historical roots that date to the 1840s and its members embrace an ideology that dates to the late eighteenth century (Bell 1979; Coogan 1987). Sinn Féin, the political wing of the IRA, dates from the early years of the twentieth century. The core belief of supporters of the IRA, that is, Irish Republicans, is that the only way for Ireland to gain complete independence from England is through military activity.

A guerrilla war, waged by the IRA and Sinn Féin, from 1918 to 1922 led to the partition of Ireland into the 6 Irish counties known as Northern Ireland and the 26 Irish counties known as the Irish Free State. The statelet of Northern Ireland maintains its position as part of the United Kingdom, but the Irish Free State seceded from the British Commonwealth in 1949 and formed the Irish Republic (the Republic, in its constitution, claims the entire island). The Irish Republic is populated predominately by Catholics, many of whom support the ideal of a unified island under one Irish government, that is, they are Irish Nationalists. In Northern Ireland, in contrast, two-thirds of the population is Protestant and identifies itself as British (Loyalist), and one-third of the population is Catholic and identifies itself as Irish (Nationalist; Moxon-Browne 1983, pp. 1-18).

The Provisional IRA and Sinn Féin are currently engaged in a guerrilla campaign in the North of Ireland.[3] The goal of this campaign is to wrest control of the North from Britain and to reunite this territory with the Irish Republic. The campaign is directly opposed by the British government and Loyalists living in Northern Ireland. Support and sympathy for the IRA comes from Irish Nationalists living in both the North (Moxon-Browne 1981) and the Irish Republic (Davis and Sinnott 1979). The IRA has more support in the North than it has in the Republic (over 100,000 Northern Nationalists voted for Sinn Féin in the 1983 Westminster general election). Although the IRA is an illegal organization in both Northern Ireland and the Irish Republic, Sinn Féin is a legal political party in both the North and South of Ireland. Sinn Féin's platform, however, does not equivocate on its support for the armed struggle of the IRA. This platform is strongly opposed by virtually every constitutional political party in the Republic and in the North of Ireland.

In 1984 and 1985 interviews were conducted with members of Sinn Féin and with people involved in constitutional politics in the Irish Republic.[4] These interviews consist of discussions of a number of topics, including why the respondents became involved in politics, the events surrounding their initial involvement in politics, and the political involvement of their families and friends. The data analyzed here are from taped interviews with fourteen IRA supporters born and raised outside of the North of Ireland, that is, "Southern Republicans," and taped interviews with six "Non-Republicans" active in politics in the Irish Republic.[5] Summary characteristics of the Republicans are presented in Table 1.

Table 1. General Characteristics of Southern Republicans

Interview Number	*Year Born** (+/−)	*Social Back-ground*	*Republican Background*	*Place of** Birth/Where Raised*	*Year Joined RM* (+/−)
1	1930	Middle Class	Yes	County Longford	1952
2	1935	Farming	Yes	County Donegal	1950
3	1935	Farming	Yes	County Longford	1955
4	1940	Working Class	No	Dublin	1969
5	1945	Working Class	Yes	County Dublin	1965
6	1955	Working Class	Yes	England	1969
7	1960	Working Class	No	County Kerry	1980
8	1960	Working Class	No	England	1974
9	1960	Middle Class	No	County Monaghan	1980
10	1960	Working Class	No	County Dublin	1981
11	1960	Working Class	No	Dublin	1981
12	1960	Middle Class	No	County Sligo	1982
13	1965	Working Class	Yes	County Louth	1984
14	1965	Working Class	Yes	County Louth	1982

Notes: * Year Born is rounded to the nearest year divisible by five in order to insure anonymity.
** Place of birth for one respondent is purposely incorrect in order to insure anonymity.

Seven of the 14 Republicans are from pro-IRA families. The approximate average age at the time of involvement in Republican politics is 20. Geographically, several different areas are represented: two persons were raised in Dublin City, and several are from smaller Irish towns or farm country. Several persons with working class backgrounds are from medium sized towns in the South (e.g., towns about the size of Athenry or slightly smaller).

The respondents involved in constitutional politics include three members of Fine Gael, one member of the Labour Party, and two members of Fianna Fáil. Of these six persons, three were elected representatives in the Irish Parliament (TDs in Dáil Éireann), and the other three are best described as full-time political activists. Summary characteristics of the Non-Republicans are presented in Table 2. Fianna Fáil is the most nationalistic of the political

Table 2. General Characteristics of Southern Non-Republicans

Interview Number	*Year* Born (+/−)*	*Social Background*	*Member of*	*Parents** Supported*
15	1945	Middle Class	Fine Gael	Fianna Fáil/ Fine Gael
16	1945	Middle Class	Fine Gael	Fine Gael
17	1950	Working Class	Fine Gael	Apolitical
18	1960	Working Class	Labour	Unknown
19	1940	Working Class	Fianna Fáil	Fáil Fine Gael/ Fianna Fáil
20	1930	Middle Class	Fianna Fáil	Fianna Fáil

Notes: * Year Born is rounded to the nearest year divisible by five in order to insure anonymity.
** For two respondents, their fathers supported one party while their mothers supported another. In these cases the mother's political party is listed after the father's.

parties represented, with the party leader and Taoiseach, until February 1992, Charles Haughey, viewed by many as a Republican. Fine Gael and Labour are less nationalistic than Fianna Fáil, and the differences between these two involve conservative versus liberal policies instead of the reunification of Ireland. In general, Fine Gael is more conservative than the Labour Party. With respect to domestic issues in the South, Fianna Fáil is often as conservative, and more so on some issues, as Fine Gael.

THE POLITICS OF SOUTHERN REPUBLICANS

Injustice in the North of Ireland: What Goes On Up There?

Examination of the interviews with the Republicans begins with a consideration of their awareness of injustice in the North of Ireland. Thirteen of the Southern Republicans were asked the question, "Would you have known about the discrimination in the North before becoming involved in the (Republican) Movement?"[6] Responses to this question are presented in Table 3. Seven of the 13 respondents state that they knew of the discrimination in the North prior to their involvement. In addition, one person states that he knew that discrimination had occurred in the past but that prior to his involvement "the worst excesses of discrimination were over."

The extended deprivation perspective suggests that all or almost all of these people knew of the injustice, and that this knowledge are an important reason for their involvement in the Republican Movement. This prediction is not supported. Instead, of the small number of respondents, almost half of them (6 of 13) were unaware of the discrimination in the North prior to their involvement, or believed that most of this discrimination had ceased. Further, this lack of knowledge is not confined to geographic areas far removed from the North since two respondents were from County Louth, a border county (Interviews 13 and 14).

Table 3. Knowledge of Discrimination in Northern Ireland Among Southern Republicans ($N = 13$)

Responses to the Question: Would you have known about discrimination in the North (before becoming involved in the Republican Movement)?

Interview Number	*Yes/ No*	*Abbreviated Response*
2	Yes	I did, at a very early age. I've experienced it as well. I used to . . . cross into Derry, into Limavady, down around there, you know?
3	Yes	Oh, well yes. At the time I'd be reading about (it in the) *United Irishman* . . .
4	Yes	I knew about it all right . . .
5	Yes	Oh, I would, yeah.
9	Yes	Yeah . . . one of my earliest memories was (going to a football game in Armagh) . . . on a Sunday, of course, and all the swings were chained.
10	Yes	I certainly did know about the discrimination . . . of Six County Catholics.
11	Yes	Well, I took it on myself to learn more about it. Obviously I wasn't going to get it from the media. So I started buying Sinn Féin literature.
8	Yes/No	Yeah, to an extent and that, because I knew Nationalists . . . .And they'd tell me, well, what the score was . . . .I didn't go to the North until about '74, '75, maybe, something like that. And therefore the worst excesses of discrimination were over . . . . So I was aware of it, but wasn't greatly aware about it. It was I was aware that the state was corrupt.
6	No	No, not really. No.
7	No	Well . . . the media in the South are totally against the Republican Movement . . . .you wouldn't actually find out exactly what the hell was going on in Ireland . . .
12	No	No.
13	No	Not really.
14	No	No . . . .after I got involved.

Evidence of this lack of awareness is presented in the two accounts that follow. The first account, from a man who knew of the injustice before becoming involved, shows that even the "informed" did not realize the full impact of injustice in th Northern Ireland.

> INTERVIEWER [hereafter, I]: Did you know about the discrimination [in the North]?
> RESPONDENT [hereafter, R]: I knew about it all right, but I never really, as I said, got interested in it too much.
> I: It didn't affect you personally?
> R: No. No, it did not. You'd feel it if you were traveling in the North all right. You'd get the hackles standing on the back of your head if you walked into any Black [Loyalist] area . . . .You'd walk into a pub and the conversation just ceased. Just stopped, you know? . . . [Because from his accent he was obviously from the South]
> I: Had you traveled up there before you got involved?
> R: I had, yeah. But we had relations in Newry and we saw them there regularly . . . .That was pre-1969. But there was nothing much in Newry, it was basically Belfast and Derry that all this was going on. That was a little bit further on than where we used to go. [Interview 4]

The second account is from a Republican born and raised in England who became a member of the Republican Movement there before emigrating to Ireland. He states first that he was unaware of the discrimination in Northern Ireland prior to his involvement, but then suggests that he did know of the discrimination. Although this may seem contradictory, it is only an indication of the complexity surrounding a simple question. He knew of injustice in the North, but he did not know how widespread and systematic this injustice was.

> I: Would you have known about the discrimination in the North? In the Six Counties?
> R: No, not really. No.
> I: No?
> R: But, you know . . . when I became of age I would have been able to think the thing out for myself and then, when you're coming into your teens and you start taking notice of the media, you couldn't help but see that there was something wrong . . . . You know, that . . . the civil rights movement was out on the streets to look for people's rights. It was obvious that the minority in the Six Counties were being discriminated against . . . . before that I didn't have much idea of . . . the British are in the Six Counties and that was it, you know? I was aware there was the Orangemen, I was aware of that. But . . . the fact that they were in such a majority and that they were actually discriminating against people, I didn't actually know about it, or know that . . . [Interview 6]

Many of the Republicans knew that "something" was wrong in the North of Ireland before they became politically active, but just what was wrong and how this influenced the daily life of Northern Irish Nationalists was not fully understood.

The deprivation perspective suggests that all or most of the Republicans knew of injustices in the North, since these injustices should have caused their political involvement. The mobilization and political process perspectives place less emphasis on knowledge of injustice, and finding that some Republicans were unaware of the injustice is not contrary to these perspectives. Investigation of additional statements made by those aware of the discrimination shows that injustice also did not greatly influence them.

Injustice in the North: Does It Influence Southern Republicans?

Six of the seven persons stating that they knew of the discrimination in Northern Ireland before they became IRA supporters were asked the question, "Would that (knowing about the discrimination) have had an influence on you getting involved?"[7] Responses to this question are presented in Table 4. These statements suggest that injustice is related to the involvement of Southern Irishmen in the Republican Movement. This injustice, however, is part of a larger, and more basic, concern that prompts involvement in the movement. Instead of the direct grievances that Northern Nationalists face being an affront to a standard of justice, self-identified national aspirations motivate the political involvement of these respondents. The account that follows demonstrates this.

Table 4. Responses to the Question: Would that (knowing about the discrimination) have had an influence on you getting involved in the Republican Movement? (Asked of those stating they knew about the discrimination; $N = 6$)

Interview Number	*Abbreviated Responses*
2	Obviously it did to a degree like, you know? It did have an affect on me, certainly. Knowing that that discrimination exists in our country. And knowing that it was occupied still by might. You know, by the gun. It was ruled by the gun and still is to this day.
3*	The one thing that I would have in mind, sort of thing there, is that the British had no right to be here . . .
4	Yeah. But . . . we have Protestants attached to the Republican Movement, too . . . So it depends on how you see things . . . . Justice is the basic thing that people are looking for.
9	No. It didn't at the time. It was one of the factors. I became involved in Sinn Féin because I think that it's the only way that we're ever going to face this . . . end this thing once and for all.
10	Yeah, it would have this part to play, obviously . . . . You know, all these things combine, uh, make up the whole, as it were.
11	At the time (I got involved) it wasn't on as broad a base as that . . . . It was just to end the killing of our people by their military.

Note: *This person was not asked the above question, but instead was asked, "If you had not of known about the discrimination do you think you still would have gotten involved in the movement?"

The following is from an individual who knew of discrimination in Northern Ireland before becoming involved in the Republican Movement. Yet, for him, a desire for national self-destiny is more important than issues like discrimination.

I: If tomorrow, somehow, it could be guaranteed that there would be civil rights, there [would] be no discrimination in the North, in the Six Counties, would you feel that the movement had achieved its goals?

R: No. They couldn't . . . the important thing to remember about the Republican Movement, and the Republican Movement support for the armed campaign, is that it intends to achieve its objectives. Its objectives are very simply the total removal of British political interference in Irish political life. And when that guarantee or that break comes, the type of reintroduction, if you like, into some centralized government that we may have here, and all the rest, would be something, I suppose, that would have to be worked on then. [Interview 5]

Injustice in the North is less important for Southern IRA supporters than expected, and several respondents even state that they were unaware of the injustice in the North prior to their involvement in the Republican Movement. Of those aware of the injustice, the data suggest that a more general concern, that is, the denial of their national aspirations, is a more important cause of IRA support than the existence of discrimination or injustice in the North of Ireland. Thus, a subtle and different kind of injustice, one more broad than "discrimination" against Northern Nationalists, is important for Southern Republicans. To examine this issue in more detail general questions concerning the North of Ireland were asked.

Northern Ireland: Its Importance for Southern Republicans

In the course of data collection it became apparent that several of the Republicans had never traveled to Northern Ireland, and that many who had were only there for brief periods of time. Because of this, some Republicans were asked the question, "Why do you even care about what happens in the North?"[8] Abbreviated responses to the question are presented in Table 5.

There are two general themes in the statements presented in Table 5. The first theme, shown in statements one through six, involves a notion of a general Irish identity in which Nationalists in the North are seen as being as much a part of Ireland as the Southern respondents. This theme parallels the findings in Table 4. The second theme in Table 5, shown in statements seven through ten, involves a general concern with injustice in which what happens in the North is compared to other, non-Irish, situations where, in the eyes of the respondents, injustice exists. These statements, to a degree, reflect the violation of some general notion of justice as suggested by the extended deprivation perspective. Thus, "any decent minded person would have to care about" Northern Ireland, just as any decent minded person would care about what is happening in El Salvador or what has happened to Jews.

Table 5. Responses to the question: Why do you even care about what happens in the North (of Ireland)? ($N = 10$)

Interview Number	*Abbreviated Response*
4*	I guess you start to realize what the people in the North are going through, and see how much the people in the North are going through . . . .Well, if you're half an Irishman at all you're going to do something.
5	Well, you see, you must realize, like, we're the family. The people of the North of Ireland, as far as we're concerned, are part of the Republic of Ireland . . . .The actual partition or British statelet that's up there doesn't really exist . . . it's just really a military machine that has to be removed.
10	At the moment (Ireland) is only partly whole . . . .And I don't believe we will have a Republic here until we can form a thirty- two county country. But certainly those people in . . . Ulster are as much a part of Ireland as I am. Or anybody else is.
3	I believe that the Treaty [partitioning Ireland], which was signed in 1921, was the biggest disaster that ever happened to this country. That it was a betrayal. That the people of the North were betrayed . . . .Now I go down to the North from time to time . . . And them people, to me, are the greatest people in . . . Ireland . . .
7	Well, they're Irish people like myself.
6	I was from an Irish background and em . . . you know, we were never brought up as English. We were never brought up to be anti-English, but we were brought up that we were Irish people living in England and through economics we couldn't live in Ireland, you know?
14	Um . . . well, it's hard to answer that . . . like I said, we should be able to like . . . a lot of Catholics, put it into a religion way, they're being treated very badly there. And like with the Jews and that. You know, I get very emotional about, say, the rights of Armagh women, the gaol . . . .That's hard . . . it just does.
12	I think that any decent minded person would have to care about it. I mean there are people screeching and roaring about South Africa and Central America, and . . . .And it's only on our own doorstep. I'm disgusted and worried and concerned about what's going on in South Africa. And certainly disgusted and worried about what's going on in the North of Ireland.
9	Because, again, I've met friends and people who are inside (in prison). I've known people who were killed . . . .And uh, you just can't close your eyes to this. Just as much as I care . . . about what's going on in El Salvador or what's going on in other parts of the world. All the more reason for one to care about what's going on in your own country.
8	. . . I would still care about South Africa, and Palestine, Nicaragua, El Salvador. And as a socialist, I think every socialist . . . if I was a socialist in [Britain] it would be still my view to take an interest in Ireland. Just as much as South Africa.

Notes: °This is the response to a more general question concerning solidarity with people in the North of Ireland.

The main theme running through the first six statements is one suggesting that the respondents were reacting to a violation of their national identity. Note the following from a respondent who was not asked the above question:

I: When you [became] involved what did you see as the goal of the Movement?

R: When I got involved . . . the only solution to our problems, and it has been my opinion all down through the years, is a united Ireland. It's the only way forward for us. There is no other way. The other way is a creeping, cringing, crawling spirit of the Irish nation. We desire freedom, we seek freedom, and it's not too much to demand. All we're seeking is our country.

Later in the interview he stated:

> . . . I've always looked at it this way, who has more right to walk the streets, or the byways, or the roads of Ireland, more than an Irishman? [Interview 2]

Indeed, the "national question," which involves both the North and South of Ireland, ideologically connects Southern Republicans with Northern Republicans. The following from a Southern Republican is similar to the above in that the goal of removing the "Brits" from the North of Ireland prompted his political involvement; social deprivation and economic factors were unimportant.

I: Did the fact that the economy [here in the South] was going bad have any affect on you getting involved?

R: Not really, no . . . .first of all it was a gut feeling that hasn't got anything to do with economics or social deprivation or anything down here, you know? I wasn't interested. All I wanted was . . . to get the Brits out. Get the Brits out of the North of Ireland. Try and help any way I could. [Interview 11]

While Southern IRA supporters may be aware of the discrimination in Northern Ireland, for many of them the national question is more important. Further, they believe that the problems in the North and the South will be solved once the national question is solved.

The last four statements in Table 5 tend to fit with the extended deprivation argument. It seems that these respondents are concerned about injustice, no matter where it occurs. Their support for the IRA, however, probably depends on more than their adhering to an abstract notion of justice. For example, two respondents state that they were unaware of the discrimination in the North prior to their involvement, and a third states that by the time he became involved most of the discrimination had ceased (see Table 3, Interviews 12, 14, and 8). They may have known of some injustice, but certainly this knowledge was not in-depth. A close examination of these cases shows that interpersonal networks greatly influenced their involvement.

The first account below is from a person with a Non-Republican political background. She states that she was unaware of the discrimination prior to her involvement. Her contact with one Republican, with whom she had a personal relationship, led to interaction with other Republicans. This, eventually, led her into the movement.

I: What was it that Kieran and the others were doing to [introduce] you to Republican politics . . . ?

R: Well, it would be just . . . a very casual kind of . . . going to pubs, then the topic would come up . . . it was just in listening to discussions, listening to people talking. And people who believed . . .You know, when you're talking to somebody who really, really, believes in something. That it's not going to profit them in any way . . . rather than that, it's going to make their lives quite a bit harder, and yet they're prepared to do what they have to do . . . That affects you an awful lot . . . When people you know or see fairly regularly, or hang around with, are more interested in the struggle than going off and getting pissed [intoxicated] and having a good time . . . They're bound to affect you. [Interview 12]

The second account also involves an individual who was unaware of the discrimination in the North before becoming involved. As above, her involvement stems from knowing someone who was (is) involved, that is, her father. Parental involvement led to the belief that Britain has no right to occupy part of Ireland, and, later, provided access to information concerning discrimination in the North. In addition, she suggests that without the involvement of her father she would have remained uninvolved.

R: Well, I started out in it [the Republican Movement] because my father was in it. And . . . I feel it's not right that a large country can come over and take part of a smaller country. That's gotta be generally it. You know, the way the British come over and took part of our land.

We also discussed her father's influence and the impact that discrimination in the North had on her involvement:

R: . . . I often wonder like if my father wasn't in the Republican Movement what way I would have went.

I: . . . You mention the discrimination of Catholics . . . would you have known about that before you got involved?

R: No.

I: No? After you got involved?

R: Yeah, after I got involved . . . . the girls I work with, they're not Republican minded, really, at all. They're not against it, but they're not Republican minded. But . . . the likes of what's going on in the prisons and that, they know nothing about it. They couldn't believe to hear some of the things that was happening, you know? So I would say I would probably have been the same as them, you know? [Interview 14]

The third account involves a Republican from a county that borders Northern Ireland who knew about discrimination in the North before becoming involved. He states, however, that knowledge of the discrimination did not influence his involvement (see Table 4, Interview 9). Instead, social networks, social responsibilities built into these networks, and injustices faced by people in these networks, led to his involvement.[9]

R: . . . in [late] 1978 I was beginning to feel that I wanted to get involved . . . . In 1979 I began working with a fellow who was on the run himself. He got involved . . . as a young fellow, 16, who had to go on the run near 18. And you know, his whole life was sitting down here in the South. And living in the same flat as him, not only working with him but living in the same flat, it began to make me think. He wasn't a particularly committed Republican, but at the same time his whole life had been destroyed because of what's happening up there. And then I began to meet other people who I knew had been in jail . . . and I thought, "Jesus Christ, this has got to be stopped" . . . definitely friendships are a big thing in it. If you know a Republican it's much more likely, I suppose, that you're going to become actively involved. [Interview 9]

The fourth account involves another Republican whose involvement was influenced by his friendship with people who already supported the Irish cause. His statement in Table 3 (see Interview 8) contrasted with the account below suggests that friendship and feelings of solidarity were more important causes of his involvement in politics than an abstract commitment to social justice.

R: . . . then I got involved with the political scene [in London] . . . the political scene sort of evolved much deeper in London . . . because you got left-wing groups, you got better party organization for the Labour Party and other sort of groups. And the Irish community there of course was far larger than in the country area where I was living . . . I just sort of developed from there. Rather than just sitting back . . . I got the view of what was going on. And I met people from the North. From both sides, Protestants and Catholics. And so like it was a fairly balanced view, as balanced as you can get without being to the North. I started to go over to the North as well . . . when I did that I said, you know, "It's okay sitting here and condemning it; you know, you have to do something about it if you really believe it's [the British occupation] wrong, get up and get involved." . . . So it's just a natural progression of reading about it, especially becoming involved afterwards, you know?

He also states the following concerning the relationship between his current friends and his involvement in politics:

> But most of my friends in adult life developed from political contact. Because I found out . . . there's a stronger bond because we were under attack for being Irish, right? So I mean, you felt under attack, although you weren't physically under attack . . . .most of my friends developed from . . . my political involvement. [Interview 8]

Three of these four persons were intimately connected with movement activists prior to their involvement, and the fourth Republican knew activists prior to his own involvement. The accounts show that the respondents reacted to ideas and beliefs that developed out of personal contact with members of the Republican Movement.

When asked why they are concerned with what happens in the North of Ireland the first six Republicans state that the North is important to them because of their own Irish identity. This identity sees all of Ireland harmed by the British presence in the North. Specific kinds of injustice or discrimination to which Northern Nationalists are subjected are less important than the belief that Nationalists in the North are "Irish people like" the respondents and, therefore, are also the victims of political injustice. The final four Republicans indicate that they were influenced by what was happening to other people. But, instead of reacting to events that harm other, unknown individuals (suggesting that they were reacting to the violation of a general standard of justice), the data show that they were reacting to discrimination and injustice faced by individuals with whom they were connected.

These findings show, first, that a direct grievance faced by generalized, or "abstract,' others did not prompt the respondents' political involvement. Indeed, several Southern Republicans state that they were unaware of the discrimination in Northern Ireland prior to their involvement, and those who knew of the injustice state that this knowledge was not a primary factor behind their involvement in Republican politics. Instead, a less immediate grievance than those usually considered by relative deprivation and equity proponents influenced the respondents, that is, the denial of national aspirations by a foreign power influenced their political involvement.

Second, the findings show that the mobilization and political process arguments fitted the data better than either a narrow or more broad interpretation of the deprivation argument. The presence of the British in the North is in itself unjust or "not right." This underlying grievance, in concert with other factors, leads to support for the Republican Movement. Specifically, because Northern Republicans also fight against this injustice a common bond links Republican sympathizers in the South to activists in the North. This bond also creates social networks which disseminate information about the North to potential IRA supporters in the South. Thus, the belief that Northern Nationalists are as "Irish" as Southern Nationalists, and the obligations and commitments that arise among those uninvolved and those already involved, leads to involvement in Republican politics.

The following account, from a Republican who knew of injustice in the North prior to becoming politically active, provides a sense of this process.

I: Why do you even care about what happens up in, say, Belfast or Derry? I mean, you can just stay down here and do your thing, and hang out and . . .

R: Hmm hmm. That's something that I had been doing. That's something I realize now which is totally wrong. And eh . . . cowardly . . . . and again, turning your back on people in the six northeastern counties of Ulster who wish to be a part of the same country that you believe in being a part of. And that is Ireland . . . . And I believe that as long as there's one person in Ulster, one person who wishes to be a member or . . . . and wishes a united Ireland, then, I think it's worth fighting for. It's worth supporting, it's worth chasing after. If there is not . . . The 26 Counties should then . . . reverse the situation and plantate, you know? But . . . that's talking fantastic . . . . But again, it's Ireland's right to rule Ireland. The island of Ireland. Geographically set aside from any other country. Nobody else has a right except the people in Ireland. [Interview 10]

National aspirations, that is, the desire for a united Ireland, and connections with individuals already involved in the movement are important motivators of the political involvement of Southern Republicans. Awareness of discrimination in the North is less important. This begs a question concerning the importance of national aspirations among the population in the Irish Republic: Since a large portion of the population in the South would like to see the reunification of the island (Davis and Sinnott 1979), why then does not the IRA have widespread support in the Irish Republic?

CONSTITUTIONAL IRISH POLITICS: WHY PEOPLE DO NOT BECOME IRISH REPUBLICANS

To ascertain why people do not become Republicans the respondents involved in constitutional politics were asked questions concerning their political involvement.[10] In general, family background and connections with individuals already involved in mainstream politics were noted as factors that led to involvement in constitutional Irish politics. Four of the six respondents mentioned familial influences, and one respondent (from a mixed political background), also noted the influence that a friend's involvement in Fianna Fáil had on him.

The following are typical of the responses to questions on this topic. The first account is from a Fine Gael member.

R: I've always been interested in politics and it was partly by family background, partly. I joined Fine Gael as a student when Declan Costello introduced The Just Society [in 1965] .... as a student I found the Fianna Fáil of the '60s corrupt and stifling. At least it appeared to me to be so, probably it wasn't. But it appeared to be so. And . . . Fine Gael, in Declan Costello's Just Society, offered a possibility of liberal reform that I favored. [Interview 16]

The following from a Fianna Fáil member shows the impact that familial influences and friendship had on his decision to become involved in politics.

R: I got involved in politics shortly after I left secondary school, which would be your equivalent of high school. Before I went on to college. I joined . . . through a friend of mine whose family were very active. And my own family, my father would have been a supporter of the Fine Gael side in politics. My mother, her family were a family tradition of a Republican family in the West of Ireland. And I suppose that her influence was stronger than my father's . . . . So I suppose it was as much a mixture of friendship and family tradition. And at the time of it, you know, it just seemed to me that in the '60s, you know, that economic development was the really important thing here and Fianna Fáil seemed to be doing that very well at the time. And listening to some very interesting people who were leading the party, who were becoming prominent in the front bench, in the cabinet. People like Charlie Haughey, who is now the party leader. [Interview 19]

These data and the interviews with Republicans show that the process of becoming involved in politics does not depend upon whether the politics are violent or constitutional (see also Gamson (1975, p. 139). While the process (working through established social networks) of recruitment into Republican and mainstream politics may be similar, the motivations that prompt some individuals into Republican politics and others into constitutional politics differ. During the interviews each respondent discussed his or her aspirations for a united Ireland. Usually this discussion followed the question: "Would you aspire for a united Ireland?" Responses to the question are presented in Table 6.

Table 6. Aspirations of Southern Non-Republicans for a United Ireland

Responses to the question: Would you aspire for a united Ireland? (*N* = 6)

Interview Number	*Abbreviated Response*
15	Well, I think that you'll find that the majority of members of our party here have the same views as I have. We, and indeed about 98 percent of the country, would have. And that's towards an aspiration of a united Ireland .... Traditionally in Irish history teaching we would have had almost inbred in us this drive towards a united Ireland. By the glorification of what our forefathers had done, and the anti-British attitude would have been instilled as well.
16	Ultimately, yes. But, I don't see it in the foreseeable future. And I also think there's a certain price I wouldn't be prepared to pay for it. And that price would be the rejection of the concept by the majority of the people living in Northern Ireland. If you put unity, bought at the price of continuing civil war, I think it wouldn't be worth that price.
17	I think the overwhelming majority of the Irish people do aspire towards a united Ireland, and I would. And explaining why is rather more difficult. Ireland's position . . . I regard as very much as the result of chance historic events .... And I don't see any need, frankly, to rush the process. It's not something that I lie in bed at night thinking about, or tossing and turning about. And in my day to day life the truth of the matter is I don't give a fiddler's damn if Ireland is ever united. It's just this thing that's in the back of one's mind, and I think that's the simple of it.
18	Personally, I am totally indifferent to it.
19	Well, I think it probably would have been, you know, it would have been an accepted thing in our house that the partition was wrong, an injustice. And that the British shouldn't have been there. And that a united Ireland was the natural way of things and that Fianna Fáil were for that . . . . However, they [Fianna Fáil] had taken the view that the gun wasn't the way to go about it.
20	Oh, I regard the issue of partition as the most important issue, the single issue, in the country. I believe it's tied up with economic progress in that the two go hand in glove together . . . . And as long as it, the island, is partitioned you will have a continuation of violence .... And I say the ongoing continuation of that is destructive in the economic and social sense as well as the political sense. So that it's just bad for Ireland, North and South, to have this arrangement that has manifestly not worked continue as a political arrangement.

The responses of the Fine Gael members are presented first, followed by the comments of the Labour Party member, and then the comments of the Fianna Fáil members. While the Fine Gael members might admit to a desire for a united Ireland, it may not be "worth" the price. Similarly, the importance of uniting the North with the South is minor for the Labour Party activist. In contrast the Fianna Fáil members express a strong desire for the reunification of the island, for example, "partition was wrong, an injustice." Only the Fianna Fáil members make statements suggesting that a united Ireland is of great importance to them. Yet, despite their personal interest in the reunification of Ireland, even the Fianna Fáil members do not support IRA violence. This suggests that more than ideology motivates the decision to become involved in the Republican Movement. Additional examination of the data shows that the expectation that IRA violence is efficacious plays an important role in whether or not a Southern Irish person supports the IRA.

Expectations of Success: Is IRA Violence Effective?

The findings of research on social protest in general (e.g., Paige 1971; Lawler 1975; Klandermans 1984), and on Northern Republicans in particular (White 1989), suggests that Southern Republicans expect the IRA to succeed while Non-Republicans expect the IRA to fail. This is what the data show. The Southern Republicans who were asked whether or not the IRA will succeed state that they believe it will. Although they are unable to say when this will be or to describe in detail what the eventual outcome will be, they do believe that in time the IRA will force the British from Ireland. The comments below are typical of the Republican view on this issue.[11]

I: Do you think that the IRA campaign will succeed in eventually driving the British out?
R: . . . .absolutely. I don't believe that it's going to be a military victory. I don't think you can talk about a military victory when you're talking about a very poorly armed force against one of the best equipped armies in the world . . . .You have all this paraphernalia of repression that they're having to use against the IRA. All of that costs. I think that they're prepared to put up with that cost in the short term, but the IRA has itself said that it's a war of attrition . . . .It's not going to be a military victory, though. It'll not be the last great field of battle or anything like that. [Interview 9]

I: Do you think the IRA will succeed?
R: Yes.
I: Really?
R: Yes. Hopefully. Eventually. I don't know if it will be in my lifetime, but I think they will.
I: On the flip side, do you think there's any hope for constitutional methods, such as the SDLP . . . ?
R: No.
I: bringing about a united Ireland?
R: No. Uh, the moves that are on at the moment, I don't know what's going to happen. I think it's a lot of talk or whatever. But if it ever, ever, happened that the Brits said, "Right,

> we are pulling out, and this is the set-up we're going to leave behind and . . . ," you know, it will all be nicely talked out and everything. They would claim that it was because it was all talked out and everything, but . . . the only reason there are any talks on at the moment is because of the war in the North and because they know they can't beat them. They've said it themselves anyway, they can't beat the IRA. [Interview 12]

In contrast to these statements note the following from two Non-Republicans. The first set of comments were made by a member of Fianna Fáil. Based on these comments, he is a strong Nationalist who under certain circumstances might be willing to support armed struggle against the British. At present such support is unlikely since he believes the IRA armed struggle will fail.

I: Would you ever have been attracted to Sinn Féin or the IRA military action as opposed to the constitutional politics of Fianna Fáil?

R: Well, I mean, there's no question about it that if there was any prospect of that being successful it would carry certain attractions. But to be successful as it was between 1916 and 1921 it had to have the great majority of the people behind it, which it had at that time . . . . there was a legitimacy about that situation in which the whole of the people and public opinion was mobilized. Which you don't have now.

Later in the interview he stated:

> We don't have the big battalions . . . I mean we can't, as a state, we can't consider invading the Six Counties. Therefore, in that situation, although all the logic of the situation impels one to the view that there should be one state, one nation here on this island, that logic, as long as it is not accepted by the British Government, is one in which we can't do much about other than in the direction [of diplomacy]. [Interview 19]

The next set of comments are from a member of Fine Gael. In contrast to the Fianna Fáil supporter above, he is at best a lukewarm Nationalist. He too believes that Republican violence will not lead to a British withdrawal.

I: Do you think political violence by the IRA will ever drive the British out of the North?

R: No.

I: No?

R: I think that it has had the effect of dramatizing the situation, of forcing the British government, I think, to a final awareness of how grave the problem is. I would blame the British government for a whole series of mistakes over the past seventeen . . . I mean sixty . . . sixty-five years. For their indifference in the early stages as to what was really happening there. Unwillingness to get involved in bringing about changes that have to be made in Northern Ireland . . . . but I don't believe at this stage that the IRA's violence will force the British government to leave Northern Ireland. I think on the contrary. [Interview 16]

Southern Republicans, and their Northern counterparts (White 1989) believe that the IRA will eventually succeed. Southern non-Republicans, whether they be ardent Nationalists or not, see the IRA as unlikely to succeed. These expectations place the nationalism of Southern Irish people and the connections of these people with the Republican Movement into a context—no matter what a given person believes about Ireland's right to self-destiny, if the person also believes that the IRA are ineffective then that person will not support the Republican Movement. In contrast, if a person is concerned about the North, or knows individuals involved in the Republican Movement, and believes that IRA violence is effective, then that person will support the IRA.[12]

SUMMARY AND IMPLICATIONS

This chapter examines the support for political violence of individuals who, based on appearances, do not have grievances. Specifically addressed is the question of why people who live in the Irish Republic support the Irish Republican Army. Using the extended deprivation/equity and mobilization/political process arguments as a guide, the analyses focus on the importance that abstract notions of social justice, connections with people involved in social movements, ideology, and perceived efficacy of violence all have on support for political violence.

The findings suggest that the violation of an abstract notion of social justice, that is, the extended deprivation and equity argument, does not prompt support for the IRA among Southern Irish people. Several of the Republicans were unaware of the discrimination in the North prior to their involvement in Republican politics, and of those aware of the discrimination, this is relatively unimportant with respect to their political involvement. Instead, it is the belief that Ireland should control its own destiny, in part a function of family background and social networks connecting potential Republicans with active Republicans, that prompted the political involvement of Southern Republicans. In sum, Southern Republicans are influenced by what they see as an injustice that affects themselves and by their personal ties to others, including Northern Republicans, who are victims of injustice. These others are not abstract victims of abstract injustice, however, and the role that social networks play in connecting non-Republicans to Republicans is consistent with resource mobilization and political process arguments.

Connections and ideology, that is, the belief that Ireland should be reunited, by themselves do not prompt support for the IRA. The data also show that expectations of success play a crucial role in the dynamic process by which people become supporters of political violence. If people do not expect the IRA to succeed they will not actively support the IRA—even if they desire the reunification of Ireland. The data suggest that three factors determine whether or not an individual supports violent or constitutional politics:

ideology, social networks, and expectations of success. Ideology appears to be a necessary cause of political violence that provides a baseline level of grievances. Social networks (either between parents and children or among friends and acquaintances), in turn, facilitate the transmission of ideology and grievances to potential social movement recruits. Depending upon one's expectations concerning the efficacy of political violence (which is influenced by social network location and ideology), then, ideology and grievances will or will not prompt support for political violence.

Perhaps the most important finding is that, despite initial appearances, the data show that the respondents do have grievances. These grievances, however, are less immediate and less direct than the usual conception of grievances. This is important on both theoretical and empirical levels. Theoretically, grievances should be more broadly conceived of than they have been in the past. Empirically, researchers of political violence and social protest cannot continue to rely solely on direct measures of grievances and injustice, for example, unemployment levels and income inequality measures.

ACKNOWLEDGMENT

I thank David Knoke, Robert Robinson, William Corsaro, Norma Shepelak, Donatella della Porta and Clovis White for their helpful comments on earlier versions of this manuscript. Special thanks go to the respondents for their willingness to participate in this research and to Terry F. White for her support, friendship, and encouragement. This research was funded in part by grant SES-8318161 from the National Science Foundation and by grants from the Indiana University Graduate School.

NOTES

1. Numerous sources document the existence of injustice in the North of Ireland that is directed against members of the Irish Nationalist community (e.g., Fermanagh Civil Rights Association 1969; Northern Ireland Civil Rights Association 1978; Darby 1983).

2. This is the original formula presented in Adams (1965). Although modifications to the formula have been suggested (Walster, Berscheid, and Walster 1973; Walster et al. 1978) the general logic involved has not changed.

3. While IRA supporters do not recognize "Northern Ireland" or "Irish Republic" as legitimate labels for the two political entities on the island of Ireland, non-IRA supporters do. "Southern Ireland," and the "26 Counties" are used interchangeably with "Irish Republic," and "North" and the "Six Counties" are used interchangeably with "Northern Ireland."

4. Some of the Sinn Féin members were veterans of the IRA. Because they had been arrested they could openly admit this. Others may have been IRA members or veterans, but because the IRA is an illegal organization they could not openly discuss their membership in the organization. Further, this paper examines why persons living outside of the North of Ireland support the IRA. Although the majority of non-Northern Republicans are found in the Irish Republic, Irish Republicans and Republican support groups are found in England, the United States, and other countries. Included in the data are interviews with three Republicans born in England, two of

whom spent their formative years in England. For simplicity, all of the respondents are considered to be Southern Republicans.

5. Some respondents may question being labeled a "Non-Republican," and it may be more accurate to refer to them as non-physical-force Republicans (Cronin 1980, p. 3). The labeling of individuals or political parties as Republican or not is difficult and questionable since the term means many things to many people. For example, the official title of Fianna Fáil, the largest political party in Ireland, is "Fianna Fáil: The Republican Party." For simplicity, people referred to below who are active in political parties other than Sinn Féin are considered to be Non-Republicans.

6. Because some questions were developed over time the first Southern Republican was not asked this question on tape.

7. Because of changes in the structure of the interview over time, not all respondents were asked this question.

8. Ten of the fourteen Southern Republicans interviewed on tape were asked this or a similar question.

9. For clarification, a Northern Republican "on the run" in the South can generally live without too much worry of being arrested. This does, however, depend on when and why a given Republican went on the run. From the early 1970s to the early 1980s Southern courts refused to extradite alleged IRA suspects to the North. This changed in 1984 and life on the run in the South is now less secure.

10. Usually the question took one of two forms, these being: "How did you get involved in politics?;" or, "Why did you get involved in politics?" With the development of questions over time one person was not asked this question.

11. In the second set of comments, SDLP is the abbreviation for the Social Democratic and Labour Party. This is the constitutional rival of Sinn Féin and the IRA in Northern Ireland. The SDLP advocates the peaceful reunification of the island. When the second respondent refers to the "talks on at the moment" she refers to events that culminated in the Hillsborough Agreement (signed in late 1985). According to the agreement, the Dublin government now has representation in Belfast, which has caused great concern in the Loyalist community. Also, when noting that the British have stated that they cannot defeat the IRA, she is most likely referring to the captured British Army document presented in Cronin (1980, pp. 339-357).

12. The belief that the IRA will succeed may develop from involvement in Republican politics. Also, the respondents provide their own description of what prompted their involvement, and this, too, may have been influenced by their involvement in Republican politics. These possibilities suggest caution in interpreting the results. However, the contrast of the statements of the Republicans with the statements of the Non-Republicans does suggest that a belief in the political efficacy of the IRA may be necessary before a person becomes involved in Republican politics (see also White [1988], [1989]). Also, it should be noted that there is evidence in support of both views of the IRA's potential for success. On the one hand, those who believe that IRA violence will bring about a British withdrawal can point to successive British withdrawals from ungovernable colonial situations (see Bell 1976). On the other hand, those who believe that the IRA will fail can point to the continued British presence in the North of Ireland despite more than 20 continuous years of IRA guerrilla warfare.

REFERENCES

Adams, J. Stacy. 1965. "Inequity in Social Exchange." Pp. 267-299 in *Advances in Experimental Social Psychology* (Vol. 2), edited by L. Berkowitz. New York: Academic Press.

Bell, J. Bowyer. 1976. *On Revolt*. Cambridge: Harvard University Press.

———. 1979. *The Secret Army: The IRA From 1916 -* . Revised and updated ed. Dublin: The Academy Press.

Birrell, Derek. 1972. "Relative Deprivation As a Factor in the Conflict in Northern Ireland." *The Sociological Review* 20:317-343.

Coogan, Tim Pat. 1987. *The IRA*. 3rd ed. London: Fontana.

Cronin, Sean. 1980. *Irish Nationalism: A History of its Roots and Ideology*. Dublin: The Academy Press.

Darby, J. ed. 1983. *Northern Ireland: The Background to the Conflict*. Belfast: Appletree Press.

Davies, James C. 1962. "Toward a Theory of Revolution." *American Sociological Review* 27:5-19.

Davis, E.E. and R. Sinnott. 1979. *Attitudes in the Republic of Ireland Relevant to the Northern Ireland Problem: Volume I, Descriptive Analysis and Some Comparisons with Attitudes in Northern Ireland and Great Britain.* Dublin: The Economic and Social Research Institute.

della Porta, Donatella. 1988. "Recruitment Processes in Clandestine Political Organizations: Italian Left-Wing Terrorism." Pp. 155-169 in *International Social Movement Research: A Research Annual,* edited by B. Klandermans, H. Kriesi and S. Tarrow (vol. 1). Greenwich: JAI Press.

Deutsch, Martin. 1975. "Equity, Equality, and Need: What Determines Which Value Will Be Used As the Basis of Distributive Justice?" *Journal of Social Issues* 31: 137-149.

Fermanagh Civil Rights Association. 1969. *Fermanagh Facts.*

Fireman, B. B. and W. Gamson. 1979. "Utilitarian Logic in the Resource Mobilization Perspective." Pp. 8-44 in *The Dynamics of Social Movements: Resource Mobilization, Social Control and Tactics,* edited by Mayer N. Zald and John D. McCarthy. Cambridge, MA: Winthrop.

Gamson, William. 1975. *The Strategy of Social Protest.* Homewood, IL: Dorsey Press.

Gurney, Joan Neff and Kathleen J. Tierney. 1982. "Relative Deprivation and Social Movements: A Critical Look at Twenty Years of Theory and Research." *The Sociological Quarterly* 23:33-47.

Gurr, Ted R. 1970. *Why Men Rebel.* Princeton: Princeton University Press.

Hewitt, Christopher. 1981. "Catholic Grievances, Catholic Nationalism and Violence in Northern Ireland During the Civil Rights Period: a Reconsideration." *British Journal of Sociology* 32:363-380.

———. 1983. "Discrimination in Northern Ireland: A Rejoinder." *British Journal of Sociology* 34:446-451.

———. 1985. "Catholic Grievances and Violence in Northern Ireland." *British Journal of Sociology* 36:102-105.

———. 1987. "Explaining Violence in Northern Ireland." *British Journal of Sociology* 38:88-93.

Jenkins, J. C. 1983. "Resource Mobilization Theory and the Study of Social Movements." *Annual Review of Sociology* 9:527-553.

Jenkins, J. Craig and Charles Perrow. 1977. "Insurgency of the powerless: Farm Workers Movements (1946-1972)." *American Sociological Review* 42:249-268.

Klandermans, Bert. 1984. "Social-Psychological Expansions of Resource Mobilization Theory." *American Sociological Review* 49:583-600.

Kovalcheck, Kassian. 1987. "Catholic Grievances in Northern Ireland: Appraisal and Judgement." *British Journal of Sociology* 38:77-87.

Lawler, Edward J. 1975. "An Experimental Study of Factors Affecting the Mobilization of Revolutionary Coalitions." *Sociometry* 38:163-179.

Markovsky, B. 1985. "Toward a Multilevel Distributive Justice Theory." *American Sociological Review* 50:822-839.

Martin, Joanne and Alan Murray. 1983. "Distributive Justice and Unfair Exchange." Pp. 169-205 in *Equity Theory: Psychological and Sociological Perspectives,* edited by David M. Messick and Karen S. Cook. New York: Praeger.

Marwell, G. and R. E. Ames. 1979. "Experiments on the Provision of Public Goods. I. Resources, Interest, Group Size and the Free-Rider Problem." *American Journal of Sociology* 84:1335-1360.

McAdam, Douglas. 1982. *Political Process and The Development of Black Insurgency: 1930-1970.* Chicago: University of Chicago Press.

________. 1986. "Recruitment to High-Risk Activism: The Case of Freedom Summer." *American Journal of Sociology* 92:64-90.

McCarthy, John and Mayer Zald. 1973. *The Trend of Social Movements.* Morristown, N.J.: General Learning.

________. 1977. "Resource Mobilization and Social Movements: A Partial Theory." *American Journal of Sociology* 82:1212-1241.

Moore, Barrington. 1978. *Injustice: The Social Bases of Obedience and Revolt.* White Plains. NY: M.E. Sharpe.

Moxon-Browne, Edward. 1981. "The Water and the Fish: Public Opinion and the Provisional IRA in Northern Ireland." Pp. 41-72 in *British Perspectives on Terrorism,* edited by Paul Wilkinson. London: George Allen and Unwin.

________. 1983. *Nation, Class and Creed in Northern Ireland.* Aldershot: Gower.

Northern Ireland Civil Rights Association (NICRA). 1978. *We Shall Overcome: The History of the Struggle for Civil Rights in Northern Ireland.* Belfast: NICRA.

O'Hearn, Denis. 1983. "Catholic Grievances, Catholic Nationalism: A Comment." *British Journal of Sociology* 34:438-445.

________. 1985. "Again on Discrimination in the North of Ireland: A Reply to the Rejoinder." *British Journal of Sociology* 36:94-101.

________. 1987. "Catholic Grievances: Comments." *British Journal of Sociology* 38:94-100.

Paige, Jeffrey. 1971. "Political Orientation and Riot Participation." *American Sociological Review* 36:810-820.

Rawls, John. 1971. *A Theory of Justice.* Cambridge, MA: Belknap Press.

Snow, David, Louis Zurcher, Jr., and Sheldon Ekland-Olson. 1980. "Social Networks and Social Movements: A Microstructural Approach to Differential Recruitment." *American Sociological Review* 45:787-801.

Tilly, Charles. 1978. *From Mobilization to Revolution.* Reading, MA: Addison-Wesley.

Utne, Mary and Robert Kidd. 1980. "Equity and Attribution." Pp. 63-93 in *Justice and Social Interaction,* edited by Gerold Mikula. New York: Springer-Verlag.

Von Eschen, Donald, Jerome Kirk, and Maurice Pinard. 1971. "The Organizational Substructure of Disorderly Politics." *Social Forces* 49:529-44.

Walster, Elaine, Ellen Berscheid, and G. William Walster. 1973. "New Directions in Equity Research." *Journal of Personality and Social Psychology* 25:151-176.

Walster, Elaine, G. William Walster, and Ellen Berscheid. 1978. *Equity: Theory and Research.* Boston: Allyn and Bacon.

White, Robert W. 1988. "Commitment, Efficacy, and Personal Sacrifice Among Irish Republicans." *Journal of Political and Military Sociology* 16:77-90.

________. 1989. "From Peaceful Protest to Guerrilla War: Micromobilization of the Provisional IRA." *American Journal of Sociology* 94:1277-1302.

Zurcher, L. A., Jr., and David A. Snow. 1981. "Collective Behavior: Social Movements." Pp. 447-82, in *Social Psychology, Sociological Perspectives,* edited by Morris Rosenberg and Ralph H. Turner. New York: Basic Books.

GOING UNDERGROUND IN ARGENTINA

A LOOK AT THE FOUNDERS OF A GUERRILLA MOVEMENT

Maria Jose Moyano

Broad generalizations about the guerrilla groups which operated in Argentina between 1969 and 1979 are virtually impossible for a variety of reasons. Initially, there were six major organizations, as well as a myriad of groupuscules. Though only two of these were still in existence by the second half of the decade because of a series of splits and mergers, it is necessary to account for the different political backgrounds of the members of the original groups. Guerrilla membership also varied dramatically. In 1969, there were approximately 150-200 active combatants. Five years later, these had turned into an army of 6,000, and by the end of the decade, membership had dwindled to 800-1,000.

Argentine guerrillas first went into action against a military government but continued operating following the country's return to constitutional rule, and were in fact partly responsible for the subsequent breakdown of democracy and the establishment of a highly repressive military regime that would become

International Social Movement Research, Vol. 4, pages 105-129.

ISBN: 1-55938-445-X

their nemesis. The patterns of violence also changed significantly over the decade. Initially, there was an emphasis on "violence against property, not persons," as the guerrillas concentrated on small-scale attacks against the security forces and "Robin Hood type" actions, such as the distribution of food in slum dwellings. During a second stage, kidnappings for ransom were favored. This in turn gave way to widespread assassinations and the staging of spectacular operations involving over 100 combatants and sophisticated technology. Not surprisingly, changes in both the nature of the regime in which the guerrillas functioned and their operational repertoire brought about concomitant changes in popular support.[1]

This paper analyzes one aspect of armed struggle in Argentina, the motivation of the individuals who launched it. However, in light of the preceeding discussion, I first provide a description of the political context in which guerrilla warfare became a salient activity as well as an account of the origins of the major groups.

POST-PERONIST ARGENTINA

On September 16, 1955, General Eduardo Lonardi staged the coup that toppled Juan Peron. For the next 30 years Argentina plunged into the most conflictive, unstable, and violent period the country had undergone since independence.[2] The heart of the matter was the debate over the role of Peronism within the polity. It was generally believed that once Peron was forced into exile, his followers would forget him. When it became apparent that this would not occur, the political elite split into two camps. One wing of the Radical Party was willing to allow Peronism to participate in elections and therefore in the political process; the military, the right, and the majority of Radicals were unwilling to do either.

With Peronism, which was supported by roughly one third of the electorate, outlawed, Argentina became a semidemocracy (Cavarozzi 1983). This period, popularly known as "the Peronist Resistance" or simply "the Resistance" is "a dominant reference point in Peronist political culture" (James 1976, p. 273, fn. 1). The Resistance saw the emergence of a left wing within Peronism, mainly as a reaction against the union bosses' willingness to ally themselves with whoever was in power in exchange for the right to maintain total control over their unions. Two sectors formed the Peronist left: the so-called combative unions and a myriad of student groupings. The combatives were a small minority within the labor movement and the student groups failed to establish a strong and unified organization. But even though the Resistance's bark was stronger than its bite, it drove home the message that if Peronist rule was unthinkable, rule without Peronism was impossible.

Between 1955 and 1966 Argentina was governed by five presidents, two generals and three civilians, none of whom finished his term: civilians were ousted and soldiers forced to retreat to the barracks and call new elections. Economic stagnation and political immobilism gradually eroded the legitimacy not only of governments but of the system. In the absence of a democratic tradition, the system was not valued per se but as long as it produced the desired results, and as the failure of democracy became apparent, the appeal of authoritarian solutions grew stronger.

General Ongania's 1966 coup, the fifth in Argentina since 1930, differed substantially from its predecessors. Traditionally, the military had intervened in politics in what were considered emergency situations, and then only to hand over power to a civilian administration after a short interval. In 1966, however, the military seized power with no intention of relinquishing it—the fact that the coup bore the rather pompous name of "Argentine Revolution" pointed to the serious transformations the military was contemplating. The Onganiato was characterized at the time as a "provisional technical dictatorship,"[3] its aim being to modernize the economy and put an end to a decade of inefficiency, corruption, disorder, and instability.[4]

Ongania began by dissolving political parties, banning all types of political activity, and launching a crusade against communism. His decision to rule out by decree the very existence of politics was due to the vision he held of his own rule within Argentina. He seriously believed he had the sacred duty to reshape and remoralize his country. This morality crusade took several forms, like the burning of books and the establishment of censorship commissions to control and eliminate corruption on television and in the cinema. The government's crusade appeared grotesquely medieval to a nation obsessed with replicating the latest European fads and cultural patterns.

The event which, to this day, epitomizes the Argentine Revolution's cultural policy was the "intervention" in all national universities, which became known as the "Night of the Long Batons."[5] When the news about the intervention became known, students at the Department of Exact Sciences of the University of Buenos Aires decided to occupy the building as a sign of protest. The military broke into the building and with an unusual display of brutality forced those students and professors present out. Over 200 people were detained and more than 30 had to be hospitalized. The same procedure was repeated at other universities throughout the country where students were diligently in class. The government attempted to justify military brutality with the excuse of a leftist provocation. This was absolutely untenable and could in no way explain, after the initial blunder, the persistent harassing of the universities by the government. University students would not forget the incident and would become the regime's main source of opposition.[6]

Three other events contributed to the radicalization of public opinion: the violent riot in Cordoba city in May 1969, known as the Cordobazo; a similar incident in March 1971, popularly called the Viborazo; and the murder of sixteen guerrillas at Trelew in 1972.

Events leading to the Cordobazo can be traced back to nationwide demonstrations in response to a government decision to raise the price of meal tickets at university dining halls.[7] In Cordoba province, student protest coincided with labor unrest due to summary dismissals. During a general strike called for May 29, students and workers took to the streets, occupied the city, erected barricades, and destroyed and burnt shops. Their progress through the city was unhampered by the police or the military until that evening. Fighting continued the following day; 14 people were killed and large portions of the city were smoking ruins. The Cordobazo was a spontaneous act by students and workers, two sectors of society which had different grievances but no channels through which these could be expressed. These two groups, which had up to that moment functioned quite independently from each other began, as a result of these events, to see the advantages of engaging in joint action.[8] The president reacted strongly, set up a military government in Cordoba, brought the insurgents before specially appointed tribunals, and closed down Cordoba university.

Ongania was deposed in 1970 in a "coup within the coup." Neither his successor, General Levingston, nor the regime's grey eminence, General Lanusse, could erase from public memory the events of the Cordobazo and its aftermath. Under Levingston, Cordoba remained the "unruly province." When Cordoba's governor delivered a speech in which he called all forces opposing the regime "subversive" and compared armed struggle to "a viper with a hundred heads," the people staged a second Cordobazo called the Viborazo, "the viper's blow." The Viborazo resulted in two days of violence (March 12-14, 1971) which brought two deaths, about thirty injured, and nearly 300 detainees.

Levingston was forced to step down—this second "coup within the coup" provided further evidence of the failure of the Argentine Revolution as the usual military retreat and call for elections took place—and General Lanusse took over. He committed a serious blunder, the Trelew massacre, which, together with the Night of the Long Batons, the Cordobazo, and the Viborazo, gave the impression of a ruthless regime intent on perpetuating itself.

On August 15, 1972, inmates of the Rawson prison in Patagonia belonging to the three most powerful guerrilla organizations carried out an escape attempt. Six guerrillas got to Trelew airport in time to board a plane and divert it to Chile, while their comrades surrendered and were taken into custody and transported to the Almirante Zar naval base near Trelew. A week later they were killed, apparently while attempting to escape. The government produced three different and somewhat contradictory versions of the events, and the federal judge in charge of the case did not order autopsies to be performed.

The incident was a premeditated murder designed to work as exemplary punishment, and as such it was viewed at the time.[9]

The intensity of antimilitary feeling which these four incidents provoked, and which manifested itself through armed struggle and collective violent protest forced president Lanusse to announce elections would be absolutely free. But he then tampered with the electoral rules in such a way that he made it impossible for Peronism's natural candidate to run. By providing the impression that Peron had once more been proscribed, Lanusse helped Peron's candidate, Hector Campora, obtain a resounding electoral victory in the March 1973 elections.[10]

THE GUERRILLA MOVEMENT UP TO 1973

Although the Ongania dictatorship provided the context in which armed struggle became a salient activity, Argentina witnessed three attempts at rural guerrilla warfare between 1959 and 1968. Throughout the decade, and emulating the Cuban example, insurgents across Latin America would attempt to establish focos, the guerrilla nuclei expected to create the conditions for revolution.[11]

The three Argentine episodes, in 1959, 1963, and 1968, would end as calamitous failures.[12] However, participants in the last rural guerrilla episode were to play a prominent role in the next decade. Organized by members of the Peronist Youth (Juventud Peronista or JP), the group planned to set up a foco in Taco Ralo in Tucuman province which would be followed by an urban guerrilla campaign. As soon as the 13 men and one woman who formed the 17 October Montonero Detachment of the Peronist Armed Forces (Destacamento Montonero 17 de Octubre de las Fuerzas Armadas Peronistas, simply known as FAP) arrived in Tucuman the police stumbled onto it while looking for smugglers,[13] but the captured guerrillas persuaded the authorities that this was simply another mad attempt at foquismo, and the urban contingent remained undetected.[14]

The year 1969, which represented a switch from rural to urban armed struggle, inaugurated a decade of uninterrupted, escalating guerrilla activity. Six major groups went into action during the year: the reconstituted FAP; the Shirtless Commando (Comando Descamisados); the Montoneros; the Revolutionary Armed Forces (Fuerzas Armadas Revolucionarias or FAR); the People's Revolutionary Army (Ejercito Revolucionario del Pueblo, ERP); and the Liberation Armed Forces (Fuerzas Armadas de Liberacion, FAL). While the last two were Marxist, the rest identified themselves with Peronism. During that first year, the groups would carry out their attacks anonymously, and would each choose a major operation in 1970 with which they made their existence known to the public.

The original Descamisados were mostly members of the youth wing of the Christian Democratic Party and heavily imbued with the ideas of radical Catholicism. This, and contacts with FAP, finalized the group's adherence to Peronism. The Descamisados remained a relatively small group which managed to combine political work in working class neighbourhoods with military actions very effectively. Their military actions were planned to the last detail—throughout the Argentine Revolution the group boasted only one death and one detention.[15]

Though it is generally believed that the Montoneros was founded by twelve individuals, the origins of the organization are more complex. Four groups coalesced before its launching; (1) a Santa Fe contingent made up of Catholic Action activists; (2) a group from Cordoba mostly made up of university students; (3) individuals from Buenos Aires province with prior activism in certain combative unions; (4) the Buenos Aires city group, several of whose members were graduates of the National Buenos Aires School, a very prestigious state school. The Montoneros went public with two spectacular operations, the kidnapping and murder of former president Pedro Aramburu and the seizure of the town of La Calera in Cordoba.

However, these two operations decimated the organization through deaths and detentions. The Montoneros were forced to seek protection from FAP, and turned to political work while they attempted to regroup. In a two-year maneuver, the organization seized control of the JP groups at the universities. This was a stroke of genius which would in no time turn the Montoneros into the only spokesman for the radicalized sectors of Peronism, an umbrella of organizations which came to be known as the Revolutionary Tendency.[16]

The founders of FAR and FAL were originally Communist Party dissidents who in 1967 had split to form the Revolutionary Communist Party (Partido Communista Revolucionario, PCR). By their own admission, both organizations had originally considered launching a rural guerrilla campaign in support of Guevara's Bolivian adventure and had subsequently reappraised their strategy in light of Che's failure (see Suarez 1970, 1971). But FAR had also proceeded to revise its views on Peronism and had become "peronised" (see Fuerzas Armadas Revolucionarias 1973). FAR first became known with the seizure of the town of Garin in Buenos Aires, a model of military precision and economy of effort which was to characterize the organization's early years. Unlike the other groups, FAL was plagued from its inception by internal squabbles which would lead to its virtual extinction by 1972, after a substantial sector calling itself Liberation Popular Commandos (Comandos Populares de Liberacion, CPL) announced it would support a future Peronist administration (*Militancia* 1973, p. 46).[17]

The ERP was the only organization established as the armed wing of a political party. In 1965 a group active among sugar cane workers in the northwest, the Popular Indoamerican Revolutionary Front (Frente

Revolucionario Indoamericano Popular, FRIP) merged with a Buenos Aires group called Worker's Word (Palabra Obrera) to form the Workers' Revolutionary Party (Partido Revolucionario de los Trabajadores, PRT). During the IVth Party Congress in 1968 the PRT split into two factions: El Combatiente advocated armed struggle; La Verdad rejected it.

La Verdad, which made up one third of the original PRT membership, was expelled from the party, and at the Vth Party Congress in 1970 the PRT decided to launch the ERP. Originally, the PRT was Marxist-Leninist while the ERP defined itself as merely anti-imperialist. But in practice these distinctions became blurred, all the more so since the leadership of the ERP tended to occupy positions in the PRT's Central Committee.[18]

EARLY GUERRILLA MOTIVATION

An analysis of guerrilla motivation must differentiate between the decision to join and the willingness to continue fighting. There are a number of situations in which armed struggle could conceivably lose some of its appeal. The group could achieve some of its objectives or, conversely, realize success is improbable. Repression might have a paralyzing effect on the group. A change in sociopolitical conditions might help de-legitimize armed struggle. And yet guerrilla groups show a marked tendency to continue operating in spite of these changing circumstances. The distinction between these two "motivational moments" becomes particularly salient in the case of the Argentine guerrilla movement, which initiated its operations fighting against a military dictatorship and increased its activity under a constitutionally elected government.

It also becomes necessary to distinguish between the first and successive generations of guerrillas, between founders and followers. I use the term "founders" to refer to those who actually launch the organization, but also to those who join when the group is in its formative stages and has not yet become a household word. "Followers" are those who join after this has occurred.

When the founders join, they do so at considerable risk. They are entering an organization that has not yet proved its worth. The nature of the state's response to the guerrilla threat might also be unclear. By the time the followers are recruited, these questions have been settled. In the followers' decision to join there is a certain element of contagion which could not be present in the founders. This was recognized by my guerrilla interviewees. Asked to evaluate if there was any difference in the motivation of those who joined before and after the March 1973 elections, they responded with variations on the following themes: "Up to 1973 the motivation was political. It was the need to espouse a political project. Afterwards, you joined for appearance's sake. Eighty percent joined because it was fashionable." "Adherence becomes more fanatical. Joining solves your life's problems. They all wanted to shoot at something." "They joined an organization with power. We created that power."

It could also be said that when the followers join the founders occupy the highest ranks in the organization. To a certain extent, the founders control the organization's resources, information, and money, and can therefore "shape" the type of follower that they want. Finally, the founders have created the group's rules and are likely to have a higher emotional involvement with the organization than the followers.

I have therefore chosen to analyze the two motivational moments with reference to the founders of the Argentine guerrilla movement. My discussion will rely on extensive interviews with ten former combatants, whom I will call A, D, E, F, G, M, O, P, S, and T. These interviews took place in Buenos Aires between October 1986 and December 1987. Except for one who joined in 1966, all the interviewees were recruited between 1968 and 1972. One never finished high school, one finished high school and went straight to work, four dropped out of university, two completed university degrees after they had already been recruited. One dropped out of the seminary and one was ordained as a priest once he had joined a guerrilla group. Except for the would-be priest, all explained the interruption of their studies through their participation in armed struggle. My interviewees were drawn from the six major guerrilla groups. Two of them made their entire guerrilla careers within one organization, while five belonged to two different organizations, two to three organizations, and one to four organizations at different times. Only two of my interviewees were women.[19]

It might also be helpful to distinguish between personal and environmental components of motivation. The personal aspect refers to the characteristics of or events in an individual's life, or in the lives or his or her close friends and relatives, that might help that individual decide to become a guerrilla. There are two types of environmental influences at work in a decision to join armed struggle, those of the immediate (in this case, Argentine society) and mediate environment.

Personal Component of Motivation

It must be strongly emphasized that the decision to join armed struggle was a collective one. Asked if there had been a particular incident in their lives which had acted as a catalyst, F was the only one to agree this had been the case: "I went on a camping trip to Corrientes province with friends. I saw people who did not have anything to eat. When I left Buenos Aires I was an upper-class kid. In a month I had made an about-face." P, S, and T remember being somewhat impressed by a particular book they had read (Ricardo Rojo's *My Friend Che,* Che Guevara's *Guerrilla Warfare*, and *The*

Art of War respectively) even though they stressed this had not provided a decisive influence.

By and large the founders did not join alone, they joined with friends. F joined with university friends, S and D with high school classmates, M with neighbourhood friends, and A, E, and O with their spouses as well as with friends. Sometimes, siblings joined, mostly as followers: A and S had one brother, and O and M two brothers, who joined their same organizations.[20] The founders also joined at a relatively early age. Five of my interviewees were born between 1931 and 1948, and the remaining five between 1950 and 1953. When they joined, two were 18 years old, one was 20, three were 21, one was 23, two were 26 and one was 37.

The founders not only joined young and joined with friends, they and their friends eventually became members of the same cell and were therefore expected to meet at least twice a week for discussion sessions, which S describes as "a time we all remember with enormous nostalgia . . . Everything got discussed, from politics to sex . . . it was almost a psychotherapy group." O adds: "In spite of the disasters you should stress that that generation displayed a solidarity that we have not seen in this country since and had never seen before." The result of this was the development of a common identity, which will be examined later in this paper.

Environmental Component of Motivation

The life histories of the founders reveal that rather than talk about an evolution towards armed struggle we should be talking about an evolution towards political involvement. Before joining a guerrilla group, all my interviewees except F were part of a legal political organization: D, E, and S in high school, A, P, and T at university, and O, M, and G among slum dwellers.[21] The founders became politically active at a time when Ongania was attempting to ban politics by decree. In an authoritarian context, joining any legal political group can be construed as a decisive step. Becoming a guerrilla appeared like the natural follow-up.

Asked to pinpoint significant developments in Argentine politics, all the founders mentioned the Cordobazo. A also mentioned the Trelew massacre and E the Night of the Long Batons as "events that shaped our generation." I says: 'You should emphasize the unique characteristics of that political moment. We were impressed by what we believed was a crisis of domination. We never realized that it was a partial crisis." E adds: "At a given moment we believed that the revolution was at hand. This was a serious error in judgment, but it was based on the impressive mass mobilizations of the time and the movement in solidarity with political prisoners."

It is difficult to say anything conclusive about the influence that the mediate environment (that is to say, political developments outside Argentina) might have had in the founders' decision to join. Asked to name any revolution or national liberation war that their own guerrilla group considered particularly important, nine mentioned the Cuban revolution and the Tupamaro guerrillas in Uruguay and seven mentioned the Algerian FLN. S, T, and O stated that "we all saw 'The Battle of Algiers' five or six times," and S went as far as to imply that there was a tendency to be overly influenced by foreign developments: "We never realized that the Algerians were fighting the French and that we were fighting the Argentines. We were destroyed by an excess of metaphors. Everything was 'in the manner of,' 'as if it were.' And we did not have an army of occupation. That would have legitimated us, but we did not have one."

And yet, asked to evaluate how their own group viewed the Chilean experience in 1970-73, P and E stated it had been considered "relevant" while the rest replied it had been "scarcely relevant" or "irrelevant." O stated that "we were not dogmatic and we did not adopt any system of thought, like historical materialism. Our national problematique was what really counted." M was more emphatic: "There were national causes for violence in the sixties. One must start in 1955 with the proscription of Peronism . . . In fact, one can go back to the nineteenth century where we start searching for an identity . . . The 1930 coup . . . the armed forces do not escape that pattern after that . . . In the sixties, the role of the universities, the importance of youth groups."

Group Ideology

Thought it might be useful to distinguish between personal and environmental components of motivation, in practice the two influence each other. The interaction between a person and his or her environment implies the development of a worldview. In the situation of small-group dynamics in which the founders operated before and after they became guerrillas, this becomes a collective task.

The outcome is the creation of a group ideology.[22] The Argentine experience leads me to believe this is the only context in which it becomes meaningful to study the ideology of groups devoted to armed struggle. Normally when we talk about ideology we refer to a rational, consistent set of beliefs which provides an interpretation of reality, past and present. The worldview of Argentine guerrillas was not very consistent. Consider, for example, the decision by a supposedly Marxist group like the ERP to refrain from attacking the Campora government while it harassed its security forces. In fact, Argentine guerrillas were capable of such ideological somersaults that it even becomes meaningless to talk about one worldview for each group.

Having said this, let me briefly rationalize the key elements in the ideology of guerrilla founders. Argentina was viewed as a standard example of a peripheral society where capitalism had exhausted its capacity to generate sustained growth. Socialism became the only way to escape dependency. Asked whether, had they lived in Western Europe, they would have identified themselves with reformist or revolutionary positions, A and D answered they did not know and the rest stated they would have been reformists. P suggested he might even have been a conservative. D hastened to add that he could not imagine himself as a member of the Red Brigades or Direct Action and E was more specific: "Argentine revolutionaries had nothing in common with European terrorists."

The other key element in the development of this group ideology was a reading of Argentine history from the vantage point of the Resistance and the Onganiato. Six of the founders emphasized the violent nature of Argentine politics. In historical terms, this is an accurate observation. Unfortunately, Argentine history was interpreted as a long series of increasingly radical popular uprisings against the dominant sectors which started with the nineteenth century provincial caudillos and inevitably led to armed struggle in the 1960s.

In this evaluation of violence there was a strong ethical component, no doubt linked to the participants age: "I was moved by a rebelliousness and a need to do things. I could have joined the Montoneros, FAP, any organization . . . Young people turned to politics in an unheard-of way. Nobody has studied why an entire generation was ready to die" (A). "What happened to me happened to many in my generation. You wanted to study and could not. You were kicked out of every place. You looked at your parents' generation and you saw hypocrisy everywhere . . . we did not want to be accomplices" (P). "It was the 'this is it, we must do something'" (T).

ARMED STRUGGLE DURING THE PERONIST INTERREGNUM (1973-76) AND THE "DIRTY WAR" (1976-1983)

With the inauguration of Campora on May 25, 1973 the left wing of Peronism appeared to be firmly in the saddle.[23] The Revolutionary Tendency had managed to get eight of its spokesmen elected to Congress and could count on the support of two members of the cabinet and of several provincial governors. However, to the Tendency the Campora administration was more valuable for what it promised than for what it actually delivered. The Peronist left had been an invaluable mobilizing force during the election campaign and its influence could certainly be felt in the final party platform.[24] This, and Campora's initial measures, seemed to point to the most radicalized administration the country had ever had. The government established diplomatic relations with Cuba, North Vietnam, and North Korea, signed trade agreements with Communist countries, and called for a new Pan-American union which excluded the United States.

In the domestic sphere, Ongania's antiterrorist legislation was abolished, and on inaugural day Campora granted a pardon for political prisoners which Congress immediately ratified. The wisdom of this measure could be debated even in those euphoric days. The ERP had already published a long declaration titled "To the People: Why and against what the ERP will continue fighting" in which the organization stated it would refrain from attacking the Campora administration but reserved the right to continue harassing the security forces (Ejercito Revolucionario del Pueblo 1973). Also, as an augur of things to come, when the Peronist bloc in the Chamber of Deputies met to discuss the projected amnesty law two days before the inaugural, the deputies began their session by standing in silence for one minute in homage to union leader Dirk Kloosterman whom the FAP had just killed (*La Opinion* May 23, 1973, p.9).

The amnesty was justified at the time on the grounds that the country had suffered a period of political and normative irregularity which rendered convictions for political offenses highly questionable. The government wished to establish new rules for the political game, in the hope that the existence of channels for more conventional forms of political participation would gradually diminish the appeal of armed struggle.

Within a month, the Revolutionary Tendency suffered its first setback: on June 20, the date of Peron's final return to Argentina, members of the Peronist right recruited to guarantee security during the ceremonies shot into the huge crowds gathered to meet him at Ezeiza airport and members of Montoneros and FAR responded in kind. The battle resulted in at least 16 dead and 433 wounded, though official figures were never released, and the thorough investigation that the government promised never materialized.[25] Peron's speech the day after the "Ezeiza Massacre" left no doubt as to his allegiances: "Those who naively think they can take control of our Movement or seize the power that the people have reconquered are mistaken . . . I advise the stealthy and hidden or disguised enemies to cease in their effort because when the people exhaust their patience they clamor for punishment."[26]

On July 13, 1973, Campora and Vice President Solano Lima resigned under the pretext that once Peron was back nobody else could be president. New elections were scheduled for September 23. Peron surprised everybody by deciding to run with his wife, Maria Estela (Isabel) Martinez. The Peron-Peron ticket received 61.9 percent of all votes cast.

Throughout the Onganiato and until the March 1973 elections Peron justified the resort to violence by what he euphemistically called "special formations" on the grounds that violence would disappear once its causes were eliminated and the Peronists were once more in power. By the time of the September elections Peron had been proved wrong—political violence increased steadily and dramatically during the three years following the return to constitutional rule, and the old politician was confronted with forces he had conjured up over which he no longer exercised control. Many of those who had voted for the Peronists in March were becoming alarmed. Peron executed a volte face, and decided the era of radical politics had come to an end.

Peron's strategy was very simple: he would build bridges with every sector of Argentine society which renounced violence, while he waged an all-out war against the guerrillas and the radicalized sectors within the labor movement. Union militancy would be fought with the Social Pact, an agreement between business and labor involving a wage increase followed by a price-wage freeze. A concomitant reform to the Law of Professional Associations guaranteed the union bosses control over the unruly rank and file.

All Peron needed to launch his offensive against the armed organizations was an excuse. This came in the form of an ERP attack against the Army Medical Corps Headquarters in Buenos Aires on September 6, 1973. Peron's offensive involved legal, semilegal and illegal means. The ERP was outlawed, left-wing publications closely associated with the guerrilla groups were closed down and in January 1974 the Criminal Code was amended and harsh penalties for terrorist offenses introduced. After the ERP attacked the 10th Cavalry Regiment at Azul in Buenos Aires province, Peron forced the resignation of the governor and the following month supported a police coup in Cordoba which resulted in the resignation of the governor and vicegovernor. The most disquieting development was the emergence of a death squad, the Argentine Anti-Communist Alliance or Triple A. The organization was officially launched on November 21, 1973, with an assassination attempt on senator Hipolito Solari Yrigoyen. Following this the Triple A published "death lists" of personalities in the arts, sciences and in politics who were suspected of left-wing sympathies and were "invited" to leave the country; and launched an assassination campaign aimed at the elimination of the regime's opponents.

In spite of these developments, in 1973 the guerrilla movement increased its membership exponentially. This was also the "great year of the kidnapping" in which standard ransoms were set at one and two million dollars. In 1974 the ERP cashed 14.2 million dollars for the kidnapping of Victor Samuelson and in 1975 the Montoneros netted 61.5 million dollars for the kidnapping of brothers Juan and Jorge Born. To a seemingly unlimited supply of combatants and money one should add the ability to operate above ground, a consequence of the amnesty.

The FAP was the only group unable to profit from these opportunities. By late 1972 the group was torn by an internal debate between the "enlightened" and the "obscure." The former argued this was a time to regroup and develop adequate ideological formulations. The latter held FAP's strength had always resided in its a-theoretical behavior. The quarrel resolved itself when the "obscure" left the FAP and joined the Montoneros. FAP suffered a further split when some of its members started advocating a policy of assassination of corrupt union bosses, expected to produce a more combative labor movement. The debate that ensued signalled the end of FAP. The organization split into those opposing the "execution of bureaucrats" who became FAP 17 October (FAP 17 for short) and those supporting it, calling themselves FAP National Commando (FAP Comando Nacional, or FAP CN) (see "Fijan su posicion las FAP" 1973, p. 8, "Se desprendio de la FAP un nucleo y da a conocer sus razones" 1973, p. 16). In 1974 FAP CN would join the ERP and the bulk of FAP 17 joined the Montoneros.

In 1973 the Montoneros were also strengthened by the incorporation of the Descamisados and the FAR (see Fuerzas Armadas Revolucionarias/ Montoneros 1973). Having already seized control of the Peronist Youth, the Montoneros began setting up front organizations: the Peronist University Youth, the Peronist Working Youth, the Union of Secondary School Students and the Movement of Peronist Slum Dwellers. These organizations reinforced the already strong ties the Montoneros had with a mass base and provided them with an enormous mobilizing power. With time these organizations became nothing more than a recruitment ground for the Mononeros, who also dictated the policies to be followed.

The ERP suffered two splits in 1973; the ERP Red Fraction (ERP Fraccion Roja or ERP FR) and the ERP 22 August, known simply as ERP 22. ERP FR, a small faction which petered out in a year, argued the PRT ought to take a more aggressive line vis-à-vis the (Peronist) labor movement (ERP Fraccion Roja 1973). ERP 22, on the contrary, accepted the fact that the working class was Peronist and supported both Peronist tickets at election time (ERP 22 de Agosto 1973). In 1974 some ERP 22 members returned to their parent organization while others joined the Montoneros. The ERP was further strengthened by the incorporation of FAP CN and of factions of FAL. But the ERP squandered its strength by deciding to open a rural front in Tucuman in May 1974. The decision was indefensible militarily and politically. It made no sense to try to emulate the "venerated Vietnamese experience" in a country where 70 percent of the population lives in urban centers, particularly when this meant transplanting city dwellers to fight in a terrain with which they were unfamiliar.

In spite of Peron's offensive, both he and the Montoneros studiously avoided an open declaration of war. The question of their relationship with Peron had produced two different answers among the Montoneros. The "movementists" (movimientistas) argued Peronism was a class alliance which derived its strength from its subordination to the leader. The "alternativists" (alternativistas) favored the construction of a truly revolutionary party. Until Peron's death the Montoneros persisted in their "movementism," albeit a hypocritical one since they continued to stage the occasional armed operation. Peron, in contrast, seems to have believed he could work by persuasion and periodically held meetings with Montonero and JP leaders in which he insisted his young followers ought to turn to their studies and prepare themselves to become Argentina's future leaders. This stance was equally hypocritical, since Peron was fully aware of the activities of the Triple A.

The break-up finally came on May Day 1974 as Peron was about to address a huge crowd at Plaza de Mayo. Constantly interrupted by Montonero slogans like "If Evita were alive she would be a Montonero," the president improvised a devastating attack on his young followers. Two months later Peron died and was succeeded by his wife. Mrs. Peron did not innovate; she merely pursued her husband's policies with greater intensity. The remaining radical publications were closed down, the government intervened in the University of Buenos Aires once more, and the provincial governors sympathetic to the Tendency who had not been ousted by Peron were deposed through federal interventions.[27] New antiterrorist legislation was passed in September 1974, and two months later Mrs. Peron declared a state of siege. Partly as a response to the activities of the Triple A, operating without any restraint since Peron's death, the Montoneros announced in September 1974 that they were going underground (see *Buenos Aires Herald* September 7, 1974, p. 7).[28]

The decision carried grave consequences. Given the high visibility acquired by militants in the Montoneros' front organizations, the return to arms turned these activists into cannon fodder. Both the Montoneros and the ERP started staging attacks against heavily guarded bases and regiments, involving over 100 guerrillas. The rationale behind this suicidal behavior was that finally the popular armies were fighting the regular army. This concentration on military "spectaculars" determined that the guerrillas remained uninvolved in the popular mobilizations which occurred as economic policy veered towards the right.

On March 26, 1976, Isabel Peron was deposed by a coup. During the following seven years, Argentina was governed by three successive military juntas collectively known as the Process of National Reorganization (Proceso de Reorganizacion Nacional). The Proceso's aims on seizing power were to reestablish order and put an end to the activities of the guerrilla organizations, to modernize the economy, to eliminate government corruption; and to carry out a vast reform of the educational system (see Spitta 1983, Corradi 1982). By 1983, when the Malvinas fiasco forced the military to call for elections, only the first of these objectives had been achieved, at the cost of 8,000-30,000 disappeared. In spite of their financial and numerical strength, the guerrillas were thoroughly unprepared for the "dirty war." To begin with, they simply expected another Ongania.[29] And when the scale of the slaughter became apparent, the guerrillas could not or would not adapt to reality.

The ERP was already decimated through the attempt to maintain the rural and urban fronts. By July 1976, it was down to 1969 operational levels. It was at that point that, purely by chance, a military detachment stumbled upon the safehouse where the ERP's top four leaders were hiding, stormed in and killed three of them.[30] For the ERP, this was the end.

Following the demise of the ERP leadership, the Montoneros' National Leadership went into exile. The rank and file was supposed to "hide among the masses." The masses, unfortunately, were in no position to offer protection from the paramilitary squads. By the time Argentina hosted the 1978 World Cup, the Montoneros had, by their own admission, lost 70 percent of their forces to the repressive apparatus ("Treve pour la Coupe du Monde" 1978, p. 61). This did not stop them from staging two final counteroffensives, one during the World Cup and one in late 1979, both abysmal failures. Thanks to the Borns' money, the Montonero leadership continued its political activities in Madrid, Rome, Mexico City, and Managua. Back in Argentina, the "dirty war" raged on, but the revolutionary war was over.

GUERRILLA MOTIVATION AFTER 1973

It is not easy to explain the Argentine guerrillas' decision to wage armed struggle against a constitutional government they had been instrumental in electing. Combatants not only wasted the unique opportunities granted them by the amnesty; they also provided the military with an excuse for the ferocious repression unleashed after 1976. It is even more difficult to account for the suicidal decision to continue fighting once the "dirty war" was launched.

After 1973, the struggle becomes "militarized." It may appear redundant to speak of militarism within guerrilla groups. However, combatants tend to view armed struggle as a means to advance political objectives through military action, and define their organizations as politico-military structures."[31] For example, reflecting on how accidental deaths during a guerrilla operation could influence the public's view of his organization, O said: "I believed it could have a very negative impact, so I always insisted we had to provide a political content to our military operations." And yet, within guerrilla groups, military considerations tend to predominate over political ones time after time.

Evidence for the development of militarism within guerrilla groups can be found at two levels, that of operations and organization. The focus of this analysis will be on the latter, more specifically on the reciprocal influence between organizational dynamics and individual behavior during the second motivational moment.[32]

As mentioned earlier, in 1973 the guerrilla groups suffered a sudden and significant increase in membership. In guerrilla jargon, this was known as the "fattening process." T, O, and D stated that the "fattening process" hurt their groups. Most of those who joined were "parsleys," which in guerrilla parlance stands for naive, politically immature individuals. F voiced similar complaints: "We recruited and recruited but did no political work." Organizational development led to increased complexity and to the emergence of the "professionals," those guerrillas who performed very specific tasks like the forging of documents or intelligence gathering. It also led to the introduction of military ranks and uniforms and the establishment of rigid authority relations.[33]

During this period the guerrillas steadily lost their ties with the outside world. Clandestinity and the emergence of the Triple A made contact with families and friends outside the guerrilla group very difficult. Romantic involvements were only possible with fellow guerrillas and in fact only likely to develop with someone in the same organizational structure. Fellow guerrillas came to act as a surrogate family. As S puts it, "life was lived to the fullest because you could die tomorrow. Besides, you had people around you whom you knew would be ready to die in order to save you. All our emotions were very intense because there was no time." It could be said that no definition of identity became possible outside the group: "The organization provided you with an identity. We argued, we fought, but we all felt one and the same" (P).

It should be stressed that strong affective ties linked the guerrillas with their dead comrades as much as with those who were still alive: "People will deny this, but if your wife or your girlfriend got killed beside you, the only thing you wanted was revenge. It happened to me after my best friend died. It is very hard to see someone die. Or you don't see him but you find out he has died . . . There is no way I can describe to you what it is like when you are at home and you get a telephone call and someone asks if you have seen so-and-so and you say 'no,' and they tell you 'he is sick' or 'he has broken a leg' which meant he was dead, and you are overcome by impotence" (S).

That the dead should carry such weight in a situation of small-group dynamics would be only natural. But this was also fostered by the groups: "In 1975 I had to carry out an operation where I only had a 50% chance of surviving. I told myself, 'this is not for me' . . . By that time we had developed a conception of heroism. What counted was no longer life but death. He who did not die was worthless" (D). A striking example of this glorification of death is provided by one of the most famous founders of the guerrilla movement, journalist Rodolfo Walsh. In 1976, while he headed the Montonero's intelligence service, Walsh wrote a "Letter to my friends" reflecting on the recent death of his daughter Victoria, also a Montonero officer, in a skirmish with the security forces: ". . . I have asked myself if my daughter, if all those who die like her, had other options. The answer springs from the bottom of my heart and I want my friends to know it. Vicki could have chosen other roads that were different without being dishonourable, but the one she chose was the fairest, the most generous, the most reasoned. Her lucid death is a synthesis of her short, beautiful life. She did not live for herself; she lived for others, and those others are millions."[34]

During this second phase the environment lost its relevance. In fact, the guerrilla group became the only meaningful environment.[35] I asked my interviewees if the evidence of popular support, or lack thereof, had any effect on their group's morale. E replied this was "decisive," F and M said popular support was important "only insofar as it helped us do our political work," and the rest considered it played no rule whatsoever. S went beyond this: "What was important was what we thought about ourselves. I admired my superiors and others admired me."

This process may not have been willed, but it was obvious to some at the time. Talking about his group's formulation of policies, O says: "We were no longer intuitively responding to reality as we had done before. We were constructing our own abstract reality. Hence the disaster." E expressed similar views on a more specific aspect, his group's sexual mores: "There was a lot of ambiguity, because on the one hand ours was the generation of the sexual revolution and there was a lot of that in the group, but on the other hand you had these extremely rigid revolutionary codes describing what the morals of the 'new man' we wanted to create should be. And that was fine, but you had to be more flexible in the face of reality."

What came to be known as the "hedge theory" provides the best illustration of this inward-looking attitude. According to this theory, which became popular after the Ezeiza massacre, Peron still supported the guerrilla groups but was driven to a confrontation with them because he was influenced by Mrs. Peron and other representatives of the Peronist right. Peron's entourage was viewed as the "hedge," preventing any meaningful contact between the leader and his radicalized young followers. That the "hedge theory" was indefensible is irrelevant. What is important is that it was formulated at all. I explains it thus: "Here our policy changed. Up until the 'hedge' the organization's development was subordinated to the development of a mass policy. With the 'hedge' the organization was, for the first time, elaborating a policy for internal consumption. The 'hedge' was meant to explain to the rank and file that the old man [Peron] was betraying us."

Perhaps the most significant factor about the "hedge theory" is that it was believed. Attempting to account for the continuation of armed struggle after 1973, former combatants and analysts of the guerrilla phenomenon have resorted to the idea of "the divorce between the leadership and the rank and file." The clearest formulation of this argument is provided by two former participants[36] who contend that, through its control of financial resources and information (and given the cellular organization known as "compartmentalization" which is typical of guerrilla groups) the leadership was able to obtain the compliance of the rank and file. Implicit here is the notion that rank and file members were lied to or betrayed by their leaders.

Compartmentalization did not in fact work as it was supposed to. As D explained, " . . . you were recruited with all your friends whom you knew since high school, so it was a joke, you were told you were not supposed to know anyone's name, and during meetings we all knew each other's names, addresses, and all that." All my interviewees also made it clear that at the time they had substantial knowledge of what went on in other organizational structures within their guerrilla group, and frequently mentioned contacts with combatants from those other structures and even with members of other guerrilla groups. This would indicate that the leadership did not have a monopoly on information.

My interviewees were not members of the top echelon of their organizations,[37] but they were not rank and file members either. All except A, D, and E were officers, where such a rank existed, or occupied positions of similar responsibility. Asked whether they agreed with the notion of the divorce between the leadership and the rank and file, only G, M., and S said they did. G did not elaborate further, M said, "this was due to the conception of "popular army," and S said, "After 1973 I wrote several papers for my superiors criticizing certain policies. Nobody responded. Besides, people simply obeyed." A stated the divorce existed only insofar as "'democratic centralism' was more centralized than democratic," an idea which P, T, and E voiced in almost the same words. But A also added that "I disagree with the thesis that the rank and file were wonderful individuals and the leadership a bunch of degenerates," a view echoed by P, O, and T.

A more likely explanation is that the powerful emotional bonds with the organization led to an obliteration of the individual conscience. Combatants ended up obeying policies decided within the upper echelons without voicing their opposition even though they might have considered those policies erroneous. "Mistakes were made both by the leadership that elaborated a policy and by the rank and file that obeyed it" (O). "You obey without questioning because life within the organization creates a militant who says 'I am opposed to this but it must be right'" (A).

The bureaucratization of guerrilla groups was undoubtedly a contributing factor. But when one individual defines his or her identity only in connection with a reference group, the pressure to conform is enormous. It also becomes difficult to conceive of an identity outside that group.[38] Asked whether they had at any given time felt they wanted to leave their guerrilla group, five of the founders said "never." D said: "Not when things went sour but in 1971. I had an attack of pacifism. It lasted for six months." F, M, and S said they first had doubts "after the Ezeiza massacre" and G "when it became clear that our policy was at odds with Peron's political project." It is significant that S waited for two years before deciding to leave, while F left immediately but continued working as a salaried employee for the group for another two years. M and G tried to garner support among their comrades so that they could create a significant split in the organization they both belonged to, but although many apparently shared their grievances, the others had second thoughts and eventually M and G were the only ones to abandon the group.

The leadership had no need to withhold information from the militants. Rather, the militants lied to themselves. The founders had a term for it: in guerrilla jargon, "to melon" is to try to recruit and/or persuade someone, through deception if necessary. After 1973, armed struggle became an exercise in "self-meloning." To some extent, this is still true today. While in 1987 they continued to haunt the same cafes they had frequented in the sixties, my interviewees referred to the guerrilla groups they had belonged to using the third person: "they were running unnecessary risks . . ."; "when they started killing off-duty policemen . . ." And while they described their groups' actions after 1973-74 with the terms "the disaster," "the foul-up," and "the delirium," they composed the following guerrilla epitaphs: "we were the generation that kicked the board and said 'this is it'"; "in spite of the things I hate, I still feel a Montonero"; or simply, "when you write about us, say that we loved each other deeply."

ACRONYMS

CPL	Comandos Populares de Liberacion Liberation Popular Commandos
ERP	Ejercito Revolucionario del Pueblo People's Revolutionary Army
ERP 22	Ejercity Revolucionario del Pueblo 22 de Agosto People's Revolutionary Army 22 August
ERP FR	Ejercito Revolucionario del Pueblo Fraccion Roja People's Revolutionary Army Red Fraction
FAL	Fuerzas Armadas de Liberacion Liberation Armed Forces
FAP	Fuerzas Armadas Peronistas Peronist Armed Forces
FAP 17	Fuerzas Armadas Peronistas 17 de Octubre Peronist Armed Forces 17 October
FAP CN	Fuerzas Armadas Peronistas Comando Nacional Peronist Armed Forces National Commando
FAR	Fuerzas Armadas Revolucionarias Revolutionary Armed Forces
FRIP	Frente Revolucionario Indoamericano Popular Popular Indoamerican Revolutionary Front
JP	Junventud Peronista Peronist Youth
PCR	Partido Comunista Revolucionario Revolutionary Communist Party
PRT	Partido Revolucionario de los Trabajadores Workers' Revolutionary Party

NOTES

1. These are also the reasons why it is difficult to characterize adequately the activities of the Argentine groups. At least until 1973, the selective nature of their operations, the widespread popular support they enjoyed, and the fact that the reaction against authoritarian rule has historically been legitimized in political as well as theological writings, make it impossible to refer to them as "terrorists." But if we assume that guerrilla warfare involves the use of hit-and-run tactics by irregular forces against a regular army, then the Argentine groups were only occasionally deserving of the name. However, given the pejorative connotations attached to the term "terrorist," I have chosen to refer to the activity as "armed struggle" and to the participants as "guerrillas," even though these are not synonyms. On issues of terminology, see Wilkinson (1986, ch. 2) and Laqueur (1987, ch.3).

2. On political and economic developments in post-1955 Argentina see Cavarozzi (1983), Diaz Alejandro (1983), Ferns (1973), Luna (1972), Potash (1969), Rock (1987), and Snow (1979).

3. See the *Ayuda Memoria. Motivaciones. Justificacion. Alcance* [Reminder. Motivations. Justification. Scope.], a document circulated among top army officers before the coup. Quoted in Rouquie (1983, vol. 2, p. 253).

4. Previous coups had by and large conformed with what Alfred Stepan calls the "moderator pattern" of civil-military relations (see Stepan 1974, especially pp. 73-84). On the difference between 1966 and previous coups see O'Donnell (1982, pp. 95-99). On the Ongania regime see Botana, Braun and Floria (1973), Castex (1981), Roth (1981), and Selser (1986).

5. Argentine universities have traditionally been governed by a council of professors, students, and graduates. "Intervention" means the removal of the governing authorities, elected by this council, and their replacement by government-appointed officials—the end of what is known as "university autonomy."

6. On the Night of the Long Batons see Selser (1986, vol. I, pp. 127-139).

7. The Cordobazo derives its name from the famous Bogotazo of 1948, which followed the death of Jorge Eliecer Gaitan. It can be translated as "the blow from Cordoba."

8. On the Cordobazo see Gonzalez Trejo (1969), Laclau (1970), and Lanusse (1977, chap. 2).

9. On the Trelew massacre see Martinez (1973), and Urondo (1976).

10. The Peronists won 20 of the 22 provincial governorships, 45 of the 65 Senate seats, and 146 of the 243 seats in the Chamber of Deputies. Campora was elected president with 49.56 percent of the popular vote.

11. There are several, works that provide an overview of the Argentine guerrilla movement: *El Terrorismo en la Argentina* (1980), Barcia (1975), Diaz Bessone (1986), Gillespie (1982a), Hilb and Lutzky (1980), Waldmann (1982).

12. The groups never had more than 20-30 members, all of whom were killed or captured by the security forces, and the activity of all three groups combined amounted to a handful of operations.

13. Personal interview with one of the leaders of the group in Buenos Aires on June 26, 1987. See also Aznarez (1987).

14. Foquismo, sometimes translated as "focoism," was the insurrectionary recipe advocated by Debray (1967) and Guevara (1973) following the success of the Cuban revolution. The recipe stated that popular forces could defeat a professional army; that it was not necessary to wait until objective conditions for revolution were present in Latin America, since the nucleus of armed insurrection, or foco could create them; that the revolutionary struggle should be waged in the countryside; and that it should be continental in scope.

15. Personal interviews with one of the founders of the group in Buenos Aires on September 1, 8 and 18, 1987.

16. On the Montoneros see Gasparini (1988), Gillespie (1982b), Giussani (1984), James (1986), Mendez (1985).

17. CPL continued staging armed operations, though.

18. On the ERP see Petras (1972), and Santucho (1974).

19. I am being deliberately vague. A table would have provided greater clarity but would have also made it easier to identify my interviewees, some of whom are now building careers in politics and the arts.

20. This phenomenon of "family dynasties" within guerrilla groups was widespread.

21. In addition, two of the founders had been heavily involved in the solidarity movement with political prisoners at Rawson. The abortive escape attempt and subsequent events at Trelew forced one of them to go underground.

22. I am borrowing the term from Klaus Wasmund (1986).

23. On the 1973-1976 period see Anzorena (1988), Bernetti (1983), Corradi, Kenworthy, and Wipfler (1976), Di Tella (1983), and Feinmann (1987).

24. For a summary of the Peronist program see the *Buenos Aires Herald* (March 13, 1973, p. 7).

25. The figures I provide result from a scrutiny of all the Buenos Aires dailies for the week following the tragedy. Newspaper coverage included lists of people hospitalized in critical condition at various medical facilities in the Greater Buenos Aires area.

26. Peron's entire speech is reproduced in Verbitsky (1986, pp. 204-209).

27. Article 6 of the Argentine constitution allows the federal government to remove all provincial authorities and replace them with federal appointees if the safety of the province in question is at stake, a procedure known as "intervention."

28. Mrs. Peron, however, waited another year before she outlawed the organization.

29. This is obvious if one considers guerrilla behavior before the coup. It was also confirmed to me by every other former guerrilla I interviewed in Argentina during 1987.

30. The fourth one escaped and eventually commanded the ERP faction that killed Somoza in Paraguay.

31. Sometimes, they explicitly do so. After 1973, the Montoneros adopted the name "Politico-Military Organization Montoneros." There is also the example of ETA's split into a "Politico-Military" and a "Military" wing. In fact, recent discussions of the internal dynamics of ETA refer to the development of militarism with an analysis analogous to the one I make here. See Ibarra Guell (1989), and Reinares (1989).

32. At the operational level, it could be said that the groups increasingly stage actions designed to show military might but lacking in clear political objectives, such as the attacks against military installations described in the previous section. One could also cite the murder of union bosses or the execution of policemen, adopted as a policy in 1974 on the grounds that they represented "symbols of authority".

33. The classic analysis of how organizational development leads to bureaucratization remains Michels (1968). See also Fox Piven and Cloward (1977).

34. The letter is reprinted in Verbitsky (1985, pp. 119-120). Walsh "disappeared" in March 1977. For a vivid description of the weight that dead comrades carry with the survivors within the Irish Republican Army see Ajemian (1981).

35. The description of a process within the Red Brigades similar to the one I have outlined here is provided by della Porta (1989, pp. 33-47).

36. See El Kadri and Rulli (1984). See also Mendez (1985) and Bonasso (1984).

37. These colleagiate bodies were known as National Leadership (Montoneros) and Executive Committee (ERP). As I have shown in the previous section, by 1974 all other guerrilla groups had coalesced around these two.

38. See Hirschman (1970), and Crenshaw (1985).

REFERENCES

Ajemian, R. 1981. "Ready to Die in the Maze." *Time* 118(7):46-48.

Anzorena, O.R. 1988. *Tiempo de Violencia y Utopia.* [Time for Violence and Utopia]. Buenos Aires: Contrapunto.

Aznarez, C. 1987. "No tropezar dos veces con la misma piedra" [Do Not Stumble on the Same Rock Twice]. *Caras y Caretas* 85(2209):23-25, 31-35.

Barcia, P.A. 1975. "Las Guerrillas en la Argentina" [Guerrillas in Argentina]. *Interrogaciones* 8:30-60.

Bernetti, J.L. 1983. *El Peronismo de la Victoria* [The Victorious Peronism]. Buenos Aires: Legasa.

Bonasso, M. 1984. *Recuerdo de la Muerte* [Souvenir from Death]. Buenos Aires: Bruguera.

Botana, N.R., R. Braun and C.A. Floria.1973. *El Regimen Militar 1966-1973* [The Military Regime 1966-1973]. Buenos Aires: La Bastilla.

Buenos Aires Herald. 1973. (March 13), p. 7.

Buenos Aires Herald. 1974. (September 7), p. 7.

Castex, M.N. 1981. *El Escorial de Ongania* [Ongania's Escorial]. Buenos Aires: Hesperides.

Cavarozzi, M. 1983. *Autoritarismo y Democracia, 1955-1983* [Authoritarianism and Democracy, 1955-1983]. Buenos Aires: CEAL.

Corradi, J. 1982."The Mode of Destruction: Terror in Argentina." *Telos* 54:61-76.

Corradi, J., E. Kenworthy and W. Wipfler. 1976. "Argentina 1973-1976: The Background to Violence." *LASA Newsletter* 8(3):3-28.

Crenshaw, M. 1985. "An Organizational Approach to the Analysis of Political Terrorism." *Orbis* 29(3):465-489.

Debray, R. 1967. *Revolution in the Revolution?* New York: Monthly Review Press.

della Porta, D. 1989. *Terrorism in Italy.* Paper presented at the conference "Terrorism in Context," Wesleyan University.

Diaz, Alejandro, C.F. 1983. *Ensayos sobre la Historia Economica Argentina* [Essays on Argentine Economic History]. Buenos Aires: Amorrortu.

Diaz Bessone, R.G. 1986. *Guerra Revolucionaia en la Argentina* [Revolutionary War in Argentina]. Buenos Aires: Fraterna.

Di Tella, G. 1983. *Argentina under Peron 1973-76.* New York: St. Martin's Press.

Ejercito Revolucionario del Pueblo. 1973. *Porque el ERP no dejara de combatir. Respuesta al Presidente Campora* [Why the ERP will not cease the fight. A response to President Campora]. Buenos Aires: n.p.

El Kadri, E. and J. Rulli. 1984. *Dialogos en el Exilio* [Dialogues in Exile]. Buenos Aires: Foro Sur.

El Terrorismo en la Argentina [Terrorism in Argentina]. 1980. Buenos Aires: Poder Ejecutivo Nacional.

ERP 22 de Agosto. 1973. "A las organizaciones revolucionaries y al pueblo" [To revolutionary organizations and to the people]. *Cronica* (July 31): 11.

ERP Fraccion Roja. 1973. "A la clase obrera y al pueblo" [To the working class and the people]. *Cronica* (July 25): 15.

Feinmann, J.P. 1987. *Lopez Rega, la cara oscura de Peron* [Lopez Rega, the dark side of Peron]. Buenos Aires: Legasa.

Ferns, H.S. 1973. *La Argentina* [Argentina]. Buenos Aires: Sudamericana.

"Fijan su posicion las FAP: Ampliar al frente nacional." 1973. *Cronica* (September 1), p. 8.

Fox Piven, F. and R. Cloward. 1977. *Poor People's Movements: Why They Succeed, How they Fail.* New York: Vintage Books.

Fuerzas Armadas Revolucionarias. 1973. "Aporte al proceso de confrontacion de posiciones y polemica publica que abordamos con el ERP" [A contribution to the process of political confrontation and public polemic that we broach with the ERP]. *Militancia* 4:35-49.

Fuerzas Armandas Revolucionarias/Montoneros. 1973. "Acta de Unidad" [Act of Unification]. *Militancia* 19:26-27.

Gasparini, J. 1988. *Montoneros: Final de Cuentas* [Montoneros: Settling Accounts]. Buenos Aires: Puntosur.

Gillespie, R. 1982a. "Armed Struggle in Argentina." *New Scholar* 8(1 & 2):387-427.

———. 1982b. *Soldiers of Peron. Argentina's Montoneros.* Oxford: Clarendon Press.

Giussani, P. 1984. *Montoneros. La Soberbia Armada* [Montoneros. The Armed Arrogance]. Buenos Aires: Sudamericana/Planeta.

Gonzalez Trejo, H. 1969. *Argentina: Tiempo de Violencia* [Argentina: Time for Violence]. Buenos Aires: Carlos Perez.

Guevara, E. 1973. *Obras Completas. Tomo III* [Complete Works. Volume III]. Buenos Aires: Cepe.

Hilb, C. and D. Lutzky. 1980. *La Nueva Izquierda Argentina: 1960-1980* [The New Argentine Left: 1960-1980]. Buenos Aires: CEAL.

Hirschman, A.O. 1970. *Exit, Voice and Loyalty. Responses to Decline in Firms, Organizations and States.* Cambridge, MA: Harvard University Press.

Ibarra, Guell, P. 1989. *La Evolucion Estrategica de ETA* [ETA's Strategic Evolution]. San Sabastian: Kriselu.

James, D. 1976. "The Peronist Left, 1955-1975." *Journal of Latin American Studies* 8(2):273-296.

Laclau, E. 1970. "Argentina—Imperialist strategy and the May crisis." *New Left Review* 62:3-21.

Lanusse, A.A. 1977. *Mi Testimonio* [My Testimony]. Buenos Aires:Laserre.

Laqueur, W. 1987. *The Age of Terrorism.* Boston: Little, Brown.

Luna, F. 1972. *Argentina de Peron a Lanusse 1943-1973* [Argentina from Peron to Lanusse 1943-1973]. Barcelona: Planeta.

Martinez, T.E. 1973. *La Pasion segun Trelew* [The passion according to Trelew]. Buenos Aires: Granica.

Mendez, E. 1985. *Confesiones de un Montonero* [Confessions of a Montonero]. Buenos Aires: Sudamerica/Planeta.

Michels, R. 1968. *Political Parties.* New York: The Free Press.

Militancia. 1973. 15(September 20): 46.

O'Donnell, G. 1982. *El Estado Burocratico Autoritario* [The Bureaucratic Authoritarian State]. Buenos Aires: Universidad de Belgrano.

Petras, J. 1972. "Building a Popular Army in Argentina." *New Left Review* 71:45-55.

Potash, R.A. 1969. *The Army and Politics in Argentina.* Stanford, CA: Stanford University Press.

Reinares, F. 1989. *La violencia politica civil y organizada en un contexto de democratizacion: consideraciones para una interpretacion del caso vasco* [Civil and organized political violence in a democratizing context: considerations for an interpretation of the Basque case]. Paper presented at the III Congrèss of Sociology, Donostia-San Sebastian.

Rock, D. 1987. *Argentina 1516-1987. From Spanish Colonization to Alfonsin.* Berkeley and Los Angeles: University of California Press.

Roth, R. 1981. *Los Anos de Ongania* [The Ongania Years]. Buenos Aires: La Campana.

Rouquie, A. 1983. *Poder Militar y Sociedad Politica en la Argentina* [Military Power and Political Society in Argentina]. 2 vols. Buenos Aires: Emece.

Santucho, M.R. 1974. *Poder Burgues y Poder Revolucionario* [Bourgeois Power and Revolutionary Power]. Buenos Aires: n.p.

"Se desprendio de la FAP un nucleo y da a conocer sus razones." 1973. *La Razon* (August 30), p. 16.

Selser, G. 1986. *El Onganiato* [The Onganiato]. 2 vols. Buenos Aires: Hyspamerica.

Snow, P.G.1979. *Political Forces in Argentina.* New York: Praeger.

Spitta, A. 1983. "El 'Proceso de Reorganization Nacional' de 1976 a 1981: los objetivos basicos y su realizacion practica" [The 'Process of National Reorganization' from 1976 to 1981: the basic objectives and their practical realization]. In *El Poder Militar en la Argentina (1976-1981)* [Military Power in Argentina (*1976-1981*)] edited by P. Waldmann and E. Garzon Valdes. Buenos Aires: Galerna.

Stepan, A. 1974. *Brasil: los militares y la politica* [The Military in Politics. Changing Patterns in Brazil]. Buenos Aires: Amorrortu.

Suarez, H.V. 1970. "FAR: Con el fusil del Che" [FAR: With Che's gun]. *Granma* (December 12): 7.

———. 1971. "FAL: El marxismo en la cartuchera" [FAL: Marxism in a Holster]. *Cristianismo y Revolucion* IV(28):73-77.

"Treve pour la Coupe du Monde." 1978. *L'Express* (April 10-16), p. 61.

Urondo, F. 1976. *Trelew*. La Habana: Casa de las Americas.

Verbitsky, H. 1986. *Ezeiza*. Buenos Aires: Contrapunto.

———. 1985. *Rodolfo Walsh y la Prensa Clandestina 1976-1978* [Rodolfo Walsh and the Underground Presss 1976-1978]. Buenos Aires: Ediciones de la Urraca.

Waldmann, P. 1982. "Anomia Social y Violencia" [Social Anomie and Violence]. In *Argentina Hoy* [Argentina Today], edited by A. Rouquie. Buenos Aires: Siglo Veintiuno.

Wasmund, K. 1986. "The Political Socialization of West German Terrorists." In *Political Violence and Terror. Motifs and Motivations,* edited by P.H. Merkl. Berkeley and Los Angeles: University of Calilfornia Press.

Wilkinson, P. 1986. *Terrorism & the Liberal State*. New York: New York University Press.

PART III

WOMEN'S STUDIES

CONSERVATIVE AND FEMINIST IMAGES OF WOMEN ASSOCIATED WITH ARMED, CLANDESTINE ORGANIZATIONS IN THE UNITED STATES

Gilda Zwerman

> *To analyze the psychology of political violence is not only extremely difficult, but also very dangerous. If such acts are treated with understanding, one is immediately accused of eulogizing them. If, on the other hand, human sympathy is expressed with the revolutionist commiting the act of violence, one risks being considered a possible accomplice. Yet it is only intelligence and sympathy that can bring us closer to the source of human suffering, and teach us the ultimate way out of it.*
>
> —Emma Goldman

Since the late 1970s, there has been a dramatic increase in the number of people incarcerated for actions of political violence in the United States. The charges include armed robbery, bombing of corporate and government buildings, assisting in the escape of radicals from prison, murder, sedition, and conspiracy

International Social Movement Research, Vol. 4, pages 133-159.

ISBN: 1-55938-445-X

to overthrow the United States government by force. Sentences range from several years to life.

Virtually all of those imprisoned—approximately 150—were active in militant sectors of the protest movements in the 1960s and eventually became part of a small segment of the "anti-imperialist" tendency of the Left. They include Black Nationalists, Puerto Rican Independentistas, and white radicals-in-solidarity-with-Third World-liberation-struggles. Nearly one-third of those incarcerated are women. Most would define themselves as socialists or communists and as having been influenced by the ideas of revolutionary nationalist leaders such as Frantz Fanon, Regis Debray, Malcolm X, and Che Guevarra. In addition to their socialist and nationalist political views, the women express a strong commitment to the goal of women's liberation.

While literature in the social sciences has paid considerable attention to acts of international political violence, there is relatively little attention to political violence within the United States, and even less to the expanding role of women in these activities.

There are, of course, a variety of reasons for this failure to document the violent actions of radical women in the current period. In part, this is due to the clandestine nature of their groups: on the one hand, public disclosure could risk the lives and future plans of those who remain underground and on the other hand, efforts to communicate with the public which do not jeopardize the organization's security—such as communiques that explain the motives and rationale of a violent protest—are ignored by the press. However, a more significant factor contributing to the dearth of material about clandestine political organizations in the United States is the extent to which conservative ideologues—in the government, the courts, and the mainstream media—control what is "known" about recent incidents of political violence and the background and motives of the individuals who are involved in these actions.

Thus, the United States public's understanding of political violence has been constructed primarily from fragmented reports of incidents involving antigovernment organizations in the Third World. Typically, the perpetrators are described by the mainstream media as members of "fanatic" left-wing, nationalist or religious groups; their targets as property or citizens or officials who represent "free," "democratic," nations, as defined by the United States government. Coverage focuses almost exclusively on the sensational aspects of the incident, masking careful analysis of the protagonists' demands. An image of irrational, pathological violence has been easily associated with these distant acts through extensive use of the "terrorist" label. Thus, when "terrorism" is applied to acts of political violence inside the United States, a plethora of conditioned hostilities and stereotypes is unleashed.

In the absence of informed public debate on the subject of political violence in the U.S., the image of individuals who engage in these actions is imbued with extraordinary levels of fantasy. And when the protagonists are women, the image is even more disquieting. It triggers not only fears and anxieties about "terrorism" in general, but about the motivations of the women who defy deeply held notions of female behavior. Political theorist, Jean Elshtain (1987) writes, "female violence slides off the edge of a divide between bounded and unbounded activity, falling into the unstructured, chaotic, marginal as something disintegrative, anomalous, threatening" (p. 169).

In the prevailing conservative view, the female "terrorist" represents, perhaps, the ultimate pariah of the modern world. She is viewed as possessing an identity that exists outside the limits of political and moral discourse. On the one hand, her connection to violence separates her from all 'legitimate' forms of social protest. She has crossed the line between "radical" and "criminal." On the other hand, her political motivations—her alliance with revolutionary movements against the state—places her in the outland of female criminality. She is considered more dangerous and incorrigible than most other types of female criminals as well as the men who engage in the same activities.

This paper will first discuss the conservative formulation of of women who engage in revolutionary political violence as it is developed in the literature of terrorist studies. Using material from interviews with women currently imprisoned for political crimes in the United States, it will examine the translation of the conservative view into government policy and procedures for handling these women in the criminal justice system. Second, this paper will discuss feminist responses to these women and identify some of the reasons why feminist activists and scholars have been unable to challenge the conservative view of women who engage in revolutionary political violence. Finally, referring to interview material from the United States cases, this paper will suggest that in contrast to both the conservative and feminist perspectives, the motives and actions of radical women associated with armed, clandestine organizations cannot be understood through the ideologically ladden, "terrorist" lens. Nor can womens' participation in political violence be dismissed as a manifestation of individual pathology. Rather, womens' participation in armed, clandestine organizations reflects a complexity of decisions and considerations involving political commitment, personal sacrifice, and emotional conflict. Most significantly, the interviews show that participation in violent actions is one of the most conflictual aspects of their experiences as revolutionaries. Their conflicts are moral and emotional, not political, in nature.

CONSTRUCTION OF THE CONSERVATIVE POSITION

Since the mid-1970s, in response to the ascendence of insurgent movements in the Third World and a perceived threat on the part of the United States and Western Europe of mounting transnational political violence, a new field of research in "terrorist studies" has been established. Emboldened by the antiterrorist hysteria of the political climate, this field is dominated by neoconservative intellectuals. The pioneers in this area hold advanced degrees from a variety of traditional academic disiciplines in the social and behavioral sciences, most noteably political science, criminology, and psychology. Through the publication of specialized journals and conference proceedings, and the establishment of a university-based curriculum, these "experts" have been successful at advancing "terrorist studies" into a recognized field of scholarship.[1]

Yet, when the content of the literature in terrorist studies is examined, its status as a scholarly field is questionable. In contrast to the standards of scientific inquiry which seeks theoretical explanations for observed phenomenon, the field of terrorist studies is more concerned with generating antipathy toward its subject than with theory or scholarship: "Let us not hear anything about root causes," runs the litany, "or deprivation, or poverty and political frustration. What we should be after is an understanding of terrorism that helps us to defeat it, not an explanation that makes us feel sorry for the terrorist" (Said 1988).

Indeed, one of the most significant aspects of the literature on terrorism is its congruency with the assumptions and "solutions" set forth by government sponsored counterterrorism policies. While complicity of academic with government policy is hardly a new theme in American intellectual life—and it is often accentuated in fields that relate to military and national security issues—the exchange of knowledge between the terrorist experts and agencies within the criminal justice system including the courts, police, FBI, and prisons, is striking. Most of the research cited in these texts is funded by government and law enforcement agencies and relies primarily on information from secondary and biased sources including intelligence and media agencies. Typically, findings are presented at conferences that are convened explicity to develop strategies for "defense and deterrence" of insurgent groups. In this context, the field of terrorist studies may be regarded as an extension of counterinsurgency thought, which borrows its formulations from politically reactionary—racist and anticommunist—ideological paradigms within traditional academic disciplines, providing a "scientific" rationale for the repressive apparatus of the state (Ahmad 1973; Schlesinger 1978; Hocking 1988).

When the dimension of gender is considered, the knowledge base in terrorist studies is broadened, although its political bias remains, combining counterinsurgency thought with antifeminist formulations of female criminality. Those who have established themselves as experts on women in the field of terrorist studies refer extensively to the well-publicized work, *Sisters in Crime* (Adler 1975). In this study, the author, neoclassical criminologist Freda Adler, attributes the rise in female criminality and the (alleged) increasing involvement of females in violent crimes in general, to the feminist movement and women's struggle for social and economic equality. Departing from the traditional view of the female criminal as either mentally incompetent or as the unwitting appendage to a male perpetrator, Adler claims that there exists a new breed of female criminal who, like their sisters in legitimate occupations, is fighting for her niche in the (criminal) hierarchy and thus is commiting more serious and more violent crimes. For Adler, the emergence of the "female terrorist" in the United States in the early 1970s is representative, par excellence, of this new criminal breed reflecting the "dark side" of women's liberation.

The new terrorist experts share several of Adler's assumptions: first, that women who engage in political violence are indeed criminals; second, that terrorism is the most serious of all crimes; third, that explanations for women's participation in such actions are rooted in the excesses of feminism and the political left combined with the pathology and personal frustrations of individual women; and finally that female terrorists are more dangerous than their male counterparts.

Benson, Evans, and Simon (1982) note that the terrorist experts have offered two types of explanations derived from Adler's model, both of which suggest that women hold power over men in insurgent organizations and pose a greater threat to the public. One explanation discusses the image of the terrorist as "amazon," and the other discusses the female terrorist as "housekeeper." In both roles, the women are . . . deadly.

Proponents of the "amazon" model focus on the profile of the middle-class educated female, primarily, but not exclusively, from the United States and Western European nations, whose political development took place within militant New Left groups of the 1960s and early 1970s and who holds a twin commitment to revolutionary and feminist politics. Representing a broad range of revolutionary movements, figures such as Ulrike Meinhof of the Red Army Faction in West Germany, Lolita Lebron of the Puerto Rican Independence Party, Dora Maria Tellez Arguello of the Nicaraguan Sandanistas, Fusako Shigenobu of the Japanese Red Army and Leila Khalid, leader in the Popular Front for the Liberation of Palestine are among those who are frequently cited as examples of the "amazon" terrorist.

H.H.A. Cooper (1979) dramatically describes this "amazon," and emphasizes the emerging prominance of women in terrorist activities:

> The female terrorist has not been content just to praise the lord and pass the ammunition; she has been, as often as not, the finger on the trigger of some of the most powerful weaponry in the arsenal of modern-day terrorism. This new woman revolutionary is no Madame Defarge patiently, if ghoulishly, knitting beside the guillotine while waiting for heads to roll. The new breed of female terrorist not only must have its hands firmly on the lever but must be instrumental in the capture of the victim and in the process of judgement, as well as in dragging the unfortunate death instrument. Women terrorists have consistently

> proved themselves more ferocious and more intractable in these acts than their male counterparts. There is a cold rage about some of them that even the most alienated of men seem quite incapable of of emulating (p. 151).

Echoing Cooper's view, Gayle Rivers (1986) describes the "new" female terrorist:

> She lives in a world of violence that was long thought to be male preserve. Therefore, there is great pressure for the female terrorist to keep proving herself. Under pressure she will pasts the point of no return, make a situation non-negotiable. If she is the leader and feels she is loosing control of the male terrorists in her command, outrage overtakes discipline. Sad to say, to preserve her status as an operative, she is more likely to kill children (p. 89).

In contrast, research by Weinberg and Eubank (1985) and Russell and Miller (1977) on women terrorists present a case for the prevailance of the "housekeeper" image. In their study, Russell and Miller (1977, p. 49) found that within insurgent groups, women still tend to take secondary roles, although they cite notable exceptions and acknowledge that the division of labor may be increasingly egalitarian. Weinberg and Eubank's study of Italian women terrorists concludes that females do not autonomously seek out participation in terrorist activity. Their research shows that more than two-thirds of the women who are recruited into terrorist organizations had husbands or male siblings who were already involved, indicating that romantic and affectional ties are important sources of motivation for the women.

Galvin (1985) also believes that it is necessary to question the degree to which women terrorists speak and act as independent subjects in revolutionary organizations. She states:

> We must ask: what makes these women become involved in terrorism and do what they do? [D]o they believe that they have a true freedom of choice in the matter? Tape recorded messages of intent expressing the will to accomplish their goal and to do so out of their own personal convictions delivered following the terrorist event can hardly be accepted as proof of the truly voluntary nature of the act (Galvin 1985, p. 3).

Galvin agrees with the findings of Weinberg and Eubank's and Russell and Miller's studies which indicate that most women join insurgent organizations because their men do and that often, the woman's role in these organizations mirrors the traditional female role in society, wherein women submit and provide support, not leadership. However, Galvin argues that the "housekeeper" is not necessarily innocent or nonviolent. The female terrorist's victimization by men in her group, Galvin believes, does not necessarily absent her from violent activities nor weaken her impact as victimizer. Galvin uses the formulation of the "provocative victim" to argue that the female terrorist may have a more disorienting and devistating effect on the victim—particularly a male victim—than her male counterpart.

> Those symtoms that follow upon a terrorist event for those directly involved in it as well as the reactions of outsiders may also be affected by the actions of the female terrorist. Some of these are in the nature of delayed reactions. Although the male victim may be able, nonchalantly, to pass off his victimization by a female terrorist to outsiders, he may be unable, personally, to cope with the degrading fact that he was overpowered by a woman. This can be a very traumatic experience, especially if the male holds a position of authority . . . In the case of the male victim/female terrorist figure, the male may find his self-concept as powerful, dominant, masculine challenged to the extent that it damages present and future relationships with wife/lover, peers and other daily relationships (Galvin 1985, p. 9).

Zawodny (1978) offers another dimension to Galvin's speculation that women may be more dangerous when they are themselves victims, secondary players, and sex objects of men in insurgent groups. He writes:

> Men who compete for women try to "outdo" each other, often initiating violence first; looking for a formalized excuse afterward. The fact that the women observe the actions as direct participants is quite an incentive. In this type of cultural setting, the presence of women within a terrorist organization is a psychological inducement to violence that is constantly present on all organizational levels (Zawodny 1978, p. 281).

Taylor's (1988) study of "The Terrorist" adds a final layer to the logic of 'victim as victimizer.' Taylor recognizes that although women's initial motivation for joining an insurgent group may be romantic or familial and that she often sees herself and is seen by others to be playing a supportive or "housekeeper" role, she is essential to the execution of violence, precisely because of the stereotypes associated with the "weaker sex." Taylor provides this scenario to illustrate the dangers posed by the "housewife."

> The mother pushing her child in a pram seems to convey all the cues of passivity possible—caring, presence of children and loving behavior. Such a situation also, of course, constitutes for the terrorist an almost perfect opportunity to move materials and weapons around in the pram. This is because the non-verbal cues in this situation make it very unlikely that the security forces will search a pram—as innocent object, you might think, as you could get. A pram also offers an excellent example of moving a bomb, which can be wheeled into some either sensitve, or populous area (carrying a baby as well as an explosive) and left (without the baby) to subsequently explode (Taylor 1988, p. 132).

In the final analysis, the terrorist experts agree that despite the role women play,—amazon or housekeeper—the level of callousness and violence of the group is either directly or indirectly intensified due to the female's participation.

The dominance of the conservative view over the field of terrorist studies has been challanged by a few.[2] These writers link Western social and behavioral scientists' concern with the "problem" of terrorism to the Reagan administration's effort to discredit and criminalize socialist and national liberation movements, particularly in the Third World. However, these critical scholars have paid little attention to the impact of counterinsurgency-based terrorist studies on social movements in the domestic sphere, particularly on the decline of radical/left-wing politics inside the United States. Nor have they examined the conservative's recent focus on women and the possible relationship between the image of the "female terrorist," as constructed in counterinsurgency literature, and the growing backlash to American feminism.

THE UNITY OF COUNTERINSURGENCY THEORY AND GOVERNMENT PRACTICE

During the first and second terms of the Reagan administration, antiterrorism became a central concern for many federal bureaucracies. Conservative and right-wing government officials sought major legislative changes that would bolster the national security establishment and intelligence community. The arrests, trials, and imprisonment of nearly 150 Black Nationalists, Puerto Rican Independentistas and white Leftists supporting armed struggle in the United States during the 1980s are linked to these changes. Indeed, conservative officials—within the executive branch of government, most prominantly Reagan himself, Edwin Meese, and William French Smith; right-wing legislators in the Senate Subcommittee on Security and Terrorism, including Jeremiah Denton, Orrin Hatch, and Samuel T. Francis; court prosecutors; the United States Marshall Service; the Federal Bureau of Investigation; state and local law enforcement agencies; and high-ranking officials in the Federal Bureau of Prisons—used these radicals as the raison d'etre for restructuring and elaborating repressive policies and proceedures within the United States Criminal Justice system (Zwerman 1989).

The right-wing's portrait of these radicals has been consistant. They are neither political dissidents nor ordinary criminals. They are home-grown terrorists who are responsive to the leadership of a host of subversive (both public and clandestine) organizations, including the Weather Underground, Black Panthers, Black Liberation Army, Republic of New Africa, Armed Forces of National Liberation (FALN), May 19th Communist Organization, United Freedom Front, Jonathan Jackson-Sam Melville Unit, Red Guerrilla Resistance, Armed Fighting Unit and EPB Macheteros, which are growing, active, and represent a broad-based leftist network, with connections, not only to each other, but also to "foreign and transnational supporters of terrorist activity including the Soviet KGB, Cuban DGI, Libyan government and Palestinian Liberation Organization (Methvyn 1984).

The exaggerated nature of this litany was recognized early on by democrats in Congress who opposed the right-wing's view, and feared that government overreaction to this small segment of radicals would result in an erosion of constitutional rights. They contended that there was "a lack of evidence to demonstrate that this narrowly defined group of individuals posed an eminent danger to American citizens" (United States Congress 1984).

The liberal presses agreed. Publications including the *Village Voice, Nation, Rolling Stone,* and even the *New York Times* emphasized the obscurity and unpopularity of the radicals' ideological beliefs and commitments. They described individual members of these groups as a "contextless, fading fringe of sixties radicalism" and the small number of "actions" they had carried out as the radicals' "last hurrah" (Berman 1981). One journalist argued that even those who participated in the most infamous action—the Brinks incident in Nyack, New York (1981) which left a police officer and two armed guards dead—should not be viewed as a vast network of terrorists but rather as "a enigmatic, tiny band of radicals whose motives were hopelessly mixed" (Castellucci 1986).

Yet, the liberals' plea for a prudent response fell on deaf ears in the climate of the growing antiterrorist hysteria of the early 1980s. The federal government hastily but ferverently constructed a new and unprecedented domestic counterterrorism program. Informed by "scientific" knowledge provided by counterinsurgency experts, domestic terrorism came to be defined in illusive yet expansive terms: the targets of the domestic counterterrorism program would include those who "associate" or "support" (other) terrorists, terrorist groups, or terrorist activity, as well as those who engaged in "pre-violent" forms of political protest that has "potential" to "evolve" into terrorism (United States Congress 1983).

Significantly, the elasticity of this definition has the greatest impact on the women, a small number (approximately 24) of suspects, defendants, and prisoners who are charged with "sedition," "conspiracy," and "criminal racketeering," and, therefore, regardless of their actual level of participation in the actions, previous criminal record, or demonstrated behavior within the courts and prisons, are subject to an array of exceptional, erratic, and experimental procedures within the criminal justice system, where no measure of security is deemed too harsh or inappropriate.

FOCUS ON THE WOMEN

In August 1985, I began to conduct interviews with a sample of women who are presently incarcerated (or recently released) in state and federal correctional institutions for their participation in acts of political violence. My research also included interviews with attorneys who were familiar with their cases, intermitant attendance at various trials and hearings, documentation of national and small local presses that covered their arrests, and documentation of government policies within the Department of Justice related to proceedures and guidelines effecting the arrest, prosecution, and imprisonment of radicals in the United States.[3]

Most striking in my findings is the degree to which (1) the conservative formulation of the "female terrorist-as-amazon" has been instrumental in the government's anticipation of security needs and "special handling" procedures during the arrest and imprisonment of the women suspects and defendants and (2) the relative powerlessness of these defendants—as women, as prisoners, and as revolutionaries apparantly increases, not lessens, the government's perceived need to exercise excessive power and force.

These themes first became apparant to me as the women described the circumstances of their arrests. For all the women, the arrest represented their initiation into their status as "terrorists" in the United States. Moreover, for most of the women, this was the first time they had been arrested.

One woman recalls the morning of her "capture."

> We were having a birthday party for my three-year-old son. He and my other two children stayed up late the night before making stuffed shells and preparing all this food—we had shopped for three days for this party. Most of the decorations were hanging and the kids were blowing up balloons downstairs in the basement and packing little paper bags with initials—thank god, they only wrote the initials—with little gifts they had picked out for the children that were coming. You know, like jacks, silly putty, superballs, little goofy things. They were playing songs by The Village People and Michael Jackson on the stereo. Everything was so festive.
>
> I was still in my bathrobe when the phone rang. I answered. The voice said "This is the F.B.I., your house is surrounded. Come out with your hands up." And I laughed and said "Hey, this isn't funny, you know. Don't make a joke like that." I was trying to hope, that it was just one of our comrades. But I knew it wasn't, this was not a familiar voice. Terror. I looked out the window. You know how when things are too hard to deal with, you think "I really don't want to be in this movie." Then I thought "this really IS happening."
>
> We lived in a quiet, working-class neighborhood, on a not-very-crowded street of double and single family homes. Outside, there were at least a dozen cars, all up and down the street and on the sidewalks. Surrounding these cars and on the roofs of some houses were men in uniform, with guns on their back, guns in their hands, guns attached to their legs. They came running out, all in formation, pointing the nuzzles at our windows. And then I saw—it really was like a movie—this soldier's tank, right there in front of the house. A big giant tank with men coming out from a door on the bottom. You wouldn't believe the things I thought about . . . . "They're wrecking my lawn."
>
> I ran downstairs to tell [my husband]. He was in the bathroom, sitting on the toilet, reading some book on Marxism and American Indians. I said, "the F.B.I. are outside and we have to go out." He jumped up and practically knocked me

> over to the side, yelling "you're kidding" as he ran upstairs.
>
> And then, there I was standing in the basement, by myself. It was probably only for a few seconds and I thought, "What am I going to do ? This is really it." I had to pull myself together.

How does a 29-year-old woman with three children "pull herself together" to face the F.B.I., a score of United States Marshalls, and four SWAT teams who have come to arrest her and her husband? Clearly, none of the women I interviewed were prepared for the haste and severity of a paramilitaristic arrest. They were particularly unprepared for the way in which their children were treated. Children as young as three, who were present during an arrest, were commanded to leave their homes with their hands in the air. Guns were trained on their heads. In some cases, they were immediately taken away and placed in state custody, unable to have contact with their parents for up to six weeks. In one case, following the arrest of his mother, an 11-year-old was interrogated by the F.B.I. for five hours. The mother of this child describes the initial period in custody following her arrest:

> When we arrived [at F.B.I. headquarters], I was cuffed and shackled. My hands were cuffed behind my back. And that's when they brought in the kids. At the time they were three, four, and eleven. They were really freaked out and starting to cry . . . . and honestly, the two little ones, I mean they were just standing there and looking at me and saying, "Mama, Mama." In chains, I can't hug them or anything. So I'm just trying to put my head against them. And they keep crying. This goes on for about five minutes and then they're taken away. I didn't see the two little ones again for over a month. (This woman went on a hunger stike while in jail in order to pressure officials into permitting a visit with her children).
>
> I saw (the 11-year-old) again, later that day when they were bringing me out into this garage at the F.B.I. Office. I was totally chained and there were weapons trained on me. Many, many weapons and a lot of agents. Right beside the car they were putting me into was another car. Sitting in it was [my child], with an F.B.I. agent, watching this whole thing. Our eyes met and I could see that while [my child] was looking at me and the agent next to him was looking at me, [my child] started to unbuckle his seat belt. The agent must have sensed something because he turned around and grabbed the door handle. Slammed it shut and drove away with (my child). Weeks after it happened and I learned that they had interrogated my kid, I started thinking that they did all that on purpose. This wasn't about an arrest or an investigation, this was about psychology, they wanted to break me.

Even weeks or months after an arrest, conditions surrounding mothers' visits with their chidren take place under security measures that traumatize both. One woman recounts a visit with her 11-month-old child that she had to insist on terminating before the alotted forty-five minute period was over:

> I hadn't been able to see (my child) for over three weeks. The first visit was going to take place under the condition that there would be no physical contact. According to prison officials, this measure had to be enforced in order to safeguard against the possibility that the children could be holding concealed weapons in their diapers. Two guards were stationed outside and carried out these orders while the child's grandparents attempted to hold them at a distance. But [my child] would not be restrained. Already a toddler, they broke loose and began to chase me around the 12 x 12 sealed room. My parents were crying, the child was screaming, and I kept trying to back away. It was unbearable.

Each woman could recount numerous traumatic experiences involving children, other family members, personal visits and other prisoners—particularly in the early period of incarceration. Journalists have documented some of these incidents in the liberal press (Nelson 1981; Bisson and O'Brien 1985). Jean Harris, herself a nonpolitical, but high-profile prisoner has written some observations about the arrival of one woman political prisoner who was given a 75-year to life sentence, without parole:

> It would be hard to describe the dither into which this [her arrival] has thrown the staff. They have been behaving like frightened rabbits for several weeks.... Anyone five feet tall who can turn a whole prison on its ear, bring out helicopters, bring special task forces to test and photograph all the fences, put the guards in bulletproof vests, cause new fences and rolls of razor wire blades to be installed, and two new ID stations to be set up at the front gate, plus a whole new security detail, armed and driving twenty-four hours a day all along the fence near the building where she is to be housed, has to be a real hotshot in the eyes of the ignorant (Harris 1986, p. 331).
>
> [She] doesn't need to escape to carry on a revolution. Her presence has caused a revolution in here without her raising a little pinkie . . . . Do they plan to keep this up for seventy-five years? (pp. 332-333).

A pertinent question. As the women await trial and in many cases, retrials, there is little respite from the drama and trauma of their "special" status within the criminal justice system. They are denied bail at a judge's discretion, under the law of preventive detention, even if they are first-time offenders and the actual charges against them are relatively minor. They are kept in maximum security facilities: in some cases the women are detained in high-security male facilities and, in other cases, new facilities have been constructed especially to house these defendants. Often they are kept in isolation—"non-punitive segregation"—from the general prison population and from each other. These measures are consistant with the exigencies of the domestic counterterrorism program.

The harsh and exceptional treatment to which women political prisoners in the United States have been subjected came to the public's attention in 1987, when the Federal Bureau of Prisons ordered the transfer of three of these women to a new, female High Security Unit (HSU) that had been constructed in an underground wing of an existing federal prison in Lexington, Kentucky (Zwerman 1988). Shortly after the unit opened, comrades, friends, and family members of the women initiated a broad-based human rights campaign to expose the conditions in the HSU. Liberal, left-wing, and feminist media published and broadcasted stories describing the horrific and intrusive conditions that characterized the HSU. Some journalists included interviews with the prisoners in their presentations. Sympathetic writers jeered at the Bureau of Prisons' rationale for designating these radical women to the HSU which, official documents indicated, was based entirely on the women's "association" with terrorist organizations, their "violence-prone" behavior, and the "threat" of escape with the aid of outside groups.[4]

Yet, left-wing, liberal, and feminist criticisms of the criminal justice system with respect to these women was sorely limited. While they did provide incisive condemnation of the HSU in terms of its ultrarepressive features and possible violation of the prisoner's constitutional rights, they offered no alternative to the conservative formulation of the identity of these women, nor did they suggest how the government might appropriately respond to women who engage in politically violent activities.

Rather, reports carefully avoided mention of the initial crimes for which these women were arrested—actions that involved the use of explosives and weapons and, in some cases, resulted in human injury and death. When charges were discussed, they focused on the superceding indictments—the explicitly political charges of "sedition" and "conspiracy"—though no one suggested that the "real" criminal charges were false. Nor were the prisoners who were interviewed forthcoming about their actions and extremist political commitments. Rather, the women prisoners were portrayed-and portrayed themselves—as victims, whose harsh treatment by the government compells leftists and feminists—for reasons that remain unclear—to "suspend" judgement about the choice to support movements advocating armed struggle in the United States. Ironically, this silence leaves progressives—as well as the political prisoners themselves—unable to effectively challenge the government's identification of these women as crazed terrorists. Why has the subject of women who engage in actions involving political violence in the United States stymied the critical skills of feminist scholars?

THE FEMINIST POSITION

In the early 1980s—before the HSU became a public issue—the defendants/prisoners in these cases, both male and female, had a difficulty drawing sustained attention from from the liberal and left-wing press. Feminists, also, showed suprisingly little interest in an objective consideration of the motives that compelled the women to get involved in acts of political violence in the United States. During the 1980s, only six books about these defendants (both the women and men) had been written by feminist and progressive writers and less than thirty articles appeared in the alternative presses.

Among those feminists who did write about one or more of these women during the pre-Lexington period (1980-86), the reaction was considerably less-than-sympathetic. OFF OUR BACKS, a well-established, radical feminist press published a commentary on the centerfold page which condemned the women associated with the Black Liberation Army/Brinks Case for jeopardizing the security of the women's community with their actions. Janis Kelly (1981) wrote this commentary, fearing that the government would convene a grand jury to investigate women in the feminist community who might have had personal or political ties to the defendants. Her comments are directed at the defendants:

> Frankly, I would like to hear some explanation of how you people justify to yourselves endangering women who do not support . . . . [ejaculatory] violence, but who will go to jail rather than sumit to interrogation.
>
> You come into our communities trailing plumes of cordite, take advantage of our nurturance, and put us at risk for things that, given the choice, we would not support. I am tired of women from male dominated, gun-slinging "vanguards" who stop off for a little R & R (rest and relaxation) in the women's community before going back to plotting bloodshed. If you still hold those values, find some other place to rest up (Kelly 1981, p. 19).

An equally condemning perspective is developed in the unauthorized biographical study of one of the female defendants, Kathy Boudin (Frankfurt 1983). Here, author Ellen Frankfort generates an image of the protagonist as a lost soul—a lonely, contextless, desparado who refused to grow up . . . "A (one-time) genuine radical with enormous energy, she could have been a thrilling leader of the feminist movement. Why did she choose to pursue the violent macho idea of revolution instead?" (Frankfurt 1983, p. 166).

In a more recent essay on the "sexuality of terrorism," Robin Morgan (1989) addresses Frankfort's question. Morgan believes that the overwhelming majority of women in the world—regardless of geographic location and the political regime in which they live—reject violence as a means of political struggle. This belief, she argues, derives from the "truth" of women's oppression which exists both before, and remains even after, "the revolution":

> Again and again, power changes hands but does not alter definition. Again and again, this is done for the sake of, in the name of, on behalf of, from, over, "the people," "the masses," "the proletariat," "the workers," "the farmers," "the

> populace"—none of whom are perceived as female . . . And they wonder why their revolutions have not "worked" (Morgan 1989, p. 164).

Morgan's argument is based on ideological notions which radical feminists, mainly in the United States, have been exploring since the late 1960s: that women, as a "group," "caste," "class," "community," have fundamentally different "political," "biological," "moral," "spiritual" interests than men . . . the belief that if women ruled the world, the world would be different and . . . . non-violent. Unwilling to concede any exceptions to this thesis, Morgan refers to women who wittingly participate and vie for power in male-dominated groups that engage in armed struggle as "token terrorists,"—women who succeed only in "becoming part of the harem of the Demon Lover," and "dancing herself toward the false liberation of death" (pp. 180-216).

The question of why a handful of radical women in countries such as the United States and Western Europe, most of whom share many sociological characteristics and political concerns with women who "chose" feminism, chose armed struggle instead, has also been explored in feminist fiction by Doris Lessing (1985) and Sarah Schulman (1984). Both focus on the image of the "token terrorist"—women experimenting with political violence in the context of a small, radical fringe group.

Alice Mellings, Lessing's protagonist, is a member of a group active in Britain in the 1970s which conducted armed propaganda—mainly bombings—in solidarity with the Irish Republican Army. As the story unfolds, the members of Alice's cell are becoming increasingly frustrated, both with their efforts to find forums in which to express their revolutionary fervor and with the tediousness of their interpersonal relationships. Morever, it becomes clear that the group's "ties" with the IRA are more fictive than real. Nevertheless, their strategy for staving off collective dispair is to plan an "action," which will resolve both frustrations: it will affirm their political commitment and regenerate group cohesion. Lessing portrays the action as nothing more than a senseless disaster, after which one cell member is dead and the others' grip on reality weakens further.

One of Schulman's central characters is Laura Wolfe, a composite of the white women in the Brinks case, who carried out "financial expropriations" under the leadership of men in the Black Liberation Army. Schulman comically depicts the bizarre ties that Laura and her small band of sister-travellers had with the feminist movement:

> I knew Laura Wolfe. We all knew Laura Wolfe. We've all known her for years as the biggest pain in the ass around. She was part of the group known as "Women Against Bad Things." They had some kind of politics which none of us understood. Whatever we did, they didn't like it and usually picketed feminist events with very long leaflets. I'd never dream that

> she would be involved is something as heavy as a bank robbery. I guess I never really took her very seriously (Schulman 1984, p. 5).

Both Lessing's and Schulman's characters are portrayed as extreme fanatics, suffering from acute sexual repression: Alice exists in a perennially enraged state as the "girlfriend" of a quasi-celibate male homosexual member of her cell and Laura is a confused, dogmatic, pansexual who moves within the realm of clandestinity as a nun. Although Alice and Laura are not completely unlikeable figures, they are, nonetheless, hopelessly pathetic anti-heroines whose motivations for making revolution are intelligible only in the context of emotional damage and personal frustrations.

THE INCONSISTENCIES OF FEMINIST THEORY AND PRACTICE

The image of the female terrorist, as created by the counterinsurgency experts, is rooted in a situational abstraction: the "horror" of the crime she has committed (or the action with which she has been associated): it does not explore the subject beyond this reality. There are no interviews with these women and few data sources. These experts rely primarily on sensationalized media accounts of the infamous event, F.B.I. files, and "incriminating" communiques of the group. Indeed, the terrorist experts' description of these women implies that obtaining first-hand knowledge could endanger the life of the researcher.

In contrast, feminist texts depicting women engaged in political violence—both fiction and non-fiction—rely on a different, yet also dubious source of data—self-knowledge or the authors' identification with their subjects. Indeed, Morgan confesses outright her source of knowledge about the token terrorist: "I know these women . . . . they walk my nightmares. I missed being one of them by what split second, what series of discontiguous, incremental changes?" (Morgan 1989, p. 241).

Through their identification with the subject, feminists offer insight about the subjective experiences of these women which pre-date involvement with armed, clandestine organizations. Feminist writers like Frankfort, Lessing, Morgan and Schulman understand and skillfully portray the frustrations of radical women longing for profound social change that will transform their own lives and the lives of those oppressed and exploited in other ways. They also understand the contradictions that often characterize the personal lives of political radicals who live in affluent yet profoundly unequal and unjust societies.

However, feminists' use of self-knowledge as a tool of inquiry is less effective as they attempt to explore their subject's involvement with violence and underground revolutionary groups. At this juncture, when the women join a plan for violence and/or going underground, moral, and psychiatric imperatives replace insight. The subject is used as a foil for feminists' conflict about violence as a form of expression in any context—a conflict which is overwhelmingly about identification with the victim, not the perpetrator.

Consequently, feminists view women who engage in political violence as having made a "wrong" choice, chosing to square-off with the "real" perpetrator—a male-dominated, violent state—on his own terms, instead of taking a more creative, humane path, or "becoming a thrilling leader in the feminist movement." For this, the subject is punished, deprived of her rationality, and forsaken of her place in and support from this movement.... until the "war" is over and she becomes a victim—in the hands of the government, the F.B.I., and the prisons. Only then is the identification of feminists with these women reestablished.

This response is worth considering not merely on a psychological level, but in light of several trends that characterize the intellectual and activist spheres of the feminist movement, relating to issues of women and revolution, crime, political repression, and political violence. First, since the emergence of the women's movement, both activists and scholars have shown a strong interest in women—of other nations and in previous historical periods—who participated in revolutionary and underground organizations. Studies of women revolutionaries who engaged in combat—Joan of Arc, the French Vesuviennes, nineteenth-century women socialists and anarchists, women of the Cumman na mBan in the Irish Republic, and more recently, Third World women who have fought in the context of guerrilla organizations in their nation's struggle for national liberation—are not scarce in women's studies literature.[5] Morevoer, these studies invariably affirm the worthiness of women's participation in the process of social change and in making history,—even when violence is part of that process, the womens' connections to the movement are mediated by men, and the outcome of the process turned out to be less-than-liberating for women. In most studies concerning contemporary Third World liberation movements, feminist criticisms of the efficacy and morality of using violence as an instrument for social change are muted by historical and cultural relativistic considerations.

Second, the field of women studies has also produced a critical literature in crime and penology in which feminists have formidably challenged psychiatric and moralistic models of female criminality (Chesney-Lind 1980). Feminists have developed a new understanding of "crimes" for which women are most frequently imprisoned—including retaliation against male perpetrators of domestic violence, prostitution, and substance abuse—in terms of patriarchal control of the family, economy, and social life. They impute a greater degree of rationality and legitimacy to women who respond in 'inappropriate' and illegal ways to their oppression and the confines of gender roles and suggest the need for society to decriminalize these behaviors. Ironically, while feminists have done much to politicize the "ordinary" crimes that women commit, they have not extended this critical analysis to the area of womens' participation in political crime. Rather, feminists appear to have a completely different, but, as yet, inarticulated, set of expectations for women—far more like themselves than "ordinary" criminals—who commit crimes in the context of revolutionary organizations.

Finally, feminists have yet to examine their predilection to "reclaim" politicos associated with unpopular and extremist organizations once they have become fugitives, exiles, or prisoners. For instance, shortly after the publication of Janice Kelly's commentary in OFF OUR BACKS, the the women defendants in the Brinks case whom she had condemned, were tried and given extraordinarily lengthy prison sentences. At that point, the OFF OUR BACKS collective felt compelled to publish a long, sympathetic, cover interview with one of the women, allowing her to spin out a self-portrait that would appeal to feminists and justify her commitment to armed struggle (Moria 1984). Similarly, while novelist Sarah Schulman was repelled by Laura Wolfe's personality and her politics in the role of public activist and provocateur in the womens movement, Laura's compatriot, Elaine Covington—a fugitive with exactly the same politics—becomes an all-consuming, exciting, sexualized obsession. Even Robin Morgan seems to cringe as she describes the tomb-like conditions which encase the women in the HSU at Lexington Prison. Condemned as "token terrorists" earlier in the text, Morgan describes the very same women in far more generous terms—as "politicos in the traditional sense"—simply because they have been put into the HSU. Apparently, their relocation and persecution by the Federal Bureau of Prisons renders the defendants—in Morgan's view—not only worthy of sympathy but of benefit-of-the-doubt as to their "actual" involvement with violence, as though charges of weapons possession and transportion of explosives may not necessarily imply intent to use this material (Morgan 1989, p. 240).

To go beyond these contradictions and inconsistencies, feminists must confront some of the unsettling realities which are generated by existing accounts of experiences women who engage in armed actions and, more typically, women who provide support for paramilitaristic revolutionary organizations. These experiences suggest that involvement with political violence and the political underground may hold specific attractions for some women (Elshtain 1987; Mullaney 1984; Randall 1981; Hobsbawm 1969; Ward 1983; Warner 1981). Moreover, in contrast to both the current conservative and feminist formulations, womens' attraction to armed struggle and clandestine life cannot be dismissed simply as masking underlying, individual pathology, amorality, or "demon-loving."

RADICAL WOMENS' ASSOCIATION WITH POLITICAL VIOLENCE

Studies by feminist historians and psychologists are correct when they note that direct participation by women in organized violence is rare (Gilligan 1982; Elshtain 1987). "War is men's: men are the historic authors of organized violence, while women are invited to turn away . . . . Whatever [most] women may finally do once wars have begun—observe, suffer, cope mourn, honor, adore, witness, work—women don't start them" (Elshtain 1987, pp. 164-166).

However, women who become involved in political movements that advocate violence are typically not forced or coerced into these organizations and activities. Rare as they may be, women seek out and sustain connections to organizations advocating armed struggle. Their decision to join socialist, national liberation, antifascist and resistance movements is often a gradual, long-considered process (Hellman 1987) and they derive satisfaction from their participation. According to Mullaney (1984), women's motives for joining revolutionary movements are totally different from those of revolutionary men. She explains:

> Yes, they may have been searching for power, but power of a different sort—the chance to exercise power not over others, but finally over themselves. [Historically], it was only within radical movements that women could prove their usefulness to society and hope to be treated as the equals of men. By choosing to revolt against the present authority structure of her society, a woman may implicitly have felt that she was working toward a newer world where the opportunities available to her as a woman would be quite different (p. 55).

My examination of the contemporary United States cases supports both theses: participation in organizations engaged in political violence is, at once, a source of affirmation and a source of fear and conflict. Women do not initiate violence. Most often, they are uncomfortable with taking an active role in an action involving violence and are spared from doing so by the men. This reality is suppressed by the government and counterterrorism experts who, for purposes of obtaining convictions and harsh sentences, fashion indictments that portray the women as "violence-prone" leaders of armed organizations, few of the women would define themselves as "combatants." Most women play peripheral or "supportive" roles in armed struggle, in part because of their conflicts about the use of violence. There does not appear to be any systematic difference in the experiences of women associated with Black, Puerto Rican, or North American groups with respect to conflict about violence.

One woman acknowledges having a "gap" between her political convictions and personal feelings:

> About the weapons, using them, the people that might be hurt . . . I had a really hard time. I tortured myself about it for a really long time, "did I have to do this?" "could I get someone else to do it ?" "could I do something else?" "what else could I do ?"

Others identify similar "gaps," "splits," "contradictions," and "schisms":

> Could I kill for the revolution ? I used to ask myself that question alot. But the fact that I had children, I always knew that I couldn't do that. I had not felt the impact of armed struggle that strongly. In one of the political orientations I attended we read this story from Mao about a nine year-old girl who had to kill her parents. I had to toss with these questions myself. Could I kill children? A member of my family—or anyone's family for that matter? These are things that deep down I feel that I could not do.

Significantly, those women who actually took active or "combatant" roles express conflicts about violence similar to those who did not, suggesting that the "choice" to be a combatant is often the result of circumstantial, not motivational, considerations. Some of these women recall feelings of dread each time an action was planned; they prayed for a cancellation; they looked for legitimate reasons to excuse themselves this one time; they promised themselves that this would be their very last action. They became anxious and upset when violence against people (as opposed to property) was used. One woman describes the first time she had been involved in action that resulted in an unintended death:

> I was not even in sight range of the action, I was parked blocks away. But I heard the shots. Bullets never sound real. Seconds later [another woman member] came running around the corner. She was in a panic. This wasn't supposed to be happening. I raised my eyes to meet hers. Her fear and distress left her voiceless as she mouthed the words. "They had to shoot someone." Then sobs came. "He's dead, he's dead." Maybe her display of terror allowed me control my own. I looked at my watch and began making a mental list of the operations still ahead. "We'll talk about it later," I said. But we never talked about it later.

What prevented this conversation from occurring? Regardless of the role they played, these women perceive themselves as having made an irrevocable choice to join and dedicate their lives to a revolutionary movement. Well before their movements embraced the strategy of armed struggle, these women had sacrificed privileges, interests, and family ties because of their commitment as revolutionaries. Each woman could provide an extensive list—of PhD's, careers in the arts or medicine, and just some of the simple pleasures of a "normal" life—which they had abandoned:

> [High] School ended and I went to a summer program for college-bound students [at a prestigious university]. I decided that this was a way I could get away from

> home, be supported and embark on a very self-conscious process of figuring out what I was going to do with my life. Was I going to define myself as a political activist or was I going to go back to what I was doing, going to school for many, many years, and becoming an academic, spending my life sitting under a tree with a book and talking about lofty ideas? I certainly could have done this. Certainly that's what my parents [were] expecting. It was 1968 and I was 16. I decided that the (political) issues were serious. It was a big-time life decision. So, I spent the summer, I took two courses, but mainly I stayed in bed, in the dormitory, starring at the walls, cogitating. When the summer was over, I joined [a radical organization]. Within weeks, I was arrested for the first time.
>
> That's my saddest thing, at my age, not to have a house, children, a family. But I made a conscious decision that I could do without those things . . . I really would like not to have done without the children. You know, this is silly but, sometimes I would get nostalgic about a house [that I was staying in]. I'd say, "oh, I liked that house, I wish that was my house and could sit and have a chat with a neighbor about the rooms and the furniture." Is that silly?
>
> I liked to draw. I still do. After I was arrested I started making these little drawings, we call them JAIL MARK cards, with little flowers and things. Sometimes I try to draw guns and guerillas and things, but I keep drawing flowers. I guess it takes all kinds of people to make up a clandestine movement.

Ultimately, these women came to believe in the necessity of armed struggle, despite the unpopularity of such beliefs among most radicals—especially women—in this country and despite serious moral and emotional misgivings about the use of violence:

> I don't have any real theories about how revolution is going to happen in this country, but we did some study about how revolution was made in other countries. It involved the formation of organized, underground cells and the ability to carry out armed propaganda.
>
> Bombings are armed propaganda. Measures are taken to make sure that no one is hurt. Warning calls are phoned in. Letters are sent to work places, warning the employees. Communiques are written and sent to newspapers and radio stations. They are written so that even if the media takes only one word or one sentence out, it would stand on its own. It would say why [the bombing] happened, that a warning call was made, and no one got hurt.
>
> It is something that really stirs things up. Its not something that people want to think about. But people have to know what these corporations stand for. They do not stand for making your life more comfortable, they stand for misery. They have to be made to understand that if you're going to support this company, this is what might happen. The message is clear that if you want to work for (a large multinational corporation), this is one of the risks that you take. There will be a warning and you'll have a chance to get out of there, but this is the risk. And if you want to be brave and run back in, you might get hurt. To me, this is a very clear thing. People have to know what they're involved in. It can't be risk-free.

> Suppose there's a bank. And suppose someone is going to expropriate monies from that bank. There are workers, customers and guards in there. If people do what they are expected to do, there are no casualties, except for the very real anxieties and internal problems people have about being in that situation. They can choose to get the hell out of the way. The big problem is when someone doesn't want to let go of something. In this case, he has made the choice to become a casualty if he looses. I wouldn't call it an act of violence, I would call it combat and self-defense. In this society, there are people who choose to align themselves with the government or with corporations and there are others, who, come hell or high water, would not do that. Everybody makes choices at some point, about how they're going to live, even people with limited choices. I'm not responsible for someone who decides to become a cop, or a bank guard, or an FBI agent .... I myself, am not a combatant, but this is what I think.

Most significantly, at times when their organization is in the midst of a crisis, or circumstances are such that they could leave without being pressured or ridiculed by others, they eschew opportunities to separate from the movement, or if they do leave, they return. One woman discusses the period when the underground organization she had supported for 15 years was disintegrating and most of its clandestine members were deciding to surface and turn themselves in. She herself was not a fugitive and could have walked away.

> For a short time, we were living in Z's apartment. Everyone was walking around in a state of shell shock. But finally Z said that she had had enough of this craziness and threw me (and others) out of the house. Most of the others weren't speaking to me either. It was late and I remember sitting alone on the curb, crying, having no idea where to go or what to do next. I knew then that something was very wrong.
>
> I actually considered getting some professional psychological help. I was more introspective in that period than for a long time before or after. But interestingly, I was not critical of the politics or the movement. I saw my doubts as weakness, as a problem of fear and insecurity that resided within me.
>
> But, you know, horrible as that time was, I could not forsee reinventing an identity for myself outside the context of a revolutionary movement. I didn't see any alternative I believed in. Many people stopped being active, though they said they wanted to check out doing other kinds of [public] political work. To me, it looked like that choice inevitably led to becoming "yuppies," professionals and intellectuals.
>
> So I started mending fences, very individually and then on a broader level, with comrades inside [prison] and [another underground] organization. With a few clandestine comrades, we began to regroup and make plans for a new practice and recruitment of new blood into the organization. At the time, it felt new and positive. Now I realize that I/we merely recreated the same type of arrangements as before.

Another woman decribes one of several attempts to leave the fold during her twenty-year connection to an armed, underground organization:

> Up until then, I felt very comfortable with what I was doing. Then came the time when there was a split in the organization. There were a lot of conflicts, a lot of killings going on. Banks were being robbed. People around me were dying or going to jail.
>
> I felt I had to back off these politics because it wasn't making sense. The very thing we said we were struggling against we seemed to become the vicitms of that very same system.
>
> So I called my mother on the phone very hysterical, crying, and told her I wanted to come home, to bring my children into safety. The family was very supportive. I stayed with them for a few months.
>
> I guess I just needed a break because soon I became restless. I missed the excitement of being involved in politics. So, just like that I quit my job and told my Mama that I was moving back. So, I took my two children and headed back and made connections with the [revolutionary] forces and got very much involved in politics again.

In contrast to the risks and dangers that accompany participation in armed actions which can produce a crisis for women who engage in violence, is the boredom of everyday life underground, which generates doubt and disillusion for the women who take peripheral roles. Since one of the requisites for survival in clandestinity is to "blend in" and maintain a low profile in the neighborhood, workplace, school, and so forth, women, particularly women living in families underground, may lead remarkably monotonous lives—most of the time. At times, their self-definitions as revolutionaries and freedom-fighters and their long-standing political commitments, are not sufficient compensation for the desire to have more social connections and productive lives.

One woman reflects on eight years of living underground with her husband and three children:

> I had a role in the underground. And I wouldn't want to ever put it down. It was an important role, but it was minimal. My role was to rent houses, buy cars and things like that. It wasn't like I went underground knowing that this was going to be my role. But because of the decisions I made, that my children were number one to me, and because of the lifestyle that required that someone had to spend a lot of time with the children, I made them my commitment. But the isolation [was the worst of it]. Because you don't want to have too many relationships. And the relationships you do have center around the kids. Always staying over [at] other people's houses and kids staying over your house. There were no restrictions on that. But still I felt it was isolation. I felt like I really wasn't hardly doing anything. I felt more like, Jesus, my whole life is about trying to survive here with kids. So I felt isolated and I didn't feel like I was doing a whole lot. I was really questioning whether I was really a revolutionary. I felt

> that I was more a community person and would like to be outside (aboveground) working.
>
> Q: What would happen when you had these doubts?
>
> [My husband] and I would discuss them. He was always willing to go with whatever I decided. He would say that we could work it out for me to surface up. But it meant a lot to do that. I would be giving up my role and breaking up my family. It felt like I was giving up. And I always said, "no, forget it."

CONCLUSION

This material suggests that the examination of the motives of women who participate in political violence must extend beyond the highly sensationalized, one-dimensional images—"terrorists," "amazons" and "demon lovers"—that have been generated by conservatives and feminists alike. In fundamental ways, these images are daunting to the goals of scholarly inquiry. They alarm and inhibit the researcher. They imply that ascertaining first- hand knowledge from and about these women presents insurmountable risks to the researcher's life and career, as if consideration of the perspective of the perpetrator would necessarily be construed as condoning her actions or alternatively, as if the protagonist herself could not tolerate efforts to place her motives and actions within a critical framework. Moreover, these images are rooted in ideological, moral and psychiatric imperatives which judge and condemn, not understand, the motives of these women.

The interviews indicate that these women do not eat their babies; they do not have histories as perpetrators of interpersonal violence; they are not entrapped victims of their male comrades; they do not exhibit any extraordinary or consistent symptoms of psychological disturbance; and most significanly, they experience conflict about violence and are capable of feeling ambivalence, guilt, and remorse.

In contrast to their feminist contemporaries in Western societies who have subordinated urges of violent retribution into moderate, pacifist, and intellectual pursuits, women who join armed, underground organizations have acted on these fantasies. Yet neither their participation in acts of political violence nor the ideological justifications they make for their actions, indicate that the women are resolved about the use of violence. The presence, self-awareness, and articulation of this conflict suggests that the examination of women engaged in political violence cannot be removed from the study of radical, feminist, and revolutionary women in general. The "extremism" of their political beliefs and their advocation of violence should not compell feminist and social movement researchers to relinquish these subjects to counterinsurgency-based criminologists and terrorist experts.

Throughout this paper, I imply that the impulse to cast women who engage in political violence as a social pariah, to shy away from a precise, self-reflexive, and critical analysis, has less to do with the women than with uncontained fascinations and intrigue on part of those who "study" and write about these protagonists, although as I indicate, the nature of involvement is different for conservatives than it is for feminists. During an interview with Newsday Press, Special Agent for the Joint Terrorist Task Force, Kenneth Walton admits that he "fantasized for years about capturing [one of these women] . . . of arresting her, putting her in the back of my car and taking her to [the F.B.I.] and saying "You looking for this girl?'" (Howell 1987, p. 3). A contrasting fantasy is articulated by feminist Sara Schulman in the conclusion of her feverish, albeit fictional, pursuit of Laura Wolf and Elaine Covington—categorically, the same women Special Agent Walton wishes to capture in the back of his car—she laments, ". . . I'll miss not having them in my life anymore . . . . these brilliant, beautiful, delicious women . . . all I want to do is love them and be good to them. But they're all so damaged. I could spend the rest of my life putting them back together again" (Schulman 1984, pp. 156-157).

Walton's fantasy well-expresses conservative (and patriarchical) "desires" in relation to women who present a direct, defiant, and symetrical challenge to his power—to stalk them, capture them, and humiliate them. Schulman's fantasies embody the feminist dilema, a double-edged desire to eroticize and repair the women who choose to square-off with the agents of state-sanctioned violence.

Ironically, both conservatives and feminists respond to these women as if she is some kind of "fifth child," possessing the worst traits of the other and none of their own. Ultimately, conservatives blame radical feminism for creating and inspiring this "amazon," and radical feminists blame the conservative/patriarchy for seducing the "demon-lover," for luring her into his world of "macho, ejaculatory violence." Yet, despite disclaimers from each side, she is their creation. In their own way, each have provided these women with reasons to support armed insurrection, to rebel against the privileges of conservatism and reject the opportunity to become a "thrilling leader" of the feminist movement. The motives of women who have chosen the path of armed struggle in the United States cannot be understood outside the context of racial, economic and sexual injustices supported by the conservative social order and the limitations of the Western feminist movement in addressing—and eliminating—these inequities.

NOTES

1. The late 1970s is marked by a significant increase in the publication of books and articles on terrorism as well as the publication of TERRORISM: AN INTERNATIONAL JOURNAL.

The field of terrorist studies is dominated by law enforcement officials, right-wing think tanks and neo-conservative scholars such as Walter Laqueur, Paul Wilkinson and Jonah Alexander.

2. For a critique of the conservative bias and the dominance of the counterinsurgency perspective in the field of terrorist studies, see Ahmad (1973); Grosscup (1986); Hocking (1988); Said (1988); and Schlesinger (1978).

3. All quotations in the following section are selected from interviews conducted by the author with women political prisoners in the United States between 1985-1987.

4. Articles condeming the HSU at Lexington Prison appeared in the Nation, Guardian, Covert Action, WomanNews as well as the local presses in Lexington, Kentucky. Programs about the unit were broadcast on Pacifica stations and National Public Radio Stations. A full-length documentary "Through the Wire" has been completed and will be aired on the Public Broadcasting Stations in 1990.

5. Within the field of Women Studies, research on women and revolution is expanding. Although many of these studies concern women who are radicals but not necessarily engaged in violent activities, for extensive discussions of women engaged in political violence see Broido (1977); Cooper, Munich and Squier (1989); Davies (1983); Engel and Rosenthal (1975); Randall (1981); Russell (1989); Strumingher (1987); Ward (1983); Warner 1981.

REFERENCES

Adler, F. 1975. *Sisters in Crime.* New York: McGraw.

Ahmad, E. 1973. "The Theory and Fallacies of Counterinsurgency" In *Taking State Power,* edited by J. Leggett. New York: Harper and Row.

Benson, M., Evans, M., and R. Simon. 1982. "Women as Political Terrorists." *Research in Law, Deviance and Social Control* 4.

Berman, P. 1981. "A Change in the Weather." *Village Voice.* (October 28) p. 22.

Bisson T. and S. O'Brien. 1985. "Children As Terrorists." *The City Sun.* (August 21-27) p. 5.

Broido, V. 1977. *Apostles Into Terrorists.* New York: Viking.

Castellucci, J. 1986. *The Big Dance.* New York: Dodd Mead.

Chesney-Lind, M. 1980. "Rediscovering Lilith: Mysogyny and the New Female Criminality." In *The Female Offenders,* edited by Griffiths and Nance. Vancouver: Simon Fraser University.

Cooper, H.H.A. 1979. "Woman As Terrorist." In *The Criminality of Deviant Women,* edited by F. Adler and R. Simon. New York: Houghton Mifflin.

Cooper, H., A. Munich, and Squier. 1989. *Arms and the Woman.* Chapel Hill: University of North Carolina Press.

Davies, M. 1983. *Third World–Second Sex.* London: Zed Press.

Elshtain, J. 1987. *Women and War.* New York: Basic Books.

Engel, B. and C. Rosenthal. 1975. *Five Sisters: Women Against the Tsar.* New York: Knopf.

Frankfort, E. 1983. *Kathy Boudin and the Dance of Death.* New York: Stein and Day.

Galvin, D. 1985. "Women Terrorists: Victims or Victimizers." Paper presented at Fifth International Symposium on Victimology. Zagreb, Yugoslavia.

Gilligan, C. 1982. *In A Different Voice.* Cambridge, MA: Harvard University Press.

Grosscup, B. 1986. *The Explosion of Terrorism.* New Jersey: New Horizon Press.

Harris, J. 1986. *A Stranger in Two Worlds.* New York: Macmillan.

Hellman, J. 1987. *Journeys Among Women.* New York: Oxford.

Hobsbawm, E. 1969. *Bandits.* New York: Delacorte Press.

Hocking, J. 1988. "Counterterrorism as Counterinsurgency: The British Experience." *Social Justice* 31.

Howell, R. 1987. "Fugitive's Hunter: We'll Get Her." *Newsday* (December 13).

Kelly, J. 1981. "Grand Juries: We All Know Too Much." *Off Our Backs.* (December).

Lessing, D. 1985. *The Good Terrorist.* New York: Knopf.

Methvyn, E. 1984. "Terror Network USA." *Readers' Digest.*

Morgan, R. 1989. *The Demon Lover: On the Sexuality of Terrorism.* New York: Norton.

Moria, F. 1984. "Judy Clark: 75 to Life, But Life Still Goes On." *Off Our Backs* (December).

Mullaney, M. 1984. "Women and the Theory of the 'Revolutionary Personality'" *Social Science Journal* 21.

Nelson, J. 1981. "Terror By Association." *Village Voice* (December 16).

Randall, M. 1981. *Sandino's Daughters.* Toronto: New Star Books.

Rivers, G. 1986. *The War Against the Terrorist.* New York: Simon and Day.

Russell, C. and Miller, B. 1977. "Profile of a Terrorist." In *Perspectives in Terrorism,* edited by L.Z. Freedman and Y. Alexander. Wilmington, Delaware: Scholarly Resources Inc.

Russell, D. 1989. *Lives of Courage: Women for a New South Africa.* New York: Basic.

Said, E. 1988. "Identity, Negation and Violence." *New Left Review* 171:47-48.

Schlesinger, P. 1978. "On The Shape and Scope of Counterinsurgency Thought." In *Power and the State.* edited by Littlejohn, Wakeford, Yarvel, and Davis. New York: St. Martins.

Schulman, S. 1984. *The Sophie Horowitz Story.* Tallahasse: Naid Press.

Strumingher, L. 1987. "The Vesuviennes: Images of Women Warriors in 1848 and Their Significance for French History." *History of European Ideas* 8.

Taylor, M. 1988. *The Terrorist.* New York: Brassey's Defence Publishers.

United States Congress. Committee on the Judiciary. Subcommittee on Civil and Constitutional Rights. 1984. *Domestic Security Measures Relating to Terrorism.* 98th Cong. Sess., 51.

United States Congress Senate. Guidelines for Domestic Security Investigations. 1983. *Impact of Attorney General's of the Committee on the Judiciary.* Subcommittee on Security and Terrorism. 97th Cong. Sess., 4.

Ward, M. 1983. *Unmanageable Revolutionaries: Women and Irish Nationalism.* London: Pluto.

Warner, M. 1981. *Joan of Arc: The Image of Female Heroism.* New York: Knopf.

Weinberg, L. and Eubank, W. 1985. "Italian Women Terrorists." *Terrorism: An International Journal* 9.

Zawodny, J.K. 1978. "Internal Organizational Problems and the Sources of Tensions of Terrorist Movements as Catalysts of Violence." *Terrorism: An International Journal* 1.

Zwerman, G. 1988. "Special Incapacitation: The Emergence of a New Correctional Facility for Women Political Prisoners." *Social Justice* 13.

Zwerman, G. 1989. "Domestic Counterterrorism: United States Government Responses to Political Violence on the Left in the Reagan Era." *Social Justice* 16(2):31-63.

LACERATIONS IN THE MEMORY: WOMEN IN THE ITALIAN UNDERGROUND ORGANIZATIONS

Luisa Passerini

INTRODUCTION

The tone of this paper owes much to a stream of ideas elaborated, together with an appropriate language, by elements of what had been the informal and intellectual left in Europe during the last years of the 1960s and the first half of the 1970s. The period that followed was characterized by the rethinking of some major aspects of the experiences of the student and worker-student movements, as well the women's movement. One of these aspects can be epitomized in a difficult question: how had members of all those movements come to take the idea of political violence literally, putting it into practice in a form they called the "armed struggle" but which turned out to be sheer terrorism?

At the same time, the remnants of what had been a new left, composed of women and men engaged in the sociohistorical sciences, reoriented their studies. Some of these scholars, myself among them, were influenced to some extent by the French Annales school in history, and by the biographical

International Social Movement Research, Vol. 4, pages 161-212.

ISBN: 1-55938-445-X

approach, in sociology and anthropology. This influence stimulated a critical reappraisal of such concepts as *mentalities* and *lifecourse*. The former, reformulated with the aim of introducing the individual into what had been a collective category, gave way to concepts such as *subjectivity* and the *imaginary*. The idea of subjectivity actually owes much to the most militant wing of the young Italian historians, who in the 1970s used it to indicate the emergence of a new culture and complex of attitudes in the social movements, especially among radical workers. Some of those historians' political objective was to claim that such subjectivity was immediately "alternative" to the existing order and could act as a foundation of a revolutionized consciousness. Others, including myself, maintained that it is necessary to distinguish between cultural and political action, and thus developed a different version of subjectivity.

I believe that my own work in oral history has contributed to understanding expressions of subjectivity as a combination of alienated thought and proposals of a new world. At the same time, the use of biographies represents a re-evaluation of the individual, if we compare our use of the biographical approach with that of the second generation of sociologists in the United States. In fact, some of us have put these qualitative tools within the context of the theoretical heritage of researchers and philosophers such as Max Horkheimer, Theodor Adorno, Walter Benjamin, and Ernesto de Martino, all of whom indicated the alienated side of the existing forms of subjectivity. The implication for our microscale is that we cannot take these forms as the foundation of "new" cultures in a revolutionary sense. All the empirical subjectivities that we study manifest both the conditioning of the existing system of power and, at the same time, some germs of novelty and change.

It should be clear, at this point, that from such a perspective memory may be treated as an expression of subjectivity and can be studied as such. I myself have explored some methodological issues connected with this interpretation of memory (Passerini 1988a). I have also tried to produce some historical writings from the viewpoint of subjectivity; my most extensive undertaking in this sense was the study of the memory of Fascism among the working classes in Turin, which demonstrated how, in the 1930s, ideology and power had penetrated into daily cultures, while at the same time an incessant negotiation and alternation of cultural resistance with compensation took place (Passerini 1987).

This paper is an experiment of the same kind but on a much smaller scale. First, I must stress its experimental nature, which is evident not only in such obvious aspects as the context of the project, its object, and our procedure, but in the particular self-interrogation awaiting those who—like use—underwent the experience of such a seminar after participating in movements that advocated violence, although in a largely metaphorical sense. And a biographical approach inevitably touches the author too, as both the short passages (see pp. 168, 180-181, 192-193, 197) and this introduction attest.[1]

Second, to avoid misunderstanding, the reader must bear in mind the tentative character of the whole operation of holding a seminar in jail on such a subject. Indeed, throughout the paper, I refer repeatedly to the need for additional research in order to develop more fully the ideas I advance as hypotheses here.

The form and content of the paper were of course influenced by the Italian context and the very specific circumstances of Italy's political and cultural history of the last two decades. Yet some element in the intellectual atmosphere that has generated such terms as *subjectivity* and provided an hospitable environment for their use seems to be shared by scholars in many European countries. That is, it seems these scholars have a common concern for the daily cultures of ordinary people—as most of us, in most ways, are—that they share an interest in trying to understand what it means to be the subject of one's own history, even if one is not directly engaged in political activities; and that there is an international effort—primarily by feminist scholar—to reassess the hierarchy between the scientific and the existential. These and related concerns are represented by small groups and individual researchers not only in Italy but certainly in France, in Britain, in what was until yesterday the German Federal Republic, in Spain, and most probably in many more places than the limits of my knowledge allow me to cite. There are indications that the same concerns are also very immediate in the East European countries as well as in Russia. Some of the researchers who demonstrated such interest are involved in oral history, but the study of subjectivity is by no mean restricted to the collection and study of memory. More compelling examinations of subjectivity might come from studies on the destiny of religion (see, for example, Gauchet 1985) or from research on the historical forms of communications (explored in the classical works of Walter Ong).

Finally, I should say that the effort to understand subjectivity in a historical perspective is as yet incomplete, our work is still marked by lacunae. For it is difficult to develop a concept both complex and subtle enough to do justice both to the enormous changes in human attitudes in this century, and to the experience of a "broken life" undergone by more than one generation in the last two decades. The narrative of this paper bears traces of both these cataclysms, traces for which the author acknowledges her own responsibility.

THE CONTEXT

In August 1985, a group of women from the area omogenea[2] at the "Carceri Nuove" prison, wrote to some lecturers and professors at Turin University proposing "a seminar of oral history" on their lives including their experience of political violence. The women expressed the need to

> give voice to the plurality of different experiences . . . to grasp and take responsibility for the motivations and inner histories of each of us, and at the same time to underline the relationship between our lives and the general movements of those years . . . to become aware of the continuities and of the breaches that we have created within ourselves as women.

The prisoners' request was not only an expression of concern with personal dissociation but a manifestation of a broad historical process, as another passage of the prisoners' letter indicated:

> there are many question marks both about the past and about the present, and all of the story is much more problematic, even for us, than it might seem.[3]

A few members of Turin University's Department of History had been teaching and conducting research on the history of the 1960s and 1970s for many years. The prisoners' proposal thus gave them an opportunity to pursue and develop some aspects of their research activities that fell within the bounds of the university's official functions. An exchange of letters between professors and prisoners as well as several meetings in prison followed the women's initial request. Permits were required from the Ministry of Justice and from the guidice di sorveglianza (a judge who decides upon prisoners' matters), as well as one from the Prison Authority, to conduct group meetings using a tape recorder for reasons of study (normally only instruments suitable for listening to previously recorded material are permitted in prison).

In November 1985 the Dean of Turin University appointed a committee to look after students in prison and to coordinate the various activities with which they would be involved, from exams to seminars. In march 1986 the Council of the Faculty of "Magistero" (Teachers' College for the Humanities) approved the program for the seminar "Women's Identity and Political Violence." Meetings and preliminary exchanges continued until all the necessary permits had been obtained, and in December 1986 the seminar series began.

Meanwhile, some of the women who had proposed the seminar had come out of prison in semi-libertà (semi-freedom). Thus two small groups were organized, one outside prison, which met at the university on Saturday mornings (and which included two members who had completed their sentences some time previously), and one inside the prison, which met on Tuesday afternoons. At the suggestion of the director of the "Nuove", a "non-political' prisoner was included in the latter group; this prisoner was also enrolled at Turin University.

From January to June 1987, with some additional meetings in the autumn, the two seminar groups proceeded simultaneously. The participants' intention was to reflect upon the proposed theme, "Political Violence and Feminine Identity" to be mediated by the historical and didactic use of oral memory.

The exceptional character of the experience requires a brief explanation of the techniques and methods used, which were agreed on in the preliminary meetings.

The participants consisted of, on the one hand, lecturers/interviewers, and, on the other, students/narrators. For several reasons, however, the latter played more varied roles than speakers who give oral testimony usually do. Their contributions were affected by, first, the manner in which the data was collected: at each setting, only one woman spoke and only one could ask questions; the others listened. Only in exceptional cases, or more generally, in the final phases of the testimony, could the others take their turn to speak. Thus each speaker was entrusted with the roles of actor and audience in turn. Secondly, each speaker also had the far from easy job of "faithfully" (as far as possible) transcribing her own testimony. This condition reduced the costs of the seminar, but more important, it forced the women to reflect—sometimes partially—on the relationship between oral and written expression. Third, the participants in the seminar were also, at least in part, required to interpret their own memories critically.

Work began with a basic reading list (compiled during the preparatory year) and a series of lectures given by the lecturers, followed by discussions on the use of oral sources in history, the history of political violence, and the history of women.[4] This phase was followed by the testimonies, with each woman's testimony lasting from one to three sessions. During the narration the lecturers followed the classical life-history approach, attempting wherever possible to obtain a spontaneous memory and asking questions only to clarify what had been said, without digressing from the main thread of the account.

At the end of this listening phase we began a third phase, in May, during which, after having reflected on the interviews as a whole, the lecturers made observations, asked questions, and expressed doubts or objections. These comments produced a series of debates, which were recorded and transcribed, as were all the other meetings. This phase was also the period of maximum tension—or more precisely the period in which the tensions that had accumulated during the preceding phase emerged—and a real exchange of viewpoints took place. The arguments raised previously were now explored in greater depth, as were intersubjective relations in the group.

The last phase of the work, which is still in progress (this paper being a part of it) concerns the analysis of the life-histories collected. By now, the group of women originally interviewed has partially dispersed; some have been moved to other prisons, others having completed their prison terms, have moved to other cities. Perhaps, however, some participants will continue to reflect and to exchange ideas; perhaps additional studies and interpretations, both historical and existential, will appear.

It is important to emphasize that the experience took place within a didactic framework. Thus, exceptional as it was, this undertaking kept its specific character of a learning experience in which one pursues research more for its methodological value than to produce definitive scientific results. This account indicates directions for further research and it contains reflections on possible sources for future commentaries, but it does not attempt to reconstruct a period or a historical phenomenon. It does, however, introduce re-elaborated concepts and an interpretative thread that tries to tie together the various strands in the history of the last twenty years.

The research approach and the type of material used reflect a primary conviction: one must not tackle the historical problem of terrorism on the factual plane alone. Studies on fascism have already shown that research must embrace the psychological and symbolic dimensions of the phenomenon. Without resorting to such categories as the unconscious, the imaginary, projection, compensation, and repression, we will never understand the relations between leaders and the masses, racial persecutions, and even present-day memories of totalitarian regimes.

We must follow a similar approach in analyzing political violence that afflicted Italy during the 1970s and the early 1980s. It appears that unless we consider psychological factors, we will find it impossible to understand certain disturbing aspects of this violence, such as the support (at the very least intellectual support) of many young people for terrorism, or the connections and differences between the social movements and this phenomenon, as well as the problem of it origins, of which explanations in exclusively political and institutional terms are not satisfactory. To place the social processes of the last twenty years—which include political violence—in a context suited to their nature and duration, we need the depth of a cultural analysis.[5] To restore to the phenomenon of terrorism its significance and complexity, we must attend to the symbolic plane.[6]

Therefore, a second important principle to follow is to reject the isolation of terrorism from the cultural climate of its time; and to try to consider it within its surrounding psychomental contexts. Not, certainly, to exonerate some actors and indict others; the historian should not in any way wish to take the judge's place. Rather, to treat the subject as revelatory of processes taking place in society as a whole, processes from which no one is exempted. The mass medias' practice of sensationalizing and spectacularizing events should suffice as an example of these processes. This practice clearly reached an extreme with terrorism, but we can study it critically only by looking beyond the perspective of this one manifestation.

For proposals concerning the analysis of the imaginary, too, we must transcend the single perspective of terrorism. A particular series of images common among perpetrators of political violence may be used to demonstrate tendencies common to other social contexts—the instrumental use of traditional attributions of femininity, for example, or, among women mimicking male models, the illusions of emancipation. The fact that the context is one of political violence does not radically change the ideological character of the supposed liberation, although it makes it even more ideological.

The analytical scheme used here is that of a history that includes the symbolic and intellectual/psychological spheres. It thus has a psychoanalytic profile, although it does not aim to be a psychological interpretation of terrorism. Nevertheless, we should not exclude this symbolic perspective, as other commentators have done (they are correct only in that they consider any formalization of a presumed type of "terrorist personality," one that generalizes particular character traits, to be unconvincing). For this perspective would regain its validity if, once again, we were to take a broader view and try to identify those psychological elements common to a specific period of time and among certain generations and social classes but which have been accentuated among members of certain movements.

To return to a well-known example, we could say that an entire era until the second World War, assigned value to authoritarian personality traits in varying ways and forms according to different national situations (and also with contradictions and inverse tendencies). To attribute the authoritarian syndrome to only one social group or to attempt to measure levels of authoritarianism present in sociological samples would clearly be limiting and misleading. In such investigations, therefore, the distinction between empirical levels of analysis and general tendencies must be carefully drawn. Having made this distinction, we could then try to deduce some traits of a "rebel personality" and of extreme psychological forms of anti-authoritarianism, as they have been manifested in Italy's recent history.

The study of this part of history, transferred to a ground that includes common attitudes and behavior, is beset with difficulties. One historiographical problem is determining the continuity or discontinuity of various phenomena and movements. Thought it is not possible to analyze this problem thoroughly here, one basic aspect can be mentioned. Twenty years after 1968—an anniversary marked with ideologies and memories but very little history—some logical connections emerge, in particular, between 1968 and the form of Marxism that preceded it, and between 1968 and the terrorism that followed. These connections require further analysis, constructed on a critical treatment of primary sources, not only on reviews of secondary sources.[7] But above all we must consider them along with the radical discontinuity between the most important part of the messages of 1968 and the messages that both preceded and followed them: that is, the 1968 movement's ethical inspiration; its insistence on speaking and being heard, on taking action and on raising the consciousness of each subject about the situation in which he or she found himself or herself; the importance of the symbolic level in tension and not in harmony with existing reality. All these elements, and others, mark the distance of the 1960s from ideological Marxism and from the privileging or organization and of violence in the 1970s.

On Tuesday afternoon we meet outside the "Nuove" and go in together. The permit is there, but each time they have to look for it in the huge registers, which don't appear to be in alphabetical or chronological order. The guard has to go through them page by page while we wait for anywhere up to twenty minutes. In the end we help him, in the tiny guard-room, three women in a man's world, the contrast emphasized by the growing pregnancy of one of us. One thing, which perhaps should be obvious, particularly strikes me: the machine guns, casually handled. I also notice the guards' difficulty in communicating with us. Gesticulation is an integral part of expression in their southern Italian speech, whereas in comparison our words are irredeemably literary, educated, distant. Each time my professional bias tells me automatically that the only qualification required of them is the elementary school certificates.

We go through two, three, seven doors ("they locked me up inside seven gates"[8]) and at each there is a different female warden. We wish them "good afternoon" as they open or close the gates, but here, too, we are aware of the same resigned distance. They aren't in uniform, but in slippers, shawls, aprons. They sit by electric fires reading comics. The atmosphere in the women's jail seems peculiarly archaic: crucifixes, holy pictures, plastic flowers, the nuns. With its archaic character, it is less sinister than a modern jail. To me it seems to be symbolic of a regression, but a regression that is necessary after there has been a serious lack of attention to some fundamental aspect. Some forms are nevertheless materially unsuitable for a regression seen as *pietas* toward the past, one's own and that shared with others.

THE ORAL, THE WRITTEN, THE IMAGINARY

We worked with ten life-histories.[9] Many of these oral autobiographies had been preceded, in 1985, by written memoirs, originating in a seminar held inside the prison by Diego Novelli and Nicola Tranfaglia. The comparison between the oral and the written accounts is significant: the prisoners' writing conserves traces of bureaucratic language, and formal turns of phrase that do not appear in their oral testimony:

> I engage in the distribution of propaganda material . . . In my experience, feminism will consolidate the word "liberation", in which subjectivity becomes "force" against the paralyzing objectivity of marginalization (Ronconi).

Certain dimensions are censored in writing. What struck me most, and what can be of help in the interpretation of the process under study, was the gap between written and oral in terms of the importance given to the imaginary. Writing almost entirely seems to censor the imaginary. What prevails is a discursive, reasonable, consequential tone. The act of writing requires the image of a reflective person who can unfold the story of his or her life in the classic form of autobiography, modeled on the *Bildungsroman* in which error is sooner or later supplanted by correct understanding and the linear structure admits no contradictions or omissions.

The oral presentation provides a different picture. The stimulus is much more strongly and immediately emotional because the interviewer is present, asks questions, or at least nods in agreement or makes signs of disagreement. But even if the listener were to remain completely impassive, the speaker would not be able to narrate without feeling that the other person was also participating. The empathy of the listener, even when accompanied by negative feelings, such as repulsion, becomes an integral part of the narration. Far from undermining objectivity, this emotional involvement provides a means of approaching it, because the very emotionality brings out those precious signs in the intersubjective relations which would otherwise be lost. Objectivity in this case amounts to a form of intersubjectivity.

In our case, speakers addressed not simply one person but a small audience, silent but full of expectations and capable of judgment. On this stage, self-representation is fundamental; the narrator chooses a role to play which combines strategy with spontaneity. The oral narrative thus dwells on nonfactual elements of the self-image. One of the life-stories opens with an almost fantastic scene: Venice, the speaker's place of birth, but a place where she never lived (and so not an everyday, ordinary, prosaic place), although she will go there at the most "storylike" moment of her life:

> It was the first trip I treated myself to after escaping, and the first place I wanted to go to get myself together again (Ronconi).

Venice becomes the focus of an identity—that is, of a cultural construction connected to the image of the speaker's mother. This evocation makes up a full-scale exordium, the first two minutes of the tape. As the woman's life-story unfolds and she recounts the escape, the dreamlike quality soon emerges:

> My memory of it is absolutely fantastic and imaginary, because each time I compare it with the others it's different . . . definitely the most beautiful moment of my life.
>
> The four of us were all in the courtyard taking the air when the charge exploded and opened the classic breach in the wall . . . . And the first thing I saw when the rain of debris thinned out was S. with a machine gun in his hand—a tremendous gun battle, bullets all over the place, smoke, uproar—he calmly said "O.K., let's go". We went through the hole and got out. Outside we couldn't see anything because there was dense black smoke due to the explosion, and as I ran toward the cars I saw all the comrades I knew, they were in a line along the road, all of them shooting because the wardens on the wall were shooting; so I run toward the car, and while I run, I see all these faces, my people, my friends' faces (Ronconi).

This description could be the account of a dream or a film. I think this cinematic dreamlike quality may reveal something about certain aspects of the terrorist phenomenon. First, it evokes the communal element, which constitutes the identity of the individual, who feels worthless, unable to exist, outside the group. I refer to communality not only in the anthropological sense—the networks of relationships that draw an individual into joining the armed struggle or that accompany her in her decision to do so (and that later become the channels along which dissociation flows)—but also in the cultural, mental, and psychic sense. The roots of the decision to espouse political violence reach right down to these communal elements and it is in light of this origin that we must [try to] understand them. They include a form of literary mentality, the illusion of a free and adventurous life, intense and spectacular, on the fringes of the law or outside it. This mentality is common among young people of various ages, and even today it is the basis for the interest that many young people have toward imprisoned terrorists, who have become the symbol of a life-style that goes against order and routine.[10]

In its allusive and enigmatic way the oral memory expresses this mentality:

> I have always had an extremely fertile imagination—I spent hours and hours alone with the dog in the garden, or telling myself stories and listening to music, which I always liked. I did classical ballet for years, ever since I was tiny. I had this extremely well developed dimension of fantasy . . . (Ronconi)

continues the same speaker. But she is not alone. Liviana Tosi, recalling her childhood in the lower Po valley, the smells of wheat and of the earth, the huge peasant family (fifteen members) and the poverty of the farm-laborer's life, says:

> I didn't have any toys, I had the immense space of the countryside . . . my games were walking around, acting out all of my stories, I had a tremendous imagination, I used to talk to dogs and cats, I invented my own fantastic stories. . . . Sometimes on a Sunday there was something on at the village theatre, but for every day I had my imagination, my fantasies.

Writing—or formal writing at any rate—does not allow this type of insight. The scripts in our possession do not devote much attention to infancy; they give a few facts and tend toward the sociological rather than the literary, thus ignoring all those significant anecdotes that, in family traditions and in the individual's repertory, constitute the actual myths about the narrator's origins. Here, these memories are illuminated by accounts of successive phases—in other words, in this context the decision to include aspects of this type in speaking about the self is not irrelevant. Let us take this point a little further. First, we must keep in mind that all except one of our oral accounts describe a happy childhood, sometimes "very happy" (De Stefano), almost as though pointing out that the decision to take up terrorism did not depend on former deprivation. This statistic is sufficient to rebut, if there were any need, the crudest interpretation that whole generations would have been corrupted by family crises. This polemic does not interest us in the cultural analysis we are attempting, but later on we will find some clearer links with this theme.

The interviews, then, contain repeated references to an imaginary and spectacular sphere. Carmen De Stefano, talking about the radical wave of protest known as the 1977 movement, recalled:

> it was something I enjoyed, I met people, we exchanged opinions, we talked ... but it all seemed to me to be a bit—to be rather a pretense. I felt that it was all like being on a stage. I don't know, we all had well-defined roles, and there are certain things that each of us had to do, but it seemed to me, somehow, that these things never got any results. I mean they never got down to the root of the various problems that existed.

As the speakers describe themselves, they "want to go into something thoroughly," and they express discontent with "only talking":

> I was rather fed up with this climate in which I had lived for years, especially at Palazzo Nuovo, of verbal extremism and incoherence, and in people's ordinary everyday lives too, so that they ended up doing exactly the opposite [of what they said they were doing] (Giulia).

Sometimes, a speaker's self-representation accentuates action, practicality, and her intolerance for long, futile political discussions: "I have always been a concrete person" (Giulia); "I have never been a great intellectual" (Mantovani).

Sometimes too we find a speaker claiming that her decision to engage in terrorism was not dictated by externally conditioned motivations but originated in a personal upsurge of rebellion:

> It wasn't the social motivations, it wasn't the fact of seeing people exploited, people suffering, no, it wasn't this. I think that it was a desire of mine to say: 'By upsetting things, breaking with things completely, you can probably get beyond them.' That, more or less, was the launching platform (De Stefano).

I think that the anecdotes about the narrator's origins, which extend the dream/film realm to what the Western medical tradition has often considered its "natural" context, i.e., mental illness and insanity, are of the same nature: rebellion interpreted as madness, "nervous breakdown" in the language of the 1950 and 1960s. Barbara Graglia reports an incident that occurred when she was fifteen and attending a very respectable private school run by nuns:

> I don't remember what actually triggered the episode, but anyhow, I had taken off my shoes, and started throwing them at the blackboard, then I took hold of this accursed uniform and I started to take it off, saying: "I can't stand it any more!" There was a uniform with white gloves and a white veil for important occasions, otherwise there was a grey flannel skirt, a dark blue blouse and socks; nylons were allowed from the fifth form upward. And anyhow, I took off these clothes and I started to say the worst swear words I could think of, insults, hard, vulgar insults too; I was trying to find the most upsetting words I could.

The result: she was taken to a psychiatrist, to a neurologist: "but," she said, 'I got over these things by myself . . . thanks to a young teacher, a left-wing Catholic."

In various ways, this sort of memory challenges the boundaries between the real and the imaginary, between the existing and the possible. I think that it does so in spite of the explicit and conscious will of the narrators, since they mistrust such connections. At this point, we would do well to clear the air of the commonplaces used by the media in the most terrible years of political violence, when there was talk of "hallucinations," "delirium," and "going mad." In emphasizing the role of the imaginary, I do not at all intend to adopt these expressions. A cross-referenced analysis of the material yields some opposing indications. In the recollections, clarity alternates with confusion but not with delirium, even during the most serious identity crises. The influence of the imaginary must not be confused with madness nor with privileging those representations that simply take the place of the principle of reality. On the contrary, the confusion of real and dream images comes about with at least the subject's partial awareness.

This partial awareness was particularly characteristic of the later period, when some women clearly understood that arrest was imminent, but they decided not to resort to flight abroad. At this point in their accounts, the terrorists' life-histories converge, for they remember debating this decision with other comrades. My interpretation attributes this decision, too, to a type of loyalty in which a maternal myth plays a strong part and is possibly even accepted with irony. Susanna Ronconi describes the divergent decisions that, in September 1980, drove one of her comrades to leave the underground organization Prima Linea (Front Line) while she remained:

> I can't accept going off on my own, it would be meaningless for me . . .
> At that moment a sort of sacrificial destiny began, which was to continue through 1982, to go to our deaths with this collective experience . . .
> In that year (1982), the situation was that the famous COLP [an underground organization founded by former Prima Linea militants were a sort of "fighting matriarchy," because women were in the majority, numerically speaking. I believe this was due to chance in the arrests. Some of us were the comrades with the longest history, and in fact it was a band of four women that was leading this group . . .
> . . . to keep everyone together, to give everyone a chance to stay sane, not to get lost. And this is a thing that S. and his group were already reprimanding us about at that time, that we had made the mistake of not sending most of the militants to France. Because a lot of the militants needed to be supported . . . it was a burden just like a large family. Regarding this debate, our position was always very entrenched—we were accused of having too maternal an attitude—entrenched on the position: "no, whatever happens, as long as we are all together, as long as we keep up a relationship, there is a chance we can hold out." This was the sort of illusion we were under, the sort of discussion we were having.

A primacy of the small community, in which friendship and sentimental ties are like blood ties, is connected with this maternal myth. In fact, paradoxically, the perception of enmity—the group's belief that it is at war with the rest of the world"[11] strengthens the group. In this case, a term such as "enmity' takes its full meaning from the realm of the imaginary[12], where the familial mentality and friendship ties are situated, and so loses the sense of being absolute, which otherwise would irrevocably assign to it a significance of madness. Thus the truculent tone of the communiqués, which did not admit of a reply, is replaced by a series of hesitant, confused and visceral expressions, justified by the imaginary, in a particular "feminine" version:

> I had always been rather terrified of going underground . . . I had only been underground for a few days, and I couldn't even make sense of having had to go underground, because they had arrested all those with whom I had strong relationships [1980] and who were the only ones in reality who could have justified the decision I was making. I wondered whether it would be better to go back to legality, but I didn't feel I could, both because it was, anyhow, dangerous—but that certainly wasn't a major reason—and because at that point in time my maternal instincts were accentuated, in the sense of staying with these young comrades who had made a difficult decision, of trying to give them confidence once more, as well as the fact that there was the problem of the comrades in jail, of managing to get them out, or anyhow of going with them, this was the main thing. One of the comrades made fun of me: if your only possible future is jail, what are you doing here? But affection, the emotional aspect, was definitely the most important (Grena).

Why do I attach such importance to the mythological dimension instead of simply to the social relations that this dimension mediates and reflects? I suggest that one cause of the "great fascination" of terrorism (see Laqueur 1987), felt above all by young people, lies in its peculiar connections with the imaginary. These connections materialize in giving literal meaning to representations shared by an individual with a group and the literalization sparks immediate action. Belief in the primary of action, which distinguishes certain fringes of youth movements (both right-wing and left-wing), goes together with the literalization of a mythology. Although this process looks like an inflation of the imaginary, in reality it turns into the exact opposite. When the symbolic sphere merges with the real, the striving to change reality, as it were, withers away. In Ronconi's words: "[from 1917 to 1980] the past was the depth which gave meaning to what I was doing, the future was not a time I lived in."

That very imagination which should contribute to the concrete overturning of the established order (or at least its modification) is lacking. The literalization and the impoverishment of the imaginary blend with the military extremism of a praxis, which thus loses its political character.

We should remember that this phenomenon appeared in Italy after an explosion of subjectivity like that which had given rise to the 1968 movement (see *Le mouvement social* 1988). Subjectivity in 1968 was seen as the quality that accentuated the value of each subject disposed to question his or her own condition, as student, young person, or worker; as the perspective that insisted on progression through unilateral positions to find a new universalism; as the practice of intersubjectivity. The deep ambivalence within the movement of 1968 coincided with the difficulty of thinking through, radically, the new subjectivity. Although subjectivity was the central theme, the activists did not make this point sufficiently clear, and above all, they did not explore its link with democracy. They proclaimed the superiority of direct democracy to representative system, but their proclamations contained serious inconsistencies and were contradicted by praxis, whereas sometimes their manifestations of praxis were not developed in theory.

The explosion of subjectivity and communication in 1968 was followed in the 1970s by the need for long-term political planning. Attempts at such planning, however, took anachronistic forms on the imaginary and organizational levels, of which third internationalism is the main example. The history of the new left groups is not only this series of anachronisms but anachronistic ritualism is one thread running through it. In the case of terrorism, which is partially included in that history, the imaginary was channeled toward different forms according to the organization, but all these forms were related insofar as they manifested the growing primacy of violence, that was mistaken for immediate action, violence that became ever more bloody and desperate. In other words, we can posit a direct relationship between the impoverishment of the imagination strength for protest and the growth of violence. That strength had certainly been present in such actions as that in which the students of Columbia University occupied the dean's office or the verbal attacks on lecturers in the German universities, but on those occasions the violence had not gone beyond the symbolic or challenged the superiority of the imagination, and it had accepted a subordinate role. In other cases, though, violence was unleashed and claimed to be the major reality, transforming itself into action and losing its innovative role.[13]

This entire process could be overshadowed by memory's claim to throw light on something that historians have not yet analyzed:

> It was the period in which I had decided to give up college, to follow the entire proletarization theory, taking things literally, almost always, and believing that every thought should be followed by an action (Grena).
>
> Until 1979, when I thought about the future—and that very rarely, absent-mindedly, because my dimension was the present—I imagined an eternal militancy in ever more open conditions, animated and full of social occasions.
>
> I lived the whole time just a little above my political and organizational capacities (Ronconi).

More detailed research might discover differences in the way the various organizations perceived of the imaginary. Ronconi speaking about her move from the Brigate Rosse (Red Brigades) to Prima Linea, as well as their different political lines, alludes to one of these differences: "the BR has no relationship to enhance the value of emerging subjectivities—and not even those already in decline!" For the scope of this article, however, it will suffice to observe that members of the various organizations lived through the symbolic in different ways, adopting different models of behavior, for example, and stressing different points about the clandestine life and the social implications of organization.[14] Nevertheless, precisely because at this time the tendency is not toward an increase in a symbolic elaboration but, rather, toward a decline in an imaginary dimension, this imaginary as a whole is subordinated to existing images that are promoted through the mass media. The everyday aspect of life is interwoven with the armed struggle not in its political aspects, but through routine experiences of small armed robberies. The way in which these robberies are experienced and imagined owes much to stereotypes of cinema and television:

> I have done quite a lot of hold-ups, in the sense that I was usually the one who went in and said the classic words from the film: "this is a hold-up," and the fact of being a woman was important, those extra two seconds more than a man when they saw me (Tosi).

The spectacular character is accentuated by a special effect: the insertion of the female figure. As in all mass cultural spectacles, the effect does not last long and in the end the element of surprise is lost:

> . . . now, I don't know, the *RAF* (Rote Aimée Fraktion), seems to be all women. So that if people see three women on the corner of a street, they say: 'that's a squad.' At that time the woman was cover. People were fooled if a woman was there. So that they always put us outside, standing guard. They always had me play that part. And it made my furious, absolutely mad. Because I wanted to go inside (Mantovani).

In clandestine conditions, the woman's identity becomes what they called "on parade"; this attitude is prompted by the woman's double desire of being present at the same level as the men and of enhancing—in the instrumental sense, also—her gender:

> I arrived in Turin in May 1979 and the first thing I remember is that I was wearing a flowered skirt, still fashionable then, with flounces. I arrived at about five in the afternoon, and everyone was looking at me, and I understood immediately that it wasn't the . . . Torinese way of dressing (Tosi).

This type of attitude is part of the accentuated sensibility to the spectacular, cultivated by the media. Although I do not want to give the "paradigm of spectacularity" an excessive role—as though it were a determinant cause of terrorism[15]—it is useful to keep it in mind as one component of a mentality, which is often deep-seated in the more or less well-known exponents of the phenomenon:

> I was arrested, they came into the house very politely, and they took me down to the police station. I remember I was a bit upset: since I lived in a very short street, there were patrols all over the place. I thought it was a bit overdone, but I said: 'Oh well, you do need a bit of show" (De Stefano).

This last quotation contains a touch of self-irony and introduces us to another characteristic that connects the oral and the symbolic dimension: the comic aspect, which in general is omitted from writing. The comic aspect appears principally in accounts of the terrorists' early involvement and always contains elements of self-derision. We find it, for example, in Ronconi's narrative in 1973. She belonged to a local group that took part in the raid on the Petrolchimico offices in Marghera:

> with the very pompous name of 'Brigata Ferretto'—Ferretto was a partisan leader on the Venetian mainland—in this group I carried out my first military operation: it is a bit ridiculous to call it a "military operation," in the sense that it was a pretty ridiculous thing, a night raid on the association head office, with the intention of taking the files. In practice, we worked at it an awful lot, as though it were a great military operation, whereas in fact we went in at night simply by breaking down the door like burglars, stealing the files, writing slogans. Incidentally, with some hilarious moments, because it was dark, we had torches,

> and this comrade had on boots which squeaked terribly . . . all going stealthily round the office, with these terrible squeaking shoes . . . we were laughing as we came out.

It appears as well in Tosi's and Grena's histories:

> My first action was done by a group involved in a project of controlling the territory, it was a "proletarian perquisition," as we called it then, of a local police station. And there the worst happened . . . I had to leave home, because I'd lost my driving license in the police station, I was wanted by the police . . . and so I ended up a fugitive from justice! (Tosi).
>
> We weren't brilliant, they were just small hold-ups which we managed to do reasonably well, respecting the criteria of not causing any serious trouble for ourselves nor for others. . .
>
> Now and again it happened that we went to do a hold-up, and someone else had already done it. I remember one morning when we had got ready, and then at the last check, at a certain point I saw the helicopter overhead, and I said: "look, they must have done the hold-up already"; I said it as a joke, but in fact it was true! Or once I remember that I was saying to a comrade: 'look, let's go this way, and I'll show you a nice little place where we just might be able to do something, to plan something" and right at that moment—luckily we hadn't crossed the road yet—we saw loads of police cars arriving! (Grena).

Sometimes the way in which an anecdote is told produces the comic effect, echoing the tones of self-irony common in the speech of present day's younger people. We can hear these tones in, for example, Anna's reference to meetings of Prima Linea which were held at her house, which neither she nor her husband had the right to attend due to their position in the group's hierarchy:

> it was rather a nuisance, too, to have to go out at half past eleven because there was a meeting in the house, and him and me taking the dogs for a walk in the park!

Self-irony is audible in various other comments as well:

> . . . a hold-up done in stages because nothing ever worked (Anna).

> . . . even in the summer, if we went down to the coast, we went there to do hold-ups, so we used to think of going to the seaside as a terrible chore (Tosi).

> I always managed to get caught, whatever I did! (Graglia).

Cora remembers her parents' visit to prison, when they had just leaned about her clandestine activity after her arrest: "the first thing they said when they came to see me: 'we thought you were intelligent.'"

These tones were to change as the narrators described the later periods, when self-irony gave way to other forms of expression or to silence. Here the women recall that element which they defined as being "on parade" in the sense that for the purpose of self-representation they select and display those aspects of the imaginary dimension which, due to their spectacularity, lend themselves to portrayal on the symbolic plane. As I have already mentioned, this symbolism is impoverished, overbalanced by an exteriorization that accompanies a rather uninspiring daily routine ("the life of a commercial traveler" [Ronconi]). There are certain characteristics both in living and in narrating all these experiences which are connected with gender, according to a hypothesis that I will try to make clear.

Perhaps in our age there has been a short circuit between the dream-memory dimension and the film-image dimension, a general process of which this very short circuit in terrorism is only one example. And although we do not have enough data to carry out the comparison that might verify the following proposition, I venture to say that the women's narration makes particular insistence upon the sequence of connections between the fantastic and the literary or cinematic aspect. One reason might lie in the fact that in recent centuries European culture has admitted women into the public sphere in the realms of literature and the spectacle (the novel, the theater, and later the cinema and television) rather than in the domain of politics. The process has left traces in the imaginary and above all in ways of self-representation, accentuated during events involving great tension, such as those we are analyzing. Here is one clue:

> I don't like the vindictive attitude. What was the process that brought me to look for another way of expressing myself in relation to things? Instead of the relationship to the male model . . . . All my story as a women comes back to me, like scenes from a film and like my own reflections—but it doesn't come out in my interview! (Grena).

The difficulty of talking about oneself and connecting the dimension of self-reflection with that of the image manifests the series of connections that we have already mentioned.

In the accounts of male terrorists, the imaginary appears to be connected to the experience of the constrictions of jail, but less frequently.[16] In the interviews of the women this process seems to be a part of a complex reelaboration that takes place in the unconscious, as well as the conscious level:

> I gradually went back, back, right back to my childhood, because, well, in jail I did it spontaneously, and everything seemed to be relevant. Then I remember that a series of dreams followed each period I was thinking about, each episode, each phase, it wasn't a linear thing, and they were a certain type of dreams, which

> took me to places connected to my childhood, or to places . . . and it meant that the problem had taken on a different characteristic inside . . . (Grena).

> . . . in 1982 there was the gap between dream and reality which was terrible, in the sense that sometimes I was dreaming and I was afraid of my own thoughts (Tosi).

Imprisonment probably intensifies the importance of dreams, as we can infer form the type of reference to dreams that we find in the life-histories:

> I once dreamt that I was in a huge museum gallery. At a certain point, two people arrived with something wrapped up in paper, they unwrapped this thing, it was a frame. They took hold of this frame and hung it up on a nail, an empty frame. And I have always connected this dream to . . . my relationship with the organization, at that moment—that is, to the fact that I was hanging an empty frame on the nail. I woke up and I connected the dreams to this type of state of mind (Giulia).

Interiorization, with no possibility of interpreting it adequately, encourages the old types of dream interpretation, belonging to traditional oneiromancy, which takes dreams as objective signs and presentiments rather than referring them to the individual's subjectivity.[17] Anna recounts a dream she had just after entering jail:

> I fell asleep for a moment, and I remember this very vivid dream which I had, in less than three seconds, that three seagulls flew away from my eyebrows. I remember saying: "how should I interpret it?" "that I will be inside for three years." In May I will have been inside for seven years!

Tosi interprets one of her dreams in a similarly objective way:

> There was a dream I had once, that at a certain point I found myself outside, there were a lot of stalls with lots of food, lots of clothes, it was night time, at a certain point the sun came out and I said: 'well! how odd for the sun to be out at night,' but I was calm. I always connect this to my first period of leave, which was shortly afterward . . . I was already under stress . . .

Although my analysis requires further documentation and further investigation, I can summarize its general direction by outlining the following hypotheses. There appear to be various stages: after 1968 and its "power to the imagination" policy, we find a dilation of the imaginary concerning the imminence of radical social upheavals; this mentality was shared by part of the new left and was associated with a panoply of heroic figures protecting the oppressed. At the same time the primacy of action was mythicized by the youth movements and probably accentuated by the misunderstanding of what the 1968 movements had proposed in terms of shifting the boundaries between theory and praxis, the political and the private knowledge and action.[18] These shared mentalities gave way—through collective and individual choices—to developments that led to the contraction of subjectivity: the gradual or sudden elimination of the distance between the imaginary and the real; the growth of the confusion that rigidifies objectivity—so much so that it can be attacked only with violence—and the channeling, with no outlet, of subjectivity into mere repetition; the confusion or loss of individual identity, and the concomitant compulsion to rely ever more strongly on the group. Grafted onto these processes, the experience of imprisonment—dramatic because it entailed evil done to others and to the self—sometimes caused further rigidity, the inability to go forward or backward, and the paralysis of subjectivity, which was evident in the narrators' obstinate silences or in their repetition of language belonging to the past. In some cases, imprisonment prompted them to redefine the boundaries between dreams and reality, a process that caused suffering and produced vacillation but also forced the subject into regression and retrospection, with the positive consequences these actions imply. At this stage group solidarity again certainly played a role, but whereas previously it had acted lethally, it now had a positive effect. Dissociation spread along the network of sociality and cohesion, prompting individuals to reassess their own experiences, and those of others; these reassessments have been difficult and are still underway.

From all this process, the memory selects some messages, sometimes with internal contradictions, and it consigns them to those who are willing to interpret them. Within the processes I have described above, certain pathways are typical of women, in terms of image and expression. Such pathways often lead to an exteriorized female identity ("on parade") of false emancipation, in part because they aim at equality with men in the existing world, and in part because their actions reenact traditional ideologies and mythologies in new contexts: the sacrificial mother, the splitting of feeling and reason, the manipulative capacity to hold together social and family relationships, the skill for organization and logistics, which women always place at the service of others, not of themselves. But this critique, concerning this group of women, has to be extended to the wider cultural context. The sharing of cultural liability and the accentuation of the imaginary do not relieve any individual of responsibility for decisions he or she has taken, but it places those decisions in a historical context.

> At the entrance of the Nuove prison there is a stone that I observe while I wait for my colleagues, and I reflect on how times have changed:

IN THIS PRISON
BETWEEN 1922 and 1945
THOUSANDS OF ITALIAN ANTIFASCISTS WERE IMPRISONED

MAY THEIR SACRIFICE NOT BE FORGOTTEN
MAY THE MEMORY REMAIN OF THE HARD PRICE
PAID TO REGAIN FREEDOM

NATIONAL ASSOCIATION OF ITALIAN ANTIFASCIST VICTIMS OF POLITICAL PERSECUTION — TURIN COUNCIL

I ask myself about the continuity, in the imaginary dimension, of a distorted idea of freedom, and about the responsibility, perhaps unconscious, which these mental processes imply historically. I am surprised to find myself, with my attention distracted as I wait, thinking again of an intellectuality of the new left, from which I come, of its limits, its taboos, the restrictions on conceiving the laicality of culture. All these ideas are tested in the experience of the seminar.

In the entrance hall, where the prison vans are stopped and checked while we wait for our permits to be verified in the registers, there is another stone, disquieting in another way:

WITHIN THESE SEVERE WALLS
SAINT GIUSEPPE CAFASSO SMILES PATERNALLY
POINTING TO THE WAYS OF THE LORD
FOR THE TRUE COMFORT
OF THOSE WHO SUFFER AND THE DEJECTED
1960

Here, too, I wonder whether our culture is able to comfort anyone, to suggest anything to him or her, to give any answers to the problems we find inside this jail.

"IGNAVA RATIO"

These life-stories reveal other stratifications of memory that include accounts of personal life and of historical experience. I think it is particularly useful to record these elements in order to document various types of continuity between the preceding period and the choices the narrators made in their lives. Among the continuities are memories of family traditions:

> I have always been fascinated by the figure of my maternal grandfather over the years: I knew him through my mother's eyes and through her tales, so to some extent I mythologized him, I suppose; but let's say he was the anticonformist of the family. My grandfather was a sculptor, he taught for years at the Academy

> of Art, he had been an irredentist, he had come from Istria and settled in Venice. He was a very handsome man, with long black hair and blue eyes. . . . in my mother's family a series of cousins, uncles and aunts take after him, and they are all very original (Ronconi).

> My family have always been communists. . . there has always been this base, not only in my family, but in the whole area [lower Po Valley]. . . some of my relatives had been partisans . . . this was the mold (Tosi).

> My grandfather is an old socialist peasant of the lower Po Valley, one of those who have been through the 1912 revolt, who deserted during the First World War, who rejected the title of Knight of Vittorio Veneto. My grandfather was a follower of Turati. My father had been a town councilor for a long time and had had experience in the Resistance, he had to go underground for quite a time. Then I have a series of uncles who were captured, who were sent to concentration camps in Germany because they were with the partisans. They were all socialists (Mantovani).

Besides—or in addition to—affirming a familial continuity, memory draws from that cultural and political environment characterized by the phrase "militant antifascism". Susanna Ronconi recalls the praxis and the discussions at the end of the 1960s, when she was already enrolled at the University of Padua and experienced the "massacre at Piazza Fontana as a significant date" in her development:

> . . . it is something that I felt and understood immediately, this idea that a part of the state is hand in glove with the clandestine fascist right wing . . . the problem of "watching out for fascists" was something that I almost immediately got into the habit of doing, and aggressively, too, in the sense that it was something I enjoyed doing.

This is a direct derivation from ideas characterized by a sort of antifascism, filtered through political interpretations, which point to the immediacy of action. Both Ronconi and Mantovani emphasize how important their association with the Padua group of the new leftist Potere Operaio (Worker's Power) in the early 1970s was for their development. Other women who experienced the same political socialization some years later, in the Turin branch of Potere Operaio, provide rather similar accounts. In the later period, however, the contrast between the tension in the group and a decreasingly militant context was more marked, and this contrast perhaps ends up making the position of the later militants' more extreme. On the one hand, the women remember their step into politics as the existential answer to a deep-seated malaise:

> for me it was a place where at last I felt united with myself, a situation and a set of relationships in which I was no longer separated from the things I did. I no longer had problems with my body, with my body language, I was no longer shy . . . I was able to speak to men and to women . . . (Graglia).
>
> I started to study, I remember that intellectually I was wide-awake, because as well as studying those academic subjects which most interested me I was also studying and reading quantities of essays. I had to read them, because the meetings of *Potere Operaio* were something that, if you hadn't read the complete works of certain people, you couldn't understand . . . so I had to! I remember a very pleasant period. . . You had to have read Tronti, Negri, the *Grundrisse*, I also remember an entire issue of *Quaderni piacentini* about the plan for development of the chemical industry (Cora).

On the other hand, they recall a sense of growing impotence ("you either destroy everything or you get nowhere") over the closing up of political spaces and the drying up of the social struggle:

> . . . in those years, 1976-77, it seemed as though the central issue had become another . . . politics, class struggle, subjectivity, liberation, were all parts of a strategy of violence, as though this could include and resolve all problems (Graglia).

The narrators refer to both continuities—the antifascist tradition and the environment of the political groups—in describing a cultural state in which violence was "natural":

> . . . in *Potere Operaio* there was a fraction that talked about force, the use of violence connected to the masses and to strikes. For me this was very natural. Violence on marches never provoked any type of breach in me. Perhaps because I have always lived with violence . . . from the violence of nature . . . I don't know, for me it was a natural thing. With my parents who had been through the wars. I remember how aware and how enthusiastic I was when I went out to throw my first Molotov (Mantovani).

Among people who shared the mentality we are describing—and in the 1970s this mentality was not limited to those who had decided in favor of the armed struggle—certain reactions to the use of violence were also perfectly "natural"; violence was to be answered with violence. These reactions were in fact so natural that even in the prisoners' recollections, we can hear on almost total lack of awareness of reflection. Mantovani again, talking about violent action during demonstrations:

> . . . at first I was sure that it was a very natural thing, and so I went home and told my mother about it, sending her into a complete panic. At the end I stopped

> telling her, but only because it upset her. My father . . . he went pale. I said to him: "At demonstrations we've done this . . . and this . . . and this." My father said to me: "You are mad, you'll never get anywhere." He told me I would end up in jail. He knew it better than I did myself. He said: "You'll never get anywhere because we have already tried and it is impossible. . . ."

Another speaker, aware that her father, ex-partisan and former member of the PCI [Italian Communist Party], had gone through a "crisis of the values of solidarity and collectivity," recalls her attempts to reestablish continuity between her father's past and her own political activity, including the violence:

> I was always so presumptuous as to explain to my father that I was right . . . I tried to explain to him that communism, the class struggle, the revolution, were right, to my father . . . (Graglia).

This naturalness in the prisoners' attitude toward violence related to the naturalness of the affection between the members of a group of comrades—essential in order to live in the rarefaction of relationships in the city—so the step into violence comes about with no break on the mental or behavioral plane:

> . . . in February-March 1977 I started to get into contact with the *Brigate Rosse*—there was no precise moment, they were just people I had met—workers in particular—who lived within the large area of *Autonomia* [Autonomy], with whom there was no difficulty in talking about violence. Partly because of the environment, and partly because of the climate of those years, it was nothing abnormal, nothing strange.
>
> At first it wasn't presented in terms of "come with us" . . . it was presented as discussion about a whole series of problems which continued the existing relationship . . . .
>
> I often used these things, theories, etc. as a "passport" to participate in the relationships with these comrades.
>
> You see, if I look back, I don't feel as though I had made a big step in my life, compared to the previous period. I found myself in the middle of it, and I accepted finding myself there. No one forced me to do anything (Giulia).

The tone of these accounts manifests a sort of indifference toward the self rather than others, as though the experiences these women had undergone or the prospects they faced justified nothing more than resignation, and acceptance of the mechanism of enduring and retaliating. This tone is evident in Carmen De Stefano's description of a visit to an imprisoned comrade whom she was having a love affair:

> In February 1981 I went twice to see this comrade in jail. I didn't feel any pain. When I went into the political section of the "Nuove" goal, he was there, and

> many other comrades, but I felt no pain. Really, the only time I felt the sort of pain which wrings your heart, I think I only felt that when I had to leave Campobasso [her home town].

It appears as well in Anna's recollections of some demonstrations that took place in 1977-78:

> . . . every time we found ourselves going down Corso Francia [outside the headquarters of the Italian fascist party] and they were using tear gas against us, my way of moving was deliberate. I wasn't afraid of what was happening, but I was outside it. In discussions I had heard during the week about what would have happened, somehow or other it was something I was completely aware of, even if I had not choice, and I had never expressed myself for or against. I seemed to know anyhow why and how it happened, in an incredibly natural way.
>
> The happy times were few, when the fact of being together, of expressing ourselves, of seeing us all together, was happy, they were very few. But the overriding feeling which I had inside was a feeling of anxiety, like a character in a soap opera would say: all of this is inevitable because it is all inevitable.

And we hear this tone again in Anna's account of her meeting with a clandestine organization, through her husband:

> . . . one evening two people arrived—it was a boy and a girl—they shook my hand and said "Please to meet you, I'm from Prima Linea." I said: "Pleased to meet you, I'm Anna." We sat down on the bed, there was some wine, I offered them some wine, and this comrade started off on a very long monologue, it was interminable, terrible, and I understood afterward that it was about the basic theory of the proletarian network, of the need to have patrols and build a sort of communication within the district which connected the broken links, and the philosophical explanations of expropriation, and so on. Now these things were always absolutely clear to me. I had always thought that the proletariat should have control of their territory.

This sort of language seems to me deeply marked by the characteristics of Anna's particular generation and social class; she was born in 1960 in the Mirafiori Nord quarter of Turin, her father was a FIAT worker, her mother a telephone operator. In her life-history she has "no memory of the time before the elementary school," where she finds herself "the last to learn to write," despite her expressive abilities, demonstrated by the passage quoted here. Her language expresses a state of mind at once of renunciation and of revolt; it is that of a person who sees herself as a stranger, who responds to signals, finds herself a place in a march, accepts what happens to her because she has no hope that anything else could happen to her. Nevertheless, she does not reject responsibility nor awareness: she responds by reducing political mediation to a minimum. But in so doing she duplicates what already exists, including violence.

In these conditions, even the search for a female identity can take the form of duplicating what is given, however courageous the women's very presence may be:

> I want to be a woman inside the things that men do. But I have always had the ambition of bringing a feminine stamp to it. Starting from my mother . . . women had to have the right to say what they thought (Mantovani).

Operating from this position, these women rejected consciousness-raising and the separate activities of the women's movement, in general, for their particular state of mind was determined by anxiety about acting, impatience with "just" talking, and confusion about their aspirations for total change. This psychological condition appeared not only in women within terrorist groups but also in groups such as Autonomia which had tendencies toward widespread violence, rather than the concentrated or focused violence of terrorist groups. Curiosity about the women's movement resulted in anger and antagonism. The study of written memories provides an outline for research on these themes. Giancarla Ceppi, for example, describes how, after going through Autonomia, she tried to approach feminism:

> I wanted to go into the square to see the women who 'wanted to take back the night' and who were dancing and singing songs alien to me. I suddenly got into a rage: everything I saw was inadequate and inconsistent. I ran to shut myself in the house in the dark, I didn't want to see anything. I felt all the violence and force compressed against the whole world growing inside me.[19]

Her account reveals "curiosity and envy" toward women, as well as her suffering due to her awareness of an internal contradiction: she is a "woman who has lived through a story of emancipation with suffering and passion," yet she is unable to share a way or a dialogue with other women; she believes she is "a militant first of all." Yet she does not understand for what and with whom she is militating.

We hear similar accents in our oral autobiographies. Barbara Graglia remembers that in discussions with a feminist comrade close to Potere Operaio, she found what seemed to her to be "artificial problems" characterized by "partiality" against "a comprehensive policy of revolution," in an opposition that could go as far as physical action:

> I participated in assemblies at the University, it was the beginning of 1977 and I used to say: "enough of consciousness-raising, there's a campaign against abortion going on". . . .

> For us at that time, the most advanced point of view was, on a march, perhaps, to burn, to break windows of cinemas showing blue films, or to go in and leave a smoke bomb under the seat, Molotovs, the so-called *lilli*, and then to talk against anti-abortionist gynecologists. We went to the Sant'Anna [gynecological hospital] and we broke up the head-doctor's study—that is, everything had an enormous appearance of liberation, the gestures we made.

Appearance, exactly. The written and oral recollections of that period and of those attitudes convey precisely the sense of appearing to move and act and yet totally failing to affect the deeper existing order; increasing the pain, material and spiritual, caused by armed violence but not initiating any process of renewal:

> In this mass of energy there was something that distorted and modified reality, even though it did not in fact displace it (Anna).

Thus the alleged feminization of the armed struggle produced distortions but not real changes, as some of the actions carried out or planned by our interviewees illustrate: for example, an attack on the head office of an association of professional women was prepared by four women but thwarted by a male leader of Prima Linea:

> . . . we were ready to go and set this place on fire. This comrade arrived and said: "It's totally out of the question," and we had a discussion in the middle of the road, practically, even though we already had the Molotov all ready. A degree of masculinity on his part which was very strong.

Or the action carried out against the female wardens of the jail, in a later period:[20]

> . . . we thought it was right that this thing, which concerned our specific female experience, be carried out directly and entirely by a group of women . . . because it seemed that the classic figure of the jailer could only be a man. From inside the jail though, it was clear that power could be wielded by women.

The judgment of the more lucid women is different:

> . . . to my mind these things [alleged "feminist" violence] were not particularly significant. I was sincerely rather disenchanted and saw no point in some comrades cutting out for themselves this feminine space. It seemed to me substantially an imaginary operation, which didn't change anything regarding our lives (Ronconi).

Ronconi continues by arguing that her position was connected with a previous "drastic decision," documented in her life-history: the decision to abandon feminism for the armed struggle because the two were truly divergent. This episode—her decision to go underground and her separation from her mother—marks a crucial point in the narrative.

> I went away saying: "I'm going away for a month," but I suppose I embraced her in a particular way . . . it was rather a treacherous kiss. And I went away at six in the evening one day . . . autumn-winter 1974, and the last thing I did was to join a demonstration of women, a torch-light procession . . . and I cried right through it, no one understood why. I went away, very torn by this, but very sure of what I was doing, too (Ronconi).

The life-stories we have collected demonstrate a fundamental feature, which also appears in other accounts of similar experiences: the progression from general activity within the movement, which includes some forms of violence (throwing Molotovs during marches, theft, destruction of the offices of other organizations perceived as hostile, threats and beatings, the so-called "expropriations"), to a specialization, for which it is necessary to go underground and which goes as far as armed robberies, kidnapping, and later wounding and murder. This progression becomes increasingly less noticeable to those who act, as the first type becomes more accentuated and more common; accordingly, the distance between the two diminishes, and the required leap from the one to the other, becomes less perceptible.[21] A few years may be enough to accelerate this progression (consider, for example, the changes from 1974 to 1977).

Tosi, too, recalls a "last feminist march" in which she participated in Bologna on March 8, 1977, which was the culmination of a "split" between her commitment to the trade union and to feminism on the one hand and to "an extremist strategy" on the other. That demonstration, Tosi says, represented a turning point because "it was attacked by the police and they beat up one of the women demonstrators.' One effect of this incident was to interrupt the debate on violence within feminist groups; another was to divide the youth movement, in which conflicting aspirations had coexisted confusedly for some time: "those who had at that time chosen violence, let us call it that" split apart from those who chose other paths, here, too, almost "naturally."

For historians who hope to reconstruct the psychomental environment of the second half of the 1970s, one of the clues provided by memory is what I have defined generically as the continuity of the cultural climate of the new left. To explore this continuity further we can take at least two directions. The first ought to follow an empirical definition of continuity and contiguity, exploring the mentalities and attitudes of people close to political violence though not directly implicated in it. This is a difficult theme, difficult even to define, since terms such as 'sympathizer' or "supporter" seem inadequate to describe these individuals.

Certain literary sources can help us here. One of the most interesting works about the decade straddling 1980 is *La mia signora* by Ida Farè (1986), in which a female protagonist, who belongs to the new left and works on a leftist daily newspaper like *il manifesto*, is put in charge of a survey "on the violence which produces bloodstains at the University, on the bridge over the Tiber, on the steps of the church an in many of the City's squares" (see note 22). The journalist investigates violence, she discovers it is part of a movement and the result of the "spirit of the times," and she finds herself invaded by it: "she absorbs and becomes blurred" with the "thing." Her lack of clarity causes her to "sympathize": a "direct and hidden thread . . . reaches her, touches her by vague exchanges, desires, emotions" (see note 22). The result will be her departure from the newspaper and her return to Milan, in residual areas of the movement, at the end of the 1970s.

At this point she finds herself writing in her diary:

> I have discovered that half of the people who come to the bar with me, in the evening, live by hold-ups, and the other half treat their women badly, half have a power mania and have entered politics by chance. Am I pure? or must I search in the mix for the part, the half, the slices of a good idealist? (Farè 1986, see note 22).

The novel, despite some weaknesses, manages to convey a climate of confusion, of incomprehension, of "scrimmage," seen by someone who might become a female subject.[22] Another novel (*Le passioni di Petra*, by Mels Freni [1985]), rather more fragile, attempts to reconstruct the parable of a young Sicilian woman who goes to the University of Padua to study psychology through the experience of political violence. Her companion dies, and she at last finds a life in the relationship with her son and in running her father's building site:

> [S]he found herself building a bridge between two generations where the distance between them was that entire time in which she had lived in the flux of passions which had nourished her years (Freni 1985).

The reconstruction is not very convincing historically or culturally, and the novel proposes a banal interpretation of a problem of the times: the roads taken by women born in the 1940s and 1950s in their search for a new subjectivity. The reconciliation in the latter novel is too quick and inconsistent (Freni 1985, p. 132). Less optimistic novels, such as *Generazione* by Giorgio Van Straten (1987) and *Via Po* by Sandro Medici (1987) offer interpretations of the cultural climate in the years following the height of Italy's violence; these works illustrate the sense of emptiness, regret, and uncertainty characteristic of the 1980s, but both have male protagonists. It would perhaps be worth looking again at a book by Dacia Mariani (1984), *Il treno per Helsinki*, which, though not one of this author's most successful works, proposes a more disillusioned and ironic interpretation of a woman's capacity for survival, when faced with the disasters of her age. The novel concludes with the image of a friend of the protagonist who has died in the so-called armed struggle because he had "believed he could change the world against the desire of the people," and at the very end the protagonist looks at "a potato in its shiny white and tender compactness," remembering a lost love.

Similar excursions through literary sources and memories might deepen our historical understanding of a particular phenomenon (e.g., the persistence of a youth movement despite the absence of wider social movements) during the uncertain period following the extinction of the left-wing groups, themselves casualties of the post-1968 climate. But if we are to understand the last twenty years, it is essential that we pursue another line of research, one that involves the history of ideas. We must investigate which traditions of thought are present in the youth movements of the 1960s and 1970s, in what form they appear and with which contradictions and variations. And we must do so with a resolute critique designed to break down that mental laziness connected with so many "revolutionary" ideologies.

The way has been opened for us by the radical thought of Hannah Arendt, who stressed very strongly how certain philosophies yield when faced with violence and its arbitrary nature, both of which are, therefore, taken for granted. Among the attitudes, Arendt criticizes is "the Marxist rhetoric of the New Left," which contrasts with Marx's position regarding violence and is modeled on the "absolutely non-Marxist conviction, proclaimed by Mao Tse Tung, according to whom 'power comes from the barrel of a gun.'" One of the best-known expressions of that rhetoric is Sartre's preface to Fanon's *The Wretched of the Earth*, which, according to Hannah Arendt (1985), is an example of the "unconscious detachment of the New Left from Marxism."

This detachment consists exactly in "a progression towards violence", which Arendt sees as the reflection, not contested by philosophical thought, of a situation of fact: the suicidal development of modern weapons. The youth movements are made up of the first generation to grow up in the shadow of the atomic bomb. Their most representative spokesmen, such as Sartre, are unaware that political "revolutionary" theories advocating violence actually duplicate existing violence. They are not afraid of writing sentences such as: "He who shoots a European kills two birds with one stone . . . the result: for a dead man, a free man." Rereading these words of Sartre's, thinking again of how they expressed a state of mind that was widely shared in the 1970s, I cannot avoid associating them with slogans current among the Italian new left in that decade and in the following one drenched with "militant antifascism": truculent sentences, bloody, arrogant.

With her libertarian thought, Arendt (1985) manages to invert the supine character of a culture that has accepted violence itself as the only answer to violence: 'If it were true, the vendetta would be the panacea for most of our ills," she observes, demonstrating the absurdity of any "revolutionary" belief that reaches such an extreme point. And she proceeds to emphasize the distance between power and violence, the inability of violence to interrupt the robot-like processes in the field of human affairs, the disappearance of the value of the individual within collective violence. In Hannah Arendt's way of proceeding, the net distance established between political action—a faculty that humanity is perhaps about to lose—and violence, which is growing in relation to that loss, seems to me essential. In her essay *On Violence* and in its appendix, the "old combination of violence, life and creativity present in the unquiet mental situation of today's generation" emerges completely unmasked (Arendt 1985, pp. 175-177, 189, 211, 236-237).

That was the generation of 1968. The depth of Arendt's analysis comes from her capacity to recognize the moral values and public happiness of which the movements of 1968 were bearers, while at the same time recognizing their darker aspects of yielding to the existing order through the acceptance of the logic of violence and death. Only the force of a similar dialectic understanding will allow us to achieve a constructive reexamination of the thought of the new left which illuminates the continuities that convinced some young people they must immediately take up violence and the instrument of death. Our aim is not to assign guilt to individual theorists nor to unload responsibility onto them; the guilt and responsibility belong to whomever acts, if he or she wants to be considered a subject in the full sense. Our purpose is rather to criticize an area of thought in its entirety, including the distances and approaches its development has involved.

A similar historical critique of the ideologies is the basis for further study. Without such a critique we cannot resolve the dilemmas posed by the conflicts we have heard narrated, for example, by women who made different decisions and who justified them with opposing ideologies: on the one hand, violence would be extraneous to women; on the other, women would be able to administrate violence in a more detached way than men. In both cases, the women would appeal to a naturalness that does not exist; or else they call "natural' something imposed by the existing world, such as women's presumed pacificism. The sphere of existence (Lebenswelt) is confused with the sphere of power; the creativity characteristic of political action and thought, which are political exactly because they do not simply react to the existing oppression, is lost.

The mental attitude of that impels one to protest to the bitter end is also part of the mere reaction of duplication.[23] Examples can be found in the field we are dealing with, where left-wing culture shows great poverty. It cannot pronounce words such as "repentance" and "forgiveness" because it believes them to be the exclusive heritage of certain historical religions against which it polemicizes; it does not realize that these words represent human values that are potentially universal. It is true, nevertheless, that, for its realization, such potential requires realization, a reformulation of those values in less objective and metaphorical terms, through a psychoanalytical and psychological perspective. These types of investigations know and analyze the inner commotion; they call it enantiodromia (a radical change that turns a life upside down) rather than conversion, but apart from the technicalities of language, they provide conceptual instruments that afford a view of cultural and psychic processes in our times (see, e.g., Musatti 1986).

No one can be legally asked or forced to repent or to forgive; such matters may not be the province of the judge or the lawyer. However, they are of interest not only to human beings in general but to those particular individuals concerned with didactics or history; it is important for everyone to contribute to and construct languages that express a critical rethinking of painful experiences and wrong ideas. Such would be the attempt to redefine "repentance" and "forgiveness" along lines coherent with their etymological meanings, but in human, rather than divine terms: to give that "something more" that is not required, beyond and above paying the penalty.[24] Intellectuals, not just those who have undergone or carried out material and spiritual violence, must contribute to this cultural effort. I believe that a certain language—and the mental attitudes it presupposes—the use of terms such as "victims," *pentitismo* (the phenomenon of the so-called "repentants"), *gambizzare* (knee-capping), duplicates violence and thus contrasts the effort to reach a real intersubjective communication on events and processes that are so tragic.

The seminar is held in a large bare room on the ground floor, separated from the outer walls by a narrow concrete courtyard. At each session we arrange the tables and stools—there are no chairs—to create a space for study and discussion.

The same room is the only covered social area for the "nonpolitical" prisoners, who are much more numerous than the "political" ones. One day we meet in the courtyard, we lecturers, the female wardens, and the members of our seminar, waiting for the "nonpolitical prisoners" to go out of the door on the opposite side; the one on our side is still locked. But inside they refuse to leave the meeting room. A violent exchange of words starts, and one of the prisoners who is with us joins in with a resolute voice and in no uncertain terms. From inside, noise, a jumble of words; we hear one phrase: "First you do a massacre, then you have a seminar about it."

It is all over in a few minutes. During the seminar, the discussion includes a reflection on political violence and ordinary violence. The presence of a woman imprisoned for a nonpolitical crime makes the subject more delicate, but also more immediate. I start a debate on left-wing culture, which has made it easier for us to accept a political assassination than an ordinary murder—if the cause, of course, is just. But I ask myself whether the usual reasoning that a just cause justifies violence should not be overturned to become: how far can a cause continue to be just despite the fact that it includes violence? It seems to me that the more thoughtful partisans I have known and listened to spoke not with triumphalism but with pain of the violence that they had been obliged to commit—a momentary suspension, forced and against all will, of universal human values. Perhaps only twenty years later a revisited antifascism has elaborated different slogans and attitudes, which excluded from value whoever was not a member of the group, such as fascists or police. In the progression to aggressive expressions and gestures, Stalin's heritage must have been considerable. But even the Resistance to Nazifascism has not been sufficiently clearly discussed on this level.

In the background there is the crescendo of violence throughout the world, the greatest potential for war there has ever been, the widespread day-to-day violence, in events, in behavior, in the symbolic realm. But each of us must start from the criticial revision of the historical tradition in which he or she finds himself/herself to reach a critique of violence in the modern world.

WOMEN'S STORIES

The prisoners' memories about female identity emerge in fragments. In their interviews some women say they had important models in their own families: the sdaura[25] aunt in the big Emilian farm (Tosi); the grandmother from southern Italy, who sat at the head of the table and was the first to be served, founder of a family of "women who all worked" (Giulia); the intellectual mother, rebellious but nevertheless fragile (Ronconi). Others portray very distant mothers, with whom they had either no contact at all or only very delayed contact, for instance, after the period of youth. This second attitude is not unusual in the self-representations of the generation of 1968.

Even the discovery of a specific female identity—beyond the illusory mimicking of male models, in the organization and in the armed struggle—comes later than the fundamental decision to get involved in political violence.

> The first people to die, in our group . . . the first to be killed . . . were women. This was a great shock . . . because in some ways we spontaneously assumed that this must be deliberate, in the sense that it was the weak element which was attacked, let's say, the "heart" . . . and it made us think a great deal (Mantovani).

This discovery often takes place in prison, both through contact with other members of political organizations—one's own and others—and through contact with the so-called 'nonpolitical" prisoners. Barbara Graglia recalls how she discovered a female universe in consciousness-raising meetings of a kind where each women told the story of her life. "I was very curious about the stories of the women, of the "nonpolitical" prisoners with their stories", she says. And referring to a "sign of the times" she sees their attitudes as "a manifestation of a way of becoming the subject of one's own life, even if on a distorted ground, the ground of . . . delinquency."

Graglia also remembers the disapproval of a comrade, who "strongly advised us to study a certain series of books, well, to commit ourselves to studying instead of wasting time in gossip and having coffee with these women."

A phase of insistence on motherhood begins in jail for some of the women. For others, however, female pride is still to be found in intellectual and political activity. This divergence gives rise to some misunderstandings, Ronconi notes:

> Some were already trying for a baby, while I kept looking at the guard on the wall to see when I could escape . . . and indeed, I committed a gaffe, a historic faux pas with G. I must tell you about this . . . because toward the end of the trial in Florence, G. went to into hospital for a scan because she was pregnant and when she came back—we were all shut in our cells—and through the peep-hole she said "two" . . . of course she meant two twins, but I didn't even think about that. I turned toward the others in the cell and said: "God, only two policemen as escort!" and I was very happy with the news: so maybe you can, perhaps on the way to the hospital you can escape!

In fact a new awareness of a female identity and a way of reconsidering one's own story will only really develop through a general acceptance of the differences between women, not through an imitation of male models.

In a final group report, a few members of the seminar state that they had not wanted to make "the mistake of seeking femininity only in those moments when the very limitation of male models caused feelings of uneasiness and difficulty". Rightly so. But the life-stories show that certain difficult situations have in fact been crucial moments of differentiation, starting points for a process that has linked the woman's perception of her body to her own individuality. Some accounts of abortions the women underwent when living underground, illustrate these turning points. In their stories solitude, suffering, and the desire to find other women characterize that memory—today—as the beginning of a different perception of the self.

The insistence on diversity becomes a recurrent theme for reflection in the most recent period, which includes prison, "dissociation" from the armed struggle, and research into the past. I think that all these considerations converge more or less directly in one perception: that female identity cannot in the end be defined on the basis of behavior or of empirical attitude. Neither the forms of emancipation as such nor the general reference to other women make the foundation of an identity possible. This identity lies rather in the continual shifts between oneself and other subjects and among various elements of one's self. The process takes place within the horizon of a common gender, with a critical attention to one's own development and through more or less successful relationships. Such a concept of identity is not governed by any established rule: women do not have to be in any particular way in order to be subjects; the sole criterion is the individuation of each woman, her full recognition of her self. Attention to individuation sets off a dialectic of equality and difference with others, in which both terms, alternately, are indispensable to the process of self-recognition.

To some extent this sort of exercise also took place in our seminar. One of the ways in which we experienced it was in the comparison between different life-stories, including the experience of one woman, whom I shall call Viola, who was in prison for a "nonpolitical" crime. Viola was born in 1957, in a lower middle-class family from southern Italy. She attended the "D'Azeglio" classical high school and joined the new leftist Lotta Continua (Continuous Struggle); she took part in this group's political activity at the Singer and Fimit factories and the occupation of flats on a council estate at the Falchera, a working-class suburb of Turin, in 1975. In 1976 she approached the women's movement, within which she joined a photography group, a consciousness-raising group, and a theater group. In the same period she enrolled at the Faculty of Humanities to read Fine Art. In the winter of 1977, Viola made a decisive choice for her life:

> I began an affair with this girl, it was very important to me, and therefore relations with my family became something like: "let's hope they won't know anything about this, let's hope they won't guess, let's hope they won't meddle" . . . there was a quite a definite choice on my part, out of love, too, of course, but anyway a very definite decision to have a gay relationship.

Describing the following period, up to 1981, Viola tells of a "search for ... areas of separateness," through travel and studies, in physical spaces and in culture. All these activities were abruptly interrupted by something that she does not explain to us, on the express advice of her lawyer.[26]

For us interviewers, this story posed a basic problem. In some ways it was very similar to the other accounts (it entailed the search for a female identity and described political work in the confused area of dissolving movements and groups), but in other ways it was very different, because of the meaning of the narrator's actions and the results of these actions. It questioned the usual hierarchy of crimes, the claim that politics can justify violence. Here, of course, the fundamental difference between right policy and wrong policy had to be introduced, but even in this case I felt reluctant to accept the supremacy of a political cause too easily. These observations did not lead us to any specific conclusion, but they stimulated further reflection on our own experiences and on the need to put the view of violence prevailing in our culture and time into its historical context.[27] Nonetheless, it is not satisfactory to reduce every king of violence to one level, because that would deny the historical differences between values, reasons, social judgments.

Accepting differences could, without giving up the construction of one's own individuality, enable one to reject violent gestures and actions firmly, but without rejecting the person who has performed them and to admit her potential capacity to become a subject. In this sense, teaching can sometimes seem like countertransference in psychoanalysis on a smaller scale: for both in teaching and in psychoanalysis the feeling and the state of mind of the participants are of people who find themselves in a dialogue potentially between equals but not in a full sense; the other alternately takes up and loses the role of subject. The dialogue is already reciprocal in so far as it aims at mutual liberation; in fact, the two subjects are continually in formation, and the difference between them does not cancel their respect for each other's rights.[28] Two individuals can reach this type of equality only if they can recognize and accept their difference (see Rossi-Doria 1987, p. 70-71).

To conclude these short notes on equality/difference, I quote one of the participants who recalled March 8, 1983, "celebrated" in Voghera top security prison at the same time as an outside demonstration was organized by a feminist group from Pavia:

> And we had thought of organizing a demonstration. A demonstration inside jail is not a very easy thing, at the beginning we thought we could interrupt the exercise period in the yard with a lot of slogans. Everything we did at Voghera had to be perfectly planned, because everything was so regimented, so controlled by the most sophisticated equipment that it was impossible to do anything without previous agreement, without some sort of plan.

The demonstration took place. The woman started shouting the slogans just a few seconds before they were called one by one to come back from the yard, and the chanting aroused

> great participation, of the whole jail—there were four completely separate sections—so you could hear these slogans like a wave, starting from one yard, bouncing to the next, then from the windows, because upstairs there were the women who came down for exercise in the afternoon.

The nonviolent and almost cheerful character of the demonstration, which created "a situation which was very intense emotionally and psychologically," was contagious because of the reaction of the female wardens and because of a peculiar form of release: laughter.

> Some of the wardens were very tense, others were bewildered, others laughed. They were laughing, laughing in the sense that . . . they were laughing . . . with us. Probably they were the same people who, shortly before going on duty, had been wished a happy women's day . . . And then, well, then we went upstairs—the squad of wardens had arrived, usually they flung insults at us as we were going up, this time they didn't even think of saying a word, it was as though they were escorting us up the staircase . . .
>
> You see, and this really was a great thing, very different, very special, and we felt it very intensely. I must say, that day was, I think, the only day that not only did we feel quite relaxed but we also felt something like a desire to surprise, by living our relation with the jail in a different way. I think it was the only time I wasn't afraid, I could have stayed outside for twenty hours, they could have dragged me in, if they could do it! No, it really was great . . . (Giulia).

The tone of this account, somewhere between the utopian and the facetious, provides new insight into the relationships between women and anticipates for a moment a different sort of awareness, which suspends the usual violent routine of insults and scorn that obliges the wardens to identify with their roles and cruelly play them out. Fear is suspended, both for the guards and for the prisoners. The interval was a foretaste of a possible world, if it were possible to find the freedom and confidence to build it.

During the phase of listening to life-stories, we interviewers more than once experienced a common impression on leaving the jail: the very facts of terrorism were absent from those recollections, as though the violence had actually been repressed. We can give contingent explanations for this absence, such as the particular dynamics of talking within a group where one seeks approval, sympathy, and legitimization to build a new identity. I think, though, that there are other causes and a global context for this phenomenon which can be better expressed through questions than statements. In a society in which violent death is so frequent, is this repression part and parcel of every kind of murder? Hasn't all previous violence, whether committed by fascism or by antifascism, been pushed aside, in a sort of collective repression mechanism?

The difficulty in speaking about all this may also be linked to the loss of "the power of the imagination" after 1968 and to the weakening of the relationship between imagination and politics. The difficulty of understanding what happened over the last twenty years, the absence of a collective willingness to accept responsibility and faults, the insistence on repeating sinister clichés, can all be connected with such processes of the imaginary.[29] In such circumstances, memory hesitates to speak and requires interpretation before it can be understood and utilized from a historical point of view.

THE MAKING OF MEMORY

At the end of one cycle of the seminar, after the first two stages, we tried a preliminary analysis of the collected life-stories. So far, we interviewers had not spoken much, but from now on we were to ask questions, make remarks, and raise objections. Our first impression was that this memory was lacerated, strewn with silences, riddled with holes, as if the recollections of the women who struck had been stricken in their turn by an internal erosion.

In the first place memory is compelled continually to update language, an effort that demands complex processes of reelaboration:

> . . . in 1973 [I belonged to] this small group of friends and comrades who began to open, you might say, a debate on arming the proletariat, as we used to say at that time, and on organizing the armed struggled in various situations . . . and a debate on the issue of information/counterinformation about the conspiracy for a coup d'état, the subversive right, etc. (Ronconi).

> . . . there was this talk, you see, about getting ready, if you like, . . . and on the topic of logistics—as we called it then—which was about getting houses equipped, and hence the talk about financing ourselves . . . (Graglia).

> Wee are two unfortunates, because here we are, in a period of full emergency—which wasn't called emergency then (Anna).

These re-elaborations do not only involve linguistic stratifications peculiar to different historical phases and characterized by swift changes. Sometimes language itself is reluctant to mention things clearly, but allusion loads them with disquieting meanings:

> . . . at home it just happens that I'm dusting and I find two things in the wardrobe, I look at them and say: "what can they be?" but I don't know what they are and I'm really scared to death. At that time they were just two black objects inside something, for me (Anna).

Besides the linguistic difficulties we encountered, we faced problems created by the emotional conflicts and lacerations of the identity, which are inherent in the interweaving of the personal and the collective, of the ethical and the existential. Consequently memory avoids visiting some of its places, as some narrators realize during the first stage of telling their life-story:

> I remember those three years with the *Brigate Rosse* just as a black tunnel.
>
> I no longer really know what happened from '78 to '80—I remember very well the kind of participation in the assaults I had, that goes without saying—but I don't know anymore . . . roughly these two years, when things become blurred . . . I don't even feel like searching my memory for them (Giulia).

Others realize this avoidance at later stages of the seminar: Valeria Cora remarks, after reading the transcript of her interview, which was in our opinion interesting and full of information: "I didn't say anything," and she insists on adding certain aspects. Originally she had claimed to have "a blank" about the decision to leave the political work in front of the factories for "an advanced phase of the struggle." She says now that it had not really been a turning point, but neither had it been totally devoid of ideological justifications, as she fears it might appear from her mention of that blank. She is also afraid that she has not sufficiently expressed her doubts, her indecision about opposing positions, when she started thinking she should abandon clandestine activity. Actually her interview mentions an "atrocious doubt" that lasted for a year, but evidently this phrase does not express strongly enough what the speaker would like to tell us about herself and her experience.[30]

Other witnesses express the same dissatisfaction, above all Grazia Grena, who was interviewed just as she was changing from prison to the state of semi-libertà (semi-freedom). Her revision of the first life-story gives glimpses of very strong conflicts of memory and the difficulty of coping with the stimuli induced in the memory by the different conditions of imprisonment, semi-libertà, and release from prison. So we can actually watch the making of a memory, in its connections, both through requests coming from the small circle of our seminar and through information coming from a wider context.

The most remarkable difference between memory in prison and that in the outer world seems to be twofold: the latter finds it easier to mention things and facts that the former avoids, but at the same time it seems to be more detached and abstracted from the depth and clarity of the recollections that the former attains. This difference, then, has to do with a process of the memory that emerges and stays on the surface, a process essential to resuming life with today's rhythms. It is dangerous to indulge excessively in the subjective sinking into one's memory which is induced by imprisonment, just as it is dangerous to do the opposite, to skip that passage altogether. The greater facility with which memory calls things by their right names after the subject has left prison may actually be the result of a new balance, obtained after a regression through dreaming and remembering.

I will give just one example of the making of memory in relation to the pressures of collective processes of information. In her life-story Susanna Ronconi does not assign to 1968 the importance of a turning point along her path; she recognizes its value in a generalized way, not specific to her decisions. As a matter of fact, we notice a certain overlap of 1967, 1968, 1969 throughout the narration; all these years seem to be interwoven in their total impact on the narrator's development. In written documents, such as a *Contributo* for the seminar on "1968 and thereabouts," organized by Salvatore Veca at San Vittore Prison in Milan and a memoir written for a videoscript[31], she takes a different line:

> My birth was in '68, my defeat was the revolutionary struggle (*Contributo*)
>
> I was born in Venice, once . . . I was born again in '68, there was a lot of us this time" (videoscript).

In the first place, the speaker's choice of these different expressions is influenced by their intended audience and aims. In the second place the oral expressions are influenced by the very fact that they are oral, and orality carries the narrative stream in directions unforeseen by the narrator, thanks to the interaction with the participants. Another influence is the specific structure of a life-story in its entirety, which supplies individual events with a general context. In sum, the first version, that of the life-story, speaks the truth in a historical-existential context; the second, of the *Contributo* and the videoscript, is valid in a symbolic-theatrical realm. The two dimensions taken together must be interpreted in their turn as characteristic features of a subject's narrative personality. These qualifications do not discredit memory, only its less wary interpreters.

To all this we owe the peculiar interweaving of self-representation, which concerns a narrative or a cultural identity, with the identity connected to a social role, acted out in working and emotional relationships. The two identities do not coincide totally, notwithstanding interlacing and cross-references (we are not all that we say we are, and we do not say all that we are). The tension between life and autobiography produces differing attitudes in different people. In the case of the seminar, it is not surprising that diversing positions came to the surface during the discussion about whether the interviews should be signed:

> Speaking only for myself, the question of making my name public is less important to me, I mean, I'm in prison under my real name and surname (Tosi).
>
> For me anonymity is not a problem at all, rather the opposite. All things considered, if I'm telling the story of my life, that's because in any case I hope I will be able to play a part, so it suits me to be the one who's going to tell it (Ronconi).
>
> I would really like to stay anonymous. My ambition in life is to get completely out of all this and to do something totally different, leaving behind me a life-story but not a name (Giulia).

The specificity of the individual's relationship with memory, particularly because of the phenomenon we are dealing with, becomes clearer if we compare the life-stories with records of a different nature.

Comparison with other sources reveals that memory complements archival records. Grazia Grena's life-story, for example, includes some references to robberies, but does not go into details. In contrast, a deposition made on January 14, 1985[32], when she decided to dissociate herself from violent political activity, naturally goes into considerable detail about them, in answer to specific questions (although the witness persists in including the facts within the wider context of her life). This judicial document is interesting because it shows the process in the making, underling how much even these official records are interwoven with memory. As to the single actions, Grena declares:

> I can reconfirm, more or less, almost all that I'm charged with, but not everything. For example, I did not take part in the robbery in Piazza Siena with which I'm charged.
> Which other action didn't you take part in?
> I don't remember.

When the questions are listed, her answers seem accurate within the investigative framework:

> Robbery at Della Foglia's jeweller's shop, Rho, 15.6.82.
> Yes.
> Robbery at the Bonassola Branch of the Cassa di Risparmio, La Spezia.
> I wasn't in the operative unit, but I knew about it.

And so on. But the mechanism gets stuck sometimes, and at such moments it becomes clear that the apparent factuality is still always based on the exercise of a personal memory:

> Robbery at Danielli's goldsmith's shop in Milan, 23.3.82.
> Yes. I suppose that was not the one in Piazza Siena?
> I don't know. I only know I didn't do that one. At the moment I don't remember any names.

Or:

> Did you participate in drafting this leaflet?[33]
> I read it and said it was all right with me when we . . .
> Reading is a subsequent moment.
> I find writing difficult, so I'm certain I didn't write it. That's why I said what I did.
> However, you participated in drafting the content of this leaflet, did you not?
> Yes, I did.
> Was it decided, was it discussed?
> I think so, but I don't remember . . . we often did that sort of thing.

The magistrate is confronted with the same problem that historians face in gathering and interpreting oral sources: memory, sometimes extremely precise, even about details, works continual fusions and short-circuits because it proceeds by associations and retotalizations. The factuality of the statements, if they are based only on memory, is therefore not a very convincing mask. On the contrary, depositions and memoirs produced at the moment of dissociation are valuable as general statements, because they really represent a breaking of the silence the individual had previously maintained toward the law. Although the language of these documents is sometimes influenced by circumstances (betraying tones of a bureaucratic or formulaic nature), they are valuable and interesting because of a twofold revelation: we see the witnesses refusing external justifications but searching for justification from within their own history.

For example, in a Memoria difensiva (defendant's note) in connection with proceedings against the crimes of the Brigate Rosse, Giulia writes:

> . . . it seems to me that in this society, not only are the 'years of lead' objectivity over, but also an entire cultural period of political short-cuts and armed solutions. Objectively finished, which doesn't mean completely ended in human experience, it rather means that the path of gratuitous destruction, of the end which justifies the means, is nothing but a dead-end track, a road leading nowhere . . .
>
> In the past I too easily schematized analyses, I too often thought of solutions in abstract terms. In fact I have changed too, since the period of armed action . . .
>
> For a time I kept this break within myself inside me, I didn't feel the need to share it. Then the movement came when I understood that it wasn't a "private fact" anymore, that it was necessary to break the old image—above all—I understood I could no longer evade my penal responsibilities, as if it were possible for me to forget crime, punishment, prison—what I live through every day.

She concludes her memoria by declaring her "willingness to answer all the questions the Court may ask, provided they concern [her] direct responsibility in the dynamics of the various actions."

In studying political violence, more than other historiographic objects, one must refer to various kinds of sources, each of which affords different and relevant elements. In the Memoria quoted above, for example, the last narrator talks about her participation in the shooting and injuring of five people and gives the names of the injured persons; in the written Note biografiche she mentions these episodes; but in the very long and exhaustive oral interview she does not mention them, although she does not deny she has participated in armed action.

The oral account is more influenced by interaction with other subjects that are the written documents—therefore implicitly taking the expectations of those other subjects into account—but it also follows different patterns of narration. Liviana Tosi's oral account for instance, simply touches on a serious episode; describing actions that were "more political" (that armed robberies) she says, "the biggest is the one at the Scuola di Amministrazione Aziendale". She immediately adds that "everything about that is already on record" and goes on to talk about some robberies. In her deposition during an interrogation on November 20, 1985,[34] however, she describes the action in terms that are logical and chronological, providing explanations and causes, from motivation to outcome. From this memory we can reconstruct the role she played in the event:

> P. and I waited in the assembly hall until a comrade came to tell us that the action was over . . . we tried to explain to these people that their sector could not be restructured.

The testimony explains that, although she did not take a direct part in the shootings, she knew about them—and the explanation is in the terrible language common to mass media and terrorism:

> . . . the purpose of the action was to exhibit *gambizzazione* (knee-capping) in order to emphasize the spectacular nature in front of the staff.

The life-story does not tell any of this. Nevertheless, when Tosi answers one of the interviewers' questions that brought the subject up again, she provides significant answers:

> . . . thinking about it very often I've come to realize that we hadn't understood the full significance of this thing . . . then, I don't know how to say it, it was a frightful sensation because I realized how much power one person could have over another.

Though they are not of great importance to justice, these statements are interesting in relation to the history of mentalities and cultural changes. They show a progressive detachment from a moral indifference, from an unawareness and a lack of adhesion to intersubjective reality. Tosi's comment about the sense of power is echoed in another interview and must be placed in the context of that loss of meaning—of politics and of existence—which above all characterized the youth movements of the late 1970s. Mantovani:

> Anyhow, I really liked the armed actions a lot. I got really thrilled. I became aware then of powers I have never been able to express since at any level. Probably because there is a total commitment, you're gambling with your life. In short, you have a thousand eyes, a thousand ears, a thousand capacities. And you feel sort of exalted, you feel great. I don't know . . . powerful, it's very gratifying. It really is true that you start to enjoy it.

Maybe this narrator can be so outspoken because she was active in a period when the Brigate Rosse did not use armed violence: "I have never fired a shot . . . It would be different if I had seriously hurt someone, and if I now realized that it had all been a waste."

The following comment measures the passing of time and reveals some inner changes:

> At that time I felt it was a fair exchange. I was ready to give my life, and so I felt I had the right . . . I know it sounds absurd now, I don't think like that anymore.

The narrators found it more difficult to describe the more serious violent actions in their life-stories not only because of the inner changes that had taken place but also because of the tone of subjective history that is characteristic of oral narration:

> I must say that my experience of homicide is atrocious, because one of the two was something that was done in Milan, a former comrade who had betrayed, so it was a boy—the thing is very hard, and, frankly, I usually deal with it by repression, except for those moments when I have obviously thought about it. And it is a terrible thing in the sense that . . . you cannot describe it very well, partly because you think about it a lot, before and after, but during it . . . these are things that only last a few minutes, and my reaction was always to suspend emotionality completely.[35]

If words are lacking in the narration of such events, previously heard expressions do emerge:

> . . . yes, its true what [an interviewer] read in the testimony of that woman during the Resistance: it's true that there's a moment when the other person understands, he knows, you see that he knows, just a few split seconds, but they are terrible (Ronconi).

For this reason, too, perhaps it would be valuable to compare the different ways partisans experienced violence, particularly those who say they felt compelled to practice it instead of exalting it. The comparison is implicit in the narratives. Graglia:

> I have no experience of violence against persons, I never took part in the shooting or killing of a human being, so I haven't got any direct experience of violence against another person . . .
>
> In any case I had accepted violence almost without questioning it when I began political activity, it seemed theoretically right because that was the way to make the revolution, probably in part because the movement hadn't yet got as far as practicing homicide, as it did later . . .
>
> Sometimes I think about my father too, who went through the experience of being a partisan, who had a direct relationship with violence, with death—he feels terrible remorse about that . . .

In the psychomental environment to which these sentences refer, the connection between violence against things and violence against persons, as well as between various types of violence, seems particularly to be lacking; here, too, the new left seems particularly slow to understand. A new awareness is slow to come to those who are involved, and it usually comes about in prison:

> I was being transferred from Messina to Voghera, and the journey being a long one, there was a halt in Rome: I asked the escort to give me a newspaper and I found out about this thing in Via Domodossola—a hold-up, with two Mondialpol guards murdered—my hair stood on end with horror and that was really the precipitating moment: "No, no, it can't go on like this, this isn't the way" (Giulia).

In the last phases of the seminar many of these issues were discussed, after a first analysis (April 28, 1987) in which we had noted that a certain mindlessness of expression ("only doing hold-ups") was already a type of silence of the memory. The language the interviewees used manifested, in addition, a suspension of judgment, and a lack of connection between past and present. Our observations clearly went beyond what is usual in the practice of oral history. Seeking each other's advice, we became aware that we were imposing an unusual procedure on the narrators: that is, we were putting their memories up for discussion, asking not only for further details from memory but also for a remixing of existential valuations. Personally, I agreed to carry this sort of intrusion so far because I thought it was essential at both a human and an educational level to make my position unequivocal and to contrast spontaneous memory, treating other women as subjects in the fulls sense. This decision was connected with the peculiar experience of that seminar and grew out as a result of a personal rethinking about my own experience within the new left (see Passerini 1988b).

The debates that followed were so rich as to show that this choice had met the needs of many, if not all, the participants in the seminar. The final group report which they wrote confirms this fulfillment for it points out a process that is underway, the dissolution of a paralysis of language and memory, and above all—and this element is what I care about most—progress toward an identity different from that of protagonists of political violence. A request for an interview, whether from the media or from historians, can constitute a trap in the sense that it is an inducement to indulge in the old identities, to think of oneself only as a character in illegal stories, to feel oneself lost, outside the old "political" image. Again, parts of the final group report testify to the force of this temptation.

Still, the process of rethinking has gone forward, thanks in part, I believe, to the contrast with different positions held by us interviewers. The belief that these processes are to some extent reciprocal is encourages for me: the fact that I, personally, learned much in the course of the seminar leads me to hope that others too have learned from it in various ways. Notwithstanding the difference between the roles of narrators and lecturers—a difference accepted and lived out with firm conviction—all of us were aware of the need to follow a path similar to the others' in terms of one's own cultural history as well as of the trajectory of political generation. The proper attitude seems to me to be one of self-understanding rather than self-criticism (a term Adorno could not bear to hear), because the latter includes tones of self-destruction and self-denigration induced by external pressures and directed toward the outside reality. Without forbearance for one's mistakes, but with the right to mourn them. It is difficult to say to what extent imprisonment affords this right and in which respects it obstructs it.

In order to restore or establish an intersubjective communication in society as a whole, we must undertake a complex psychic and cultural process: we must analyze, study, and understand, so as to comprehend the suffering both of those who have been stricken and of those who have struck. This process of reflection is broader and of a different nature than the juridical process, but the two processes should be reciprocal. And both processes should have one characteristic in common: to follow worldly ways of communication rather than those of the Lord, as Giuseppe Cafasso was entitled to do. Therefore, they will be difficult, insecure, risk, and tortuous ways, enlightened only by the use of historical reasoning that does not recoil when facing emotions, the imaginary, the inner dimension.

ACKNOWLEDGMENTS

I wish to express my thanks to Dr. Giuseppe Suraci, Director of the "Nuove" prison in Turin, and to Sister Lucia of the Women's wing; to the magistrate Dr. Fornace; to Dr. Buscemi of the Bologna prison; to Monica Fuggetta, who helped us to type some handwritten manuscripts and to transcribe some material from the outside group; and to the Department of History of the University of Turin, which kindly made available facilities for photocopying.

My thanks as well to Francis Cooper for her care in translating this essay; to the director and editorial board of *Revista di storia contemporanea* where this essay originally appeared (vol. 2 [1988]) for permission to translate it; to Jane Mills for her very kind advice on the difficult problem of rendering certain expressions into English; to Martha Linke for editing it. Finally, part of the funding for the reproduction of oral and written material, comes from a research fund provided by the Italian Council foir Researches (Consiglio Nazionale delle Ricerche, CNR) for research on oral and written sources for recent history. I want to thank the CNR for its help.

NOTES

1. The original version of this paper had in fact no introduction, but the editor of this volume and I agreed that, for its publication in English, a preface would help to provide a background for the discussions that follow. However, some of the subtleties appropriate to the question of Italian terrorism are not rendered in the English translation.

2. Aree omogenee are sections of a prison where former terrorists could—at their own request—serve their sentences together [translator's note].

3. All the documents mentioned in this introduction, together with transcripts of the life-stories and the debates, will be deposited in the sound archives of the Department of History at the University of Turin.

4. Our work included a commentary of the "Segnalazione bibliografica," Roberta Fossati (1983), and the following texts: Lotman (1985); Passerini (1987, 1988a); and Marcuzzo and Rossi-Doria (1987).

5. We can propose an interpretation of terrorism on the symbolic level thanks to previous work carried out on other levels, especially the social and political. For useful sociological and political analyses see in particular the essays in Bonanate (1979) and Pasquino (1984) and Ferrarotti's article in Galleni (1981).

For a historical approach see Galli (1986); the essays by Angelo Ventura, Giancarlo Caselli and Donatella della Porta, and Nando Dalla Chiesa, in della Porta (1984); and Nicola Tranfaglia's article in Galleni (1981). Important quantitative data can be found both in this latter volume and in della Porta and Rossi (1984). Although it is weak on the Italian situation, Laqueur (1987) provides useful information on the general context.

For an analysis of the ideological and psychological dimension see Calvi and Martini (1982), and Vasale (1980).

6. The problem of terminology indicates how difficult this undertaking is: "political violence" seems too general a term, because it refers to phenomena of widely varying intensities; "armed struggle" seems to dignify these acts, because it was originally used in reference to liberation and resistance movements; and "terrorism" ignores the differences between Left and Right. In this paper I use all these terms, depending on the context, and try to be aware of their respective nuances.

7. Collecting primary sources for recent history presents quite a serious problem: some, such as periodicals, are available; others, when they exist, are not always easily accessible, for example, television or radio recordings, Police documents are obviously not available for consultation, while judiciary papers, although accessible in principle, are often incomplete or difficult to find. Private archives, which are of the utmost importance, involve problems of classification and organization, as well as of confidentiality. Sources consisting of photographs or films are also difficult to find and consult. And finally, the interpretation of oral sources regarding recent history is particularly hazardous and complex.

8. Verse from a folk song about a women's prison.

9. The ten women were born between 1950 and 1960; three of them came from the Brigate Rosse, six from *Prima Linea,* one was in prison for a nonpolitical murder. Their parents were: farm laborers, shop-keepers, originally farm laborers and then worker/housewife, manager/housewife, clerk/teacher, owner and manager of a small firm, worker/dressmaker, peasant, and worker. Grazia Grena's story derives, with comments and additions, from the interview by Donatella della Porta which was part of a research program conducted by Raimondo Catanzaro for the Institute Cattaneo in Bologna on political violence in Italy (*La violenza politica in Italia*). My thanks to them both for their permission to use the interview. I interviewed Nadia Mantovani who had been transferred to a Bologna prison.

10. On the importance of relational networks and on the significance of mythological aspects (in right-wing movements) see, respectively, Claudio Novaro (1988) and Bruno Osella (1990), two

papers presented to the Congress of the Istituto Cattaneo (Bologna, 3-4 June 1988), which concluded the reseach for La violenza politica in Italia.

11. On the concept of "absolute enemy," characteristic of the mentality of supporters of political violence, see Luigi Manconi's (1988) contribution to Congress of the Istituto Cattaneo (Bologna, June 3-4, 1988).

12. The theses concerning the imaginary are based on Lacan's distinction between the imaginary and the symbolic; the former is characterized by "animal psychology" and moves toward disillusion, whereas the latter represents the successful distinction between subjective and objective, with the consequent formation of a subject. On the tensions and the mutual interpenetration between the real, the imaginary, and the symbolic, see Lacan (1975).

13. In pursuing this line of research further, we find an important antecedent in the relationship between the movements of 1968 and the artistic and literary historical avant-gardes of the time, in particular concerning the breakdown of the usual boundaries between thought and action, art and life, theory and praxis. To determine the consequences of the 1968 movements one would have to analyze the passage from the imagination to the imaginary and the loss of subjectivity during the 1970s.

14. On the differences among terrorist organizations, specifically their different ways of living and thinking, see Nicola Tranfaglia's introduction to Novelli and Tranfaglia (1988).

15. See the contribution by Carlo Marletti in Pasquino (1984, esp. pp. 124-30).

16. I mean, for example, the kind of writing in Curcio (1984), in which we find the themes of dreaming, the outlook typical of the imaginary, and the literary "release" of the unconscious. Another very important example is Balestrini (1987), a sophisticated literary reworking of a life experience. The continual progression backward and forward between the present, in prison, and the past, within the movement, perfectly recreates a dream atmosphere, although the content of the description is strictly factual. Some phrases point up this alternation clearly: "then a flash and I see in front of my eyes the page of a pamphlet' (p. 15); "suddenly a fixed confused image . . . it must have been filmed at night" (p. 25); here memory and the television images are meaningfully superimposed; "the symbolic aspect is much in evidence during these things during the searches" (p. 31). The lack of punctuation corresponds to the associative process characteristics of the imaginary

17. On the utility of dreams as indicators of the imaginary, see, for example, Patlagean (1987) and Le Goff (1985), chaps. 8 and 9. For the relationship between the dream world and literature, see the anthology by Almansi and Béguin (1988).

18. See the article by Massimo Martini in Calvi and Martini (1982) which reinforces this interpretation: "a 'deprivation of ideals'—that is, an ever-clearer consciousness of the gap between reality and values learned during the formative years—can cause forms of political radicalization, particularly in those with a good education (pp. 122-123).

19. See Ceppi (1980, p. 97). Other works related to this theme are: Federici (1986), Perrini (1986), Sasso (1986), all of which deal with women's memoirs.

20. "On 5 February 1979 at about 7:20, in Turin, R.F., who was a female warden at the local prison, had just left home when she was approached by two women, armed but with faces uncovered. The warden, not the least afraid, asked the two unknown women whether it was a carnival stunt, but they shot her several times and hit her in the area of the left buttock . . . responsibility for the attack was claimed the same day by the organization *Prima Linea*, which had sent a leaflet to a journalist on a local newspaper for the purpose . . . this document stated that 'a firing group . . . made up entirely of women' had struck." (From a sentence of the second assize court of Turin, December 10, nos. 4 and 7/83, General Register, no. 16.83, Register of Sentences.)

21. The essays edited by Melucci (1984) illuminate the nature of the movements "of the metropolis" in the second half of the 1970s and the first half of the 1980s.

22. See Farè (1986, pp. 59, 61, 83). The same author collaborated with Franca Spirito to produce a collection of interviews and other material (Farè and Spirito).

23. Again, Balestrini (1987) has described the atmosphere and the state of mind of generalized protest: "around the headquarters groups of comrades come and go the night is lively noisy with our shouts songs music and coloured by our jackets scarves skirts hair the walls are continuous graffiti drawings and slogans mixed and overlapping on all the walls against the bosses against irregular work against all work against ghettoes against the clergy against the mayor against the trade unions against the parties against the local government against men against heroin against the fascists against the fuzz against the judges against the state against poverty against repression against prison against the family against school against sacrifices against boredom" (Balestrini 1987, p. 201).

24. The etymology of these words can be given a lay reformulation: "repentence" as a recognition of a lack, something missing, and "forgiveness" as a donation par excellence, something extra. These two psychic activities are reciprocal: the reelaboration performed by the first permits the emotional delivery of the second, and the two feed one another, as different parts of the same subjective process.

25. *Sdaura* is the word used in Emilia Romagna to define the woman who governs the big peasants' houses.

26. Viola is in prison for the murder of the woman whom she talks bout in her life-story. Her lawyer is one of the lecturers present at the seminar, Bianca Guidetti Serra. (The third lecturer is Patrizia Guerra.)

27. My thanks to Gianni Perona for having drawn my attention to an article that was useful in the discussions during the seminar, since it analyzes a political assassination that was at the same time motivated by love: see Loraux (1985, p. 3ff.) for a discussion of Thucydides' narration of the murder of Hypparcus, son of Pisistratus, by Armodius and Aristogito, in 514 B.C.

28. I take these terms from Trevi (1988).

29. One example of repetition is the article by Fortini (1988) in which he opposes consciousness to knowledge and to action, devaluing the dimension of inner morality. Fortini's reduction of the interior aspect to only two elements, conscience and morality, does not stop him from resorting to the category of psychological repressions in accusing those who have abandoned their previous opposition to existing society. This sort of reasoning was commonly found in a large part of the New Left, which, for example, persisted in the illusion that the rejection of the violence of the system could take place "before and beyond the choice for or against institutions", whereas in fact in post-World War II Europe this rejection is acceptable only if it takes place within the institutions of parliamentary democracy.

In relation to my arguments in the present essay, Sergio Segio's answer to Fortini is relevant, since it mentions being "dissociated also in the psychological sense" (Segio 1988).

30. A Postilla (annotation) testifies to the persistence of her dissatisfaction. The witness added the following to her life-story in order to emphasize the specific nature of her experience:

> Compared to the members of the group my story is rather different, because militancy and jail for me took place during the initial phase of armed struggle in Italy, and so I don't have a dramatic experience of the entire period, of the clandestine life, of the armed organization, and violence has only 'touched' my life, rather than coming heavily into it, although ideological adhesion to certain forms of struggle, and to certain steps in this, was complete. From when I left jail to the time of the seminar, nine years have passed, during which I have tried to build something of completely different value, but which still had some aspect of social and personal renewal [political work within a working-class quarter, the effort to invent a different sort of world]. . . . When it was suggested that I join the outside group of this seminar I willingly accepted. I felt the need to reflect on a part of my life and to find a continuity between my distant past, my recent past, and my present.

> To rebuild memory by following also the thread of my dreams and of the major dream of my 'adolescence-youth': to quickly, immediately cancel all the horrors of the world, to regain its richness, to rebuild affectionate ties and to reunite all my pieces which seemed to be split . . . in order to suffer those years again, the betrayals, my abandoning the struggle, the defeat, and to reflect on it with an adult's awareness.

31. This is a letter within the videoscript of *Lettura ad alta voce*, produced by Gabriella Rosaleva. (Program for the third television channel of the RAI-TV.)

32. The transcription I was able to consult is countersigned B 3/1 (141-769), LA/52-55.

33. The witness was accused of "crimes related to propaganda, apology of subversion and public instigation, related to the distribution of leaflets under the signature *Coordinamento situazioni communiste*." Regarding the latter charge, the woman stated: "The fact that there was that signature, I can't understand it myself."

34. Transcription B 17 (1614-2299), LA/44-46. The attack on the business management school in Turin took place on December 11, 1979; the press reported that among the attackers were "three girls". Public opinion was struck by the particular ferocity of this episode of the two hundred people who were held, ten were chosen at random and wounded in the legs. The city reacted with a huge demonstration, and a strike was called by the Trade Union Federations CGIL, CISl and UIL, with a communiqué including the following observations: "In the historical memory of the Italian people, the bestiality of the action can only find an echo in the Nazi brutalities." See the shocking accounts and photographs in *La Stampa*, December 12 and 13, 1979.

35. It is interesting to compare the oral expression with the tone of a judicial account:

> On the morning of 7.2.80 three armed persons, among them a woman, accosted W. Waccher, who had just come out of his home, and shot at him several times with a revolver. The young man fell to the ground wounded, and the murderers came up to him and shot several "finishing shots." . . . Responsibility for the homicide was claimed by *Prima Linea* and justified by the character of certain statements to the judicial authorities made by Waccher, supposedly a delator (Third Assize Court, Milan, no. 43/84 of the Sentence 50/82 + 64/82 + 40/83 +41/83 + 56/83 + 21/84 R.G.; hearing of October 23, 1985 and March 8, 1986, sheet 575).

This last source reveals that Susanna Ronconi was condemned to life-imprisonment for this crime, too; the sentence was commuted to 29 years' imprisonment for her "profound critical revision" confirmed by "many declarations made by the accused: these show a total detachment from the practice of violence and, more, manifest a convinced denial of her previous behavior, through reflections which have been completed over several years" (sheet 1597-1598).

My warm thanks to Dr. Maurizio Laudi for having made it possible for me to consult the cited judicial acts.

REFERENCES

Almansi, G. and Béguin, C. eds. 1988. *Teatro del sonno* [Theater of Sleep]. Milan: Garzanti.

Arendt, H. 1985. *Politica e menzogna.* Milan: SugarCo. [Italian translation of *Crises of the Republic*]. San Diego: Harvest/HBJ Books, 1969.

Balestrini, N. 1987. *Gli Invisibili* [The Invisible]. Milan: Bompiani.

Bonanate, L. 1979. *Dimensioni del terrorismo politico* [Dimensions of Political Terrorism]. Milan: Angeli.

Calvi, G. and M. Martini. 1982. *L'estremismo politico* [Political Extremism]. Milan: Angeli.

Ceppi, G. 1980. *Non abbiamo sognato* [We Did Not Dream]. Verona: Bertani.

Curcio, R. 1984. *WKHY*. Rome: Fatamorgana.

Della Porta, D. ed. 1984. *Terrorismi in Italia* [Terrorisms in Italy]. Bologna: Il Mulino.

Della Porta, D. and M. Rossi. 1984. *Cifre crudeli. Bilancio dei terrorismi italiani* [Cruel Figures: A Reckoning of Italian Terrorism]. Bologna: Instituto Cattaneo.

Farè, I. and F. Spirito. 1979. *Mara e le altre. Le donne e la lotta armata: stories interviste riflessioni* [Mara and other Women. The Armed Struggle: Stories, Interviews, Reflections]. Milan: Feltrinelli.

Farè, I. 1986. *La mia signora* [My Lady]. Milan: SugarCo.

Federici, A. 1986. *Lettere ai miei* [Letters to My Dear Ones]. Pordenone: Studio Tesi.

Fortini, F. 1988. "Non è solo a voi che sto parlando" (It is not only you I am speaking to). *Il manifesto*, (March 24).

Fossati, R. 1983. "Segnalazione bibliografica" [Bibliographic recommendations]. Pp. 120-26 in *Fonti orali e politica della donne: storia ricerca racconto* [Oral Sources and Women's Politics: History Research Narration], Acts of the conference of Centro Di Documentazione, Ricerca e Iniziativa Della Donne, Bologna, October 1982. Bologna: CDRID.

Freni, M. 1985. *Le passioni di Petra* [Petra's Passions]. Florence: Vallecchi.

Galleni, M. ed. 1981. *Rapporto sul terrorismo* [Report on Terrorism]. Milan: Rizzoli.

Galli, G. 1986. *Storia del partito armato 1968-1982* [History of the Armed Party, 1968-1982]. Milan: Rizzoli.

Gauchet, M. 1985. *La désenchantement du monde*. [The Disenchantment of the World]. Paris: Gallimard.

Lacan, J. 1975. *Le séminaire. Livre I. Les écrits techniques de Freud (1953-1954)* [The Seminar. Book 1. Technical Writings by Freud]. Paris: Seuil.

Laqueur, W. 1987. *The Age of Terrorism*. London: Weidenfeld & Nicolson.

Le Goff, J. 1985. *L'imaginaire médiéval* [The Imaginary in the Middle-Ages]. Paris: Gallimard.

Le mouvement social. 1988. Special issue on "Mémoires et histoires de 1968" [Memories and histories of 1968]. Issue no. 143.

Loraux, N. 1985. "Enquête sur la construction d'un meurtre en histoire" [Enquiry into the construction of an assassination in history). *L'écrit du temps* 10:3-21.

Lotman, J. M. 1985. "Il diritto alla biografia" [The right to biography]. Pp. 181-99 in *La semiosfera*. Venice: Marsilio.

Manconi, L. 1988. "Il nemico assoluto. Antifascismo e contropotere nella fase saurorale del terrorismo di sinistra" [The absolute enemy: Anti-fascism and counter-power at the Dawn of left-wing terrorism]. *Polis* 2:259-286.

Maraini, D. 1984. *Il treno per Helsinki* [The Train to Helsinki]. Turin: Einaudi.

Marcuzzo, M.C. and A. Rossi-Doria, eds. 1987. *La ricerca delle donne* [Women's Research]. Turin: Rosenberg & Sellier.

Medici, S. 1987. *Via Po*. Turin: Cooperativa il manifesto anni 80.

Melucci, A. 1984. *Altri codici* [Other Codes]. Milan: Il Mulino.

Musatti, C. 1986. *Enantiodromia: processo dialettico e ambivalenza* [Enantiodromy: dialectics and ambivalence]. Paper presented to the congress Presenza ed eredita' culturale di C.G. Jung [The Presence and Cultural Heritage of C.G. Jung], Milan. December 6-7.

Novaro, C. 1988. "Reti amicali e lotta ramata" [Friendship networks and armed struggle]. *Polia* 2:287-320.

Novelli, D. and Tranfaglia, N. 1988. *Vite sospese. Le generazioni del terrorismo* [Lives in Abeyance: The Generations of Terrorism]. Milan: Garzanti.

Osella, B. 1990. "L'autorappresentazione ideologica degli eversori di destra" [Ideological self-representation by Right-wing terrorists]. In *Ideologie, movimenti, terrorismi* [Ideollgies, Movements, Terrorism) edited by R. Catanzaro. Bologna: Il Mulino.

Pasquino, G. 1984. *La prova della armi* [The test of arms]. Bologna: Il Mulino.

Passerini, L. 1987. *Facism in Popular Memory*. Cambridge: Cambridge University Press.

———. 1988a. *Storia e soggettività* [History and subjective]. Florence: La Nuova Italia.

———. 1988b. *Autoritratto di gruppo* [Group's self-portrait]. Florence: Giunti-Astrea.

Patlagean, E. 1987. "Bisanzio X-XV secolo." Pp. 420-483 in *La vita Privata dall'impero romano all'anno Mille*, edited by P. Ariès and G. Duby. Rome-Bari: Laterza. [Italian translation of *Histoire de la vie privé* I. De l'Empire romain à l'an mil. Paris: Seuil, 1985. ed. P. Ariès and G. Duby. English translation, *A History of Private Life,* Vol. 1, *From Pagan Rome to Byzantium.* Trans. A. Goldhammer. Cambridge, MA: Harvard University Press.]

Perrini, A. 1986. *Cuci e taci* [Sew and Be Silent]. Turin: I libri del gambero.

Rossi-Doria, A. 1987. "Mi è cara l'idea di uguaglianza" [I cherish the idea of equality]. *Noi donne* (September): 70-76.

Sasso, C. 1986. *In rosa* [In Pink]. Susa: Tipolito Melli.

Segio, S. 1988. "Lotta armata e giudizio morale" [Armed struggle and moral judgment]. *Il manifesto* (July 4).

Trevi, M. 1988. *Forme e limiti del controtransfert in psicoterapia* [Forms and limits of countertransference in psychotherapy]. Paper presented to the seminar of the Institute for Psychotherapy and Psychoanalysis, Discorso amoroso e practica del transfert [Love Discourse and the Practice of Transfert]. Turin. February 27.

Van Straten, G. 1987. *Generazione* [Generation]. Milan: Garzanti.

Vasale, C. 1980. *Terrorismo e ideologia in Italia* [Terrorism and Ideology in Italy]. Rome: Armando.

PART IV

COMPARATIVE STUDIES

LEFT-WING AND RIGHT-WING TERRORIST GROUPS: A COMPARISON FOR THE GERMAN CASE

Friedhelm Neidhardt

INTRODUCTION

Terrorism is a small stimulus with big impacts. It is practiced by relatively small groups. Because their activities consist of resorting to violence and claiming that it is legitimate, they collide not only with the general taboo on violence but also—and this is the political crux of the matter—with the modern state's claim to a monopoly on violence. That latter challenge lends terrorist actions social fascination and provokes state prosecution. In the ensuing conflicts many variables that affect the course of events come into play, not least those conditions that arise only with the social and political responses to terrorism (Neidhardt 1985).

The analysis in this paper focuses on the action system that produces terrorism: the terrorist group itself. The primary question concerns its forms of organization, the circumstances from which it stems, and what it actually accomplishes. The interrelation of these variables will be analyzed by comparing several left-wing and right-wing terrorist groups that were active

International Social Movement Research, Vol. 4, pages 215-235.

ISBN: 1-55938-445-X

in the Federal Republic of Germany in the 1970s. The analysis will begin with general background information.

The history of terrorism in the Federal Republic of Germany begins at the end of the 1960s. Although violent acts and attacks had been carried out even before that point, especially on the fringes of extreme right-wing movements, they lacked the coherence of overall planning and organization. These qualities developed at the other end of the political spectrum from the sometimes turbulent events surrounding the student movement and the "extraparliamentary opposition" (Ausserparlamentarische Opposition, APO). Arson attacks and bombings by left-wing and anarchist groupings had increased since the autumn of 1967, particularly in West Berlin. The first terrorist organization, the Red Army Faction (Rote Armee Fraktion, RAF, also known as Baader-Meinhof Group) was founded in 1970, and soon after already-active groups of the antiauthoritarian, anarchist scene in West Berlin joined to form the Movement of June 2 (Bewegung 2. Juni). In 1973 a third faction formed within leftist terrorism, the Revolutionary Cells (Revolutionaeren Zellen, RZ), which recruited their members among supporters of the RAF and the Movement of June 2 but which experimented with new strategies of underground warfare. Despite extensive manhunts and continual losses of members, all three factions managed to establish themselves in the underground for a few years. By 1980 several hundred attacks on individuals and property had been attributed to these groups, which were the main representatives of German terrorism. They were the ones who preoccupied and worried the German public and political establishment the most.

In 1977, however, rightist terrorism began to increase, climaxing in 1980. The militancy of neo-Nazi groups had been on the rise even before that point, but now some groups formed with the express intention of preparing and carrying out terrorist attacks. They were the Kühnen-Schulte-Wegener Group, the Otte Group, and Manfred Roeder's German Action Groups. Only some of the members could be arrested before committing terrorist acts. This scene is credited with having carried out about thirty attacks from 1977 to 1980. Rightist terrorism did not achieve a stable social structure in this period either, however. Its capacity to establish itself underground remained slight, a failing described and explained in greater detail below.

MEMBERSHIP

This study focuses on the RAF, the Bewegung 2. Juni, and the RZ on the left, and the Otte Group, the Kühnen-Schulte-Wegener Group, and the German Action Groups on the right. To gain an initial insight into the factors determining their degree of cohesion and their performance capability, one can compare the social characteristics of their members. In view of the data base, the analysis can only include statistical information on age, sex, and education. But these characteristics and their distribution can be interpreted as group-specific indicators of conditions and possibilities if the relations they indicate can be validated with additional material.[1]

Age Distribution

The years of birth listed for the persons labeled terrorists in this text (Table 1) are only unreliable indicators of the age at which these individuals joined the terrorist scene and became active in it. Most operations of left-wing terrorists began in the early 1970s; those of right-wing terrorists, toward the end of that decade. Despite the impression given by Table 1 most left-wing terrorists (especially those in the Bewegung 2. Juni) were "young people." To that extent, my material does not contradict the image of the "terrorist personality" that emerged from Walter Laqueur's extensive analyses of terrorist groupings of many different countries and periods:

> In short, there have always been a most diverse array of character traits [and] intellectual and psychological elements among terrorists. One can say with certainty only that terror was (and is) practiced by young people and that in most other respects the differences between the terrorists are more striking than what they have in common (Laqueur 1977, p. 125).

For comparing groups, however, the average age of the members is much less salient than the age distribution. In this regard, members of left-wing terrorist collectives were much more similar in age. By contrast, the age distribution of right-wing terrorists as a whole peaked at two different points, a multigenerational composition also reflected in most of their individual action groups. It is to be assumed that the corresponding age span complicated the social cohesion of right-wing terrorist groups in ways unknown or less severe in left-wing terrorist groups. Such problems would seem to be a handicap particularly for underground existence with its routine difficulties of living in close quarters.

Table 1. Age Distribution and Age Brackets of Left-wing and Right-wing Terrorists (In Percentages)

Year of Birth	*Right-wing Terrorists*	*Left-wing Terrorists*	*RAF*	*Bewegung 2. Juni*
1965 or later	51	3	3	2
1951-1955	12	29	15	41
1946-1950	4	34	36	39
1945 or earlier	33	34	46	17
(1930 or earlier)	(12)	(0)	(0)	(0)
N	51	223	74	41

Gender Profile

The differences between left-wing and right-wing terrorist groups in their sexual composition were remarkable (Table 2), with the share of women being considerably higher in left-wing terrorist groups. In the right-wing scene almost all groups were purely male organizations. Only the German Action Groups had female members—who were, however, clear patriarchal annexations as girlfriends, fiancées, daughters, or wives of male members. Their function in the German Action Groups was correspondingly subservient; essentially they were to carry out assignments and give support. Leftist groupings were different. Not only did they have significantly more women, they also granted them clearly equal status in the decision-making structures. Many of their leaders have been women.

The reasons for the sex differences in the memberships of left-wing and right-wing terrorist groups are inevitably rooted in the dissimilar philosophies of the two sides. Rightist extremism expresses the belief of "natural orders" attributed to a hierarchy of race as well as sex. "Men make history." Women remain behind the scenes of battle, and when they do come forward, they must serve. All this is expressed among right-wing extremist combat groups in the very swagger of their language, in the masculinization of their clothing as military uniforms, and, overall, in a militarization of communication, which consciously emphasizes the difference between the sexes. By contrast, leftist philosophy in general embraces equality and emancipation of the repressed and the leveling of traditional strata and hierarchies. So it is not surprising that a few members of the increasingly militant women's movement of the 1960s and 1970s tended to find a home and function in left-wing rather than right-wing extremist movements and, eventually, in their terrorist activities (Eaubonne 1978).

Table 2. Composition of Left-wing and Right-wing Terrorist Groups by Sex (In Percentages)

Sex	*Right-wing Terrorists*	*Left-wing Terrorists*	*RAF*	*Bewegung 2. Juni*
Male	90	67	66	61
Female	10	33	34	39
N	51	223	74	41

Apart from these reasons, the high proportion of women in left-wing terrorist groups fulfills secondary functions of no small significance for long-term underground struggle. The presence of both sexes provides for the satisfaction of emotional and sexual needs within the group, allowing it a degree of autonomy that in many ways enhances the capacity to lead a subversive existence. Love relations with nonmembers not only imperils security because they leave additional tracks, they imply the development of competing loyalties. An underground group is bound to be jealous of such relations and to urge homogamy. The fact that right-wing terrorist groups are largely unable to satisfy emotional and sexual needs within their ranks because they consist of only one sex would seem to be one more limitation on their possibilities for successful subversive activity.

Educational Background

Further differences between the terrorist movements become apparent if the educational backgrounds of their members are compared (Table 3). On average, right-wing terrorists clearly have a lower level of education than left-wing terrorists. That may partially explain why the theoretical quality of statements by right-wing terrorists is only rudimentary. Conversely, it is certainly no accident that the most serious literature came from the group with the highest educational standard, the RAF.

The dissimilar styles of reflection evidenced by left-wing and right-wing terrorists is also explained in part by the fact that their educated members tend to come from different academic subcultures, as can be seen from their courses

Table 3. Educational Level of Left-wing and Right-wing Terrorists (In Percentages)

Educational Level	*Right-wing Terrorists*	*Left-wing Terrorists*	*RAF*	*Bewegung 2. Juni*
Elementary School	49	17	15	22
Tenth Grade Technical or Business School	22	15	12	25
College Prep	17	19	22	17
University	10	42	50	29
No Information	2	7	1	7
N	51	227	74	41

of study. The liberal arts figure prominently among left-wing terrorists: educational science (26 percent), languages and cultural sciences (24 percent), and social sciences (20 percent). The five right-wing terrorist academics in the group examined in the present text had studied engineering, medicine, mineralogy, law, or economics.

To summarize, the statistical analysis of the social backgrounds represented by members of terrorist organizations, shows that the individual groups differed in several ways that do not appear to be random. The highly intellectualized RAF had a status of its own, and there is a conspicuous difference between left-wing and right-wing terrorist groups. Though most terrorists are young people, several right-wing terrorist circles were conspicuous for the number of male members over fifty years of age who linked group dynamics to Nazi ideology in the cases examined. The largely male-dominated character of nearly all right-wing terrorist combat groups also fit that ideology. The ideological basis of these groups acquired no theoretical underpinnings of great repute in part because they all lacked the kind of humanist intellectuals that the RAF had been able to attract as ideologists.

As for the effectiveness of left-wing and right-wing terrorist groups at conducting illegal struggle and adapting to its conditions, the composition of right-wing terrorists organizations suggests that they could be more prone to internal tensions and problems. Given the age ranges of their members and their lack of women, they seem perhaps less suited to prolonged underground activity. This weak conjecture, however, must be examined by analyzing other conditions that are probably more decisive for the potential of terrorist groups to act.

THE SOCIAL INFRASTRUCTURE OF TERRORIST ACTIVISTS

A certain minimum amount of resources is required for practicing terrorism. Terrorists need weapons and explosives, must have money with which to acquire them and to finance other things, have to provide hideouts and means of escape, and must develop firm, reliable interpersonal relations and loyality. The question is whether someone will help do it—and who.

Backgrounds of Left-wing and Right-wing Extremism

One could expect to find a reservoir of support for terrorists primarily among left-wing and right-wing extremists because it can be assumed that they are the most likely people to sympathize with the general objectives of terrorists. The relation between political extremism and militant terrorism is more complicated than it appears to be, however, as is shown when one analyzes whether and to which extent members of terrorist groupings had been also members of extremist legal organizations.

To some extent, the biographies of terrorists show that extremist organizations have played an obviously militarizing role in their careers as "flow heaters" in which a kind of presocialization to militancy must have taken place. Among left-wing extremists, they did not encompass the relevant, familiar organizations of orthodox communists, and only in exceptional cases did they include organizations of the "New Left." The most frequent recruitment fields for left-wing terrorists were local splinter groups of the APO and a multitude of political "politcommunes" and "red cells." At the end, recruitment was done almost exclusively in organizations that specialized in the support of terrorists in prison, the so-called torture committees and antifascist groups (ANTIFA).

The "recruiting field" of right-wing terrorists seems to be even more diffuse. About three quarters of the 51 right-wing terrorists included in the present study came from a number of right-wing extremist organizations. However, there have also been cases in which the commitment to rightist terrorism came about privately for the most part through family relations or friends, not through connections with any right-wing extremist organization. This is true, for example, of the German Action Groups, into which the two initiators wove a private network of comrades-in-arms, including friends of both sexes, sons-in-law and daughters, as well as friends and fiancées.

On the whole, one can make out a general pattern in the history of the origins of both right-wing and left-wing terrorist groups. The vast majority of terrorists had a record of involvement with extremist circles. In these cases, however, where precursory organizations of the rightist and leftist extremism militarized later terrorists, the road to terrorism was not taken as a career in these organizations but as a step by individual members. True, various right-wing extremist circles and organizations were recruiting fields for leftist and rightist terrorism but did not become terrorist organizations themselves. Individuals coming from these groups and organizations decided to engage in illegal activities, while the majority remained more or less uncertain or disapproving. As revealed by material on the origins of individual terrorist groups, some of the factors determining the people who made that switch evidently had little to do with the political objectives of terrorism. Whereas many persons refrained when approached or deserted when things became really serious, others took part out of personal loyality and sometimes because of intimate ties. Aside from all other circumstances, friendships, love affairs, and kinship were probably the aspect that was able to tip the scales from ambivalence to participation. Further analysis reveals remote motives for ultimately deciding in favor of terrorism, and it is not at all certain whether the people in question were aware of them. The nature of the circumstances that paved their way to terrorism, suggested it to them, and made it possible can be explained in structural terms. Without such circumstances, the motives of the terrorists could have led to quite different careers.

Support Circles

Some of the social structures observed for the recruitment of terrorist groupings are repeated in the patterns of their support. As far as hideouts, supply, and defense are concerned, private aid is not to be underestimated. The category of people from which it comes cannot be identified precisely. Their willingness to help is essentially of an unpolitical nature, coming as it does from relatives and friends as well as people who empathize if they feel that terrorists are being hunted and persecuted. This category accounted for a considerable share of the 6 percent of those who, in a 1971 survey of a representative sample of the population, responded that they were prepared to "take in for one night" a member of the Baader-Meinhof Group being sought by the police (Kepplinger 1974, p. 777). The willingness of these "sympathizers" to help certain terrorists must not be confounded with sympathy for their terrorism. To that extent their willingness to help is limited and rather defensive; it is a kind of emergency reserve for individual predicaments.

As hinted in the previous section's examination of terrorism's recruiting mechanisms, the circle of left-wing and right-wing extremists lending support to terrorism was not a reliable reservoir. All in all, their attitude toward terrorism is ambivalent at best. Certain objectives and no doubt also the aversion to the "persecutors" were shared, but most extremist organizations and groups repudiated terrorism on strategic, political, or even moral grounds. This stance was particularly true, for example, of all orthodox communist organizations as well as of the right-wing extremist National Democratic Party of Germany (Nationaldemokratische Partei Deutschlands, NPD). But even more militant organizations did not give any ideological and political backing as a rule.

It is significant, though, that there were strategically important exceptions in this regard. If the social infrastructure of left-wing and right-wing terrorists are compared with this in mind, differences emerge. On the fringes of the left-wing extremist camp alone, there were organizations clearly supporting terrorist activities. Their development began with the founding of "torture committees" in 1973 and continued after their dissolution with the rise of the International Defense Committee. A few attorneys representing terrorists who were serving sentences played a major role in the militarization of these and other organizations. This militarization took on significant dimensions with the formation of the ANTIFA, groups of the "legal RAF sphere," which at the end of the 1960s were operating with 150 members in 12 cities (mostly university towns) and which were considered to be the instigators and organizers of several militant events. The RAF, in particular, had been recruiting its new members almost exclusively from the "torture committees" and the ANTIFA since 1975. Organizations obviously supporting terrorism in the right-wing extremist camp had not yet differentiated and crystallized to the same degree. The lines of support ran more through individuals who belonged to different organizations or who were "unaffiliated."

On the whole, then, the infrastructure of rightist extremism has remained more diffuse and less organized than that of leftist extremism. Just what the "hinterland" of rightist terrorism was nonetheless capable of delivering is shown, among other things, by the donations that flowed to the militant circle around Roeder (even since his arrest after the terrorist acts committed by his German Action Groups). According to investigations conducted by security authorities, approximately 700 persons donated a total of about DM 84,000 (currently more than $50,000) from the summer of 1979 through the summer of 1980. Pensioners accounted for 45 percent of the donors; 12 percent of the donors lived abroad.

Foreign contacts in the support of German terrorism play a role that cannot be neglected. It is notable that the Palestinian Liberation Movement, with its training camps in the Near East, served as a port-of-call and training center for both left-wing and right-wing terrorists, which would never have been conceivable without the militant antizionism they shared. As early as 1969-70 members of the RAF and the Bewegung 2. Juni underwent considerable military training in camps of the Palestinian Front for the Liberation of Palestine. The "international faction" of the RZ has conducted joint operations with Palestinian commandos, and all leftist terrorist groupings have probably received money and weapons from this source. As for right-wing terrorists, there is proof of contacts established in Lebanese camps by dispersed members of the Wehrsportgruppe Hoffmann after it was banned (see Hoffman 1982, p. 20). By 1980 foreign contacts of right-wing terrorists were not capable of doing much. Aside from weapons deliveries arranged by Swiss friends of similar persuasion, they have not played a significant role in right-wing terrorist activity to date. In this respect as well, the infrastructure of the German rightist terrorism is still underdeveloped compared to that of leftist terrorism, whose links to militant movements in the Near East as well as in almost all Western European countries (especially France, Italy, and Holland) have been a decisive factor in its operations in recent years. Foreign contacts arranged not only hideouts but also many kinds of cooperation.

Organizational Capacity of Left-wing and Right-wing Militancy

The infrastructures serving leftist and rightist terrorism in the Federal Republic of Germany were unequal in quality in the 1970s. The difference was primarily that rightist terrorism, unlike leftist terrorism, was unable to build and guard an illegal underground and was therefore much more vulnerable to government manhunts.

One reason for this difference was that rightist terrorism was more recent than leftist terrorism and had thus not yet been able to establish itself as well. But this answer does not explain why leftist terrorism had a developmental headstart in the first place. The premise—the capacity to maintain a stable underground—is simply taken for granted, yet here must have been structural conditions encouraging this capacity to develop disproportionately on the left rather than the right.

The reasons must be sought at several levels. It is important to note that rightist extremism, which probably had about as much latent potential in the population of the Federal Republic of Germany as that of leftist extremism, was less organizationally capable of developing militancy because of its sociostructural roots. First, rightist extremism was far more deeply seated than leftist extremism in higher age brackets, that is, those including socially established people for whom family ties and jobs make illegal activities and underground existence far more costly than is the case with leftist students. Under these circumstances, rightist extremism was more apt to remain latent, and that for a longer period. Second, rightist extremism was geographically more dispersed in that it did not possess the regionally and socially effective media for crystallization that leftist extremism had primarily through the university. By concentrating the potential of leftist extremism and offering the freedom guaranteed by relatively anomic structures, universities gave it opportunities to mobilize (Allerbeck 1971). Rightist extremism had no comparable sanctuary. The situation of right-wing extremists was similar in some ways to that of the French peasants under Louis Bonaparte. Seeking to determine why they were incapable of "pressing their class interests . . . in their own name," Karl Marx wrote that they were "a mass" of many elements in tune with each other "but in many respects without rallying to one another. Their mode of production isolates them from each other instead of bringing them to interact" (Marx [1852] 1960, p. 308).

A third point that should not be overlooked when examining the organizational capacity of the right-wing extremist movement is that the theoretical stature of their ideology was much less developed than in leftist extremism. It subsisted on just a few powerful affects over which cognitive control was relatively weak. This ideology may have been a good stimulant for precisely that reason, but it scarcely lent itself to deriving strategic and tactical programs of action. The cognitive structures of this ideology had little capacity to exert control. That is why reasoning seemed to play a conspicuously small part in the communication between right-wing extremists. Issues were decreed more than described; conclusions were commanded more than derived.

At the social level, such lack of cognitive structure corresponds to the appreciation in the status of leadership. Leaders are a kind of functional equivalent for a normative theory of action. When it is accepted, decisionism is legitimated. To that extent leadership elicits extraordinary discipline and precise organization, provided the charisma of the leader is believed in. It thereby solves the problem of institutionalization also associated with the establishment of a terrorist infrastructure.

This point brings up the fourth aspect in understanding the difference in the quality of the infrastructure drawn on by leftist and rightist terrorism in the Federal Republic of Germany in the 1970s. A major shortcoming of the right-wing extremist movement in postwar Germany is that it has never found a recognized leader. As stated in a special issue of Thies Christophersen's Bauernschaft, "We can officially found an NSDAP [Nationalsozialistische Deutsche Arbeiterpartei] only when a new Führer is there. . . . We have enough parties. What we are missing are personalities who could assume a role as Führer." As long as they are not found, rightist extremism in the Federal Republic of Germany will be weakened by rivalries between ambitious would-be leaders and will be limited in its ability to mount prolonged, collective, large-scale operations. Conversely, this means that its stature could soar with a new Führer.

GROUPS AND GROUP PERFORMANCE

As populations, right-wing and left-wing terrorists constitute nothing other than a statistical category, namely, a mathematical summation of individuals. To which extent and in which manner they are capable of planning and carrying out terrorist activities depends, along with everything else (such as the stature of the members and the quality of the infrastructure), mainly on whether and how the individuals relate to one another, form groups, build organizations, and develop solidarity. Such systems give rise to additional capacities. They permit more than the mere summing of forces, they allow for a division of labor and for specialization as well as for mutual emotional support. That means an enormous gain in power. The question is to which extent and in which manner the terrorists identifiable by 1980 knew how to convert it.

Group Formations and Degrees of Organizations

The scope and nature of the social linkages among persons directly involved in carrying out terrorist acts can be broken down into the following types of social group formations:

- Anomy: There is no specific purpose linking the actors (loners).
- Loose networks: Various actors form a loose chain of largely one-on-one contacts, thus comprising no common identity with the system and no finite system.

- Primary groups: The social link between individuals crystallizes into direct relations between all members, creates collective identity within the group (the "we-feeling") and excludes outsiders through clear membership criteria.
- Organization: A streamlined structure links individual actors and subgroups to a system based on the division of labor, establishes responsibilities and positions, and develops management structures.

If these categories and the criteria used to define them are used to describe the social connections of left-wing and right-wing terrorists, significant differences emerge. Interpreting the sequence of categories as a scale on which the actors' degree of organization is plotted between zero (anomie) and one hundred (organization), one could develop the general thesis for the 1970s that the actors of rightist terrorism in the Federal Republic of Germany tended to be on the lower half of the scale in the 1970s, whereas those of leftist terrorism tended to be on the upper half.

The striking thing about rightist terrorism is that the number of loners was higher than for leftist terrorism, especially before 1978. The rise of the Kühnen-Schulte-Wegener Group, the Otte Group, and Roeder Group indicates a more developed degree of organization in rightist terrorism from 1978 to 1980. But even then, they cannot be considered unconditionally as primary groups in the sense defined above. They are more like loose networks having only a very small core group at the center. In all three groupings, for example, it is typical that ad hoc recruits suddenly join in the operations because a member of the "inner circle" knew them to be cut well enough for the job—and subsequently fade almost entirely from the picture.

Similar ad-hoc recruitment was not observed for leftist terrorism. Its three principle groupings—even the most loosely structured one, the Bewegung 2. Juni, which initially experienced great fluctuation within a widely spun network of accomplices—formed well-defined *primary groups* in the sense defined above. Some of the reasons for leftist terrorism's higher degree of social crystallization have already been cited in a different context: greater homogeneity of the members, greater local concentration, and freer social availability of the members due to their lower average degree of occupational and familial ties and other commitments. At the same time, there is a special aspect that is both a condition and an effect of social crystallization in leftist terrorism. Unlike rightist terrorists, leftist terrorists went underground and were able to persevere there despite the imprisonment of many of them. That called for a minimal capacity for group cohesion, but it also pulled the members together the moment life as total outlaws had begun. This was a fundamental reaction to the feeling of mortal danger engendered by the pressure of being hunted.

Although the RAF, the Bewegung 2. Juni, and the RZ were born of closely knit left-wing movements whose members identified strongly with one other, these three groups did differ in the degree of organization with which they linked individual members together appropriately and efficiently in their diverse parallel and auxiliary groups and these, in turn, with each other. These variations stemmed from unequal capacities and different fighting strategies. The RAF had (and still has) the highest degree of organization, so it was able to set the most demanding objectives. It achieved the greatest degree of centralization and continuity—despite an almost 100 percent turnover in membership. Except in the beginning, its operations were carefully prepared and planned well in advance. The individual subgroups were marshaled onto a common course in an increasingly laborious process of consensus-building, one that was conceptually established far more in the RAF than in all other groupings. It was even published in part; there was and still is "RAF theory," whatever one may think of its quality.

The Bewegung 2. Juni cannot compare in this regard. Naturally, this contrast stems from the anarchist views of the group's leading figures. Their subgroups remained relatively autonomous, lacking even the beginnings of some sort of center. Between these two poles of left-wing terrorist organization fall the RZ. On the one hand, they emphasized a decentralized structure, wanting to organize "opposing power in small cores that work autonomously in the different areas." On the other hand, they attempted to link and coordinate the subgroups, whose most conspicuous medium for a time was the newspaper Revolutionärer Zorn (Revolutionary Wrath) put together by the delegates of various local groups. It seems, however, that the desired integration was very incomplete and became more and more difficult as police pressure grew.

Walter Laqueur (1977, p. 83) has stated that the "ideal model" of terrorist organizations is "strong, central leadership that deals with general strategy but leaves the details to the local groups." If the quality of what the three left-wing terrorist formations have accomplished is measured against that maxim, then the problem of the RAF would have to have been overcentralization; that of the Bewegung 2. Juni and the RZ, mainly undercentralization. Although undercentralization has the advantage of greater and more variegated ability to adapt to the demands of local environments and the needs of individual members, it compromises the division of work and cooperation. Overcentralization achieves both but entails the danger of becoming isolated from the environment. Indeed, it can be shown that the internal integration to which the RAF was compelled was linked with the group's self-isolation from the outside world. This self-isolation, in turn, was a key factor in the group's ever more absolutist overestimation of itself, its increasingly ideological perception of reality, and its more and more fictitious objectives (Neidhardt 1982, chapts. IV and V). These changes were precisely what the RCs and the Bewegung 2. Juni persistently criticized.

Stability and Solidarity

The differentiations between left-wing terrorist formations lie at a group level that none of the right-wing terrorist groupings achieved in the 1970s. This dissimilarity is expressed in the different quality of group accomplishments, both internally with regard to the creation of stability and externally with regard to the execution of appropriate activities.

In terms of the relation between the level of the groupings and their chance of stabilizing, the finding for the formations of rightist terrorism is clear. They survived their first terrorist activities for only a short time, often not even getting beyond the planning stage before they were broken up. The decisive external factor of this instability stems from the loose network structure of their coalitions and the resulting openness of their outer boundaries, which government spies were able to penetrate to a greater degree than was apparently the case with any left-wing terrorist group. Some of these agents even managed to attain positions within the core of the groups. Evidently, such infiltration succeeded in the leftist extremist scene only before left-wing terrorist groups crystalized, that is, in a situation where network structures dominated on the left as well. In any case, it is plain that the speed and rate of imprisonment were significantly higher in the right-wing terrorist sphere.

Another fact is also plain, one that can be considered an indicator of the minimal degree of group solidarity achieved. The percentage of members of right-wing terrorist groupings who "sing" and "squeal" as soon as they are arrested is much greater than that of members of such groupings on the left. Interrogation records, indictments, and court findings pertaining to the right-wing terrorist formations studied here (the Kühnen-Schulte-Wegener Group, the Otte Group, the Roeder Group, and the "network" around Eisermann) reliably show in each case that several members divulged detailed information about the internal workings of their groups, incriminating each other considerably despite all previous oaths of loyalty and all threats of reprisals for betrayal. Obviously, these groups never managed to forge steadfast loyalities.

In these and other respects, the differences with left-wing terrorist groupings are remarkable. To be sure, severe reprisals were threatened as part of the established control measures in left-wing terrorist groups, too, and in at least one case (the Schmücker murder) a traitor was even liquidated. In left-wing terrorist quarters, however, this mode of discipline cannot be regarded as either typical or even dominant. For maintaining internal security and discipline, left-wing terrorist groupings, particularly (but not only) the RAF, had functional alternatives to violence to a greater extent than did right-wing terrorist "circles." The very recruiting practices of left-wing terrorist groups were more sophisticated and stringent. The group boundary drawn by restrictions on communication excluded even active supporters. Furthermore, the creation of group loyalities undoubtedly succeeded better in leftist terrorism. Despite the miserable conditions of underground existence and the danger of being pursued, only a small minority of the several hundred members and active supports of leftist terrorist groupings have become "defectors," and when imprisoned or interrogated only very few of those individuals have revealed details of their terrorist practices. When they did inform under interrogation or in publications, they rarely divulged secrets that could have endangered their former groups.

At first glance such feats are incredible, but what makes them possible? Several factors can be suggested. As soon as leftist terrorist groups are driven underground, they are under strong pressure to hold together. Each member must be able to rely on the other, if only for his or her own sake. And the longer this situation persists, the more possible it is for common experience "on the front" to nurture cohesion and mutual support with deep emotional roots. Intrinsic reasons probably also contribute to this solidarity. One gets the impression that left-wing terrorists, at least in the 1970s, were imbued with a stronger and more stalwart sense of their political mission than right-wing terrorists were. That may have to do with the greater reflection characteristic of left-wing extremist theories, perhaps also with the greater lure of their moral principles. In leftist terrorism, the ultimate objectives of "freedom, equality, and brotherhood" are the classical virtues of the Enlightenment, which are certainly easier to idealize and less assailable today than an apotheosis of nation and race (Lübbe 1980). The impression is that left-wing terrorists and their comrades therefore found it easier to assuage their consciences about their criminal activities. Whatever doubts they may have had, they managed to define themselves as a "moral community" (Neidhardt 1981).

Terrorist Operations

It is necessary to develop internal cohesion and stability if serious programs of actions are to succeed. Where group processes are nipped in the bud and where the members begin to operate against each other under the pressure of impending court cases, the minimal amount of continuity that would be necessary just to accumulate experience cannot build. It is thus a further indication of the unequal strengths of the terrorist formations considered here that tricks of the militant underground trade were collected in the left-wing terrorist scene—and only there—in a virtual textbook, the *Kröcher Paper*, nearly two hundred pages containing a wealth of detailed lessons on everything that seems important for a "guerilla fighter" to know under the then current conditions of being on the run.[2]

The compilation of such a "textbook" presupposes not only a relatively long history of practical "field experiments" but also a social infrastructure that permits the findings to be collected, systematized, and written up. This would have been inconceivable in rightist terrorism. It is therefore not surprising that right-wing terrorist operations, when they came off at all, were simple and downright amateurish compared to those of the RAF in particular (Hoffmann 1982, p. 13).

This is not to say that the danger of right-wing terrorist operations was negligible. In 1980 eighteen people died as a result of right-wing terrorist attacks (though it is possible that some of these casualties, not being planned in this way, were due to amateurism). As far as the willingness to kill is concerned, no overall differences between left-wing and right-wing terrorists are discernible at present. Nor do there seem to be any general differences in terms of selective mechanisms inhibiting action against noncombatants—who constitute a politically instructive category that reveals the systematically derived notions that both sides have about who should not be hurt by their actions.

The assertion, which contradicts prevailing theses in the literature, needs to be thoroughly discussed. It is widely held that terrorists in general, and right-wing terrorists in specific, can be characterized by their wanton choices of goals and victims. As Peter Waldmann (1977, p. 72) states,

> One of the major general traits of terrorist procedure is their capriciousness and lack of predictability. Terror befalls its victim as it were. The arbitrariness in the choice of targets, which is accentuated by the disregard of all legal and humanitarian axioms, is not based on some cult of spontaneity indulged in by terrorists or on their inability to plan and control violence; they make it an outright principle. In the name of this principle, they go above all for innocent people like children and the elderly who have not the slightest thing to do with the conflict at hand.

My material contradicts such butcher theories about terrorism. It documents abiding reflection on both sides not only about the targets that are tactically and strategically appropriate to attack but also about systematically definable taboos on attacks. It was inconsistent with the political concepts of liberation held by left-wing terrorists when "ordinary people" were injured, and when that nevertheless happened in attacks, serious conflicts and even sanctions resulted within the terrorist ranks. Among right-wing terrorists, there were certain thresholds inhibiting attacks against the terrorists' own race, especially against "national comrades" (except certain categories of Germans, particularly politicians considered to be "mercenaries" of foreign powers). Attacks on residences and other targets, for example, were often not carried out if it could be assumed that Germans would be endangered. It is therefore rather unlikely that the bloody massacre at the Oktoberfest in Munich in September 1980 was consistent with any kind of logic of right-wing extremist act of violence. In this case, which cannot be cleared up completely, an accident caused by a loner was probably involved. Of course, it is no coincidence that "accident" and "loner" are important categories precisely in the sphere of rightist terrorism. Both are consistent with the vacuous character of the system behind German rightist terrorism. Given its minimal degree of organization, its self-imposed limits are not reliably enforcable. In that sense, elements of "capriciousness and lack of predictability" come into play that have to do with "inability to plan and control violence."

The fact that normative operational ground rules in German terrorism prevented actions against certain targets was also manifested in the deliberate aim taken at others. Aside from the larceny, bank robberies, and other crimes that both sides committed to equip themselves, the left wing and the right wing often had different targets for attack. The left concentrated on large firms and capitalists, book stores of the NPD, and installations of the West German military, for example; the right, on such things as shelters for foreigners and refugee camps, the Berlin Wall, and an "Auschwitz memorial exhibition."

Sometimes the choices of leftist and rightist terrorism overlapped, indicating the ways in which the resentments of the two sides also converged. Targets of both left-wing and right-wing terrorist attacks included Jewish facilities; foreign troops, especially installations of the U.S. army; buildings of the security authorities as well as police and judges; and institutions of the government and the established political parties in general. True, such operations differed in their technical quality and motives. Antizionism was motivated on the right by antisemitism; on the left, by anti-Israeli sentiment (not least out of consideration for the cooperation of Palestinian liberation movements). And to right-wing extremists, the U.S. army was an "occupation regime;" to the leftists, a symbol of imperialist wars, among other things. Nonetheless, the aggressions complemented each other and at times ran parallel. To that extent, there was not only hostility between left-wing and right-wing extremist groupings but also common elements and sympathy (as could be observed on the right).

Partial consonance of this sort becomes comprehensible in view of the formally similar strategic determinants of leftist and rightist terrorism. The aim was "to undermine the state from within, to make the population feel insecure" (Otte), to force the state to the defensive measure of "martial law" so that it would "turn the masses against itself by its own terror, thereby sharpening contradictions [and] compelling the revolutionary struggle" (Meinhof). The differences between left-wing and right-wing terrorists began essentially only thereafter. Until that point, however, they played into each others' hands. How successful they were at it and which side had the greater impact was not determined solely by the results of their own doings. The success of terrorism depends above all on how society reacts to it. It is a function of the population's indifference, the sense of justice and the power of political instances, the perceptions of the pursuers, and, not least, the mass media's sense of political responsibility.

THEORETICAL IMPLICATIONS AND FINDINGS

What has theory gained by this empirical analysis? It seems to be of limited value to make generalizations pertaining to the specifically German manifestations of leftist and rightist terrorism. The constellations of circumstances on the left and right under which terrorism emerged in the Federal Republic of Germany in the 1970s can change over time. Only certain aspects remain the same. Many features of German rightist terrorism, including its operational weaknesses and lack of success, certainly have nothing in principle to do with its ideological position but rather with the fact that right-wing extremist ideology appears to have been largely discredited by the German history of national socialism in the eyes of the population. Only a few decades after the end of Nazi rule, rightist terrorism in Germany is having a particularly hard time finding members, supporters, and sympathizers. Hence, its peculiarities can be generalized in the international framework only to a limited degree. Nonetheless, a theoretical analysis can benefit from a German comparison of leftist and rightist terrorism at a higher level of abstraction. In a systematic comparison of terrorism's leftist and rightist characteristics, the key analytical point is for theoretically relevant variables to vary enough to make their relations conspicuous and identifiable.

Such variables were specified through a selective perspective related to the patterns of "resource mobilization theories" in research on social movements (McCarthy and Zald 1973, 1977; Oberschall 1973). It directs attention to the central units of action of terrorist formations—namely, the active terrorist groups—examines the organizational processes of their action, and ascertains the organizational efficacy that can be empirically documented particularly as a function of environmental conditions that are salient in terms of "resource mobilization." The empirical analysis can thus be understood ex post as a practical application and acid test of elements of the resource-mobilization approach. A few comments about it are in order.

(1) To ensure a clean, empirically testable analysis, it seems advantageous to focus on active groups that conduct terrorism (as in Crenshaw 1985, p. 467; see also Gurr 1988, p.128). An investigation of these groups reveals pivotal differences. Terrorist groups in the Federal Republic of Germany are remarkable for the wide variation in the scope of their organization, that is, the degree to which they have socially structured division of labor, cooperation, and leadership. Among other things, the categorization that Ted Gurr (1988, p. 129) expressly calls for should thus be scaled according to this criterion. As in the analysis of German terrorist groups, one could thereby distinguish between (a) anomy, (b) loose networks ("quasi groups"), (c) primary groups, and (d) organization. It must be kept in mind that an increasing degree of organization does not imply the organizational style of centralization. Advanced decentralization, too, can be strictly organized.

(2) The analytical purpose of such a typology stems from the hypothesis that the degree of organization of terrorist groupings correlates highly with their effectiveness. This is plausible in at least two ways. If terrorist groupings are interpreted as production companies, then their primary organizational objective is the production of terrorist operations. Resorting to random violence is not enough to destroy anything. As political entrepreneurs, terrorist groupings depend on reaching the right "targets" and using violence against them in a way that is simultaneously tactically and strategically efficient and symbolically meaningful. In addition to everything else, that is a technically difficult undertaking, and terrorist groupings are capable of managing it only under certain organizational conditions. Bruce Hoffman (1982, p.13), for example, bears out the present analyses of right-wing and left-wing terrorist groups:

> The right-wing terrorists' favorite weapon is the bomb. This may be an indication that the terrorists are still at a somewhat primitive stage—unable, because of lack of expertise, organizational skills, or logistical deployment, to carry out more sophisticated operations (e.g., kidnappings and assassinations).

It must be remembered that terrorists in modern societies are under the enormous pressure of pursuit by professional criminologists and that some of their politically most attractive targets are heavily protected. Having to cope with an overwhelmingly hostile environment, the key achievement of terrorist groups, their fundamental premise is just to survive as a system of action. Probably, most of their work consists of ensuring their clandestine existence so that they can continue to exist (see Crenshaw 1985, p. 473). Given the conditions of underground life, this means being constantly on guard against the outer world and one's own comrades-in-arms. They must not know too much and under no circumstances must they want to betray what they do know. The level of organization must be high enough to tighten both group cohesion and group control as much as possible.

(3) It is unimaginable that the small terrorist groups that are operating are capable of stabilizing themselves and mounting terrorist attacks without outside help. Although there are indications in our analysis that terrorist groupings differ in their degree of autonomy depending on the size and composition of their membership, none of them can exist on their own power alone. Besides the fact that they need to recruit new members from time to time, they need social support for "resource mobilization"—places to go into hiding, the provision of material assistance, the supply of information and specialized expertise, and, no doubt, also social recognition and moral support.

Our analysis shows that the differences in the ability to mobilize such resources are largely responsible for the unequal organizational capacities of German terrorist groups. It also shows that general sympathies with the objectives and actions of terrorists on the part of the population are not sufficient. Much as in the case of social movements (see McAdam, McCarthy, and Zald 1988, p. 709), terrorism requires at least some organized social infrastructure of preparatory and supporting networks, groups, and organizations functioning as intermediate linkages. It is clear that the outstanding viability and efficiency of the RAF is connected mainly with the fact that it has possessed this infrastructure more than the other groups mentioned in the present context.

ACKNOWLEDGMENTS

This article is a revised and abridged version of a previous analysis (Neidhardt 1982, pp. 434-476). The original text was produced in a work group appointed by the Federal Ministry of the Interior, with the results presented in five volumes. The present version omits most of the original report's descriptive sections and their detailed data on the forms and actions taken by the individual terrorist groupings. The newly written concluding section is an attempt to relate the theoretical results of the comparative analysis to new concepts of and approaches to research on terrorism.

NOTES

1. Most of the sociological statistics in the following sections have been taken from a survey of biographical information compiled through content analysis of files on terrorists. Commissioned by the Federal Minister of the Interior in 1979, the work was conducted by federal and state officials of that Ministry. The group to be investigated for this purpose was defined as all persons who had been sought, accused, or convicted on the grounds of having violated paragraphs 129 or 129a of the criminal code by the end of 1978. This group embraced 250 persons, of whom 227 can be classified as left-wing terrorists and 23 as right-wing terrorists. To raise the number of right-wing terrorists on record by 1978 to a level acceptable for statistical analysis and to take account of the increase in activity in this sphere in 1979 and 1980, the group of 23 right-wing terrorists was widened by the author to include names of persons that had come to police attention in the last two years mentioned. Most of the persons were members of the Otte group, the "German Action Group," and a grouping (Hepp, Riedel, among others) that had formed in the Stuttgart and Karlsruhe areas, and whose members had been captured and charged with belonging to a criminal organization (paragraph 129 of the criminal code). The population of right-wing terrorists in the study thereby increased to 51.

2. Examples from the contents of this compendium for terrorists are: "A Few Words about Tactics"; "Ways of Attacking a Man" (with illustration); the equipment of the "Cops," with a subsection titled "Experimental Police Weapons"; "Security of Underground Conferences"; "Exchanging Messages"; information about techniques of "Surveillance" and "What One Can Do To Counter It"; "What To Do in a Police Street Raid"; "Setting Up Telephone Espionage" (with many technical details and sketches); "Encoding Communications," with a number of code systems; tips on uncovering "Bugs" and intercepting "Cop Radio Transmissions"; description of the contents of an "Emergency Suitcase" and "Tool Vests"; "Setting Up Depots," with a section on "Clandestine Apartments, Illegal Production Centers, Secret Supplies, etc."; "How to Guard against Informers"; "What To Do under Arrest and Interrogation"; "Behind Bars": What to Expect," "What You

Can Do," "How to Start a Prison Revolt"; "Rent a Car (without Formalities)"; "Assassinations," with a section on "Weapons and Their Use," "Improvised Explosive Charges," "Booby Traps," "Delayed Fuses"; "Manufacturing Explosive Materials and Detonators," with information on "Calculating the Charge" and "Safety Instructions"; "Emergency Treatment of Injured Persons" (with numerous illustrations).

REFERENCES

Allerbeck, K. 1971. *Soziale Bedingungen für studentischen Radikalismus* [Social Conditions of Student Radicalism]. Ph.D. dissertation, University of Cologne.

Crenshaw, M. 1985. "An Organizational Approach to the Analysis of Political Terrorism." *Orbis* 29: 465-489.

Eaubonne, F. de 1978. *Feminismus und Terrorismus* [Feminism and Terrorism]. Munich.

Gurr, T. R. 1988. "Empirical Research on Political Terrorism: The State of the Art and How it Might be Improved." Pp. 115-154 in *Current Perspectives on International Terrorism,* edited by R. Slater and M. Stohl. New York: Macmillan.

Hoffman, B. 1982. *Right-Wing Terrorism in Europe.* Santa Monica: Rand Publication Series.

Kepplinger, H. M. 1974. "Statusdevianz und Meinungsdevianz. Die Sympathisanten der Baader-Meinhof-Gruppe" [Deviation of Status and Opinion: The Sympathizers of the Baader-Meinhof Group]. *Kölner Zeitschrift für Soziologie und Sozialpsychologie* 26: 777-800.

Laqueur, W. 1977. *Terrorismus* [Terrorism]. Kronberg.

Lübbe, H. 1980. "Freiheit und Terror." Pp. 239-260 in H. Lübbe, *Philosophie nach der Aufklärung* [Philosophy after the Enlightenment]. Düsseldorf: Econ.

McAdam, D., J.D. McCarthy, J.D.; and M. N. Zald. 1988. "Social Movements." Pp. 695-738 in *Handbook of Sociology,* edited by N. Smelser. Newbury Park: Sage.

McCarthy, J.D. and M.N. Zald. 1973. *The Trend of Social Movements in America. Professionalization and Resource Mobilization.* Morristown: General Learning Press.

———. 1977. "Resource Mobilization and Social Movements: A Partial Theory." *Americam Journal of Sociology* 82: 1212-1241.

Marx, K. 1960 (1852) 1960. "Der achtzehnte Brumaire des Louis Bonaparte" [The Eighteenth Brumaire of Louis Bonaparte]. Pp. 222-318 in *Ausgewählte Schriften in zwei Bänden* [Selected Writings in Two Volumes], vol. 1 Berlin: Dietz.

Meyer, T. 1980. *Am Ende der Gewalt? Der deutsche Terrorismus. Protokolle eines Jahrzehnts* [At the End of Violence? German Terrorism: Records of a Decade]. Frankfurt am Main: Ullstein.

Neidhardt, F. 1981. "Über Zufall, Eigendynamik und Institutionalisierbarkeit absurder Prozesse. Notizen am Beispiel der Entstehung und Einrichtung einer terroristischen Gruppe" [On Chance, Inherent Dynamics, and Institutionalization of Absurd Processes: Notes on the Inception and Establishment of a Terrorist Group]. Pp. 243-257 in *Soziologie in weltbürgerlicher Absicht* (Sociology in Cosmopolitan Intention). Publication in honor of René König, edited by H. von Alemann and P. Thurn. Opladen: Westdeutsches.

———. 1982. "Soziale Bedingungen terroristischen Handelns: Das Beispiel der Baader-Meinhof-Gruppe" [Social circumstances of terrorist action: The example of the Baader-Meinhof Group]. Pp. 318-392 in *Gruppenprozesse* [Group Processes], vol. 2 in the series Analysen zum Terrorism [Analyses of Terrorism], edited by W. von Baeyer-Katte et al. Opladen: Westdeutsches.

———. 1985. "Große Wirkungen kleiner Reize" [Big Impacts of Small Stimuli]. Pp. 322-333 in *Soziologie und gesellschaftliche Entwicklung* [Sociology and Social Development], edited by B. Lutz. Frankfurt am Main: Campus.

Oberschall, A. 1973. *Social Conflict and Social Movements.* Englewood Cliffs: Prentice Hall.

Waldmann, P. 1977. *Strategien der Gewalt* [Strategies of Violence]. Stuttgart: Kohlhsmmer.

ETHNIC AND SOCIOREVOLUTIONARY TERRORISM:

A COMPARISON OF STRUCTURES

Peter Waldmann

The scientific debate about terrorism and terrorists suffers from the overuse of the term *terrorism,* which scholars have invoked to describe too many and varied phenomena. If we accept the costumary definition of terrorism—a definite strategy of action designed to cause deep fear by exemplary application of violence to specific groups (Duvall and Stohl 1988; Fromkin 1977)—we face the question: Which actors resort to this procedure and for what reasons? We can initially classify the relevant actors by differentiating between state terrorism and insurgent terrorism as well as between leftist and rightist terrorism. This differentiation, however, is by no means definitive, as we must still determine the validity of political terms of daily usage, such as those just mentioned.

In this paper I try to analyze more thoroughly the distinction that frequently appears in the literature between ethnic terrorism, or terrorism inspired by

---

International Social Movement Research, Vol. 4, pages 237-257.

ISBN: 1-55938-445-X

nationalistic motives, on the one hand, and terrorism with sociorevolutionary goals on the other (Waldmann 1983).

I begin by contrasting one example of sociorevolutionary terrorism (the RAF in West Germany) with two examples of ethnic terrorism (the ETA of the Basque region and the IRA in Northern Ireland). This contrast provides the foundation for a comparative typology that juxtaposes several basic features of both types of terrorism. Having delineated this typology, I then test its comprehensiveness by critically analyzing three other examples of sociorevolutionary and ethnic terrorism (Action Directe in France, the Red Brigades in Italy and the Front de Libération in Quebec) to see if, and how, they fit the terms of our scheme.

CONTRASTING EXAMPLES OF SOCIOREVOLUTIONARY AND ETHNIC TERRORISM

The Rote Armee Fraktion (RAF)

The character of leftist terrorism in an industrialized western country is exemplified by the political violence that occurred in West Germany in the 1970s. The facts about this outbreak of violence are well known and documented in many scientific studies.[1]

In the 1970s, West Germany became the setting for a series of politically motivated assassinations, kidnappings, attacks on public institutions, and assaults on banks and savings institutions. Three organizations were responsible for these attacks on the state and society: the RAF, which grew out of the Baader-Meinhof group, the Movement of June 2nd, and the Revolutionary Cells. These three organizations, all of which emerged from the declining student movement and the extraparliamentary opposition of the 1960s, rejected the West German system because of its supposed fascism and imperialism. Their revolutionary ideology entailed in part anarchistic elements and in part features of class struggle. The aim of the terroristic attacks was to liberate the German working class and the poor, exploited masses of the Third World countries from the capitalist yoke.

The RAF was the most influential of the three groups, because of the impact of its many ideological documents justifying terrorist attacks. The RAF was a centrally organized group of limited strength whose members were fanatically devoted to the revolutionary cause and were united by strong emotional links. The prosecution to which they were subjected made these links even stronger. Even the early imprisonment of its leaders could not undermine the suggestive force of the example provided by this group and the charismatic influence of its most important members. On the contrary, even after their apparent defeat, the terrorists of the RAF succeeded in rebuilding a new organization from their cells; they won new adherents and instigated new acts of violence. Considering the continuity and number of its attacks, we find that, all together, the group showed surprising cohesion and effectiveness throughout more than a decade, manifesting clear signs of decline only in the 1980s. Nevertheless, we should not overestimate the size of the circle of sympathizers and adherents from which the RAF recruited its followers: its number probably never exceeded a few hundred. The RAF brutal acts were vehemently repudiated not only by the extreme Left but also by all the working class—the group that the RAF supposedly favored. The reasons for their limited appeal were, one, the artificiality of their thesis asserting the repressive-fascist character of the West German state, a thesis whose complicated theoretical deduction was difficult to understand and contradicted by the everyday experience of the common individual; and, two, the elitist arrogance and missionary touch of the RAF intellectuals, which alienated even those who were basically sympathetic to their cause.

This second reason brings us to the individual features and qualities of the terrorists. Thanks to the systematic analysis of police and judicial records (Jaeger, Schmidtchen, and Suellwold 1981; Neidhardt 1988), we have relatively complete information about the character and background of these terrorists. The great majority of them came from middle- or upper-middle-class families. Many grew up in broken homes (the father was killed in the war or the parents were divorced). Because of their parents' high social status, German terrorists typically grew up largerly free from material concerns and received a liberal education. At the same time, they were brought up with high expectations for their performance in schools and elsewhere. Several signs indicated that a great number of the terrorists were unable to live up to such expectations; as a result, they rebelled and tried to satisfy their ambition for status by opposing the established order. In many cases the future terrorists' rupture with the parental home occurred early in life, primarily, because of conflicts with the father. Although approximately two-thirds finished high school or attended university, they often had checkered academic careers, and this frequent failure in school coincided with irregularities and rebellious conduct that incurred disciplinary sanctions and even juvenile sentences. Another indicator of their future lives as terrorists was the obvious restlessness and instability that gradually separated them from their parental home, whether by interrupting their study, or by over-extending it (as a result of frequent changes), or by impelling moves from one work place to another. Only by joining with others who shared their political sympathies, generally in a large city or university, and then developing an extremely critical concept of state and society, did the future activists gain a new direction and orientation. They thus entered a phase of intense political engagement on the border of legality. In general, they became affiliated with a terrorist group as the result of a fortuitous constellation of connections based primarily on relations to someone already within the group.

Most terrorists were juveniles and were either protestant or atheists. A large percentage of the activists were women, who often occupied high ranking positions. Many of the arrested terrorists possessed to a considerable degree those organizational and technical abilities and skills that are needed to operate any underground organization.

The "Euskadi ta-Askatun" (ETA)

The average profile of the German terrorist—someone who is incompletely socialized and poorly integrated into his society but has a great deal of ambition that does not find adequate fulfillment within the established social order and professions—contrasts sharply with the characteristics of the ethnically motivated terrorist. Let us consider, for example, a member of the Basque underground organization, ETA:

> J.A.E. was born in 1944 in Elgueta, a town in the province of Guipúzcoa, near the border with the province of Vizcaya. He was the second of nine children. His father had a small farm and worked successively in various small factories. Basque was spoken within the family. The slight yet strong J.A.E. lived at his parents' farm until he was 30, except for the time he spent in military service. He held various jobs: dock-worker, worker in a textile factory, lorry-driver, and, in 1974, at the age of 30, he became a teacher in a driving school. He gave most of his income to his parents.
>
> J.A.E. enjoyed a good reputation in his home town. He was known as a reliable person with a cheerful and sociable disposition. His work companions appreciated him, and it was said that he had a talent for cheering up people, for organizing and getting things going. In games he was famous for his determination, his abilities to impose himself, and his strong will to succeed—qualities that seemed typical of his character in general. He was secretive: not even the closest members of his family suspected he was affiliated with the ETA until his arrest.
>
> J.A.E. neither read nor traveled. Ideological problems did not interest him, nor did he belong to a political party. He was called *abertzale,* which means patriot. J.A.E. showed great initiative in implementing the construction and the financing of a Basque school (*icastola*) in Elgueta. He was a passionate hunter, mountain climber, and *pelota* player.
>
> In 1976 J.A.E. was arrested under suspicion of having participated in an assault on the Guardia Civil. He was repeatedly tortured and finally released on bail. Afterward he fled, crossing the border to France, where he spent the last four years of his life as a *liberado* in the clandestine movement. His family kept in touch with him and visited him frequently, bringing him food, clothing, wine, and all the necesseties for his subsistence. He refused, however, to comply with his mother' s wish that he return to Elgueta, arguing that he wanted to continue fighting for the liberation of the Basque Country. On April 28, 1980, at the age of 35, J.A.E. was killed in an assault on a policeman.[2]

J.A.E. is typical of the 80 members of the ETA about whom I collected data for a sample which I analyzed according to sociostatistical criteria (Waldmann 1981, p. 45; see also Clark 1986). According to this sample, the majority of ETA members came from a purely Basque social and family background, which is quite remarkable since approximately 50 percent of the inhabitants of the Spanish Basque region are immigrants or descendants of immigrants. The "typical" etarra (Basque soldier) was raised on a farm or in a small town or village environment; his parents generally belonged to the lower or lower-middle class and were farmers, craftsmen, tradesmen, skilled workers, or employees. His own level of education was modest; normally he did not go beyond secondary school or a specialized technical school. Only a few ETA members grew up in a middle-class family, finished college, and completed a university degree. Until 1980 (the latest year for which I have date) the organization recruited part of its new members from seminaries and the Basque clergy. Here we should note that in the profoundly Catholic Basque region the church represents one of the classic channels of social advancement for the members of the lower class. Apart from the eclesiastic institutions (among them the Jesuit university of Deusto in Bilbao) the favorite reservoir of new members of the ETA were hiking clubs, mounting climbing and other sport clubs, scouting groups, choirs, and cultural associations. All these groups are deeply rooted in Basque society. Accordingly, it was only natural that the ETA and its members enjoyed full and unqualified acceptance among the middle and lower social classes of the Basque population. Even today they have the unconditional support of about 20 percent of the inhabitants.

If we look for evidence of inadequate socialization during childhood or other signs of poor social integration among these Basque activists, we look in vain. Indeed, the etarras moved about in the Basque society like "fish in the water" (to use Mao Tse-tung' s famous quote about communist guerrillas), at least during the Franco era. Their integration into their environment was due, in no small part, to their ties to the cuadrilla, the group of friends of the same age in which each activist grew up, and which accompanied him throughout the successive stages of his personal evolution and, indeed, for the rest of his life. As a rule, the etarras were not teenagers but young adults (the average age was 25 years). The great majority were men; within the ranks of the organization, women were the exception and exercised only auxiliary and supporting functions.

The Irish Republican Army (IRA)

We can fill out our picture of ethnic terrorism by adding to this brief sketch on the ETA data from my study on the IRA in Northern Ireland (Waldmann 1989, also for further bibliographical references). Like the etarras, almost all the members of the provisional IRA, the most militant branch of the movement, come from a lower-class environment. Many of them are unemployed, others work on a temporary basis or are permanently employed in manual labor. Again like ETA members, IRA members are representative of the Catholic population of their country in general. If they differ in any way from the average Catholic in Northern Ireland, it is in their "positive" qualities, such as initiative, a sense of responsibility for the community, a talent for organization and leadership. Another significant characteristic, which underlines the parallel between the IRA terrorist and the Basque etarra, is the IRA member' s strong bonds with primary groups: family and friends, the neighborhood community, collegues of the clubs to which he belongs, and so on. An individual joins the group usually after a period of uncertainty and undecision, most often as an act of solidarity with a friend or a family member (the father or a brother, for example, may have already fought against Great Britain). IRA members are usually married, and while their wives are well aware of their husbands' risky activities, they themselves do not participate in terrorist acts. Like the ETA, the IRA is an entirely male organization.

The respect and trust that members of the IRA received from the Catholic population in Northern Ireland were even greater than that which the *etarras* received from their ethnic community in the Basque Country. As potential martyrs who defend the idea of a United Ireland in the most pure and uncompromising way, and as preservers of the centuries-old tradition of resistence to the United Kingdom, they are regarded almost with veneration. Resorting to violence as an expression of protest and insurrection has become a central element in the culture and way of life of the lower Catholic classes. In this context, killing a British soldier does not represent a crime but, on the contrary, an heroic act, or—to put it in a less emotionally weighted way—an obligation within the political military service to be fulfilled at a certain stage of the terrorist' s life. To obtain both recognition of the military political character of their assaults and the corresponding status in the eyes of British authorities, quite a few IRA prisoners staged hunger strikes that ultimately cost some of them their lives.

AN ATTEMPT TO CONSTRUCT A COMPARATIVE TYPOLOGY

At this point we can attempt to summarize the preceding information about the different organizations and their members in a comparative typology. Although derived from only a few cases, our scheme may potentially have a more general heuristic value. Leaving aside the features common to both ethnic and leftist revolutionary terrorism (i.e., the terrorists' youth, similar strategies and tactics), I will base this typology on the differences between the two.

Like Donatella della Porta (1988, pp. 32 ff.), I assume that terrorism is the product of the interaction of two categories of variables: those which refer to the actor and those which refer to the environment. Thus in our typology one group of categories—"Goals," "Motivation," "Identification," and "Membership"—is related to the actor, while a second groups—"Supporting Environment" and "Political Culture"—deals with the terrorists' environment.

The result of the interaction of these two kinds of variables constitute a third group, which includes "Function of Violence," "Dynamic of Violent Processes," and "Biographies of Terrorists." This scheme tries to demonstrate not only that there is more than one type of terrorism but that we must reckon with different functions and patterns of violence, depending on the motives, social background, and goals of the violent groups and on the environmental structures within which they operate, structures that in turn effect the career of the typical terrorist.

As for the description of the actor, a few remarks about some categories used in the scheme should be specified. The question of "Identification" is central for an understanding of the terrorist groups (Schmid 1983, p. 195; Münkler 1985). Only those individuals who have radically detached themselves from their own society and state are capable of fighting its representatives ruthlessly. Not by accident, then, does the general population have much less sympathy for guerrilla movements that attack the internal elites in power than for movements whose goal is to free the country from foreign occupation. Münkler's expression "a supposedly interested third" points to the fact that the intellectuals who support leftist terrorism very seldom have any real connection to those levels of society whose "liberation" they champion. Moreover, in describing the supporting groups, I depend primarily on Wolfgang and Ferracuti' s (1969) theory of subculture of violence according to which the lower social classes not only tolerate but even foment violence, whereas the middle class rejects and punishes violence. My comparison refers to the majority of terrorists in question, and to the group or social level that generally dominates the organization. In both the ETA and the IRA, several students and intellectuals from the middle class made repeated efforts to guide the organization into a different course, one oriented more toward the idea of class struggle (we recall the ETA político-militar and the "official" IRA of the 1970s). These efforts failed, however, and the military wing, represented by the members of the lower class, succeeded each time in retaining control, even if necessary by effecting a fait accompli through the use of violence, and so forcing the rest of the group to follow their line. At the present, intellectuals of both these nationalistic movements find their field of action within two parties—respectively Herri Batasuna and Sinn Fein—which support the terrorist organizations by flanking them in their political arena.

As for the categories that deal with the terrorists' environment, in "Supporting Environment" I compare the cross-generational solidarity characteristic of the ethnic protest movements to the generational conflict typical of leftist terrorism in the industrialized nations. Although this distinction is basically correct, it does require some qualifications. Ethnically motivated rebellions, too, are affected by friction and dissent between generations. These elements, for example, contributed to the separation of ETA from the conservative national Basque party at the beginning of the 1960s.

Table 1. Comparison of Structures of Ethnic Terrorism (Basque Region, Northern Ireland) and Left-Wing Terrorism in Highly Developed Industrialized Societies (West Germany)

Ethnic Terrorism	*Left-Wing Terrorism*
Goals	
Greater autonomy, even independence from the oppressor state.	Sociorevolutionary transformation of society.
Motives for Rebellion	
A real or fictive threat to the ethnic group from such external factors as repression by the state, detrimental economic and linguistic policies, foreign infiltration	As a result of a change in their consciousness, activists come to see their own social class and society at large as sick, corrupt, and repressive. They consequently conclude that neither is worth preserving. Terrorists thus search for alternative models of society.
Terrorists identify with their own group (ethnic, religious, or regional) because of a directly experienced threat to that group. The enemy is "external" to one's own social group.	Terrorists detach themselves from their own social class and society, identifying themselves with a "supposedly interested third group"—that is, the working class or the oppressed masses of the Third World countries. This identification is accomplished primarily through ideology. The object of identification is "external," while the enemy is "internal."
Group Membership	
Members of terrorist groups are recruited mainly from the lower or the lower-middle class. They are almost exclusively men who, lacking any other means of self-expression, regard violence as the medium to defend oneself and impose one's views. Family ties (e.g., brother, brother-in-law) between terrorists are quite common. Members who come from the middle class are usually the group's leaders and theorists.	Terrorist groups recruit their members mainly from the middle class. A large percentage of the members are women. Strong emotional ties between the sexes are common. Because the members' readiness to use violence is not based on socialization or education but must be "artificially" implanted by ideology, intellectuals, as producers of ideologies, play a key role in leftist terrorist organizations.
Supporting Environment	
Terrorists remain embedded in their social milieu of origin they move about like "fish in water." They rely on the support and sympathy of a great percentage of the populace who share the terrorists' ambitions and are closely linked to them through primary group relations. Solidarity between generations is typical. Ecclesiastical institutions, certain districts, and rural hideaways serve as zones of protection and retreat throughout the region. External connections with other terrorist groups are rare.	Dissidents must create their own sociopolitical milieu within the protest movement. The generational conflict reinforces the terrorists' alienation from the rest of society. University and artistic-intellectual subcultures provide zones of protection and a field of experiment for the resistance, which is concentrated in large urban centers. Support for terrorism remains low among the population in general since the working class—the group the terrorists are most anxious to engage—shows hardly any response. Because left-wing terrorist groups lack support, they develop external connections to the international terrorist network.

Political Culture	
Ethnic terrorists operate within a tradition of more or less intensive conflicts between minority and majority or center and periphery. For the militant sector of the minority, members of the majority represent the "enemy"; thus, violent actions against them are considered legitimate and quite often are a traditional component of the political culture.	Left-wing terrorism arises in industrialized societies characterized by the state's monopoly on violence and by the dominance of the middle classes. The central values of such societies are material and physical security, legalism, and the reliance on the verbal expression of conflicts. Terrorist actions thus have a shocking and strongly disruptive effect.
Function of Violence	
Violence has a primarily "instrumental" significance and is used as a means to reach a certain goal.	Terrorist acts are intended primarily as messages to the poor, oppressed masses; they are meant to agitate the oppressed and to incite them to fight. Accordingly, violence has a "communicative" or symbolic rather than "instrumental," character.
Dynamic of Violent Processes	
Rebellion is the result of permanent discrimination and/or oppression ("violence of defense"). Once the dynamic of the violent process has exceeded a certain limit, it is almost impossible for external agents to stop or control it, because terrorism is perpetuated by continuous and sustained recruitment. The process is part of the development of a protest movement.	The leftist terrorism of intellectual middle-class groups follows the pattern of the so-called J-Curve of J.C. Davies. It is caused by unfulfilled expectations ("violence of aspirations"), and throughout its course it remains subject to the momentary political situation, especially to the attitudes of the state's security forces. Left-wing terrorism is less the expression of a protest movement than the product of such a movement's decline.
Biography of a Terrorist	
Generally, ethnic terrorists join the terrorist organization only after evaluating the situation carefully and giving their decision much thought. Terrorists do not exhibit psychopathological particularities, nor can they be categorized as a particular psychological type. Certain qualities, however, do appear to be characteristic: determination and initiative, the ability to impose oneself, and an authoritative mental structure. Ethnic terrorists rarely have criminal records; rather, they are sociable and well adapted. Generally, they are quite representative of the milieu of the lower or lower middle classes from which they come and in which they remain (they maintain close connections with their family and circle of friends and remain within a limited geographical area).	Left-wing terrorists go through a complicated process of gradual detachment from their middle class origins, whose rules and norms they cannot adhere to or are unwilling to comply with. This process consists of various stages: a period of diffuse resistance and a general lack of orientations; a stage at which the individual enters the political counterculture; and, finally, the point at which he or she joins a terrorist group. At this stage, at the latest, a consistent resocialization (re-evaluation of all values) or late socialization occurs. The terrorists' intellectual and psychic mobility is complemented by their psychical mobility: often these terrorists have left a country or village environment, gravitating toward the large cities. Only those youths who became alienated from their place of origin at an early age have a statistical "chance" of being incorporated into the milieu of militant protest. It is for this reason that the biographies of left-wing terrorists typically manifest several anomalies: deficient socialization, interrupted studies, a history of erratic employment, conflicts with public institutions and the police.

Generally, however, in the ethnic terrorist groups the elements of continuity prevail, and the new generations are integrated into the adults' world. In contrast, the West German student movement of the 1960s and its terrorist branches vehemently opposed the affluent society represented by the activits' parents.

"Political Culture" is a wide and complex category; its elements vary from case to case, and it can include traditional attitudes and patterns of conduct in dealing with violence. As far as the political culture is concerned, we should note that the militant nationalists of the Basque Country and Northern Ireland operate on assumption that their ethnic or religious group is in a state of permanent warfare with its opponents. Therefore, they feel no more remorse for killing a Spanish policeman or a British soldier than any soldier fighting in a declared war would feel at the death of his enemy. In this context, the key role of identification—that is, the process of designating friends and foes—becomes evident. Left-wing terrorists instead attribute their society' s rejection of violence to the dominance of the middle class—a view that oversimplifies the existing conditions, even in the case of West Germany.

In describing the "Function of Violence" among ethnic terrorists as "instrumental" I mean that these terrorists use violence to cause enough enemy casualties and inflict enough damage on the oppressor state to force it to withdraw from the disputed region. The IRA and the ETA, for example, wage a continuous campaign designed to irritate and ultimately expel the British and the Spanish state. The logic behind the sociorevolutionary terrorists' use of violence is, in comparison, much more complicated. On the one hand, their attacks are designed to induce the state to overreact; on the other hand, they represent a call for a general uprising of the "oppressed and exploited masses." To assign these particular functions exclusively to each type of terrorism is, of course, to oversimplify the nature of both. Ethnic terrorists sometimes use violent attacks as a means of communication, while many of the RAF' s actions can be seen as instrumental attacks on the very heart of the state. A last remark refers to the pattern of the J.C. Davies' s J-curve, mentioned in the "Leftist" column of "Dynamic of Violent Processes," which belongs to the classical theories of revolution. In brief, it indicates that revolutions do not usually break out when the economic situation is precarious but rather when a sudden break occurs after a period of continuous economic growth. By that time, people have come to expect further improvement in their situation, and they blame the elites in power when their expectations are not fulfilled (Davies 1973, p. 185 ff). I believe that Davies' s theory possibly holds true for the middle classes, for whom time is a dynamic element that holds the promise of change but not for the lower classes, whose position is more static, tied to the maintenance of the status quo.

Summarizing what has been said so far, ethnic terrorism is carried out by people directly affected by the conditions they protest and is characterized by their claim that their collective—be it a region or an ethnic group—is threatened by a real (or supposed) menace. Thus the individuals who offer armed resistence to this danger can rely on broad support among their social group. Violence in this case appears to be more or less the natural expression of the self-assertion of a collectivity. Consequently, this form of self-defense can hardly be brought under control or be limited from outside, once it has been generally accepted by the group.

In comparison, leftist terrorism—which reaches its climax in the 1970s in the industrialized western nations and disappeared almost completely thereafter—was from its very beginning much more unstable and precarious, mainly because the primary supporters of this terrorism—the leftist intellectuals—were not themselves affected by the deplorable conditions they sought to correct (i.e., class exploitation or the imperialist subjugation of Third World countries). They functioned as advocates of social groups that had never asked them to take over their defense. And because they were not victims of the evil they were so ready to combat with weapons, their relationship to violence remained purely ideological and thus easily manipulated from outside.

The intensity of this type of protest violence depends on several factors, among them: the extent to which concepts and slogans that stimulate aggression appeal to the population at large, and the extent to which they are diffused throughout that population; the reaction of the state' s security forces to provocation by the rebels; and the movement leaders' estimate of the political situation. Because left-wing groups operate in an environment in which their violence is not accepted as a legitimate defence against the conditions that threaten their existence, their form of terrorism faces the ever-increasing danger of becoming detached from its original motives—that is, of becoming self-justifying.

But ethnical terrorism is no less susceptible to this danger. And the longer a terrorist campaign lasts, the greater the danger becomes. Here we reach the limit of the predicative capacity of the comparative scheme, for at this point ethnic and sociorevolutionary terrorism begin to resemble each other more and more closely. Clandestinity by its very nature produces adaptive constraints and structural standardized trends that no terrorist organization can escape, regardless of its original concept and purpose. The need to resort to criminal acts (such as bank robberies) to obtain the means of survival; the terrorists unavoidable isolation from the rest of the protest movement, which continues to pursue legal forms of protest; the interdependence of group members and their convinction, through mutual reinforcement and the constant repetition of arguments and slogans of the righteousness of violence, and above all the self-imposed obligation to combat the state and its representatives with violence—all these elements reduce the differences between ethnic and sociorevolutionary terrorism and determine that, in the long run, the two will evolve in an identical way. Consequently, in every terrorist group the members' deeds and ambition become channeled in only one direction: to prepare and implement "military actions."

ANALYSIS OF THREE ADDITIONAL CASES

To test the usefulness of the comparative scheme, we can examine three additional cases of terrorism. Two cases prima facie fall within the spectrum of sociorevolutionary terrorism—Action Directe (AD, Direct Action) in France and Italian terrorism as represented mainly by the Brigate Rosse (BR, Red Brigades). The third case—the Front de Libération du Québec (FLQ, Liberation Front of Quebec), which was active in the province of Quebec during the 1960s—belongs to the ethnic type.

Action Directe (AD)

During the past three decades, France was the scene of several types of terrorism: the ethnically motivated violence of Corsicans and Bretons; terrorism from international organizations, which perpetrated attacks mainly in Paris; and, finally, the attacks of the sociorevolutionary group AD (see, among others, Hamon and Marchard 1983; Cerny 1981; "La documentation francaise" 1989; Paas 1988). Action Directe appeared somewhat later than comparable West German and Italian terrorist groups. Its first actions, which caused only material damage, took place in 1980. Shortly after these attacks, the leaders of the organization were arrested and imprisoned. Freed in 1981 under a governmental amnesty, they resumed their attacks after a short interval. Their assaults increased between 1983 and 1986 and culminated in some dramatic assassinations of policemen and representatives of the state and economy. Finally, in 1987, the police succeeded in putting the leaders of the organizations behind the bars. Without its leaders, the group eventually dissolved.

The characteristics of AD correspond largely to those of leftist terrorism. Its "Goals" and "Motives of Identification" indicate that AD obviously pursued a communist agenda: its objective was the destruction of the "bourgeois imperialistic" French state in the name of the national proletariat and the exploited masses of the Third World. As for "Group Membership," AD, like the RAF, recruited its members not from among hard-core radicals and leaders of the political protest of the 1960s and the 1970s, but from the marginal sector of this movement.

The "Biographies" of AD members reveal that they grew up in the provinces, in Algiers or in Morocco, and had come a long way—in the intellectual and spiritual as well as in the geographical sense—before meeting each other within AD in Paris. The sociological literature provides little information about their social status and milieu of origin. We know that some of them had wealthy parents; and that the organization included quite a few students. Yet, reviewing the data we do have, one gets the impression that the great majority of the members of AD belonged to the middle and lower-middle class rather than to the higher level of society. For the rest, most of the features of the group conform to the profile of sociorevolutionary terrorism elaborated in the scheme. We find, for example, a considerable number of women in the ranks of AD as well as many couples among the terrorists.

If we consider the "Function of Violence" and the "Dynamics of Violent Processes" in AD, we see further correlations with our typology: AD had close connections with its German and Italian counterparts; its attacks were primarily symbolic; and, last if not least, it was almost totally—perhaps totally—isolated not only from the working class but also from the entire anti-authoritarian, libertarian political protest movement, whose strong arm it claimed to be.

If there are discrepancies between the "typical" features of sociorevolutionary violence highlighted above and the features of AD, they are to be found in the sociopolitical context in which French terrorists operated. In France this context, which our scheme includes under the categories "Supporting Environment" and "Political Culture," was distinctive in several respects. First, French industrial workers have a tradition of militancy which goes back to the early nineteenth century or even further. There has always been a militant sector that expressed its discontent not only by means of frequent strikes but also through public demonstrations and occasional barricades battles. And so the protest movement of the 1960s in France, unlike that in West Germany, was not confined to students and intellectuals but included factory workers as well. The revolt of the intellectual youth in May 1968 was accompanied by a general strike that paralyzed all public life. Consequently, for the radical Left in France, 1968 did not mark the beginning of the decline of the protest movement; rather, they were seen as evidence of the movement's success. This fact helps to explain why, in France, the demonstration of 1968 did not trigger any paroxysmal reaction as a result of unfulfilled expectations. Even after 1968, the students who worked toward sociorevolutionary changes were always eager to keep in touch with the working class. In France, therefore, it was the inclusion of the radical Left in a tradition of limited violent protest which, paradoxically, helped to prevent terrorism.

A second distinctive feature of the French context was the presence of a large group of leftist intellectuals who also had a mitigating effect on the conflict. The most famous example of a leftist intellectual serving as a buffer or mediator between impatient academic youth and a mainly conservative majority was Jean Paul Sartre's key role in absorbing the frustrations produced by the official prohibition of the Proletarian Left in 1970. By expressing sympathy and understanding for the cause of the juvenile rebels, the intellectuals gave the student movement a certain respectability in the public opinion. At the same time, they explained to the young rebels that one can change the society and the state through means other than pure violence.

The third element responsible for moderating the course of the disputes between the protest movement and the "status quo" forces in France was the French state itself. A self-assured, centralized, strong state that can draw on a 200 year tradition of dealing with social discontent, the French state does not need—at least at first glance—to defend itself against leftist accusations that it is "fascist." This self-confidence explains one of the main differencies in the way France and West Germany responded to terrorism. West Germany, a less consolidated state, burdened besides with a historical fascist mortgage, was convinced that it had to prove its strength to political challengers by intervening forcefully and energetically. While the inflexible and unnecessarily harsh actions of the West German police contributed to the escalation of the conflicts in that country, in France volatile situations were repeatedly defused by the subtle, concerted action of the head of the police and the leaders of the protest movements, as both sides wanted to avoid unnecessary bloodshed. Thus France was able to cope with the restless 1960s and 1970s, which were marked by innumerable street battles and confrontations, without additional security laws and without a state of emergency.

Slow changes in the environmental conditions mentioned above explain the rise of a rudimentary terrorist organization and subculture at the beginning of the 1980s: as a result of the general shift in political sentiment toward the Right, the leftist intellectual milieu, which had arised after the war, gradually began to dissolve; and the state took harsher measures against the radical Left, especially after the failure of the amnesty laws of 1981. In addition, by the early 1980s the so-called "autonomous" movement—a radical protest movement that had copied themes and forms of action from its Italian counterpart and had dominated the leftist scene in the 1970s—had begun to show clear signs of weakness, and its decline too was conducive to the emergence of AD. Thus AD confirms a general feature of leftist terrorism in our scheme: it was an accidental outgrowth of a vanishing era and of the decline of a sociopolitical movement.

The Brigate Rosse (BR)

The Italian terrorism also falls in the category of sociorevolutionary violence. Italian terrorism however generated many more actions than did French terrorism, and over a longer period of time.[3] Two cycles of violence occurred in Italy, the first from 1970 to 1974, the second from 1975 to 1982. The number of attacks during the first cycle was not very high and, above all, cost few human lives. During the second phase violence escalated considerably. In the decisive years 1977 and 1978, terrorists perpetrated 34 and 57 attacks respectively against people, and the number of actions inflicting material damage rose into the hundreds. Both cycles coincided with the demobilization of protest movements: the first cycle fell within the period of decline of the student movement; the second, which had a broader base and was more radical than the first, emerged after the so-called autonomous movement had passed its climax. As a number of more or less clandestine groups had existed in Italy since the mid 1970s, anyone determined to fight the state by violent means found easy access to radical organizations. This fact provides an explanation for the rapid increase in violent actions after 1975.

Looking first at characteristics of the protagonists, we find that Italian terrorism essentially remains within the scheme we developed above, although it exhibits several peculiarities. The "Goals" of the rebels were marked by an anarchistic and antiauthoritarian tendency. Among their "Motives for Rebellion" was the desire for a profound sociopolitical change that would bring the proletariat into power. The proletariat was the main object of "Identification." As for the "Group Membership," approximatly 50 percent of the rebels were university and high-school students and professional people. The other 50 percent were workers, technical employees, and elements of the subproletariat (i.e., the unemployed and former prisoners) (Weinberg 1986). Members of the poorer classes joined the terrorist groups particularly during the second cycle but the leadership and style were still determined primarily by young intellectuals. As in West Germany and France, the structures within the terrorist groups were characterized by close personal relationships and especially by couple relationships. Twenty-five percent of terrorist were women.

We can infer what the Italian activists perceived as the "Function of Violence" when we see that, typical of middle-class youth, they were impatient, convinced that some concrete action should follow endless talking, and ready to question traditional authorities and norms.

The typical "Biography" of these terrorists reveals that many grew up in a small-town, Catholic environment and had come a long way, both geographically and intellectually, before finally joining in a violent radical Marxist organization in one of the large cities of Northern Italy.

For the most part these data accord with our scheme, if we leave aside an important fact related to the "Dynamics of Violent Processes": in Italy the appeal of terrorism reached across the boundaries of the students' and intellectuals' milieu and attracted adherents in other strata of the population. If we seek the reasons for this diffusion, which were also responsible for the intensity and the length of the terroristic campaign, we come back (as in the case of France) to peculiarities in the sociopolitical conditions under which the terrorists operated—that is, to the "Supporting Environment" and the "Political Culture" in our typology.

A first peculiarity was the chronic weakness of the Italian state and its lack of authority. If the French view their state with detachment, most Italians feel an absolute aversion to and contempt for their state and its political representatives. They regard state dominance as a kind of alien domination and the demands of the state as questionable and illegitimate. This attitude is a response to, among other things, the traditional inefficiency and corruption of the state' s apparatus, which has been in the hands of practically a single political party (the Democrazia Cristiana) since the end of World War II. In addition, Italians remember the historical role of the political elite as an instrument of fascism, a role it seemed to be reassuming when, around 1970, the number of assaults launched by the radical Right increased and a rightist coup d'état became at least a latent danger. The brutality of the badly equipped Italian police also rekindled the hatred of the Left towards the state.

Out of this leftist political camp a powerful protest movement arose during the 1960s and the 1970s—the second decisive factor in Italy' s sociopolitical context. This movement represented the confluence of several historical elements: the permanent agrarian rebellion and rural anarchism in the south was supported by a working class of traditionally very militant industrial workers in the north. A third element, from recent Italian history, was the model of the Resistance that emerged at the end of World War II, which had also espoused sociorevolutionary ideas. In the late 1960s, a general loss of confidence and crisis of values, produced by rapid industrialization and by the accompanying generational conflict, added to these historical factors and set the protest in motion. Until the 1960s, the groups of the extreme Left had some institutional support from the communist party (PCI), which basically rejected the postwar bourgeois democratic system. For many years, the PCI had played the same moderating role in Italy that the leftist intellectuals had played in France, but when it accepted capitalism and was transformed into a social democratic party, the groups of the extreme Left were left virtually homeless and began openly to incite violent revolution. The idea of such a revolution found extensive acceptance within the extra-parliamentary opposition.

Despite its rhetoric of riot and violence, and even though terrorist opposition to the state was deeply rooted in various social groups, sociorevolutionary terrorism in Italy is now a phenomenon of the past. Remarkably enough, the political system was able to bring it under control even while preserving the rules of the constitutional state. Thus the "Dynamic of the Violent Process" indicates another decisive difference between leftist terrorism and at least the two cases of ethnic terrorism we have already examined, the Basque ETA and the IRA in Northern Ireland, for unlike the relatively short-lived leftist terrorist groups, these two are still active even after twenty years.

But to acquire a more complete view of ethnic terrorism we should consider at least one additional example. The problematic case of the French-Canadian FLQ is instructive.[4]

The Front de Libération du Québec (FLQ)

The FLQ was a loose association of violent groups that were responsible for about 170 assaults in the French-Canadian province of Quebec between 1963 and 1970. The great majority of these attacks were directed against institutions, buildings, and other material objects. Not until 1970 did the FLQ directly endanger human life, kidnapping two high-ranking political figures, one of whom was eventually murdered. The indignant reaction of the whole population and the energetic measures that the Canadian state took against the terrorists put an early end to the FLQ.

At first glance, the organization and actions of the FLQ seem to represent a variety of terrorism that does not correspond exactly to either of the two types our scheme describes but instead combines elements of both. On the one hand the FLQ' s "Goals," "Motives of Rebellion," and "Identification" fit the ethnic model: the declared goal of the "Felquists" was to liberate the French-Canadian province of Quebec from the yoke of Anglo-Canadian imperialism and to lead it to independence from the state. Although the FLQ also pursued social revolutionary changes for the French-Canadian society, its main objective was to eliminate the cultural, economic, and political oppression to which, in its opinion, the Anglo-Canadian majority subjected the French-Canadians. On the other hand, the FLQ displayed several features that could be considered typical of sociorevolutionary terrorism. If we look at its "Membership," for example, we find that the group was composed almost exclusively of students and intellectuals of the middle class, although many of them originally came from the lower class; workers were hardly represented at all. Accordingly, the Felquists' violent activism grew out of their impatience with Quebec' s slow rate of progress and was aimed at winning greater independence for Quebec within the Canadian confederation. This nationalism was fostered by a change in consciousness among the French-Canadian middle classes, which caused them to perceive Quebec' s situation in a "negative" light. As for the "Function of Violence" in the FLQ, its attacks were meant as "propaganda by action," intended to arose the French-Canadian masses from their indifference.

A look at the "Supporting Environment" and the "Political Culture" in which the FLQ operated raises additional questions about the validity of classifying this group as an example of ethnic terrorism as defined by our scheme. Its members never gained a widespread support in French-Canadian society; they were not able to move about like "fish in the water" in some sectors of the population but in fact were decidedly rejected. Only some of the Québécois students expressed their solidarity with the organization. Thus the situation of the FLQ was more like that of the RAF in West Germany than that of the ETA or IRA.

French-Canadian society, which was strongly influenced by the values of the new middle classes, continued to cultivate an image of its history in which its own ethnic group appeared in continuous and sometimes even violent rebellion against the Anglo-Canadian hegemony. But it had in fact adopted the democratic rules for solving conflict peacefully, so much so that it regarded the FLQ' s attacks as revolting and risky. It found its authentic voice in Réné Léveques, who promised to achieve the province' s multiple goals for greater economic and political independence by peaceful means through his Parti Québécois.

The FLQ, however, only seems to depart from the model of ethnic terrorism elaborated in our scheme. In fact, it represents a period in the development of this type of terrorism which lies ahead of the stage that the scheme intends to describe. In Northern Ireland and the Basque Region, ethnic rebellion was initiated by the protest of dissatisfied groups of the middle class, most of them students or independent intellectuals. This protest, originally moving through peaceful channels, provoked such a vehement reaction from the Protestant majority (in Northern Ireland) and from the central state (in Spain) that it created the threatening situation described in the scheme. Only at this stage did members of the lower and lower middle classes begin to defend their ethnic group by violent means, and only at this point did many groups among the population express their solidarity with the violent activists. It is difficult to tell how the lower classes of Quebec would have reacted had the Canadian government taken extreme and repressive measures to counter the FLQ's attacks. But for once, general solidariety with the terrorists was besides the point because the central government in Ottawa took moderate yet energetic steps to avoid the eruption of violence, and also because the protesters had recourse to a peaceful instrument of change in the form of an independent party which promised to continue the struggle for independence by legal means.

FINAL CONSIDERATIONS

Has our scheme fulfilled its purpose to offer a comparative typology that justaposes several basic features of ethnic and sociorevolutionary terrorism? It is surely too early to reach such a conclusion. To test it further we would have to examine additional examples of terrorism which might introduce data that would require changes in one or the other of the proposed features. For the moment, however, I think we can justify three deductions:

1. Basically, it seems useful to distinguish between ethnic and sociorevolutionary terrorism. Because the two types of terrorism stem from different motivations, each allows for and requires a different form of

identification and engagement; each attracts different groups, which are embedded in different segments of the population; each looks to different situations to justify violence and impose it; each attributes different function to violence; and in each, violent process follow a different course of development.

2. Although we can justify the distinction between ethnic and sociorevolutionary terrorism primarily by referring to the different types of actors—to their goals, for example, or the motives they represent—we must remember that to understand and explain the real extent, the course, and the meaning of violence we need to consider the sociopolitical conditions under which the terrorists act. Our examples of both ethnic and sociorevolutionary terrorism revealed considerable variations within each type depending on the national political tradition and culture, the state's reputation and role, the militancy of the working class, and the general climate of values and orientations. The examples have thus proved the utility of separating the variables referring to actors from those referring to structure.

3. In testing the validity of the individual features elaborated in our scheme, we found that the second group of examples confirmed our models only in part, for we also saw some notable deviations (e.g., in the composition of the supporting groups, and in the depth and extent of the support for violence in the general environment and in the political culture). To anticipate any objections to the scheme arising from these deviant cases, we should, I think, consider this scheme as merely a framework for the comparison of both types of terrorism. This framework underlines their extreme forms and features but also accomodate less well-defined profiles and combined forms of political violence.

NOTES

1. See the results of "Analysen zum Terrorismus," (Fetscher and Rohrmoser 1981); Jaeger, Schmidtchen and Suellwold (1981); Baeyer-Katte, Claessens, Feger and Neidhardt (1982); Matz and Schmidtchen (1983); Sack and Steinert (1984).
2. The curriculum is an excerpt from an article of Werner Herzog ("Basler Zeitung," August 23, 1980). In general on ethnic conflicts, see Rokkan and Derek (1983), Esman (1977), and Smith (1981). On ETA, see Waldmann (1982).
3. For the Italian terrorism, see, among others: Hess (1988), Weinberg and Eubank (1987), Weinberg (1986), della Porta and Pasquino (1986); della Porta (1988), Ferracuti and Bruno (1983.)
4. On the FLQ, see Laurendeau (1974), Latouche (1971), and Waldmann (1989, pp. 49 ff, 137 ff).

REFERENCES

Baeyer-Katte von, W., D. Claessens, H. Feger, and F. Neidhardt. 1982. *Analysen zum Terrorismus. Gruppenprozesse* [Analyses of Terrorism: Group Processes]. Opladen: Westdeutscher.

Cerny, P. 1981. "France: Non-Terrorism and the Politics of Repressive Tolerance." Pp. 91-118 in *Terrorism: A Challenge to the State,* edited by J. Lodge. Oxford: Martin Robertson.

Clark, R. P. 1986. "Patterns in the Lives of ETA Members." Pp. 283-310 in *Political Violence and Terror: Motifs and Motivations,* edited by P. H. Merkl. Berkeley: University of California Press.

Davies, J.C. 1973. "Eine Theorie der Revolution" [A theory of revolution]. Pp. 185-204 in *Empirische Revolutionsforschung* [Empirical Research on Revolution], edited by K. von Beyme. Opladen: Westdeutscher.

della Porta, D. 1988. "Protestbewegung und Terrorismus in Italien" [Protest Movement and Terrorism in Italy]. *Aus Politik und Zeitgeschichte* 45:21-34.

della Porta, D., and G. Pasquino. 1986. "Interpretations of Italian Terrorism." Pp. 169-190 in *Political Violence and Terror: Motifs and Motivations,* edited by P. H. Merkl. Berkeley: University of California Press.

Duvall, R. D., and M. Stohl 1988. "Governance by Terror." Pp. 231-269 in *The Politics of Terrorism,* edited by M. Stohl. 3rd ed. New York and Basel: Marcel Dekker.

Esman, M. J., ed. 1977. *Ethnic Conflict in the Western World.* Ithaca: Cornell University Press.

Ferracuti, F., and F. Bruno 1983. "Italy: A System Pespective." Pp. 287-321 in *Aggression in Global Perspective,* edited by A. P. Goldstein and M. M. Segall. New York: Pergamon.

Fetscher, I., and G. Rohrmoser. 1981. *Analysen zum Terrorismus. Ideologien and Strategien* [Analyses of Terrorism: Ideologies and Strategies]. Opladen: Westdeutscher.

Fromkin, D. 1977. "Die Strategie des Terrorismus" [The strategy of terrorism]). Pp. 83-99 in *Terrorismus. Untersuchungen zur Strategie und Struktur revolutionaerer Gewaltpolitik* [Terrorism: Research on Strategy and Structure of Revolutionary Political Violence], edited by M. Funke. Bonn: Bundeszentrale fuer politische Bildung.

Hamon, A., and J. Marchand. 1983. *Action Directe. Du terrorisme francais a l'euroterrorisme* [Direct Action. From French terrorism to Euroterrorism]. Paris: Seuil.

Hess, H. 1988. "Italien: Die ambivalente Revolte" [Italy: The ambivalent revolt]. Pp. 9-165 in H. Hess et al., *Angriff auf das Herz des Staates. Soziale Entwicklung und Terrorismus* [Attacks at the Heart of the State: Social Development and Terrorism], vol. 2. Frankfurt am Main: Suhrkamp.

Jaeger, H., G. Schmidtchen, and L. Suellwold. 1981. *Analysen zum Terrorismus. Lebenslaufanalysen* [Analyses of Terrorism: Analysis of Careers]. Opladen: Westdeutscher.

"La documentation francaise." 1989. *Quinze ans de terrorisme et d'antiterrorisme en France* [Fifteen Years of Terrorism and Antiterrorism in France]. Special issue, no. 149.

Latouche. D. 1971. "Violence, politique et crise dans la société québécois" [Violence, politics and crisis in Québécois society]. In *Essays on the Left,* edited by L. La Pierre. Toronto: McClelland and Stewart.

Laurendeau, M. 1974. *Les Québécois violents* [The Violent Québécois]. Montreal: Edition du Boréal Express.

Matz, U., and G. Schmidtchen. 1983. *Analysen zum Terrorismus. Gewalt und Legitimitaet* [Analyses of Terrorism: Violence and Legitimacy]. Opladen: Westdeutscher.

Münkler, H. 1985. "Guerrillakrieg and Terrorismus" [Guerrilla warfare and terrorism]. *Neue politische Literatur* 25: 299-326.

Neidhardt, F. 1988. "Linker und rechter Terrorismus. Erscheinungsformen und Handlungspotentiale im Gruppenvergleich" [Left-wing and right-wing terrorism: Forms and potential of action in group comparison]. In F. Neidhardt, *Gewalt und Terrorismus: Studien zur Soziologie militanter Konflikte* [Violence and Terrorism: Studies on the Sociology of Militant Conflicts]. Berlin: Wissenschaftszentrum fuer Sozialforschung.

Paas, D. 1988. "Frankreich: Der integrierte Linksradikalismus" [France: The integrated Left]. Pp. 167-292 in H. Hess et al., *Angriff auf das Hertz des Staates. Soziale Entwicklung und Terrorismus* [Attacks at the Heart of the State: Social Development and Terrorism], vol. 1. Frankfurt am Main: Suhrkamp.

Rokkan, S., and U. Derek 1983. *Economy, Territory, Identity. Politics of Western European Peripheries.* London: Sage.

Sack, F., and H. Steinert 1984. *Analysen zum Terrorismus. Protest und Reaktion* [Analyses of Terrorism: Protest and Reaction]. Opladen: Westdeutscher.

Schmid, A. P. 1983. *Political Terrorism: A Research Guide to Concepts, Theories, Data Bases, and Literature.* Amsterdam: Swidoc.

Smith, A.D. 1981. *The Ethnic Revival in the Modern World.* Cambridge: Cambridge University Press.

Waldmann, P. 1981. "Mitgliederstruktur, Sozialisationsmedien und gesellschaftlicher Rueckhalt der baskischen ETA" [Membership structure, media of socialization, and social support of the Basque ETA]). *Politische Vierteljahresschrift* 22: 45-68.

———. 1982. "Sozio-oekonomischer Wandel, zentralistische Unterdrueckung und Protestgewalt im Baskenland" [Socio-economic change, centralistic pressure, and violent protest in the Basque Country]. Pp. 199-286 in P. Waldmann et al., *Die geheime Dynamik autoritaerer Diktaturen* [The Secret Dynamic of Authoritarian Dictatorships]. Munich: Voegel.

———. 1983. "Terrorismus" [Terrorism]. In *Woerterbuch zur Politik. Westliche Industriegesellschaften* [Political Dictionary: Western Industrial Societies], edited by M. G. Schmidt. Munich and Zurich: Piper.

———. 1989. *Ethnischer Radikalismus. Ursachen und Folgen gewaltsamer Minderheitenkonflikte am Beispiel des Baskenlandes, Nordirlands und Quebecs* [Ethnic Radicalism. Origins and Consequences of Violent Minority Conflicts with the Basque Country, Northern Ireland, and Quebec as Examples]. Opladen: Westdeutscher.

Weinberg, L. 1986. "The Violent Life: Left- and Right-Wing Terrorism in Italy." Pp. 145-168 in *Political Violence and Terror: Motifs and Motivations,* edited by P. H. Merkl. Berkeley: University of California Press.

Weinberg, L., and W.L. Eubank. 1987. *The Rise and Fall of Italian Terrorism.* Boulder and London: Westview.

Wolfgang, M.E. and F. Ferracuti 1969. *The Subculture of Violence.* London: Tavistock.

POLITICAL SOCIALIZATION IN LEFT-WING UNDERGROUND ORGANIZATIONS:

BIOGRAPHIES OF ITALIAN AND GERMAN MILITANTS

Donatella della Porta

INTRODUCTION

Most studies of terrorism have been concerned with the structural origins of the phenomenon; many with the problem of controlling consequences; a few with the characteristics of militants of the underground organizations. Research in this last category has addressed the topic mainly from a psychological perspective, focusing on individual personalities. This study, as well as other studies published in this volume, attempts to link macro and micro levels of analysis by considering both individual motivations and the structural context in which they arose. The subjects of this study were militants of left-wing underground organizations in Italy and West Germany. Although I compare some characteristics of the Italian and German militants, my primary

International Social Movement Research, Vol. 4, pages 259-290.

ISBN: 1-55938-445-X

aim here is not a systematic comparison of militancy in the two countries. Rather, using data on the Italian and German militants mainly for the purpose of illustration, I propose some general hypotheses about individual motivations for joining a left-wing underground group and about the social dynamics which reinforce this commitment.

My research was guided by few definite assumptions about “becoming a terrorist,” which I think it helpful to summarize before I present my empirical analysis. My first assumption concerns the *intentionality* of a militant’s behavior and choices. In its most obvious sense, “intentionality” means that militants are not prisoners of their environment. The intentionality of choices is probably the only way to explain why only a few of those who shared the same structural locations and cultural affinities joined a terrorist group. I also assume that, to a certain extent, militants “knew” what they wanted: they were first of all political activists aiming at political goals. For most of the individuals, joining a terrorist organization was a last step in a “career” characterized by legal forms of political commitment. Thus, they considered the “armed struggle” an appropriate political means to reach political ends.

My second assumption is that the militants’ belief in the historical necessity of “taking up arms” was the outcome of an *interactive* process. The external conditions in which the political socialization of the future militants took place influenced individual motivations to join the underground groups. The militants of the underground organizations were in fact part of a generation whose political socialization occurred in a climate which was generally conducive to violence. Moreover, loyalty and commitment to their underground organizations were forged during their experiences within much larger political groups.

My third assumption is that the effects of these interactions are mediated by the militants’ *perception* of the reality in which their political involvement developed. The main tool for determining the link between individual motivations, at the micro level, and environmental conditions, at the macro level, is in fact the analysis of the militants’ perception of this reality, of the dynamics that intensified and radicalized their involvement, and of their role as “freedom fighters.” By taking the militants’ perception into account, I did not imply that I “trusted” everything they say about their reasons for joining the underground. Quite the contrary, my approach aims at “discovering” the characteristics of the militants’ images of reality and the way in which these images were created. Here, then, I will consider mainly the militants’ images, leaving aside the important question, How do the images compare with the “real” preconditions for the development of underground organizations in the two countries.

My fourth assumption is that an individual’s conversion to terrorism must be understood within the context of his or her entire *political career* (Matza 1969), during which collective identities are built and, during collective processes, transformed. Conversion to terrorism requires, in fact, a specific definition of reality, which is produced by new beliefs and values. The possible meanings of external reality therefore evolve within dense social networks and create positive attitudes toward the "armed struggle." Accordingly, commitment is a process during which new collective identities are built. Affective, normative, and cognitive mechanisms contribute to the identity-building process.

My principal source for this study has been biographies of former militants of left-wing underground groups.[1] For information on the Italian militants, I used 28 life histories of members of the Brigate Rosse (BR, Red Brigades), Prima Linea (PL, Front Line), and other minor groups active in Italy during the 1970s and early 1980s.[2] I have integrated material from these sources with information from published biographies.[3] For information on the German militants, I relied on the results of a research project sponsored by the Bundesministerium des Innern—including interviews of seven militants (Jaeger and Boellinger 1981)—and on printed autobiographies and biographical interviews.[4] Other sources provided supplementary information. For the Italian militants, I used quantitative data from a data bank on about 1,200 militants of underground organizations which I built from trial records (see della Porta 1990a). For the German militants, I referred to the quantitative data—provided by the study sponsored by the Bundesministerium des Innern—on 227 left-wing militants sentenced on the basis of article 129 Strafgesetzbuch (Neidhardt 1982b; Schmidtchen 1981); the biographical accounts on 50 militants provided by the Bundeskriminalamt (Jaeger 1981); press information on 14 militants (Jaeger 1981); and the interrogation records of 9 militants (Neidhardt 1982a). These studies refer to militants of the Rote Armee Fraktion (RAF, Red Army Fraction), Bewegung 2. Juni (Movement of June 2), and Revolutionaere Zellen (RZ, Revolutionary Cells).

POLITICAL SOCIALIZATION IN THE NEW LEFT: THE CREATION OF A COUNTERCULTURE

One essential fact about the militants of the left-wing underground organizations in Italy and West Germany is that they all had political motivations. In both countries, those who joined the armed struggle had already been involved, often for many years, in legal radical Left organizations. My research on Italian militants has shown that 38 percent of them had been involved in the New Left—especially in two radical groups, Potere Operaio (Workers' Power) and Lotta Continua (Continuous Struggle)—and as many as 84 percent in the small groups of the so-called Autonomia (Authonomy) (della Porta 1988c, pp. 161-162). In West Germany too, most of the terrorists had participated in New Left organizations. The founders of the RAF and of the Bewegung 2. Juni had previous experience in the student movement; and many from the "second generation" had been active in groups close to the so-called Spontis, such as the squatters' movement groups or the Rote Hilfe (Red Help), or in the semi-anarchist Rebels of the Hashish and Schwarze Hilfe (Black Help). Quite a large number of recruits came from the Sozialistisches Patientenkollektiv in Heidelberg.[5] As the German criminologist Wilfried Rasch observed: "At the outset of these careers stood a serious social engagement which did not confine itself to verbal propagation of revolutionary goals but was realized in practical social work" (Rasch 1979, p. 81).

By exposing the future militants to vital formative experiences, the political and social activities in which they participated helped to create a peculiar political counterculture. The future militants of the underground groups shared, first, strong political identities—that is, political commitment was an essential constituent of their personality—and, second, a political socialization to violence—that is, their political ideology and activities did not exclude the use of physical violence (della Porta 1987b; 1988a; and 1988c). I will illustrate the environmental preconditions for the development of this counterculture by describing not the "objective" reality but the subjective images of the actors. These subjective images, however, were by no means peculiar to the future militants of the underground; indeed, they were shared by many within the larger environment of the New Left.

Politics as a Totalistic Activity

As we examine the process of political socialization, we see that an individual's decision to join an underground group was often influenced first of all by strong affective ties. Italian clandestine organizations, in fact, recruited their militants within dense networks of social relations, where political ties were strengthened by primary solidarity based on friendship and kinship relations.[6] Among the German militants, too, "recruitment in political groups sometimes started for nonpolitical reasons on the basis of personal sympathies" (Jaeger 1981, p. 147).

How were these friendship ties created? How did they become so important in determining the individual's decision to join the armed struggle? From the very beginning of the process of political socialization, emotional motivations play a decisive role. For instance, one Italian militant, talking about his recruitment to a radical group, said: "I never made an ideological choice, ideology always came later on. . . . If I had met a PCI member whom I had liked more [than the radical militants], today I would be a PCI member myself" (Life history no. 1, p. 43). Former RZ member Klein wrote in his autobiography: "Most of the comrades of my group called themselves 'anarcho-trade unionists,' and so did I, although I did not really understand what it meant" (Klein 1980, p. 149).

Participation in small legal political groups strengthened these friendship ties. Even when an individual belonged to friendship networks external to the political milieu, their importance to him diminished as he became more politically socialized. In a spiral of mutual determinations, the more time an individual spent in political activities, the greater number of contacts he made with comrade-friends. At the same time, the strengthening of friendship ties within the political environment augmented the value of political involvement, and accordingly people would dedicate more and more time to political activities. This commitment weakened other ties, which thus lost their power to exert a countervailing influence on the formation of the personality. In a process characteristic of other experiences of political socialization (Keniston 1968), commitment to underground organizations involved a gradual isolation from the outside world, which enforced the members' loyalty to the new group. The individual's comrade-friends became his or her most important and influential peer group.

Sharing the activities of everyday life further strengthened affective ties among members of the legal left-wing groups. Interviews with Italian former militants often include such statements as:

> Obviously the relations at the personal level were built in the environment in which you spent your everyday life. I mean that *with the comrades . . . you built, day by day, affective ties* (Life history no. 13, pp. 35-36; here and in all following quotations, emphasis is mine).
>
> In that period *friendship coincides with politics*. It is difficult for me to distinguish between friends and comrades, because politics occupied every moment of my life (Life history no. 9, p. 30).
>
> My most beloved friends are those with whom I handed out leaflets in front of the factories (Life history no. 9, p. 32).

In West Germany in particular the youth counterculture was a seedbed of critiques of the "conformist" society. For many German militants, strong affective ties developed within the communes, or *Wohngemeinschaften*,[7] where, often, countercultural attitudes ultimately found expression in political involvement. Former RAF member Volker Speitel, for instance, described the countercultural context of his politicization in the *Szene* of Stuttgart:

> At this time I lived . . . in a commune that was absolutely apolitical. . . . Correspondingly, life was chaotic in that commune and as an orientation or aid for solving the many conflicts that arose we smoked a joint or took a trip. . . . We dreamed of a farmhouse in the country, nature, love, peace, and at the same time we liked any armed action. We wanted everything and at the same time nothing. . . . We were as far away from the radical left as a Bavarian priest from a small village, and nevertheless we felt part of it. *The affinities were based on a formal connection: the same habits, the same music, the same slang and slogans* (Speitel 1980a, pp. 36-37).

The political socialization of former Bewegung 2. Juni member Bommi Baumann similarly began in the youth counterculture; he was radicalized by the feeling that he had been rejected by the "adult" society:

> For somebody like me, with my long hair, when I went out in Berlin, it was like being in the skin of a negro. They threw us out of public places, they spit on us, they insulted us, they annoyed us . . . completely unknown people, people you had never done anything against. . . . For many people, politics appeared with the demonstrations against the Vietnam war on the Kudamm. All us from the Gedaechtniskirche permanently met on the Kudamm. During the marches, we were therefore forced to meet each other. Since the very beginning, some took part in the marches. They were street affairs. . . . First of all, it was a lot of fun (Baumann 1976, pp. 30-42 passim).

How did politics become a totalistic experience? The accounts of former militants highlight three main contributing factors: the acceleration of the politicization process, the large amount of time devoted to political activities, and the transformation of everyday life. Apropos of the first factor, an Italian militant recalled: "There is also something which I find hard to explain: it is *the very high speed at which I precipitated* [into the movement]. From this [my] first approach, from this curiosity about the new environment, to the more totalistic activism, to my embracing political militance, immediately in the groups of Lotta Continua, there are three or four months" (Life history no. 18, p. 16). Speitel described how his involvement in Stuttgart's Rote Hilfe rapidly changed his life: "Through this combination of discussion and working together, *our whole life practically changed in a period of only three or four months"* (Speitel 1980a, p. 38). Caught up in this rapid evolution, the militants no longer perceived themselves as making a deliberate choice:

> There was not a moment in which I chose, I said "now." It was an *evolution toward a model of life, which became extremely exacting for the rest of my life.* From that moment on, I did only that, full time, concentrating there not only all my physical energies . . . but also all my attention (Life history no. 29, p. 15).

As the political group began to demand more and more of the militants' time, they gradually gave up all other activities—social, athletic, or musical. Recalling the years of their militance, both Italian and German militants commented on the intensity of their activism:

> In those years, *I participated in nothing else but political activities:* I went to every single mass demonstration that took place in those years. . . . A single strike meant ten general assemblies, meetings at Palazzo Nuovo, in the schools, in the coordinatory committees, leaflets and discussions (Life history no. 18, p. 31).

> Eventually, I was involved in this *crazy activism*, I did not have time to sleep anymore (Life history no. 5, p. 9).

> *Political activity was on a 24-hours-a-day basis*. . . . It was a big game, a big game in which we felt involved, willing to give all ourselves. In that period politics transformed our dreams into reality: [it gave us] the feeling of being influential, of being many, of having power . . . (Life history no. 13, pp. 22-23).

> *We did nothing else, for 14-16 hours a day,* but work on a leaflet, produce information material for the media, organize meetings or discussions in support of the hunger strike (Speitel 1980a, p. 40).

Not only did political activity absorb all the militants time, political experience "determined" every aspect of their lives. In the words of former RAF member Juenschke, "*everything was political in that period*" (1988, p. 153). In the political groups, also a search for a new value system took place. In a television interview, former RAF member Horst Mahler expressed his fascination in observing "the way in which human beings can, in a very short time, change so profoundly" (cited in Jaeger 1981, p. 148). In another interview, Mahler observed: "A very important experience has been the transformation of human relations, the big openness: to see how barriers between people fall down and how the greatest loyalty and reciprocal affection are created" (cited in Jaeger 1981, p. 149).

The former militants recall this period of their lives as extremely exciting.Coinciding with their first experience of independence from the family, the militants' life within the group was, they remember, very happy; they use often the words "party" and "play" to describe it. Hints of this party-like atmosphere appear in the following recollections of two Italian militants:

> My life was in many ways marked by political experiences. I mean that my friends were all comrades with whom I lived everything together with. . . . I have to admit that in those years, in my high-school years, *I had such a good time* (Life history no. 28, p. 11);

> I remember that summer holidays were felt as . . . very boring because they interrupted that continuous cycle which had represented your entire existence for the whole year; the meetings of Lotta Continua, the meetings at my school, the student assemblies, the marches, the demonstrations (Life history no. 13, p. 33).

The situation of the German activists was very similar. Baumann described the atmosphere in the Kommune 1 as "always nice, and even fantastic when we planned some political actions, and when an action succeeded, then there was a real party at home" (Baumann 1976, p. 51). Klein remembered new relationships characterized by "solidarity," "love," "self-transformation":

> Two years after having being organized in a group, in a political group, I had acquired completely new experiences and knowledge. I do not mean here study and political understanding but the *practice of solidarity, love and reciprocal respect without competition and its anxieties.* Help even for the weakest members of the group, instead of defense against them. That really was a fantastic experience for me. . . . On one side there was solidarity

> toward the others instead of the everybody-for-himself [ethic] practiced until then. On the other side there was love and good-will for the others, also if they were weaker and had their defects (Klein 1980, p. 144).

The frequent use of the word "family" in these recollections testifies to the emotional importance of the relations within the political groups. Italian militants, for instance, affirmed: "the comrades became my family" (Life history no. 5, p. 35), "Potere operaio was a small family" (Life history no. 16, p. 71); "It is the sense of a family . . . we questioned the family, but looked for new certainty inside the group, which replaced what we criticized" (Life history no. 26, p. 16).

The peer group composed of comrades-friends therefore come to exert more and more influence on the most important personal choices. At the same time, the group became more and more isolated from the external world. Boellinger summarized this development in the biography of one of his interviewees: "The group became always more closed in on itself . . . and an enormous pressure came from the union of private and public life. Any refusal, any private conflict was criticized as political weakness" (Boellinger 1981, p. 181). Or as an Italian militant put it: "The sense of the group has always been very strong. It determined personal choice and concrete behavior toward society" (Life history no. 26, p. 5). Moreover, many of the small networks that had sprung up within the counterculture began to compete among themselves, and as a result the group became smaller, closer, and more insular sects. As one German militant acknowledged,

> In my radicalization, I became very intolerant. When I met comrades who had made different choices, I let them down. Eventually, *I became completely closed.* Everything was political to such an extent that I did not meet human beings on a human basis anymore. . . . We lost a lot of our sensitivity (Juenschke 1988, p. 153).

The fact that these small groups of the left-wing and youth counterculture were responsible for selecting and processing relevant political information also contributed to the militants' loss of sensitivity. As an Italian interviewee put it, "ghettos" were created: "You built a network of friends, of personal relations always inside this circle. I think that already at that moment a kind of unconscious ghetto-like isolation took place" (Life history no. 13, p. 6).

The Legitimation of Political Violence

Although the militants of both Italy and West Germany found a legitimation for the use of violence in their political experiences in the counterculture, militance in the two countries differed in several, and remarkable, ways. For reasons I do not discuss here, political violence surely was more widespread in Italy than in West Germany. Nevertheless, similarities also existed, at least in the evolution of some small and radical groups. I will focus on two of these similarities that legitimized political violence: the image of a "violent" and "unfair" state, and the everyday practice of political violence.

The Image of a Violent State

Militants found a justification for violence in the widespread belief that the state had broken the rules of the democratic game, and that revolutionary violence was therefore the only way to oppose an increasingly authoritarian state. In this context the "real" attitude and behavior of state apparatuses and governments is irrelevant; my concern here is the images that were diffused in the counterculture and influenced the attitude and behavior of the militants. The image of a violent state was created, first af all, by the militants' vivid memories of police brutality. Reminiscences of the public marches in Italy are full of such details as "a policeman who aimed his gun at my belly" (Life history no. 21, p. 31); "my burned hand, when I tried to throw back a squat candle" (Life history no. 3, p. 19), "eyes red from smoke of the tear gas" (Life history no. 12, p. 11). In his autobiography, Klein described police violence as he experienced it during house squattings in Frankfurt: "I was passing near the Grueneburgweg just when the policemen started their orgy of clubs. I threw myself in the battle. Two minutes later I found myself in an ambulance" (Klein 1980, p. 199). Police "brutality" dominates the early reminiscences of both a German and an Italian militant, who present similar descriptions of their first participation in a public march:

> . . . *a pandemonium: tear-gas, cries, blows, people who ran everywhere* . . . this Milan in a light in which I could have never imagined it, with the smoke of squat candles and a really *ghostly scene: torn placards, broken road-signs, and people wounded in the streets* (Life history no. 12, p. 11).

> I had never been at a march, and it was almost by chance that I passed near to that one. And there, I saw *three policemen who were beating a girl.* I think if it had been a boy, I would not have felt so shocked (Klein 1980, p. 57).

In Italy, several members of leftist legal and illegal groups died during police actions or fascist attacks, and for the militants these deaths acquired a highly symbolic value as expressions of the degeneration of the state. Among the events that helped to radicalize the attitudes of the Italian militants—eventually impelling them to join the underground groups—were the "April days" of 1975, which one militant described in his biography: "Three days of fighting . . . following the assassination of the young Varalli by a group of neofascists and of Zibecchi, crushed by a police car in front of the MSI [neofascist party] headquarters" (cited in Novelli and Tranfaglia 1988, p. 163). Another militant recalled that "the days of the death of Zibecchi in Milan, Boschi in Florence and Micciche' in Turin were the moment when rage and the desire to rebel came to possess all of us. . . . Those deaths gave us a strange feeling, almost as if it were not possible to go back anymore" (cited in Novelli and Tranfaglia 1988, p. 206).

The militants also found another justification for the use of violence in the shared belief that it was necessary to resist the violence of the police: "We reacted with stones against those who had guns and squat candles and clubs," one militant remembered. "This difference was for me a justification: it *legitimized the defensive use of violence*" (Life history no. 9, p. 26). They found an even stronger justification, however, in the belief that the state was involved in a sort of dirty war. This belief was in fact grounded in reality: in Italy, in the outbreaks of neofascist violence, which were widespread at that time; in West Germany, in the historical experience of Nazism and the incomplete "denazification." Moreover, in Italy, the belief that members of the state apparatuses had tolerated, and even helped, the neofascists was held not only by the Left but also by part of the "liberal" public opinion.

Neofascist violence in Italy took three forms: the "squadrismo" of bands of young radicals, the massacres carried out by right-wing terrorists, and several plots for a coups d'etat. Several life histories describe how left-wing militants increased their military skill in the cruel fights with right-wing radicals. The following account is typical:

> The physical struggle with the political counterpart, I mean with the fascists, was a matter of almost every single day. . . . It was therefore *unavoidable that we started to equip ourselves in a military way* . . . because those were the days of militants being killed during the marches, the years in which comrades were killed in fascist assaults (Life history no. 13, pp. 29-30).

This "spiral of revenge," or "merciless man hunt" (Life history no. 6, p. 29), radicalized the forms of action the militants used as did the neo-fascist massacre of Piazza Fontana (on December 12, 1969, in Milan). Proof of the involvement of the Italian intelligence service in the protection of the assassins had the same effect. In the leftist political culture, the state became the "state of the massacre," which used a "strategy of tension" to repress democratic protest. It therefore became *"right, there in Italy, to use mass violence* against those responsible for the 'massacre perpetrated by the state'" (Life history no. 12, p. 10).

The conviction that the ruling class was going to organize a coup d'etat and that thus it was necessary to equip oneself for resistance was also widespread, as a number of biographies indicate:

> *"What to do when there is a coup d'etat"* was the classic book that all the comrades had hidden in their book-shelves (Life history no. 6, p. 19).

> We assumed a *conspirational identity,* typical for that kind of situation in which we lived, for that particular climate that we experienced . . . the *paranoia of a golpe* (Life history no. 18, p. 47).
>
> Everyday life was interwoven with this atmosphere: I remember periods when I had my backpack already prepared under my bed, false alarms for a non-broadcasted radio-news, chains of telephone calls more or less reassuring (cited in Novelli and Tranfaglia 1988, p. 122).
>
> The "black" plots from Piazza Fontana on made that perspective [of a golpe] almost imminent. How many people—I do not refer only to the comrades of the extra-parliamentary left—did not sleep at home; how many eyes were pointed at the barracks . . . (cited in Novelli and Tranfaglia 1988, p. 204).

In West Germany, the counterculture worked to delegitimize the state by emphasizing the state's continuity with the Nazi regime. Activists and scholars described the rise and the radicalization of the student movement as reactions to an always authoritarian state. Horst Mahler, for instance, explained this relation in an interview:

> How could young people, enthusiastic about the universal good, feel OK in a *state that had already shown itself as a murderous Leviathan,* as the institutionalized crime against humanity? This is the reason why this form of terrorism . . . appeared rightly in West Germany, Italy and Japan . . . It was not a lack of reverence or a presumed naughtiness of the young people which prevented their identification with the German state and the German people. It was instead the traumatic memories of fascist cruelty, the absence of an antifascist revolution in West Germany and the continuity of the state involvement in imperialism (Mahler 1980, pp. 26-27).

In interpreting the state's reactions to protest and terrorism, militants repeatledly invoked images stressing continuities with Nazism or a return to Nazism. The perception of a "fascistization of the state" began to spread as early as 1967, when a protester, Benno Ohnesorg, was killed by the police; and this perception was enforced after an attempt on the life of the leader of the student movement, Rudi Dutschke. Baumann recalled:

> [After the attack against Rudi Dutschke] the street lightened by the torches and the shout "Rudi Dutschke" meant to me: "this bullet was directed against you also. *For the first time, they fired against you"* (Baumann 1976, p. 72).
>
> The turning point of the State apparata, which was concretized in Ohnesorg's and Rudi's cases, proved that the state was ready to do anything and that *its fascist face appeared* as soon as it felt in danger for whatever reason (Baumann 1976, p. 81).

In 1973, the treatment of "isolation" of the RAF prisoners was perceived as evidence of the process of "fascistization" of the state. As former RAF member Klaus Juenschke put it:

> The acceptance of special prison units also legitimates all other means aiming at the same goal: constriction therapies, brain surgery, genetic manipulation. The inadequate reflection

> on German history from 1933 to 1945 corresponds to this lack of sensitivity toward the complete control of human beings, toward total dominion over human beings (Juenschke 1988, p. 131).
>
> Those in command positions in economy, politics, army, police, secret service, church, science, media, and so on, are ex-Nazis or those responsible for Nazism (Juenschke 1988, p. 136).

Experiences with Political Violence

Justifications for the use of violence also emerged from the militants' concrete, everyday experiences of political violence. Italian former militants stressed that their personal experiences with political violence preceded their involvement in the underground groups:

> The qualitative jump in the use of violence produced an internalization of the idea that *violence was legitimate for any communist militant,* that it was a legitimate instrument, a practice of everyday life (Life history no. 13, p. 28);
>
> You talked everyday about the use of physical force and *everyday you practiced it* (Life history no. 8, p. 35);
>
> *Every morning I left home, I went to fight the police in the street battles,* I came back home for lunch, and went back to fight in the afternoon and until night. It was a Londonderry, I mean a series of battles carried out with molotov-cocktails and stones to conquer five meters of land (Life history no. 27, p. 26).

The life histories reveal the symbolic value that violent actions had for the militants and the influence of these actions on the militants' political socialization. "Hard pickets," "people's trials against the factory bosses," and "sabotages" often provided the militants with direct experience in the use of physical coercion as a political form of action. Violence was justified, first of all, as a practical and defensive need. Especially at the end of the long and intense cycle of strikes that lasted from 1968 to 1973, some very radical forms of action sporadically appeared (della Porta and Tarrow 1987). One of the older militants recalled the violence during the strike pickets: "The picket often took violent forms, . . . often we chose the way of physically opposing those who wanted to break the lines, because we thought that it was the right way to get what we wanted" (Life history no. 9, p. 39).

During this cycle of industrial protest, radical forms of action spread from the factory to other economic sectors and social groups. For many New Left militants distributing propaganda supporting prisoners' and soldiers' protest was their first experience of "underground" actions. Violent episodes also took place during strikes in public hospitals, house squattings, and actions against heroin dealers. In these cases too the militants justified violence for its instrumental value:

> I was among those who organized the pickets in front of the schools. And we tried to split drug dealers' heads. *It was a pratical matter; it was the only way to succeed in what we wanted* (Life history no. 8, p. 35).

> If there is not enough personnel . . . and if they do not want to reduce the places, we will do it ourselves. So we did. And we had charges for this (Life history no. 15, p. 26).

> In San Basilio there was this famous squatting during which the people living there fired with guns against the police (Life history no. 12, p. 20).

In the minds of the militants, these episodes became mythical examples of the presence of a revolutionary consciousness, and as such, they in turn contributed to the radicalization of the movement. Further, they begun to regard violence as a positive symbolic value. Inside the big factories, violence came to express the "power of the workers," as the following account illustrates: "We organized a people's trial against the foremen. . . . We marched inside the factory and captured some of them, others escaped. . . . There was this people's trial against the bosses. Some of them were acquitted, others were sentenced to be expelled from the factory. But we just bound them to the gate, outside in the rain" (Life history no. 29, p. 24).

As the cycle of protest evolved, political violence became more and more organized. Inside the factories, "squads of 'Volante rossa' were founded in Turin . . . they were groups of workers, often members of the trade unions that during the marches inside the factories . . . destroyed the headquarters of the right-wing trade unions or beat the most detested foremen" (Life history no. 29, p. 20). Ouside the factories, a levy of the very young militants for the underground organizations was composed of those who had been socialized to politics in the highly violent second half of the 1970s. Long before joining the terrorist groups, many of these militants had been involved in armed marches and so-called proletarian expropriations—mass hold-ups in big stores defined as protest actions against conspicuous consumption and a class society. These actions were widespread and organized:

> It was a happening. . . . It was "what do we do on Saturday? do we occupy the *curia* for the week-end? do we organize a proletarian expropriation?" (Life history no. 3, p. 63).

> We were a sector of the movement that did incredible things, we carried guns at any public march; during every single event organized by the movement we were armed with pistols and sometimes with rifles (Life history no. 28, p. 54).

> I had the feeling that everything was going to precipitate: guns in the streets had became as common as the sticks of the flags some time before, and the guerrilla attacks that started with marches and then returned back to marches were an everyday practice (cited in Novelli and Tranfaglia 1988, p. 294).

One important difference between terrorism in Italy and West Germany was that the use of violent repertoires by legal organizations was much more frequent in the former than in the latter. This fact is probably one of the main reasons terrorism was more widely diffused in Italy than in West Germany. But political violence occurred in West Germany too, although it was not as extensive and involved a much smaller number of people. And in West Germany as in Italy, it was quite common for future militants of the underground groups to have participated in violent events. According to Schmidtchen's data (1981, p. 47), 32 percent of German future terrorists (as against 4% of the comparable population) had taken part in nonauthorized marches; 17 percent in squattings (as against 1%); and 63 percent in confrontations with police (as against 8%). In addition, such experiences as acting as marshalls in demonstrations accostumed German militants to violence. Klein, for instance, recalled that he was always one of those who "protected the end of the cortege as far as we could, or [we] freed the comrades. How many times had I freed comrades fighting with the policemen and how many time was I criticized because of my militant combativeness" (Klein 1980, p. 163). Referring to the RAF militants, Ulrike Meinhof observed: "All of us come from there: from the street battles of Berlin students in 1967/68 against the police, from the sit-ins, and from the attempt . . . to make socialist politics at the limit of legality" (cited in Neidhardt 1982a, p. 339).

In both Italy and West Germany, the militants' earlier involvement in violent political activities provided them with the "skills" they needed to organize the "armed struggle" and so made their passage to the underground less traumatic, even, in some cases, imperceptibles. Another effect of this familiarity with violence was prosecution by the judges and the police, which itself became a precipitating cause for recruitment in terrorist organizations.

RECRUITMENT IN THE UNDERGROUND: SOME PRECIPITATING FACTORS

So far I have concentrated on the political socialization of future militants of the underground. I already emphasized that membership in the political counterculture was in no way typical of those who later joined the underground. To the opposite, radical groups were only small minorities of mass movements: a few thousand people in Italy, a few hundred in West Germany. Our next step, then, is to define the specific characteristics of those who actually made a choice of the underground. As I stressed in my introduction, a sociological analysis cannot offer a "complete" explanation for individual choices, which depend to a great extent on the consciousness of each individual. It can, however, provide an important part of the explanation. I will illustrate two "precipitating" causes: the social networks to which a militant belonged and the militant's perception of a situation of emergency.

The Loyalty to Friends in Danger

The decision to join an underground organization was very rarely an individual one. In most of the cases, it involved cliques of friends. My research has shown that, for the Italian militants, in at least 843 cases out of 1,214 the people who decided to join an underground group had at least a friend already participating; moreover, in 74 percent of these cases the new recruit had more than one friend, and in 42 percent more than seven (della Porta 1988c, p. 158). The situation among the German militants was very similar in this respect. Although no one has ever conducted a systematic study of the recruitment of German militants, there is widespread agreement that "most terrorists, in fact, ultimately became members of terrorist organizations through personal connections with people or relatives associated with appropriate political initiatives, communes, self-supporting organizations, or committees—the number of couples, and brothers and sisters is astonishingly high" (Wasmund 1986, p. 204). Similarly, Neidhardt described those who joined the RAF as "tied to each other to form a network, by means of personal acquaintances, of shared participation in communes, also of love stories, and in some case also of a shared social work" (1982a, p. 341).

In some cases, recruitment was determined by the individual's solidarity with an "important" friend who was arrested or had to go underground. Bommi Baumann's explanation is typical of these recruits: "I had joined the group because of Georg. I knew that he had decided to do some things and I did not want to abandon him" (Baumann 1976, p. 185). In addition, many of the German militants of the second generation became involved in the underground groups to express solidarity with friends—often comrades of the same commune—imprisoned during the first wave of arrests (Jaeger 1981). Even asides from the impetus provided by personal acquaintances, the death of the RAF militant Holger Meins during a hunger strike was a motivating factor for many of those who had worked in the radical groups that focused on the problems of "political prisoners":

> I was for the first time personally struck by the situation of the prisoners. I really saw tortured and tormented prisoners, in their totally isolated cells, where they wanted to destroy them slowly by means of scientific methods. . . . Then the day came when Holger Meins died. . . . For us this death was a key experience . . . *The death of Holger Meins and the decision to take arms were one and the same decision. Reflection was not possible anymore.* It was only the emotional pressure of the last few months which pushed us to react (Speitel 1980a, p. 41).

> If all I needed for not only propagating the armed struggle, but also for taking it up myself was the right "kick," then Holger Meins was this "kick." With his death my sense of powerlessness in front of the state grew so much that I felt overwhelmed. I had had enough of legal politics and I was ready to fight (Klein 1980, p. 256).

The deaths in prison of the RAF leaders Ulrike Meinhof, in 1976, and Baader, Ensslin, and Raspe, in 1977, had a similar effect on the following "generations" of German militants.

The Italian militants described the decision to join an underground organization as the effect of a "growing responsibility for friends" and a search for a shared, "equal punishment":

> [There was] a deep change and distortion in my life because, by *devoting all myself to this kind of involvement spiritually related . . . to my friend who had to go underground,* to this idea of our feverish lives . . . I had these images of the necessity, the rightness, the beauty of that kind of sacrifice (Life history no. 18, pp. 58-59).

> It was when S. was arrested that I found the emotional energy that pushed me to carry out the first actions for the organizations (Life history no. 17, p. 15).

In Italy more than in West Germany, several members of the same small political group would all decide to join a terrorist organization, sometimes after a general meeting and a vote. The probability of becoming involved in the underground was thus higher for the activists in the small groups that were "in contact" with terrorist organizations. Strong ties among peer groups composed by comrades-friends encouraged the kind of fidelity manifested in the following statement: "There are many things I cannot explain by analyzing the political situation, or the social conditions in a city . . . as far as I am concerned it was up to emotional feelings, of passions for the people I shared my life with" (Life history no. 21, p. 28). The very fact that the choice was a collective one made it less perceivable and therefore less traumatic: "A choice [made] in cold blood, such as 'now I will become a terrorist,' does not exist. It was *a step-by-step evolution, which passed through a kind of human relation* which I had with Guido, and with the people I worked with" (Life history no. 17, p. 31).

The Risk of Being Arrested

The militants' decisions to go underground were also often determined by their perception of being involved in a personal emergency—that is by the lack of alternative solutions. Many militants in fact perceived that they were personally at risk, in danger of being arrested and prosecuted because of their participation in radical political activities. Those who went underground were therefore often those who had already been charged with crimes of political violence, such as, among the German militants, Baader and Ennslin, who had received prison sentences for setting fire to a Frankfurt department store; or Mahler, whose professional career was ruined after he was sentenced to pay 250.000 DM for damages produced during a violent demonstration (Krebs 1988); or Ulrike Meinhof, who went underground after the police linked her to the liberation of Baader (Krebs 1988). Many Italian militants also went underground because they thought they were in danger of being arrested. As one Italian woman said: "I could not stay at home and be quiet while waiting for them to come and take me" (Life history no. 15, p. 29).

PERSISTENCE OF COMMITMENT: THE "FREEDOM-FIGHTER" IDENTITY

Having described the ways in which people became involved in underground organizations we must still explain what made them persist in their commitment. Journalistic literature has often overemphasized the degree to which the threat of physical punishment, as retaliation, deterred people from leaving terrorist organizations. In both Italy and West Germany, for many years militants were not at risk when they quit their organizations, provided they did not collaborate with the police, "steal" arms or money, or try to persuade others to "desert." But by the second half of the 1970s in West Germany and the beginning of the 1980s in Italy, militants did feel they risked retaliation if they quit. When some among their members collaborated with the police, the terrorist organizations reacted by punishing the "traitors" or "suspected traitors" (Caselli and della Porta 1984). According to many of the interviewees, the threat of punishment often delayed the decision to leave the underground.

Persistence of commitment, however, can be attributed less to the fear of negative sanctions than to the existence of positive "incentives" (della Porta 1988b). As we will see, terrorist organizations fostered a sense of collective identity in which every member became a "freedom fighter;" that is, individual identities became grounded in a larger community of those who supported the armed struggle.

The "Sense of the Group"

Affective ties within the terrorist organizations were vital in preserving loyalty to the group. While recruitment to underground organizations usually involved groups of friends, frequent and often exclusive interactions inside the underground organizations maintained and even strengthened solidarity ties among small groups of militants, primarily in the first stages of individual involvement and at the beginning of the clandestine groups' stories. Similarly as everyday life in legal left-wing groups, Italian militants characterized also their relations with comrades of the same underground group as "absolute human relations," "solidarity even in the small things," "relations free from any material interest," "affective generosity." They also remembered the time spent with fellow comrades as a very happy one; former militants spoke of "parties that followed some actions," a "large component of conviviality," a "merry brotherhood," and so on. A German militant defined the RAF as a "family" that had anticipated the "right forms of life for the future," pushed for "nonrepressive and open relations," and fought against "the imperialism that is inside ourselves" (cited in Boellinger 1981, p. 202).

The exposure of friends to danger was another factor that strengthened the affective ties in the underground groups. Among the Italian interviewees, maintaining solidarity with friends who had been arrested was an important reason for remaining in a terrorist organization:

> I believe that if G. had not been in prison since 1977, L. and I would have not continued for such a long time. . . . The fact that Chicco was in prison was an important element for continuing, because he was a friend of ours (Life history no. 26, p. 68).

> This kind of involvement with my friends means that, at the end of the game, *either we are all outside or we are all inside* [prison], because if some of us are out and some of us are in, I don't give up my friends. . . . This meant that if my friends had drowned because of a belief that I shared with them, I would decide to drown; well if they are there and I can't help them, I prefer to be with them (Life history no. 18, pp. 58-59).

Former German militants also explained the persistence of commitment in terms of "human solidarity" (Boock 1981, p. 113), and "loyalty toward people one knew from before and would not want to be defined by as a pig" (Speitel 1980c, p. 34).

Not all the former militants described relations within the terrorist organizations as positive—life underground was especially stressful and a very hierarchical structure provoked strong personal conflicts—but their accounts reveal that these organizations definitely developed a "sense of the group," and the group came to include the whole "community" of "freedom fighters." As one RAF member put it: "Anybody who fights is one of us" (cited in Boellinger 1981, p. 202). Loyalty to the group preserved commitment:

> The identity or identification with the group is like an alarm clock that always rings an "I keep going" in this choice you always make when, with a residual spark of self-preservation, you ask yourself "why." . . . you cannot cut the thick threads the group has covered you with in the course of time. *One's whole existence was first of all in the group* . . . the whole existence of all of us was first of all the group (Speitel 1980c, p. 34).

The militants came to identify not only with their own comrade-friends, but with all members of underground groups. "The group," a German criminologist explains, "offers this type of identification-object in the form of comrades and leading personalities" (Boellinger 1981, p. 223). The comrades became mythical people. A German interviewee declared: "My involvement did not come only from my head but also from my belly. It was wonderful to belong to those who had a complete understanding of the world and who really started to work hard, instead of sitting and complaining" (cited in Boellinger 1981, p. 189), it was exhilarating to be one of "these extremely intelligent comrades with an iron will" (Boellinger 1981, p. 202).

It was not only comrades who acquired a mythical status. The underground organizations created "heroes," comrades who had died during terrorist actions. And reference to these shared heroes strengthened the militants' loyalty. The death of a fellow member produced strong emotional strains and feelings of "revenge," as it is evident in this statement of an Italian rank-and-file militant: "The deaths of Matteo and Barbara . . . had such a strong emotional impact. . . . Then you are inside *a spiral of revenge and retaliation,* because when you are in that game, you have to play it" (Life history no. 17, p. 35).

Further, underground groups stuck together because their members shared a "sense of being responsible" for each other. The militants outside prison felt responsible for the destiny of their comrades in prison, whether they knew each other or not. Any desire to quit the terrorist organization was considered "betrayal of those who were in prison." At the same time, the militants in prison felt a "sense of becoming responsible" for those who, outside, risked their lives to free them. The following two passages describe this reciprocal emotional blackmail. The first, from the account of one of the leaders of the Italian PL, describes the feelings of those outside. He remembered that even in the early 1980s, when the defeat of the organization was more than evident,

> We continued to fight above all for our comrades who were in prison. . . . *Choices of death, of individual death, were based on this very thing: solidarity with those who were in prison.* Because for all these people, it would have been much better if they had escaped abroad or surrendered. And instead they made this unbelievable choice. It is not by chance that the whole story finished in October 1982 in Florence [in the Florence prison] when we all met [for a trial], and therefore, all together we could decide that it was over, that we would quit. We did not have the problem of a reciprocal blackmail anymore, of a solidarity that . . . had become reciprocal blackmail between those who were inside and those who were outside (Life history no. 26, p. 69).

Meantime, those who were in prison had very similar feelings for their comrades outside:

> It was a situation in which we were all for declaring the dissolution of the organization, the end of the experience of the armed struggle. But at that point the comrades outside wrote a very radical document for "continuing" the struggle, and rejecting their demands seemed to us immoral. So, all that happened many years later (Life history no. 29, p. 48).

A New Value System

The "freedom-fighter" identity, however, consists not only of feelings toward other members of the underground but also of shared values and images of the external world. Jaeger and Boellinger (1981) rightly state that we can understand the dynamics of terrorism more clearly if we consider terrorist groups as subcultures with a peculiar value system. Actually, the militants of the underground behave just as "normal" people do but within an alternative value system: "In terrorist groups there is not only the breakdown of normality but also the development of a counterculture, of an alternative system of norms and aims that establishes the frontiers, reduces the constraints, imposes compliance, and—in the situation of complete isolation from the external world—replaces the normal standard of right and wrong, good and evil, by means of a different or alternative value orientation" (Jaeger 1981, p. 157). A counterculture's main instrument for developing a new value system is the ideology, which "has a twofold function, namely, to give an outward expression of the group's legitimacy and to act as a means of inner rationalization within the group itself. . . . Through group ideology, a pure criminal act is reinterpreted into a 'political act,' or rather it is only then that it gains political dimensions. An ideology conveys to the terrorist the conviction that a meaning lies behind his action" (Wasmund 1986, pp. 218-219). In addition, values and ideology interact to produce images of external reality which justify the "necessity," the "correctness," and the "beauty" of the "armed struggle."

Accordingly, we must now examine the interactions among values, ideologies, and alternative images of the external world which took place within the terrorist counterculture. These interactions generated three images that the terrorists used to legitimize their armed struggle. The first image is the enemy as a "nonhuman being"; the second, the militant as an heroic "example"; and the third, the situation as a "war."

Depersonalization of the Victims

The militants justified their use of political violence by depersonalizing their victims, defined in the documents of the underground groups as "tools of the system" and, later, as "pigs" or "watch dogs." They were therefore considered not as flesh and blood human beings, but as symbols. Their victims thus dehumanized, the militants could deny committing any injustice: "By declaring your enemies 'non-persons,' and by denying their human qualities, moral scruples are blocked from the beginning" (Wasmund 1986, p. 215). The most frequently quoted German terrorist slogans were those that emphasized the "fight of the human beings against the pigs in order to free humankind" and proclaimed that "humanity toward the enemy of humankind is inhuman" (cited in Jaeger 1981, p. 162). Ideological statements such as these were internalized by the militants:

> What I liked in that activity was the fact that it was possible, in some moments, to overcome the inhibitory restraints . . . . Even today, I do not feel any general scruple concerning

> a murder, because *I cannot see some creatures*—such as, for instance, Richard Nixon—*as human beings* (a German militant, cited in Boellinger 1981, p. 203);

> We say that policemen are pigs, that guy in uniform is a pig; he is not a human being. And we behave toward him accordingly (Meinhof, cited in Juenschke 1988, p. 164).

One important difference between Italian and German terrorism is that the Italian groups, having a much larger reservoir for recruitment, tried harder to find a legitimation among the radical Left. For this reason, their language remained for a long time much more "political"—that is, they tried to explain the necessity of the "armed struggle" by using symbols and drawing on meanings that they shared with the mass radical movement. At the same time, however, Italian terrorists relied to a great extent on "depersonalization" of the victim to justify their actions. Although they did not resort to terms such as "pig" until the 1980s, when the underground groups were growing increasingly isolated, since the very beginning of this wave of Italian terrorism, however, the militants defined the victims of their attacks as "wheels of the capitalist machine." The following passage from a biography clearly illustrates how the definition of the victims as "small wheels of a machine" enabled the militants to dismiss the idea that they had killed other human beings. Recounting her own participation in a murder, a militant said:

> We lived the problem of death inside a grand ideology . . . . I am one of those who killed the policeman Lo Russo in Turin . . . . Well, I lived that murder inside this logic of the function, because he was a warden, and he was well known as a "torturer," as we used to say, so I had all the justifications of the ideology . . . . For me it was a routine job. And this is the very aberration of the ideology; on one side, there are your friends; and on the other, there are your enemies, and *the enemies are a category, they are functions, they are symbols. They are not human beings.* And so they have to be dealt with as absolute enemies; so that you have a relation of absolute abstraction with death (Life history no. 26, pp. 62-63).

An Heroic Elite

Ideology also offered images of the "self" which, interiorized by the militants, helped them persist in their commitment. Implementing the idea of "depersonalizing the enemy" was the image of a "cold executioner" who must fullfil his duty. Italian and German militants alike describe how this "bureaucratic" perception of their role eliminated moral scruples in their everyday life:

> You make a political analysis, but then you need a victim. If you want to hit the Christian Democracy in a neighborhood, you need a target . . . therefore, you start to look for this victim . . . you read the newspapers, you infiltrate their meetings, and you try to find out. Then you have singled out your victim: he is physically there; he is the one to be blamed

> for everything. In that moment there is already the logic of a trial in which you have already decided that he is guilty; you only have to decide on his punishment. So you have *a very "emphatic" sense of justice;* you punish him not only for what he has done but also for all the rest. Then you don't care anymore which responsibilities that person has; you ascribe everything to him . . . he is only a small part of the machine that is going to destroy all of us" (Life history no. 27, p. 45).

> Most of the fear you feel disappears in the phase of the planning and repetition of the exercise until perfection . . . . *Then you become nothing more than a working gear* (cited in Boellinger 1981, pp. 189-190).

The militants further justified their activities by invoking quasi-existentialist explanations that emphasized the "extraordinary" role of a small minority. Like in other political sects, the underground groups idealized such tenets as the value of living outside normal standards; the idea of courage, as a duty of the true believer, and of sacrifice as a shared suffering (Kanter 1968, 1972). How these ideas became embodied in images is evident in, for example, the glamour that guns held for the militants: "the gun . . . gives you more strength," one militant explained (Life history no. 27, p. 33); "arms have a charm . . . that makes you feel more macho," said another (Life history no. 16, p. 79); you can feel "very secure of yourself because you keep a gun in your hands . . . a crazy self-confidence," reported a third (Baumann 1976, p. 165).

The more isolated the militants felt from the external world, the more firmly they came to see of themselves as a few heroes with an important symbolic role. In West Germany, the militants self-defined image of their role as "freedom-fighters" in the metropolis was soon superseded by another kind of symbol: "Eventually," Neidhardt observed of the RAF, "the group perceived itself less as a real instrument of liberation than as an example of self-liberation. It presented itself as a lighthouse" (Neidhardt 1982a, p. 357). Consequently, the group now emphasized "activism." Ulrike Meinhof, for instance, talked of the "supremacy of the praxis": "The Rote-Armee-Fraktion states the supremacy of the praxis. The question if it is right to organize the armed resistance now depends on the fact if it is possible, and the question if it is possible is only a practical question" (cited in Neidhardt 1982a, p. 355).

In Italy, too, as the terrorist groups became increasingly isolated at the end of the 1970s, they found a rationale for underground militance in the need to "keep alive the revolutionary movement" by "opposing pacification." One interviewee clearly described the "underground" state of mind at that time:

> *From 1980 on, the only aim is to resist* . . . . There is no longer the idea of an advancing revolution: "Let's go on, we are many, we are beautiful;" we are not beautiful, we are not many; we are only poor chaps who meet and say "O.K., let's try to do something while we wait, let's try to create again a revolutionary situation." . . . If we want to synthesize that in a slogan, it was *to resist at any price,* without allowing them to reabsorb the movement and to impose social peace (Life history no. 6, p. 50).

Thus the Italian militants too glorified the idea of an adventurous and active life. The dangers involved in participating in a terrorist organization were considered "the expression of a dynamic and interesting life," in contrast to the dullness of normal life. According to a militant, this "diversity" was the foundation for group identity: "the group was made homogeneous by this peculiar attitude; it found in this diversity its identity and its sublimation. These attitudes were therefore exalted and became its raison d'être" (Life history no. 6, p. 46).

The War Analogy

As underground groups grew more and more isolated, they shifted their rationale for the "armed struggle" from the "instrumental" role of violence in a revolutionary process to the "symbolic" value of violence as an expression of conflicts. Italian and German militants, however, viewed this rationale in different ways. In Italy, where, it has been often noted, the underground groups had a larger reservoir for support, the militants initially justified the "armed struggle" as part of the tradition of the working-class movement, supporting their argument with frequent references to the "fathers of socialist thought":

> We were supported in this also by famous quotes from Marxist literature, in which violence appeared as absolutely legitimate, as part of the history of the working class. Once it is decided that the historical conditions allow for that kind of organization, the rest is only a technical consequence (Life history no. 12, p. 21).

Moreover, throughout the 1970s, the Italian underground groups cultivated a more than optimistic image of the success of the "armed struggle." The documents of the groups were full of such statements as "the worst, the better," "the near victory of the working class," "the forthcoming revolution." This internalized optimism emerges even in the militants' present-day recollections, which include several statements affirming the "mass" support for the armed struggle: "hundreds of people supported us," "we were deep rooted at Fiat and Pirelli," "we were in contact with the working class," "there was a very widespread legitimation for our actions," "our hypothesis was going to be accepted at a mass level." For a long time the militants had few doubts about the victory of their organization, of the working class, of the revolution. Indeed, they denied defeats describing them simply as indicators of the need to "shift to a new phase of the struggle."

The West German militants paid less attention to the development of a justification through traditional Marxist theory, than did their Italian counterparts. For the German underground it was not the "corrupt working class of the Metropoli" but the marginal Lumpenproletariat and the people's liberation movements of the Third World that represented the "revolutionary subject." They defined urban guerrilla warfare as "a method of revolutionary intervention for altogether weak revolutionary forces" (cited in Neidhardt 1982a, p. 355). But whatever the ideological differences with the Italian terrorists, the German militants resembled them in at least one way: they too refused to acknowledge defeats. As Neidhardt observed, the RAF's emphasis on the Third World in the anti-imperialist fight allowed for a "pretence of success." According to the RAF, in fact, revolution could happen only in the Third World, and the Left in the Metropolis had the role of building the "international brigades for the victory of the people's war in Quan Tri and Hue, Palestine, Lebanon, Angola, Mozambique, Turkey" (cited in Neidhardt 1982a, p. 357)

In both the Italian and the German underground, this unreal image of the external world was the product of each group's selection and restriction of its sources of information. Clandestinity, in fact, drastically reduced external contacts to such a degree that a militant's only source of information would be his or her own organization:

> The majority of the group was closed towards some topics. They could not get information (Boock 1981, p. 114).

> It was *a sum of small lies*. In fact, each of us . . . tried to give credit to the image of an underground organization that was deep rooted in society, which enjoyed more popularity, more support, more consensus. This did not happen through big lies but through the small lies we told each other . . . : "but do you know that . . . the concierge understood that I am a member of the Red Brigades and not only does she not denounce me but rather, if she sees a policeman, she manages to warn me? Do you know that the people of that cafe understood who I am and, when I go there, the barman offers me a drink? Do you know that in that factory, when we wounded that foreman, they opened a bottle and toasted?" (Life history no. 11, p. 38).

As time went on, and the militants saw increasing evidence of the isolation of their political project, they found it more and more difficult to use images of "political" victories as a rationale for the "armed struggle." Thus they substituted the image of a "war" between the underground groups and the state. This change took place much earlier in West Germany than in Italy. The use of war terms became widespread and internalized:

> In clandestinity, one lives in a completely changed world. . . . *You see the world only inside a military model,* as a freed zone, or as a dangerous area. You do not see human beings so often any more . . . . When the world becomes so illusory, then you have to change yourself (Mahler, cited in Horn 1982, p. 149).

> They talked about depots, infrastructure, new structures, and battle structure; they talked about cadres, units, and commandos *in a military terminology that suggested, at least to me, that something like that really existed* (Speitel 1980a, p. 41).

By equating their situation with war, the militants hoped to eliminate inhibitions and guilt about their physical attacks against individuals. As Mahler declared in an interview: "We were from our point of view in something like a war. We therefore defined ourselves as soldiers in order to be able to face the problem of death" (cited in Jaeger 1981, p. 164). For the RAF founders as well as for the militants of the RZ, training periods in the Near East strengthened the "Kriegsanalogie" that subverted the "normal" way of judging right and wrong. One German militant recalled, "In Jordan, the feeling that you do not have to be afraid became stronger. When you are afraid of breaking the law, then you are in a weak position. The dominant feeling was instead that that was a thing for a military command, a military action. Therefore, there was the certitude that the law was on our side" (cited in Jaeger 1981, p. 164). According to Speitel, the request of the RAF members in prison to be treated as "prisoners of war" expressed this attitude: "It was not a request by which we pursued the improvement of prisoners' conditions. Quite to the contrary, this slogan should convey the sense of the armed struggle" (Speitel 1980b, p. 32). In defining the situation as a war, the militants grounded the entire ideological system on an absolute opposition of "friend and enemy" (Manconi 1988), of total good and total evil, which justified the militants' more radical actions. Boellinger explains the psychology of this warlike stance: "As a further defense mechanism the group cultivates collective projections: the enemy is therefore as powerful and as ideal as oneself . . . one's own importance and authenticity are related to the 'dimension' of the enemy" (Boellinger 1981, p. 204).

Finally, analogies with war allowed the militants to define "successes" and defeats strictly in military terms. They could thus evaluate the effectiveness of the armed struggle on the basis of its military achievements. "Satisfactions" and "gratifications" came from military success. An Italian militant, for instance, remembered that during a bombing "the very fact of seeing that thing burning and falling down, that made me happy" (Life history no. 2, p. 28). And another militant acknowledged: "We had this tendency to find our gratification only at the military level; therefore we went and did what had to be done" (Life history no. 5, p. 57).

Reviewing the factors that influenced the militants' commitment, we can see that the group's definition of the external situation enforced the militants' perception of their role as "freedom-fighters." It provided them with a collective identity. Conversely, an individual who quit the underground organizations would have implicitly transformed a "positive" identity into a "stigmatized" (Goffman 1963) identity—that is, he or she would have been confronted with his or her definition as a "terrorist," and therefore murderer, crazy, cruel criminal. The biographies describe the many obstacles militants faced in quitting the underground. Even when the deep crisis of the organization increased the perceived costs of participation, "the idea of quitting the organization produced feelings of guilt because," an Italian militant observed, "after having already paid such a price, to quit meant to admit that all that we had done had been useless" (Life history no. 19, p. 2/63). Persistence of commitment came to mean a search for redemption:

> *The only chance for redemption I have, from a moral point of view,* both for the violence I produced and the violence I suffered . . . *is to go right to the end* (Life history no. 18, pp. 73-74).
>
> [I had] this ideological belief that *I had to pursue the way I had undertaken* in order to find—or better to try to find—a reason for my previous participation in a murder (Life history no. 14, p. 19).

Loyalty to the "revolutionary community" in fact allowed militants to ignore the price they had already paid. Moreover, it could obscure the militants' perceptions of some "material" costs by presenting the imprisonment as a step in the fight for freedom. Boock, for instance, took this perspective in describing his situation in the high-security prisons:

> Those who are kept in the high-security units develop a logic of their own in order to make understandable and bearable an unbearable prison situation. *These hostile conditions become more bearable only if the prisoner can consider himself part of a larger community, of a somehow overdetermined truth, which allows one to see one's own existence as prisoner as only a temporary one.* I am a member of the Rote Armee Fraktion, an anti-imperialist urban guerrilla, who fights against the Federal Republic of Germany, because the FRG, side by side with the imperialist USA, represses its own people and exploits the Third World peoples. Because I was and I am part of this struggle, the state has taken me as a prisoner, almost as a hostage, and is keeping me in these inhuman conditions in prison. Any small compliance with their wishes in this situation will be taken as a sign of weakness, and used against me and my comrades. There can not be an individual solution for me: my only support is the group, the solidarity with the other comrades, and the continuation of the common struggle, even in these constrictive conditions . . . . *Only insofar as I keep my loyalty to the aims of the group, can I keep my identity and the hope that the situation will change* . . . . The prisoner has only this choice between capitulation, which means destruction of the self and despair, and the spasmodic attachment . . . to the group and its aims (Boock 1988, pp. 97-98).

It seems therefore that the militants' very high initial investment reduced the likelihood that they would leave their organization, or choose what Hirschman (1970) called an "exit" option. That is, since they had already paid a very high price, they had a strong need for an adequate reward. When they did not obtain such a reward, a psychological mechanism impelled them to "raise the bid" rather than quit. Thus, they persisted in their involvement, because surrendering implied "losing" everything they had already paid as the cost for entering the underground.

POLITICAL SOCIALIZATION IN THE UNDERGROUND: A CONCLUSION

The preceding analysis has demonstrated that Italian and German militants were motivated to join the underground for very similar reasons and through very similar processes, which I will now summarize. Jaeger and Boellinger have observed that the "political socialization of terrorist groups' members . . . is to be seen as part of a transformation in the reference system, i.e., as a gradual process of individual exit from the majoritarian culture and integration in a political counterculture with divergent norms, values and loyalties, and a particularly rigid pressure to conform" (Jaeger and Boellinger 1981, p. 232). In this article, I have examined the way in which this "transformation in the reference system" took place. During the phase of statu nascenti (Alberoni, 1984) in the late 1960s and early 1970s, *political countercultures* developed in which the future militants of the underground organizations first became involved—usually at a very young age—in political activities. In the extraordinary atmosphere of those phases of high-collective mobilization, dense social networks of comrade-friends proliferated and alternative value systems emerged. Both Italian and German militants had had long political careers in New Left organizations before joining the underground. The interactions between social movements and institutional actors created among the activists an image of the state as a violent and unfair enemy. Several activists engaged in violent forms of collective action. In this volatile environment, the use of political violence became legitimate.

Within many small circles of individuals support for political violence escalated, gradually and sometimes without the members' conscious intent, until these people joined the underground groups. A militant's recruitment to the underground was therefore often facilitated by *precipitating factors,* such as the arrest or assassination of a friend, a friend's decision to go underground, and the risk—or perceived risk—of being arrested oneself.

The underground organizations secured the commitment of their members by developing a value system that rejected "normal" definions of good and evil, replacing them with their own. Wilfried Rasch has described the importance of the group in sustaining the terrorist's career:

> The group provides back-up when other support is eradicated. Within the group several psychological variables become essential: solidarity, complicity and reality perception. Group membership means obligatory acceptance of a certain system of values and norms, deviations from these are sanctioned. The group dynamics of complicity catalyze actions which any one member would hardly have been able to accomplish alone and which he has difficulties understanding later on. He acts within a set of mutual expectations and role assignments. Being forced . . . underground the group lives in isolation and, working in close cooperation, evolves new models for the interpretation of reality which acquire a binding character for the group members (Rasch 1979, p. 82).

My comparative analysis confirms the validity of this description. I can add another important observation: it was these group dynamics that produced the *freedom fighter identity*. The militants began to perceive themselves as members of a heroic community of generous people fighting a war against "evil." Their image of reality was enforced through affective dynamics, which strengthened solidarity among comrades involved in the same mythical destiny, and through cognitive dynamics, which made the small circles of underground activists the militants' source of values and information.

To conclude, in both Italy and West Germany the militants of the underground organizations had political motivations—that is, they aimed at producing political changes in the external reality. Although they retained these political motivations throughout the different stages of their militancy, their perceptions of the external reality changed. During the process of political socialization, their image of politics as the expression of social conflicts gradually gave way to an image of politics as the result of a military conflict. One can observe this trend both in individual biographies and in organizational evolution. In both, one can detect a loss of the sense of reality—that is, the creation of images further and further removed not only from the "dominant" culture but also from the counterculture.

This loss of the sense of reality merits a few additional observations. First, the militants' sense of reality became more and more tenuous with the passage of time.[8] This interval was shorter for the German militants than for the Italian. *The longer the individual's involvement and the older the organization to which the terrorist belonged, the more removed from the reality he or she became.* Second, this loss varied with the degree of "clandestinity" an individual experienced; that is, it varied according to both the organizational model chosen by the terrorist group and the personal conditions of a militant. Both in West Germany and in Italy, these dynamics were more visible in some organizations—namely, the RAF and the BR—than in others. *The more compartimentalized an organization was, and the more involved in the clandestine life a militant was, the greater the militant's loss of the sense of reality.* Third, this phenomenon was in general more pronounced among German militants than among Italian militants.

More generally, we can conclude that the *degree to which the underground group is isolated* is the single variable capable of explaining the differences in the perception of the reality. In other words, the more isolated the underground organization, the weaker its members sense of reality. Although the decision to go underground is always a strategic choice of isolation from the external environment, a terrorist organization's degree of isolation changes according to the conditions of its environment. As we have noted, the political environment in Italy was more favorable to underground organizations than was the German environment, because Italy had a greater tolerance for political violence than did post-World War II West Germany, whose degree of tolerance for political violence was, indeed, extremely low. The different environmental conditions in the two countries influenced the origins and evolution of their respective underground organizations, and the militants' motivations and perception of external reality. Nevertheless, Italian and German militants ended up with very similar—and similarly "absurd" or alienated—images of the external world. Isolation, in fact, appears to be an unavoidable consequence of the decision to function clandestinely in a democratic regime. Clandestinity produces a gradual, although not total, loss of the sense of reality and a consequent shift in the motivational structures of the members of terrorist organizations.

ACKNOWLEDGMENTS

My thanks to Bert Klandermans, Friedhelm Neidhardt, and Herbert Reiter for their comments on an earlier draft of this paper. For the opportunity to carry out my research, I am grateful for a research grant at the Carlo Cattaneo Institute in Bologna, a research fellowship at the European University Institute in Florence, and the Harry Frank Guggenheim Foundation's Career Development Award at the Wissenschaftszentrum Berlin fuer Sozialforschung.

NOTES

1. On the use of life histories, see della Porta (1987a, 1990b).
2. These life histories have been collected through interviews with former militants, as a part of a research project sponsored by the Regione Emilia Romagna at the Istituto di studi e ricerche Carlo Cattaneo and coordinated by Raimondo Catanzaro. The life histories of left-wing militants were collected by a research team composed of Donatella della Porta, Giuseppe De Lutiis, Patrizia Guerra, Luigi Manconi, Domenico Nigro, Claudio Novaro, and Luisa Passerini. The quotations from "Life history no. . . . " which appear throughout this article refer to the transcription of these interviews, which are stored in the archives of the Istituto Cattaneo.
3. I refer to 18 biographies of former members collected by Diego Novelli and Nicola Tranfaglia during a two-year seminar in the Turin prison (Novelli and Tranfaglia 1988), and to the summary of nine biographies of female militants collected during a seminar directed by Luisa Passerini in the same prison (published in a special issue of "Rivista di storia contemporanea" 1988).
4. I refer to the written autobiographies of Bommi Baumann, from the Bewegung 2. Juni in Berlin; Peter Juergen Boock, from the RAF in Hamburg; Klaus Juenschke, from the RAF in Heidelberg; Hans Joachim Klein, from the RZ in Frankfurt; Horst Mahler, from the RAF in Berlin; Volker Speitel, from the RAF in Stuttgart. Two other biographies of German militants are summarized in Billing (1984) and Krebs (1988).
5. According to Schmidtchen's data, German left-wing terrorists had been members of the following types of legal groups: 27 percent had belonged to prisoners' help organizations, 10 percent to New Left organizations, 8 percent to student organizations, 7 percent to K-Gruppen (Schmidtchen 1981, p. 71). These percentages are doubled if we exclude the 48 percent of missing values from their computation.

6. See della Porta (1987b and 1988c). Novaro (1988) found similar results in his analysis of the biographies of militants coming from a region—the Val di Susa in Piedmont—where the Partisan movement against the German occupation had been very strong.

7. Schmidtchen (1981) observed that 47 percent of future left-wing terrorists had lived in Wohngemainschaften (against 15% for people in the same conditions), and 41 percent in Kommunen (against 5%).

8. On the evolution of underground organizations, see, for Italy, della Porta (1990a) and, for West Germany, Neidhardt (1981).

REFERENCES

Alberoni, F. 1984. *Movement and Institution.* New York: Cambridge University Press.

Baumann, M. 1976. *Tupamaros Berlin-Ouest* [Tupamaros West-Berlin]. Paris: Les Presses d'aujourd'hui.

Billing, O. 1984. "The Case History of a German Terrorist." *Terrorism* 7:1-10.

Boellinger, L. 1981. "Die Entwicklung zu terroristischem Handeln als psychosozialer Prozess" [The Evolution toward Terrorist Actions As Psycho-social Process]. Pp. 175-231 in *Lebenslaufanalysen* [Analysis of the Careers] edited by H. Jaeger, G. Schmidtchen, and L. Suellwold. Opladen: Westdeutscher.

Boock, P. 1981. "Im Schuetzengraben fuer die falsche Sache" [In Trench for the Wrong Thing]. *Der Spiegel* no. 9:110-125.

________. 1988. *Schwarzes Loch im Hochsicherheitstrakt* [Black Hole in the High-security Section]. Hamburg: Rowohlt.

Caselli, G. and D. della Porta. 1984. "La storia delle Brigate Rosse: strutture organizzative e strategie d'azione" [The History of the Red Brigades: Organizational Structure and Action Strategy"]. Pp. 153-221 in *Terrorismi in Italia* [Terrorism in Italy], edited by D. della Porta. Bologna: Il Mulino.

della Porta, D. 1987a. "Storie di vita e movimenti collettivi. Una tecnica per lo studio delle motivazioni alla militanza politica" [Life Histories and Collective Movements. A Technique for the Study of Motivation in Political Activism]. *Rassegna italiana di sociologia* 28:105-131.

________. 1987b. "I militanti delle organizzazioni terroriste di sinistra in Italia" [The Militants of Left-Wing Underground Organizations in Italy]. *Rivista italiana di scienza politica* 17:23-55.

________. 1988a. "Protestbewegung und Terrorismus in Italien" [Protest Movement and Terrorism in Italy]. *Aus Politik und Zeitgeschichte* 45: 21-34.

________. 1988b. "Gli incentivi organizzativi nella militanza in organizzazioni clandestine" [Organizational Incentives and Militancy in Clandestine Organizations]. *Polis* 2:233-258.

________. 1988c. "Recruitment Processes in Clandestine Political Organizations. Italian Left-Wing Terrorism." Pp. 155-169 in *New Social Movements in Western Europe and the United States,* edited by B. Klandermans, H. Kriesi, and S. Tarrow. Greenwich, CT: JAI Press.

________. 1990a. *Il terrorismo di sinistra* (Left-wing Terrorism). Bologna: Il Mulino.

________. 1990b. *Biographies of Social Movement Activists: State of the Art and Methodological Problems.* Paper presented at the ECPR Joint Sessions, Bochum, April.

della Porta, D. and S. Tarrow. 1987. "Unwanted Children. Political Violence and the Cycle of Protest in Italy. 1966-1973." *European Journal of Political Research* 14:607-632.

Goffman, E. 1963. *Stigma: Notes on the Management of Spoiled Identity.* Englewood Cliffs, NJ: Prentice-Hall.

Hirschman, A.O. 1970. *Exit, Voice and Loyalty.* Cambridge, MA: Harvard University Press.

Horn, M. 1982. *Sozialpsychologie des Terrorismus* [Social-psychology of Terrorism]. Frankfurt am Main: Campus.

Jaeger, H. 1981. "Die individuelle Dimension terroristischen Handelns" [The Individual Dimension of Terrorist Action]. Pp. 120-174 in *Lebenslaufanalysen* [Analysis of the Careers] edited by H. Jaeger, G. Schmidtchen and L. Suellwold. Opladen: Westdeutscher.

Jaeger, H. and L. Boellinger. 1981. "Thesen zur weiteren Diskussion des Terrorismus" [Theses for a Further Discussion on Terrorism]. Pp. 232-242 in *Lebenslaufanalysen* [Analysis of the Careers] edited by H. Jaeger, G. Schmidtchen and L. Suellwold). Opladen: Westdeutscher.

Juenschke, K. 1988. *Spaetlese. Texte zu Raf und Knast* [Late Vintage. Texts about RAF and Prison]. Frankfurt am Main: Neue Kritik.

Kanter, R. M. 1968. "Commitment and Social Organization: A Study of Commitment Mechanisms in Utopian Communities." *American Sociological Review* 33:499-517.

________. 1972. "Commitment and the Internal Organization of Millennial Movements." *American Behavioral Scientist* 16:219-243.

Keniston, K. 1968. *Young Radicals: Notes on Committed Youth.* New York: Harcourt, Brace and World.

Klein, H. 1980. *La mort mercenaire. Temoignage d'un ancient terroriste ouest-allemand* [The Mercenary Death: Testimony of a West-German Former Terrorist]. Paris: Seuil.

Krebs, M. 1988. *Ulrike Meinhof. Ein Leben im Widerspruch* [Ulrike Meinhof: A Life in Contradiction]. Hamburg: Rowohlt.

Mahler, H. 1980. *Per la critica del terrorismo* [For Criticism against Terrorism]. Bari: De Donato.

Manconi, L. 1988. "Il nemico assoluto. Antifascismo e contropotere nella fase aurorale del terrorismo di sinistra" [The Absolute Enemy. Anti-Fascism and Counter-Power at the Dawn of Left-Wing Terrorism]. *Polis* 2:259-286.

Matza, D. 1969. *Becoming Deviant.* Englewood Cliffs, NJ: Prentice-Hall.

Neidhardt, F. 1981. "Ueber Zufall, Eigendynamik und Institutionalisierbarkeit absurder Prozesse. Notizen am Beispiel der Entstehung und Einrichtung einer terroristischen Gruppe" [On Chance, Inherent Dynamics, and Institutionalization of Absurd Processes: Notes on the Foundation and Establishment of a Terrorist Group]. Pp. 243-257 in *Soziologie in weltbuergerlicher Absicht* [Sociology in a Cosmopolitan Design], edited by A. von Alemann and H.P. Thurn. Opladen: Westdeutscher.

________. 1982a. "Soziale Bedingungen terroristischen Handelns. Das Beispiel der 'Baader-Meinhof-Gruppe' (RAF)" [Social Circumstances of Terrorist Action. The Example of the Baader-Meinhof Group (RAF)]. Pp. 318-391 in *Gruppenprozesse* [Group Processes] edited by W. von Baeyer-Katte, D. Classens, H. Feger and F. Neidhardt. Opladen: Westdeutscher.

________. 1982b. "Linker und rechter Terrorismus. Erscheinungsformen und Handlungspotentiale im Gruppenvergleich" [Left-wing and right-wing terrorism. Forms of manifestation and potential of action in group comparison]. Pp. 434-476 in W. von Baeyer-Katte, D. Classens, H. Feger, and F. Neidhardt, *Gruppenprozesse* [Group Processes]. Opladen: Westdeutscher.

Novaro, C. 1988. "Reti amicali e lotta armata" [Friendship Networks and Armed Struggle]. *Polis* 2:287-320.

Novelli, D. and Tranfaglia, N. 1988. *Vite sospese. Le generazioni del terrorismo* [Suspended Lives: The Generations of Terrorism]. Milano: Garzanti.

Rasch, W. 1979. "Psychological Dimensions of Political Terrorism in the Federal Republic of Germany." *International Journal of Law and Psychiatry* 2:79-85.

"Rivista di storia contemporanea" 1988. *Special Issue,* vol. 17, no. 2.

Schmidtchen, G. 1981. "Terroristische Karrieren" [Terrorist Careers]. Pp. 14-77 in *Lebenslaufanalysen* [Analysis of Life Careers] edited by H. Jaeger, G. Schmidtchen, and L. Suellwold. Opladen: Westdeutscher.

Speitel, V. 1980a. "Wir wollten alles und gleichzeitig nichts. I" [We Wanted Everything and at the Same Time Nothing. I] *Der Spiegel* 31: 36-49.

———. 1980b. "Wir wollten alles und gleichzeitig nichts. II" [We Wanted Everything and at the Same Time Nothing. II] *Der Spiegel* 32:30-39.

———. 1980c. "Wir wollten alles und gleichzeitig nichts. III" [We Wanted Everything and at the Same Time Nothing. III] *Der Spiegel* 33:30-36.

Wasmund, K. 1986. "The Political Socialization of West German Terrorists." Pp. 191-228 in *Political Violence and Terror: Motifs and Motivations*, edited by P.H. Merkl. Berkeley: University of California Press.

JAI PRESS

Volume 2. Organizing For Change: Social Movement Organizations in Europe and the United States
1989, 442 pp. $63.50
ISBN 0-89232-964-5

CONTENTS: Preface. SOCIAL MOVEMENT ORGANIZATIONS, *Bert Klandermans.* **STRUCTURE AND CHANGE,** *Bert Klandermans.* **Spontaneity and Democracy in Social Protest,** *Naomi Rosenthal, College at Old Westbury and Michael Schwartz, State University of New York at Stony Brook.* **Environmental Movement Organizations in West Germany and France: Structure and Interorganizational Relations,** *Dieter Rucht, University of Munich.* **The Development, Change and Decline of the Dutch Catholic Movement,** *Ton Duffhues and Albert Felling, Catholic University of Nijmegen.* **MANAGEMENT OF SOCIAL MOVEMENT ORGANIZATIONS,** *Bert Klandermans, Vrije Universiteit.* **Resource Acquisition and Allocation in U.S. National Associations,** *David Knoke, University of Minnesota.* **Contradictions Between National and Local Organizational Strength: The Case of the John Birch Society,** *Pamela Oliver and Mark Furham, University of Wisconsin.* **Exit-Behavior in Social Movement Organizations,** *Gerrita van der Veen and Bert Klandermans, Vrije Universiteit.* **Realities, Images and Management Dilemmas in Social Movement Organizations: The Three Mile Island Experience,** *Edward Walsh, Pennsylvania State University and Sherry Cable, University of Tennessee.* **LEADERSHIP AND DECISION MAKING,** *Bert Klandermans, Vrije Universiteit.* **Organizing Activity in the Women's Movement: An Example of Distributed Leadership,** *M. Helen Brown, The Tavistock Institute of Human Relations.* **Leadership and Decision Making in a Strike Organization,** *Jean Hartley,University of London.* **The Struggle Within: Conflict, Consensus and Decision Making Among National Coordinators and Grassroots Organizers in the West German Peace Movement,** *Joyce Marie Mushaben, University of Missouri at St.Louis.* **INTERORGANIZATIONAL NETWORKS,** *Bert Klandermans, Vrije Universiteit.* **Multi Organizational Fields and Recruitment to Social Movements,** *Roberto M. Fernandez and Doug McAdam, Universuity of Arizona.* **Integration into Voluntary Associations and Incentives for Political Protest,** *Karl-Dieter Opp, University of Hamburg.* **Conflict in Interorganizational Systems: On the Logic of Trade Unions and Employers' Associations in the 1984 Metal Strike in West Germany,** *Hajo Weber, University of Bielefeld.* **ORGANIZATIONAL EFFECTIVENESS,** *Bert Klandermans, Vrije Universiteit.* **The Influence of Social Movements on Government Policy,** *Leo W. Huberts, University of Leiden.* **Effectiveness and the Structure of New Social Movements,** *Peter Gundelach, University of Aarhus.*

Research in Social Movements, Conflicts and Change

Edited by **Louis Kriesberg,** *Department of Sociology, Syracuse University*

Volume 11, 1989, 339 pp. $63.50
ISBN 0-89232-945-9

CONTENTS: Bringing the Crowd Back in: The Nonorganizational Elements of Social Movements, *Pamela E. Oliver.* **The 1960 Sit-Ins: Protest Diffusion and Movement Take-Off,** *Anthony Oberschall.* **"Threats to Homes" as Grievance: Targets and Constituencies,** *Barbara Schmitter Heisler and Lily M. Hoffman.* **Intellectuals and Leadership of Social Movements: Some Comparative Perspectives,** *Maurice Pinard and Richard Hamilton.* **Defensive Revolutionaires: The Moral and Political Economy of Basque, Breton and Quebecois Nationalism,** *Michael S. Kimmel.* **Bonapartist Elites in Communist Revolutions: Implications for Social Theory,** *J. David Edelstein.* **The Institutiionalization of Social Movements in Voluntary Organizations,** *Maren Lockwood Carden.* **Consensus Movements: City Twinning and Derailed Dissent In the American Eighthies,** *John Lofland.* **Power and Practice in Peace Movement Discourse,** *Michael Blain.* **Atomic Scientists and Protest: The Bulleting as a Social Movement Organization,** *Frances B. McCrea and Gerald E. Markle.* **Some Remarks to the Perception of International Relations: Bacon and the Global System,** *Tamas Szecsko.* **The Choice Between Coercive and Noncoercive Actions in Disputes,** *Martin Patchen.* **A Structural Analysis of International Conflict and Cooperation,** *Thomas F. Mayer and Adele G. Platter.* **Peace and Deterrence,** *Matthew Melko.*

Volume 12, 1990, 344 pp. $63.50
ISBN 1-55938-065-9

CONTENTS: Microstructural Bases of Recruitment to Social Movements, *Roberto M. Fernandez and Doug McAdam.* **Ambiguity and Crowds: Results from a Computer Simulation Model,** *Norris R. Johnson and William E. Feinberg.* **Alternative Social Movements in Contemporary Poland,** *Bronislaw Misztal.* **The Historical Structuring of a Dissident Movement: The Sanctuary Case,** *David Kowalewski.* **Strategies in the Italian Peace Movement,** *Carlo E. Ruzza.* **Rebels and Theorists: An Examination of Peasant Uprisings in Southern Peru,** *Benjamin S. Orlove.* **Conflict Over Housework: A Problem That (Still) Has No Name,** *Marjorie L. DeVault.* **The Sudanese Settlement: Reflections on the 1972 Addis Araba Agreement,** *C.R. Mitchell.* **Genocide and Social Conflict: A**